Lecture Notes in Computer Science   13273

More information about this series at https://link.springer.com/bookseries/558

Mohammad Reza Mousavi ·
Anna Philippou (Eds.)

Formal Techniques for Distributed Objects, Components, and Systems

42nd IFIP WG 6.1 International Conference, FORTE 2022
Held as Part of the 17th International Federated Conference
on Distributed Computing Techniques, DisCoTec 2022
Lucca, Italy, June 13–17, 2022
Proceedings

 Springer

Editors
Mohammad Reza Mousavi ⓘ
King's College London
London, UK

Anna Philippou
University of Cyprus
Nicosia, Cyprus

ISSN 0302-9743   ISSN 1611-3349 (electronic)
Lecture Notes in Computer Science
ISBN 978-3-031-08678-6   ISBN 978-3-031-08679-3 (eBook)
https://doi.org/10.1007/978-3-031-08679-3

This Springer imprint is published by the registered company Springer Nature Switzerland AG
The registered company address is: Gewerbestrasse 11, 6330 Cham, Switzerland

Foreword

The 17th International Federated Conference on Distributed Computing Techniques (DisCoTec 2022) took place in Lucca from June 13 to June 17, 2022. It was organised by the IMT School for Advanced Studies Lucca. The DisCoTec series is one of the major events sponsored by the International Federation for Information Processing (IFIP), the European Association for Programming Languages and Systems (EAPLS), and the Microservices Community. DisCoTec 2022 comprised three conferences:

- COORDINATION, the IFIP WG 6.1 24th International Conference on Coordination Models and Languages
- DAIS, the IFIP WG 6.1 22nd International Conference on Distributed Applications and Interoperable Systems
- FORTE, the IFIP WG 6.1 42nd International Conference on Formal Techniques for Distributed Objects, Components and Systems

Together, these conferences covered a broad spectrum of distributed computing subjects, ranging from theoretical foundations and formal description techniques to systems research issues. As is customary, the event also included several plenary sessions in addition to the individual sessions of each conference, which gathered attendants from the three conferences. These included joint invited speaker sessions and a joint session for the best papers from the three conferences.

The DisCoTec 2022 invited speakers were:

- Muffy Calder, University of Glasgow, UK
- Maarten van Steen, University of Twente, The Netherlands
- Luca Viganò, King's College London, UK

Associated with the federated event, five satellite events took place:

- BlockTEE 2022: Workshop on Blockchain Technologies and Trusted Execution Environments
- CoMinDs 2022: Workshop on Collaborative Mining for Distributed Systems
- FOCODILE 2022: Workshop on the Foundations of Consensus and Distributed Ledgers
- ICE 2022: Workshop on Interaction and Concurrency Experience
- REMV 2022: Workshop on Robotics, Electronics and Machine Vision

Moreover, we also had a number of short tutorials on hot topics:

- An Introduction to Spatial Logics and Spatial Model Checking by Vincenzo Ciancia
- A Gentle Adventure Mechanising Message Passing Concurrency Systems by David Castro-Perez, Francisco Ferreira, Lorenzo Gheri, and Martin Vassor

- Smart Contracts in Bitcoin and BitML by Massimo Bartoletti and Roberto Zunino
- The ΔQ Systems Development Paradigm by Neil Davies, Seyed Hossein Haeri, Peter Thompson, and Peter Van Roy
- ChorChain: A Model-driven Approach for Trusted Execution of Multi-party Business Processes on Blockchain by Alessandro Marcelletti

Of course, all of this could not be done without the precious work of the Program Committees of the three main conferences and the five workshops, and of the Steering Committee and Advisory Boards. Many thanks to all of them, they are too many to mention. However, I would like to thank personally the Program Committee Chairs of the main conferences, namely Maurice ter Beek and Marjan Sirjani (for Coordination), David Eyers and Spyros Voulgaris (for DAIS), and Mohammad Mousavi and Anna Philippou (for FORTE). They have managed to select an excellent set of research papers.

The organization of DisCoTec 2022 was only possible thanks to the dedicated work of the Organizing Committee, including Marinella Petrocchi, Simone Soderi, Francesco Tiezzi (Workshops and Tutorials Chair) and Giorgio Audrito (Publicity Chair). But a special thanks has to go to Letterio Galletta, the Chair of the Local Organizing Committee, who, in many cases, because of my absence, acted also as General Chair. Finally, I would like to thank IFIP WG 6.1, EAPLS, and the Microservices Community for sponsoring this event, Springer's Lecture Notes in Computer Science team for their support and sponsorship, EasyChair for providing the reviewing framework, and the IMT School for providing the support and the infrastructure to host the event.

June 2022   Rocco De Nicola

Preface

This volume contains the papers presented at the 42nd IFIP WG 6.1 International Conference on Formal Techniques for Distributed Objects, Components, and Systems (FORTE 2022), held as one of three main conferences of the 17th International Federated Conference on Distributed Computing Techniques (DisCoTec 2022) during June 13–17, 2022. The conference was organized by the IMT School for Advanced Studies Lucca.

FORTE is a well-established forum for fundamental research on theory, models, tools, and applications for distributed systems, with special interest in

- Component- and model-based design
- Cyber-physical systems, autonomous systems, and AI-enabled systems design and trustworthiness
- Object technology, modularity, software adaptation
- Self-stabilization and self-healing/organizing
- Software quality, reliability, availability, and safety
- Security, privacy, and trust in distributed and/or communicating systems
- Service-oriented, ubiquitous, and cloud computing systems
- Verification, validation, formal analysis, and testing of the above.

The Program Committee received a total of 28 submissions, written by authors from 19 different countries. Of these, 12 papers were selected for inclusion in the scientific program. Each submission was reviewed by at least three Program Committee members with the help of 18 external reviewers in selected cases. The selection of accepted submissions was based on electronic discussions via the EasyChair conference management system.

As program chairs of FORTE 2022, we actively contributed to the selection of the keynote speakers for DisCoTec 2022:

- Muffy Calder, University of Glasgow, UK
- Maarten van Steen, University of Twente, The Netherlands
- Luca Viganò, King's College London, UK

We are most grateful to Muffy Calder for accepting our invitation to be the FORTE-related keynote speaker. This volume contains the abstract of her talk entitled "30+ years of FORTE research: a personal perspective".

We wish to thank all the authors of submitted papers, all the members of the Program Committee for their thorough evaluations of the submissions, and the external reviewers who assisted the evaluation process. We would also like to express our appreciation to the Steering Committee of FORTE for their advice and suggestions. Last but not least, we thank the DisCoTec General Chair, Rocco De Nicola, and his organization team for their hard, effective work in providing an excellent environment for FORTE 2022 and all other conferences and workshops.

June 2022   Mohammad Reza Mousavi
                                                                   Anna Philippou

Organization

Program Committee

Étienne André	Université de Lorraine, CNRS, Inria, France
Nathalie Bertrand	Inria, France
Georgiana Caltais	University of Konstanz, Germany
Yu-Fang Chen	Academia Sinica, China
Louise Dennis	University of Manchester, UK
Adrian Francalanza	University of Malta, Malta
Hubert Garavel	Inria, France
Fatemeh Ghassemi	University of Tehran, Iran
Ebru Göl	Middle East Technical University, Turkey
Ákos Hajdu	Meta Platforms Inc., UK
Arnd Hartmanns	University of Twente, The Netherlands
Marieke Huisman	University of Twente, The Netherlands
Peter Höfner	Australian National University, Australia
Wen Kokke	University of Edinburgh, UK
Barbara König	University of Duisburg-Essen, Germany
Annabelle McIver	Macquarie University, Australia
Massimo Merro	University of Verona, Italy
Claudio Antares Mezzina	Università di Urbino, Italy
Mohammad Reza Mousavi (Chair)	King's College London, UK
Catuscia Palamidessi	Inria and LIX, France
Kirstin Peters	TU Darmstadt, Germany
Anna Philippou (Chair)	University of Cyprus, Cyprus
Sanjiva Prasad	Indian Institute of Technology Delhi, India
António Ravara	Universidade Nova de Lisboa, Portugal
Ana Sokolova	University of Salzburg, Austria
Mahsa Varshosaz	IT University of Copenhagen, Denmark
Mahesh Viswanathan	University of Illinois at Urbana-Champaign, USA
Tim Willemse	Eindhoven University of Technology, The Netherlands
Ingrid Chieh Yu	University of Oslo, Norway

Additional Reviewers

Abel, Andreas
Bocchi, Laura
Ciancia, Vincenzo
Di Stefano, Luca
Grigore, Radu
Kamburjan, Eduard
Kohlen, Bram
Koppula, Venkata
Lang, Frédéric

Mota, João
Puthoor, Ittoop
Ringert, Jan Oliver
Shilov, Nikolay
Stramaglia, Anna
Thomsen, Michael Kirkedal
van Dijk, Tom
van Glabbeek, Rob
Zhang, Minjian

30+ Years of FORTE Research: A Personal Perspective (Abstract of Invited Talk)

Muffy Calder

University of Glasgow
`muffy.calder@glasgow.ac.uk`

I attended the first FORTE conference in Scotland in 1988, and have published in several FORTE conferences since then. Over the past 34 years the field has changed, and so has my own research. Using six example applications, from 1989 to 2020, I reflect on how my own research in fundamental research on theory, models, tools for distributed systems has evolved, and where we might focus research in the future.

Contents

Monitoring Hyperproperties with Circuits

Luca Aceto[1,3], Antonis Achilleos[1], Elli Anastasiadi[1(✉)],
and Adrian Francalanza[2]

[1] ICE -TCS, Department of Computer Science, Reykjavik University, Reykjavik,
Iceland
{luca,antonios,elli19}@ru.is
[2] Department of Computer Science, University of Malta, Msida, Malta
adrian.francalanza@um.edu.mt
[3] Gran Sasso Science Institute, L'Aquila, Italy
luca.aceto@gssi.it

Abstract. This paper presents an extension of the safety fragment of
Hennessy-Milner Logic with recursion over sets of traces, in the spirit of
Hyper-LTL. It then introduces a novel monitoring setup that employs
circuit-like structures to combine verdicts from regular monitors. The
main contribution of this study is the definition of the monitors and
their semantics, as well as a monitor-synthesis procedure from formulae
in the logic that yields 'circuit-like monitors' that are sound and violation
complete over a finite set of infinite traces.

1 Introduction

The field of runtime verification concerns itself with providing methods for checking whether a system satisfies its intended specification at runtime. This runtime
analysis is done through a computing device called a *monitor* that observes the
current run of a system in the form of a trace [4,12]. Runtime verification has
recently been extended to the setting of concurrent systems [1,5,7,16] with several attempts to specify properties over sets of traces, and to introduce novel
monitoring setups [2,6,11]. A centerpiece in this line of work has been the specification logic Hyper-LTL [9]. Intuitively Hyper-LTL allows for existential and
universal quantification over a set of traces (which describes the set of observed
system runs). The properties over one trace are stated in LTL, with free trace
variables, and then made dependent on properties of other traces via the quantification that binds the trace variables.

We define the linear-time specification logic Hyper-μHML, as a counterpart to Hyper-LTL, building on previous studies of monitorability and monitor

The authors were supported by the projects 'Open Problems in the Equational Logic of
Processes' (OPEL) (grant No 196050–051) and 'Mode(l)s of Verification and Monitorability' (MoVeMent) (grant No 217987) of the Icelandic Research Fund, and 'Runtime
and Equational Verification of Concurrent Programs' (ReVoCoP) (grant No 222021),
of the Reykjavik University Research Fund. Luca Aceto's work was also partially supported by the Italian MIUR PRIN 2017 project FTXR7S IT MATTERS 'Methods and
Tools for Trustworthy Smart Systems'.

© IFIP International Federation for Information Processing 2022
Published by Springer Nature Switzerland AG 2022
M. R. Mousavi and A. Philippou (Eds.): FORTE 2022, LNCS 13273, pp. 1–10, 2022.
https://doi.org/10.1007/978-3-031-08679-3_1

synthesis for μHML [1,13], which are necessary for the kind of correctness and complexity guarantees we aim to achieve in this work. However, just like Hyper-LTL, Hyper-μHML can define dependencies over different traces, which intuitively causes extra delays in the processing of traces as the properties observed on one of them can impact what is expected for another. For example, if a property requires that an event of a trace is compared against an event occurring in all other traces then the processing cost of this event becomes dependent on the number of traces. In this approach, we keep the processing-at-runtime cost (as defined in [17]) minimal by restricting the type of properties verified to a natural fragment of Hyper-μHML, but applying no assumptions on the system under scrutiny. This comes in contrast with the existing research, where the runtime verification of such properties is dealt with via a plethora of modifications and assumptions made over the monitoring setup, such as being able to restart an execution or having access to all executions of a system.

Our monitor setup is engineered for the studied fragment of the specification language, by utilizing circuit-like structures to combine verdicts over different traces. The fragment of the logic restricts the amount of quantification that can be applied to the properties of individual traces and thus limits the dependencies between them. This naturally induces circuits with monitors from [1] as input nodes and simple kinds of gates at the higher levels, with the resulting structure having constant depth with respect to the corresponding formula, which is considered efficient in the field of parallel computation [14]. Thus, each step taken by such a monitor in response to an event of the system under scrutiny takes constant time, which makes the monitors 'real time' in the sense of [17].

2   The Logic

Our logic is defined in the style of Hyper-LTL as presented in [9]. The quantification among traces remains the same, but the language in which local trace properties are stated is μHML. We consider the following restriction to a multi-trace sHML logic (the *safety* fragment of μHML [1]), with no alternating quantifiers, called HYPER[1]-SHML. We can similarly define the cHML (co-safety) fragment, and the HML fragment.

Definition 1. *Formulae in* HYPER[1]-SHML *are constructed by the following grammar:*

$$\varphi \in \text{HYPER}^1\text{-SHML} :: = \exists_\pi \psi \qquad | \ \forall_\pi \psi \qquad | \ \varphi \sqcup \varphi \qquad | \ \varphi \sqcap \varphi$$

where ψ stands for a formula in sHML *and π is a trace variable from an infinite suppy of trace variables $\mathcal{V}$. $\sqcup$ and $\sqcap$ stand for the regular $\vee$ and $\wedge$ boolean connectives, only usable at the top syntax level. Although the syntactic distinction is cosmetic, it allows us to keep the synthesis function in Definition 4 clearer.*

Semantics. The semantics of Hyper-μHML is given over a finite set of infinite traces T over ACT and it is a natural extension of the linear-time semantics of μHML. The existential and universal quantification happens via the trace variable π which ranges over the traces in T. The extension of the μHML linear-time semantics from [1] to the Hyper-μHML semantics is done in the style of Hyper-LTL. This semantics applies to HYPER[1]-sHML, which is a fragment of Hyper-μHML. We only consider *closed* formulae in HYPER[1]-sHML and for these we use the standard notation $T \models \varphi$ to mean that a set of traces T satisfies φ (and similarly for $T \not\models \varphi$).

Example 1. The HYPER[1]-sHML formula $\forall_\pi [a]\text{ff} \sqcap \exists_\pi [b](max\ x.([a]\text{ff} \land [b]x))$, over the set of actions $\{a, b\}$, states that for any set of traces T, none of the traces in T start with a, and $b^\omega \in T$.

3 The Monitors

The intuition behind our monitor design is the following (we recommend following this intuition along with the example given in Fig. 1). Over a finite set of traces T we instrument a circuit-like structure. Each trace $t \in T$ is assigned a fixed set of regular monitors that correspond to the properties in sHML to be verified. These regular monitors are connected with simple gates which evaluate to *yes*, *no* or *end* based on the verdicts produced by their associated regular monitors. Once some of these gates start evaluating to verdicts, they communicate with more complex gates, connected in a circuit-like graph, which propagate input verdicts though logic operations until the root node of the circuit reaches a verdict as well. The formal definition of a circuit monitor is given in the style of computational complexity circuits [18, Definition 1.10].

Definition 2. *The language* $C\text{MON}_k$ *of k-ary monitors, for $k > 0$ is given through the following grammar:*

$$M \in C\text{MON}_k ::= \bigvee[m]_k \quad | \quad \bigwedge[m]_k \qquad | \quad M \lor M \quad | \quad M \land M$$
$$m ::= \quad yes \mid no \mid end \quad | \quad a.m,\ a \in \text{ACT} \quad | \quad m+n \quad | \quad rec\ x.m \quad | \quad x$$

$C\text{MON}$ *is the collection of infinite sequences* $(M_i)_{i \in \mathbb{N}}$ *of terms that are generated by substituting* $k = i, \forall i \in \mathbb{N}$, *in a term M in* $C\text{MON}_k$.

We use $M, M' \ldots$ to denote the monitors (infinite sequences of terms generated by the first line of this grammar), and refer to them as circuit monitors, and $m_1, m_2 \ldots$ to denote the regular monitors described by the second line. The notation $[m]_k$ corresponds to the parallel dispatch of k identical regular monitors m, where $k = |T|$, with $T = \{t_1, \ldots, t_k\}$.

Given a monitor $M \in C\text{MON}$, we will call each syntactic sub-monitor of M a gate. For example, we have inductively that over the monitor $M' \lor M''$ we have the gates $M' \lor M''$ and all gates contained in monitors M', and M'', while for the monitor $\bigvee[m]_k$ we have the gates $\bigvee[m]_k$ and gates $m_{[i]}$ for $i \in \{1, \ldots, k\}$. For $M \in C\text{MON}$ we define a set of *program variables* G_M, where one variable $g_{M'}$ is assigned to each gate M' of M.

For readability purposes we will be omitting the naming g of the program variables and call them by the name of the gate they represent. We use $m_{[i]}$ to mean the regular monitor m instrumented over the trace t_i. It is important here to see that $g_{m_{[i]}}$ will be the *name* of the gate assigned to one such monitor and stays unchanged while the actual monitor advances its computation as trace events are read. This will be clarified later, through the instrumentation rules.

A program variable related to gate M, can be assigned the following values: *yes*, *no*, *end*, and j, with $j \in \{0, \ldots, 2^{(\ell+1)} - 1\}$, ℓ being the number of immediate syntactical sub-monitors of gate M. Number j is encoded in binary, and is used to carry the information of which sub-gates have given some verdict (this means that the encoding of j has $\ell + 1$ bits). The value of the $\ell + 1$-th bit of j is reserved to encode that one of the sub gates has outputted an *end*. The information that j carries is very important for the evaluation of a gate, as often this evaluation depends on the verdicts of more that one sub-gate, as well as what these verdicts are (see Fig. 1). A variable g_m can only take the values *yes*, *no* and *end*, produced by the relevant monitor instrumented over a trace.

A **configuration** of monitor M is an array s_M containing a value for all program variables g of M. We denote the set of all configurations for a monitor M as $\mathcal{S}_M$. We use the notation $s[M \backslash i]$ to denote the update of a configuration s where gate M stores some value j to one where the i-th coordinate of j is 0, while all other variables have the value they had in configuration s. Similarly, we use the notation $s[M \backslash end_i]$ to refer to a configuration where the update $s[M \backslash i]$ has taken place *and* the value of the $\ell + 1$-th bit of j is set to 1, and we also use the notation $s[v/M]$ with $v \in \{yes, no, end\}$, to mean a configuration where the value of the variable for gate M is updated to v,

All gate variables in a circuit monitor are initialized to $2^\ell - 1$ (a sequence of ℓ-many zeros), to represent that all sub-gates are waiting to give some output and $s_{M_{init}}$ stands for the initial configuration of M. Since M is a family of circuits, we have that the initial configuration of each monitor M_i in the family corresponds to a different initial configuration $s_{M_{i-init}}$.

Example 2. In Fig. 1, we give an example of a circuit monitor and its evaluation.

Semantics. The semantics of a regular monitors is as presented in [1]. Each regular monitor corresponds to an LTS, and a transition labeled with $a \in \text{ACT}$ corresponds to a regular monitor observing the event a when instrumented with a system p that produces it. The semantics of a circuit monitor is given as a transition relation $\rightarrow \subseteq \mathcal{S}_M \times \mathcal{S}_M$ and the instrumentation $\lhd$ takes place over a set of regular monitors $\overrightarrow{m}$ instrumented over a set of traces T, denoted $M(T)$.

We define $M(T) := s_{M_{|T|-init}} \lhd \overrightarrow{m}_{[i]} \lhd T$, where $\overrightarrow{m}$ is the set of regular monitors that occur in M, and $\overrightarrow{m}_{[i]}$ is $\overrightarrow{m}$, instrumented over the trace $t_i \in T$. When m is a regular monitor then $\lhd$ stands for the existing instrumentation relation from [1]. The transition and instrumentation relations are defined as the least ones that satisfy the axioms and rules in Fig. 2. Due to lack of space, we only include the rules giving the semantics of the $\bigvee[m]_k$ monitor. Those for the other operators follow the same structure. The proof in Appendix A could help with the understanding of the more intricate instrumentation rules.

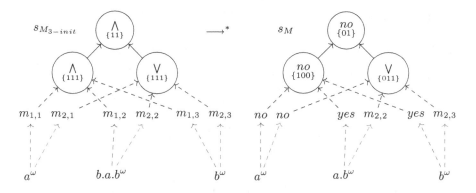

Fig. 1. The circuit monitor for the formula from Example 1, over $T = \{a^\omega, b.a.b^\omega, b^\omega\}$.

Monitor semantics:

$$\frac{s[m_{[i]}] = yes}{s \to s[yes/\bigvee_{[m]_k}]} \qquad \frac{s[m_{[i]}] = no}{s \to s[\bigvee[m]_k \backslash i]} \qquad \frac{s[m_{[i]}] = end}{s \to s[\bigvee[m]_k \backslash end_i]}$$

$$\frac{s[\bigvee[m]_k] = 0}{s \to s[no/\bigvee_{[m]_k}]} \qquad \frac{s[\bigvee[m]_k] = 2^k}{s \to s[end/\bigvee_{[m]_k}]}$$

Instrumentation:

$$\frac{m \xrightarrow{\tau} m'}{m \triangleleft t \xrightarrow{\tau} m' \triangleleft t} \qquad \frac{m \xrightarrow{a} m'}{m \triangleleft a.t \xrightarrow{a} m' \triangleleft t} \qquad \frac{\forall j \in \{1, \dots r\}, \; m_{j[i]} \triangleleft t \xrightarrow{a} m'_{j[i]} \triangleleft t'}{s \triangleleft (\overrightarrow{m} \triangleleft T) \to s \triangleleft (\overrightarrow{m}[m'_{j[i]}/m_{j[i]}, \forall j] \triangleleft T[t'/t])}$$

$$\frac{s \to s'}{s \triangleleft (\overrightarrow{m} \triangleleft T) \to s' \triangleleft (\overrightarrow{m} \triangleleft T)} \qquad \frac{s \triangleleft (\overrightarrow{m} \triangleleft T) \to s \triangleleft (\overrightarrow{m}[v/n_{j[i]}] \triangleleft T[t'/t])}{s \triangleleft (\overrightarrow{m} \triangleleft T) \to s[v/g_{m_{j[i]}}] \triangleleft (\overrightarrow{m}[v/n_{j[i]}] \triangleleft T[t'/t])}$$

Fig. 2. Operational semantics of processes in CMON.

A monitor is required to be *correct* with respect to some specification formula φ. The notions of correctness we use in this work are defined below.

Definition 3. *Given a monitor $M \in$ CMON, and a set of traces T.*

- *M **rejects** T (resp. **accepts** T) denoted $rej(M, T)$ (resp. $acc(M, T)$) iff $M(T) \to^* s \triangleleft \overrightarrow{n} \triangleleft T'$ for some $s, \overrightarrow{n}, T'$, where $s[M] = no$ (resp. $s[M] = yes$).*
- *Given a formula $\varphi \in$ Hyper-μHML, M is **sound** for φ if $\forall T$, $acc(M, T) \implies T \models \varphi$, and $rej(M, T) \implies T \not\models \varphi$.*
- *M is **violation complete** for φ if $\forall T$, $T \not\models \varphi \implies rej(M, T)$.*

Synthesis: Given a formula φ in HYPER[1]-sHML, We synthesize a circuit monitor M through the following recursive function $Syn(-) :$ HYPER[1]-sHML $\to$ CMON.

Definition 4 (Circuit Monitor Synthesis).

$$Syn(\exists_\pi \varphi) = \bigvee[m(\varphi)]_k \qquad\qquad Syn(\forall_\pi \varphi) = \bigwedge[m(\varphi)]_k$$
$$Syn(\varphi_1 \sqcup \varphi_2) = Syn(\varphi_1) \vee Syn(\varphi_2) \qquad Syn(\varphi_1 \sqcap \varphi_2) = Syn(\varphi_1) \wedge Syn(\varphi_2)$$

Where $m(-)$ is the monitor synthesis function for sHML *defined in [1].*

Proposition 1. *Given a formula φ in* HYPER[1]-sHML, *we have $Syn(\varphi)$ is a sound and violation-complete monitor for φ.*

Proof. The proof is by induction on the structure of φ. We present here a characteristic case and give more details for some of them in the Appendix A. Assume that $\varphi = \exists_\pi \psi$, with $\psi \in$ sHML and that we have a set of traces T s.t. $T \not\models \varphi$. From the semantics of HYPER[1]-sHML, we have that $t_i \not\models \psi$, for all traces t_i in T. However $\psi \in$ sHML and thus from [1] we get that m_ψ is a violation complete monitor for ψ. This means that for all $t_i \in T$, there exist $t_i' \in$ ACT* and $t_i'' \in$ ACT$^\omega$, such that $t_i = t_i'.t_i''$, such that the monitor m_ψ rejects t_i'.

From the rules in Fig. 2 we see that each gate $g_{m_{\psi[i]}}$ will reach the value no as enough events over the trace t_i' will occur. I.e. $s_M \lhd \overrightarrow{m_{\psi[i]}} \lhd T \to^* s_M \lhd \overrightarrow{m}_{[i]}[^{no}/m_{[i]}] \lhd T[t_i''/t_i]$, witch propagates to the evaluation of $g_{m_{[i]}}$ to no, for all i. We now study the transitions $s_M[^{no}/g_{m_\psi[i]}]$ since those can be then composed with this instrumentation via the fourth instrumentation rule. Applying the SOS rules yields that the update $\backslash i$ takes place for all i at the gate $\bigvee[m]_k$ which means that the value of j stored in it becomes 0. This finally yields that the value of the final gate $\bigvee[m]_k$ becomes 0, i.e. $s_M[^{no}/g_{m_{[i]}} \forall i] \to s_M[^{no}/\bigvee[m]_k]$. Since this transition can be composed with the discussed instrumentation we have that $s_M \lhd \overrightarrow{m_{\psi[i]}} \lhd T \to s_M[^{no}/g_{\bigvee[m_\psi]_{[i]}}] \lhd \overrightarrow{n} \lhd T'$ for some $\overrightarrow{n}$ and T and we are done. □

3.1 Runtime Costs

The monitor synthesis in Definition 4 provides a family of circuits that can be instrumented appropriately on an arbitrary set of traces to analyze the events occurring in them. Ideally, the runtime cost of monitoring resulting from our constructions should be bounded by a constant that does not depend on the parameters of the system (such as the number of available traces, or of the events observed so far) [17]. In this way, if a monitor is launched along with the system components, it will only induce a feasible computational overhead.

We already know that the regular monitors instrumented with individual traces analyze the system events they observe with a constant overhead [13]. Regarding the computational cost of the circuit part, since we are given k many traces, it must be that the necessary computation performed from a circuit monitor can be performed in parallel, distributed over the components that produced the traces in the first place. This means that we can only concern ourselves with the *circuit complexity* [18] of a given monitor, which encapsulates the parallel processing power necessary for its evaluation.

We now observe the synthesis function. There, a formula φ in HYPER^1-sHML will be turned into a family of circuit monitors where, for each connective of the original formula φ, the output monitor increases in size based on the size for the monitors of the sub-formulae of φ. However, for each connective of the formula, the *depth* of the circuit is only increased by 1 which means that the output circuit monitor has a depth bounded by the size of the formula φ. Since the gates of the output monitor can have either a fixed amount of sub-gates $(\vee, \wedge)$, or k many $(\bigvee, \bigwedge)$, we have that the output circuit is in the complexity class AC^0 [18]. Thus, the monitor only adds a constant computational overhead when executed over the computational resources of the distributed components of the system.

4   Conclusion and Future Work

We expect that the fragment HYPER^1-sHML is maximal with respect to violation completeness, which means that any monitor in CMON is monitoring for a formula in HYPER^1-sHML. However, the ultimate goal of this work is to extend the collection of monitorable properties by allowing alternating quantifiers in the syntax. This is a very important aspect of any work in this field, as the more interesting hyperproperties, such as the property "at all times, if one trace encounters the event p then all traces do so as well" which is a necessary component for the expression of properties such as noninference [8,15], require alternation of quantifiers.

A way to tackle this would be to project such properties into the HYPER^1-sHML fragment. However this procedure is not formally yet defined, or trivial and one could argue that since every hyperproperty has been shown ([9]) to be the intersection of a liveness and a safety hyperproperty, (and since liveness and safety properties are widely accepted as independent [3]), an elimination of alternating quantifiers can only take place in very few cases. Thus, our main purpose is to extend the logic and the consequent monitors in order to express and monitor for the most general class of such properties. The main objective of the logical fragment we give here is to establish a formal baseline which we will attempt to extend in future work.

Our approach to an extension would be to allow a notion of synchronization rounds among the regular monitors (or equivalently a round of communication). This would enable more complex dependencies between traces, as now the properties required of a given trace can be impacted by the state of the ones monitored for on a different one. However, the analysis of communications among the monitors is a complicated extension, as their exact content plays a significant role to our insight over the system, as well as the processing at runtime cost. We plan to implement this therefore by utilizing dynamic epistemic logic [10] in order to perform this extension formally and soundly.

A   Appendix: Cases for the Proof of Violation Completeness

Here we give some more insight on the remaining cases of the violation completeness proof. First we highlight that the second base case of our proof, for formulae of the form $\forall_\pi \psi$ is completely analogous to the one we give and thus omitted.

We will here give an important lemma necessary for analyzing both remaining cases, and then present the high level details for the case of $\sqcap$. The intuition of the importance of the lemma is that the monitors $Syn(\varphi_1)$ and $Syn(\varphi_2)$ should not have their computation affected from the fact that they are run in parallel over a set of traces T.

Lemma 1. *If*

- $s_{M_1} \lhd \overrightarrow{m_1}[i] \lhd T \rightarrow s'_{M_1} \lhd \overrightarrow{m_1}[i]' \lhd T'$, *and*
- $s_{M_2} \lhd \overrightarrow{m_2}[i] \lhd T \rightarrow s'_{M_2} \lhd \overrightarrow{m_2}[i]' \lhd T'$

then

- $s_{M_1 \vee M_2} \lhd \overrightarrow{m_{12}}[i] \lhd T \rightarrow s'_{M_1 \wedge M_2} \lhd \overrightarrow{m_{12}}[i]' \lhd T'$, *and*
- $s_{M_1 \wedge M_2} \lhd \overrightarrow{m_{12}}[i] \lhd T \rightarrow s'_{M_1 \wedge M_2} \lhd \overrightarrow{m_{12}}[i]' \lhd T'$,

where $\overrightarrow{m_{12}} = \overrightarrow{m_2} \cup \overrightarrow{m_2}$ *and* $\overrightarrow{m_{12}}' = \overrightarrow{m_2}' \cup \overrightarrow{m_2}'$ *respectively.*

Proof. We note here that a configuration for $s_{M_1 \vee M_2}$ is identical to one for $s_{M_1 \wedge M_2}$ except the root variable, as all other variables they both contain are $s'_{M_1} \cup s'_{M_2}$.

The key aspect of this proof is the third rule of the instrumentation relation. There we can see that in order for a configuration instrumented over a set of regular monitors, instrumented over a set of traces, can only advance its computation, if all monitors instrumented over the same trace progress with their computation synchronously by reading the next trace event.

Thus, form the assumptions of this lemma we get that for all $j = \{1, \ldots r\}$, where r is the total amount of different regular monitors occurring in M_1 and M_2 the premise of our rule is satisfied and thus the cumulative configuration of variables amounting for the union of variables of the two circuit monitors M_1 and M_2 (including the root variable), can perform the necessary transition to the new state, where all regular monitors (those both from M_1 and M_2) assigned to trace t_i have processed the event a, and we are done.   □

Having the above lemma streamlines our inductive step for the rest of the cases. Assuming a non-base-case formula in HYPER[1]-sHML we can clearly see that it must be of the form $\varphi = \varphi_1 \sqcap \varphi_2$ or $\varphi = \varphi_1 \sqcap \varphi_2$. We only analyze one of the two cases as they are symmetrical. For any set of traces T, such that $T \not\models \varphi$, from the semantics of HYPER[1]-sHML, we have that $T \not\models \varphi_1$ and $T \not\models \varphi_2$. Since the synthesized monitor for $\varphi_1 \sqcap \varphi_2$ can reach a configuration where the values of the gates for $Syn(\varphi_1)$ and $Syn(\varphi_2)$ are the same as they would be for the individual monitors instrumented over T, and by inductive hypothesis (which guarantees that $Syn(\varphi_1)$ and $Syn(\varphi_2)$ are violation-complete) we have necessary conclusion by combining the two negative verdicts of the individual monitors via the semantics.   □

References

1. Aceto, L., Achilleos, A., Francalanza, A., Ingólfsdóttir, A., Lehtinen, K.: Adventures in monitorability: from branching to linear time and back again. Proc. ACM Program. Lang. POPL **3**(52), 1–29 (2019)
2. Agrawal, S., Bonakdarpour, B.: Runtime verification of k-safety hyperproperties in HyperLTL. In: IEEE 29th Computer Security Foundations Symposium, CSF 2016, Lisbon, Portugal, June 27–July 1, 2016, pp. 239–252. IEEE Computer Society (2016)
3. Alpern, B., Schneider, F.B.: Recognizing safety and liveness. Distrib. Comput. **2**(3), 117–126 (1987)
4. Bartocci, E., Falcone, Y., Francalanza, A., Reger, G.: Introduction to runtime verification. In: Bartocci, E., Falcone, Y. (eds.) Lectures on Runtime Verification. LNCS, vol. 10457, pp. 1–33. Springer, Cham (2018). https://doi.org/10.1007/978-3-319-75632-5_1
5. Bocchi, L., Honda, K., Tuosto, E., Yoshida, N.: A theory of design-by-contract for distributed multiparty interactions. In: Gastin, P., Laroussinie, F. (eds.) CONCUR 2010. LNCS, vol. 6269, pp. 162–176. Springer, Heidelberg (2010). https://doi.org/10.1007/978-3-642-15375-4_12
6. Bonakdarpour, B., Finkbeiner, B.: The complexity of monitoring hyperproperties. In: 31st IEEE Computer Security Foundations Symposium, CSF 2018, Oxford, United Kingdom, July 9–12, 2018, pp. 162–174. IEEE Computer Society (2018)
7. Cassar, I., Francalanza, A., Mezzina, C.A., Tuosto, E.: Reliability and fault-tolerance by choreographic design. In: Francalanza, A., Pace, G.J. (eds.), Proceedings Second International Workshop on Pre- and Post-Deployment Verification Techniques, PrePost@iFM 2017, Torino, Italy, 19 September 2017, vol. 254 of EPTCS, pp. 69–80 (2017)
8. Clarkson, M.R., Finkbeiner, B., Koleini, M., Micinski, K.K., Rabe, M.N., Sánchez, C.: Temporal logics for hyperproperties. In: Abadi, M., Kremer, S. (eds.) POST 2014. LNCS, vol. 8414, pp. 265–284. Springer, Heidelberg (2014). https://doi.org/10.1007/978-3-642-54792-8_15
9. Clarkson, M.R., Schneider, F.B.: Hyperproperties. J. Comput. Secur. **18**(6), 1157–1210 (2010)
10. van Ditmarsch, H., van der Hoek, W., Kooi, B.: Dynamic Epistemic Logic, 1st edn. Springer, Dordrecht (2007). https://doi.org/10.1007/978-1-4020-5839-4
11. Finkbeiner, B., Hahn, C., Stenger, M., Tentrup, L.: Monitoring hyperproperties. Formal Methods Syst. Des. **54**(3), 336–363 (2019)
12. Francalanza, A., et al.: A foundation for runtime monitoring. In: Lahiri, S., Reger, G. (eds.) RV 2017. LNCS, vol. 10548, pp. 8–29. Springer, Cham (2017). https://doi.org/10.1007/978-3-319-67531-2_2
13. Francalanza, A., Aceto, L., Ingólfsdóttir, A.: Monitorability for the hennessy-milner logic with recursion. Formal Methods Syst. Des. **51**(1), 87–116 (2017)
14. Håstad, J.: Computational Limitations of Small-Depth Circuits, vol. 53. MIT Press, Cambridge (1987)

15. McLean, J.: A general theory of composition for a class of "possibilistic" properties. IEEE Trans. Softw. Eng. **22**(1), 53–67 (1996)
16. Mezzina, C.A., Pérez, J.A.: Causally consistent reversible choreographies: a monitors-as-memories approach. In: Proceedings of the 19th International Symposium on Principles and Practice of Declarative Programming, PPDP 2017, pp. 127–138, New York, Association for Computing Machinery (2017)
17. Rabin, M.O.: Real time computation. Israel J. Math. **1**(4), 203–211 (1963)
18. Vollmer, H.: Introduction to Circuit Complexity - A Uniform Approach. Texts in Theoretical Computer Science. An EATCS Series. Springer, New York (1999)

Process Algebra Can Save Lives: Static Analysis of XACML Access Control Policies Using mCRL2

Hamed Arshad[1]([⊠]) , Ross Horne[2] , Christian Johansen[3] , Olaf Owe[1] ,
and Tim A. C. Willemse[4]

[1] University of Oslo, Oslo, Norway
`{hamedar,olaf}@ifi.uio.no`
[2] University of Luxembourg, Esch-sur-Alzette, Luxembourg
`ross.horne@uni.lu`
[3] Norwegian University of Science and Technology, Gjøvik, Norway
`christian.johansen@ntnu.no`
[4] Eindhoven University of Technology, Eindhoven, Netherlands
`T.A.C.Willemse@tue.nl`

Abstract. This paper proposes an approach to formally verify XACML policies using the process algebra mCRL2. XACML (eXtensible Access Control Markup Language) is an OASIS standard for access control systems that is much used in health care due to its fine-grained, attribute-based policy definitions, useful in dynamic environments such as emergency wards. A notorious problem in XACML is the detection of conflicts, which arise especially when combining policies, such as when health institutions merge. Our formal translation of XACML policies into mCRL2, using our automated tool XACML2mCRL2, enables us to verify the above property, called consistency, as well as other policy properties such as completeness and obligation enforcement. Verifying policy properties statically allows us to resolve inconsistencies in advance, thus avoiding situations where an access request is denied in a critical situation (e.g., in an ambulance, when lives may be put in danger) just because of incomplete or inconsistent policies. The mCRL2 toolset is especially useful for modeling behaviors of interactive systems, where XACML would be only one part. Therefore, we verify an access control system together with the intended health care system that it is supposed to protect. For this, we exemplify how to verify safety and liveness properties of an assisted living and community care system.

Keywords: XACML · Access control · mCRL2 · Process algebra

1 Introduction

Access control is a fundamental security mechanism that protects resources based on access control policies. Access control systems are normally part of the authorization process that checks access requests against policies to ensure

© IFIP International Federation for Information Processing 2022
Published by Springer Nature Switzerland AG 2022
M. R. Mousavi and A. Philippou (Eds.): FORTE 2022, LNCS 13273, pp. 11–30, 2022.
https://doi.org/10.1007/978-3-031-08679-3_2

that only authorized users get access to resources of a system. One of the more recent and expressive access control models is the Attribute-Based Access Control (ABAC) [18,24], which provides fine-grained protection based on attributes of subject, object, and action. ABAC offers numerous advantages over conventional access control models and has reached the maturity of OASIS standards with the eXtensible Access Control Markup Language (XACML) [24] and the Security Assertion Markup Language (SAML) [8].

In this paper we focus on e-Health, were ABAC is a popular choice due to the flexibility given by the attributes and the way they cater for fine-grained access control in emergencies [3,15,27]. ABAC can handle quite complex access policies, such as for collaborative access control, where multiple subjects are involved (e.g., a doctor needs to be present/logged-in in order for a nurse to perform a procedure). An important feature of the XACML standard architecture is the use of obligations to perform actions before granting/denying access. For example, detailed auditing of health-care processes (such as administering medicines, preparing operation rooms, or home visits) can be done using obligations.

At the heart of ABAC are the access control policies, which can be specified using the policy language provided by the XACML standard. However, developing XACML policies is complex and error-prone because the policies grow in complexity at the same rate as the complexity (not the size) of the systems they are intended to protect. This is exacerbated by the XML-based verbose syntax and the extensive collection of features in XACML. The consistency and completeness of policies are important properties, e.g., a doctor cannot access the medical records of a patient due to inconsistent policies, or a caregiver cannot open the door lock of an elderly in home-care scenarios due to incomplete policies.

Resolving conflicts is currently done at runtime by employing one of the several XACML combining algorithms. For example, the DenyOverrides combining algorithm states that if several applicable rules result in both Permit and Deny, the final decision would be Deny. Such strategies of defaulting to deny access requests may be good for ensuring confidentiality, but they can be detrimental to the availability of the system. In complex and dynamic systems as in e-Health we wish to minimize the number of times that such conflicting situations appear, so to increase the availability of systems where unavailability may put lives at risk. This issue can be addressed by static analysis of access control policies, since the static analysis allows the states to be explored before the system is executed.

This paper presents an approach, and a tool, for verifying XACML policies integrated into their e-Health processes. Our approach is based on a process algebra, called mCRL2 [7,12,14], for modeling the behavior of distributed protocols and systems [1,10]. Using mCRL2 has the advantage of featuring time and (custom) data types, which we use for specifying XACML policies. The mCRL2 process language is accompanied by a powerful toolset, enabling us to simultaneously model XACML policies and e-Health processes subject to such policies, as well as specifying the properties we wish to verify.

Our goal is to formally verify access control policies and resolve inconsistencies in advance. Static analysis of policies helps to discover inconsistent and incomplete policies before their actual use. Counterexamples generated by the verifier can help security administrators to correct their policies. This paper provides also a tool for automatic transformation of XACML policies into mCRL2 specifications. Our tool, which we call XACML2mCRL2, can be added to the mCRL2 toolset to make it possible to automatically verify XACML policies.

A second goal, which also motivated our choice of process algebra, is to not only verify XACML policies independently, but together with the system that these policies are supposed to control. Since process algebras, like mCRL2, are particularly useful for modeling behaviours of distributed systems, the translations that our tool provides can be combined with models of, e.g., e-Health systems. Formal verification of such systems enables us to prove properties such as liveness or safety, which are relevant for the availability and confidentiality.

Structure of the Paper. Section 2 provides basic information about the XACML policy language. Section 3 presents our approach for the specification and verification of XACML policies using mCRL2. It first describes the procedure for mapping XACML policies into mCRL2 (Sect. 3.1), then it formulates the desired properties of the XACML policies using the modal μ-calculus (Sect. 3.2), next it explains how to verify the XACML policies (the mCRL2 specifications and properties) using the mCRL2 toolset, and finally, some example policies are analyzed based on the proposed approach. Section 4 explains how to analyze the behavior of the systems employing access control schemes using the same approach explained in Sect. 3. Related work is discussed in Sect. 5.

2   Background on the XACML Policy Language

The XACML standard describes (besides other things such as a reference architecture) a policy specification language, which we will simply refer to as XACML in this paper. As represented in Fig. 1, XACML has a hierarchical structure, with the main elements being: PolicySet, which includes one or more Policies or other PolicySets, and Policy, which includes one or more Rules.

Every PolicySet, Policy, and Rule has a Target, which determines the requests to which they are applicable. A Target may include a conjunction of AnyOf elements, each consisting of a disjunction of AllOf elements. An AllOf element is a conjunction of pairs (attribute-name, attribute-value), as XACML policies are based on the attributes of subjects, objects, actions, and the environment. The Target of a Rule may be empty, making the Rule applicable to all requests filtered based on the Targets of the PolicySet and Policy.

A Rule, normally meant to express a very simple access control policy, has a Condition part as well as an Effect that is either Deny or Permit. If the attributes provided in a request match those needed by the Target and the Condition of a Rule, then the Effect of the Rule will be returned to the parent Policy. In the case the attributes do not satisfy the Condition or if an

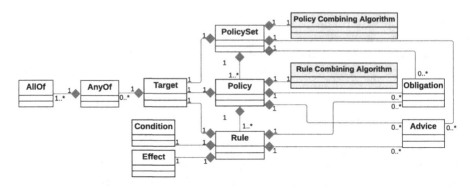

Fig. 1. XACML policy language model [24]. As explained in Sect. 3.1, the proposed approach does not translate gray boxes to mCRL2.

error occurs, `NotApplicable` or `Indeterminate`, respectively, will be returned to the parent `Policy`. `Conditions` are more powerful than `Targets` because XACML provides numerous functions (such as *integer-greater-than, integer-less-than-or-equal, n-of, not, anyURI-starts-with*) that can be used inside conditions, in addition to the OR/AND constructions that `Targets` are limited to.

`Obligation` or `Advice` expressions may be attached to every `PolicySet`, `Policy`, and `Rule` in order to enforce extra constraints. For example, a `Policy` may use an `Obligation` to require to log successful access to patients medical records. An `Advice` is the same as an `Obligation` with the difference that the `Advice` is optional, i.e., the policy enforcement point (PEP) can ignore an `Advice`, whereas it must always execute all `Obligations`.

Since multiple `Rules` (or `Policies`) with different `Effects` may be applicable to the same request, conflicting rule `Effects` (or decisions) may be reached, which indicates inconsistencies between `Rules` and `Policies`. The XACML standard does not offer any solution to detect such inconsistencies when authoring access control policies. Instead, it provides several combining algorithms, i.e., `Rule Combining Algorithms` and `Policy Combining Algorithms`, to combine contradictory decisions and reach a single decision.

3   Modeling and Analyzing XACML Policies

The mCRL2 toolset [7] can be used for analyzing software and concurrent systems [13]. Its main input language is an ACP-inspired process algebra that also has built-in support for frequently-used data types and operations on these, as well as facilities for users to specify their own data types. Properties of systems modeled in the mCRL2 language can be expressed in the first-order modal μ-calculus. For a detailed account of the mCRL2 language and the property language, we refer to [12–14]; in the remainder of this paper, we explain the relevant syntax and concepts as we go along.

In this section we show how to specify and verify XACML policies using the mCRL2 toolset (version 202106.0). We first explain how we map XACML policies into mCRL2 processes; this is the essence of our tool XACML2mCRL2 [4]. Then, we formally define three desired properties for XACML policies and in the end analyze three example policies.

3.1 Mapping XACML Policies into mCRL2

We encode the XACML components into mCRL2 concepts as follows. An attribute can be considered as a name-value pair. A Rule can be considered as a tuple ⟨*RuleID, Target, Condition, Effect, Obligation*⟩, where *Target* and *Condition* are sets of attributes, and *Effect* can be either *Permit* or *Deny*. The last element is abstracted as a pair of *ObligationID* and a *FulfillOn* element with value either *Permit* or *Deny*, specifying the decision for which the obligation is applicable. A Policy can be abstracted as ⟨*PolicyID, Target, Rules, Obligation*⟩, and similarly a PolicySet as ⟨*PolicySetID, Target, Policies, Obligation*⟩, with both *Rules* and *Policies* being sets. PolicySet, Policy, and Rule can also include advices. However, since the policy enforcement point can ignore enforcing an advice, it can be ignored when analyzing XACML policies.

An mCRL2 specification begins with a declaration of the required data types and actions. We start by defining the following data types for the subject, object, and action attributes:

```
1  sort SAtt = struct attribute(name:SAttName, value:SAttValue);
2  sort OAtt = struct attribute(name:OAttName, value:OAttValue);
3  sort AAtt = struct attribute(name:AAttName, value:AAttValue);
```

The keyword **sort** is used to define new data types. We use the keyword **struct** because these are structured data types (functional data types), defined using other data types for names and values. Normally, all attribute names and values used in the policies that are going to be analyzed need to be listed in the definitions of these sorts. For the sake of simplicity in the text here, we consider the following values for these sorts.

```
1  sort  SAttName   = struct  subjectid;
2  sort  SAttValue  = struct  CareGiverA|Doctor;
3  sort  OAttName   = struct  resourceid;
4  sort  OAttValue  = struct  HealthData;
5  sort  AAttName   = struct  actionid;
6  sort  AAttValue  = struct  Read;
```

We define a data type **Decision** containing the two possible rule effects.

```
1  sort  Decision = struct  Permit|Deny;
```

The following sort lists obligation identifiers. Here we keep this list minimal, but our tool populates this with all the obligations found in the XACML files.

```
1  sort  ObgID = struct  email|log;
```

We model the main elements of an XACML policy, i.e., PolicySet, Policy, and Rule, as separate processes (starting with keyword **proc**). All the actions performed by these processes need to be declared at the beginning of the mCRL2 specification. If an action is parametrized by some data, then the type of the parameter needs to be stated as well. Below, the `Request` action carries three sets of attributes (i.e., subject, object, and action attributes), whereas a `Response` action carries in addition also a decision. We use finite sets, defined with *FSet*, with the type of the elements specified as parameter.

```
1  act  Request : FSet ( SAtt )# FSet ( OAtt )# FSet ( AAtt );
2       Obligation : FSet ( SAtt )# FSet ( OAtt )# FSet ( AAtt )# ObgID ;
3       Response : FSet ( SAtt )# FSet ( OAtt )# FSet ( AAtt )# Decision ;
```

The policy decision point evaluates an access request against the policies and reaches a decision based on the values of attributes provided in the access request. Hence, we define the above-mentioned processes as parametrized processes, where a process carries a set of attributes provided in the request.

The `PolicySet` process checks whether the attributes that exist in the received request match those requested by the target of the policies. If a policy is applicable to a request, the corresponding `Policy` process will be called (i.e., the `PolicySet` process will behave as the corresponding `Policy` process). For example, suppose that a `PolicySet` (e.g., `PolicySet_PLS1`) contains two policies, e.g., `Policy_PL1` and `Policy_PL2`, where the target of the first one is applicable to the requests that contain a subject attribute `attribute(A, B)` and the second one is applicable to the requests containing an object attribute `attribute(C, D)` and an action attribute `attribute(E, F)`.

```
1  proc PolicySet_PLS1(RS : FSet(SAtt), RO : FSet(OAtt), RA : FSet(AAtt))=
2       ((attribute(A, B) in RS) ->
3                               Policy_PL1(RS, RO, RA))
4     + ((attribute(C, D) in RO && attribute(E, F) in RA) ->
5                               Policy_PL2(RS, RO, RA));
```

In the above, the `PolicySet` process consists of non-deterministic choice operator + and the ternary if-then-else construct c -> A <> B, where the evaluation of the Boolean condition c determines the behavior. If the condition c holds, then the process behaves as the process A; otherwise, it behaves as the process B. Note that c -> A is equivalent to c -> A <> `delta`, where `delta` denotes a process that cannot perform any action. The *in* operator is used to check if an attribute exists in the received request including sets of subject attributes, `RS`, object attributes, `RO`, and action attributes, `RA`. Figure 2 shows how every element of a simplified version of the corresponding XACML specification is transformed to mCRL2 (please note shapes, colors, and labels). Our standard for naming mCRL2 processes is {PolicySet/Policy/Rule}_{PolicySetId/PolicyId/RuleId}, where PolicySetId, PolicyId, and RuleId will be extracted from the XACML specification. The red dashed lines box in Fig. 2-a represents a logical AND between two conditions; hence, it is transformed to && in mCRL2. In XACML, `access-subject`, `resource`, `action` categories are for, respectively, subject, object, and action attributes (`RS`, `RO`, and `RA` in our mCRL2 specifications).

A `Policy` process also checks the target of its rules to call the `Rule` processes that are applicable to the received request. Suppose that `Policy_PL1` has `Rule_R1` and `Rule_R2`, where `Rule_R1` and `Rule_R2` are applicable to

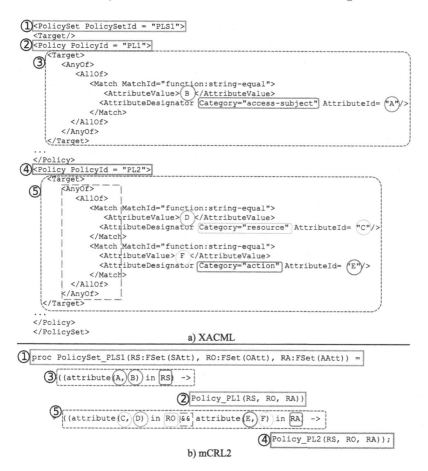

Fig. 2. A simplified piece of an XACML specification and corresponding mCRL2 specification.

the requests containing object attributes, respectively, `attribute(G, H)` and `attribute(I, J)`.

```
1  Policy_PL1(RS:FSet(SAtt), RO:FSet(OAtt), RA:FSet(AAtt)) =
2    ((attribute(G, H) in RO) ->  Rule_R1(RS, RO, RA))
3  + ((attribute(I, J) in RO) ->  Rule_R2(RS, RO, RA));
```

A `Rule` process checks whether the received request satisfies its condition. If the request satisfies the condition of the rule, then the `Rule` performs the `Response` action, which reflects the effect of the rule. However, if there is an `Obligation` associated with the `Rule`, then the `Rule` performs the `Obligation` action (which carries the request and the obligation ID) before the `Response` action. In the XACML policy language, an `Obligation` might be included in a `PolicySet`, a `Policy`, or a `Rule`. In our mapping, we move an `Obligation` from the `PolicySet` and `Policy` levels to the `Rule` that activates them. For example, suppose `Policy_PL1` has an obligation, which mandates writing a log when an access is granted (Obligation ID = log, FulfillOn = Permit). The effect of `Rule_R1` and `Rule_R2`, which are included in `Policy_PL1`, is `Permit` and `Deny`, respectively. Moreover, the condition of `Rule_R1` and `Rule_R2` includes action attributes `attribute(K, L)` and `attribute(M, N)`, respectively. In the following specification, the symbol . denotes the sequential composition. Figure 3 also represents the relation between a simplified version of the corresponding XACML specification and the generated mCRL2 specification (follow the shapes, colors, and labels). As shown in Fig. 3, the `log` obligation of `Policy_PL1` is moved to the applicable rule, `Rule_R1` (see the red box that is labeled with 7).

```
1  Rule_R1(RS:FSet(SAtt), RO:FSet(OAtt), RA:FSet(AAtt)) =
2  ((attribute(K, L) in RA) ->
3  (Obligation(RS, RO, RA, log).Response(RS, RO, RA, Permit)));
4
5  Rule_R2(RS:FSet(SAtt), RO:FSet(OAtt), RA:FSet(AAtt)) =
6  ((attribute(M, N) in RA) -> Response(RS, RO, RA, Deny));
```

An mCRL2 specification ends with the initialization of the system. The system can be initialized by considering all possible combinations of attributes and excluding empty sets for subject, object, and action attributes as follows.

```
1  init sum RS:FSet(SAtt).sum RO:FSet(OAtt).sum RA:FSet(AAtt).
2  (RS !={} && RO !={} && RA !={}) ->
3  Request(RS, RO, RA).PolicySet_PLS1(RS, RO, RA);
```

In mCRL2 specifications, the initialization section starts with the **init** keyword. The summation operator, `sum`, is used for considering all possible values for attributes in `RS`, `RO`, and `RA`. In mCRL2, `!`, `{}`, and `&&` denote the negation, empty set, and logical AND, respectively.

We have implemented a prototype, XMACL2mCRL2, for automatic transformation of XACML policies into mCRL2 specification using Java. Since XACML policies are in XML format, XMACL2mCRL2 uses the declarative eXtensible Stylesheet Language Transformations (XSLT) (version 1.0) to define a set of template rules specifying how XACML policies should be transformed into mCRL2. XMACL2mCRL2 may further be integrated into the mCRL2 toolset as a new tool for analyzing XACML policies. The completeness of our transformation tool (and our proposed approach) can be evaluated in terms of the number of XACML policy elements that are covered/supported in the translation from XACML to mCRL2. Our transformation tool covers all elements of the XACML policy model represented in Fig. 1 except `Policy Combining Algorithm` and `Rule Combining Algorithm`. The combining algorithms are intentionally not modeled because one of our goals is to find inconsistencies between policies and fix them when authoring policies, i.e., statically before the access control system is put into production.

The XACML standard offers several functions that can be used in the condition part of rules to form more complex conditions. However, the current version of our implementation may not cover all of them. For example, we can now check whether or not the request contains attribute (Role, Doctor). However, some policies may use other functions, such as *greater-than* or *less-than*, e.g.,

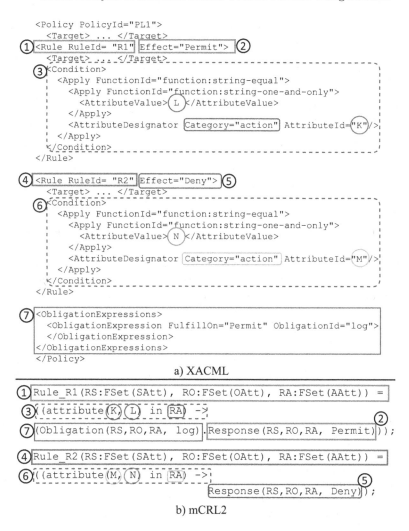

Fig. 3. a) A simplified XACML specification and; b) the corresponding mCRL2 specification.

a policy might be applicable to requests issued by adults (age > 18). Since all the functions offered in the standard can be specified/modeled in mCRL2, the current version of our transformation tool can be improved by considering the remaining functions for the condition part of the rules.

3.2 Specifying the Properties of XACML Policies

This section formulates our desired properties of XACML policies using the first order modal μ-calculus. The properties that we consider are policy-completeness, policy-consistency, and obligation-safety as defined below.

Property P1 *(Policy-Completeness). A set of policies is complete if it covers all the access requests.*

More formally, for every `Request` action, the policy set will inevitably provide a `Response` action. This can be formalized as follows.

```
forall rs:FSet(SAtt), ro:FSet(OAtt), ra:FSet(AAtt).
[Request(rs, ro, ra)]mu X.
([!exists d:Decision.Response(rs, ro, ra, d)]X && <true>true)
```

In the above formula, the symbols `forall` and `&&` denote the conventional first-order logic constructs and can be interpreted as usual. The modal operators `[_]_` and `<_>_` allow to reason about the behavior of the process. A state satisfies formula `[A]`ϕ if all states reached by an action taken from a set of actions `A`, satisfy formula ϕ. Sets of actions are described using first-order logic; for instance, `true` describes the set of all actions, `exists` denotes set union and the `!` operator denotes set complement. The subformula `[Request(rs,ro,ra)` `]`ϕ captures exactly those states whose `Request`-successor states satisfy ϕ. The operator `<A>`ϕ is dual, and holds true of a state if it has some `a`-transition (with `a` taken from set `A`) leading to a state satisfying ϕ. Note that the state formula `true` holds true in all states. A state therefore satisfies `<true>true` whenever it can execute *some* action. Finally, the subformula shaped `mu X.([!A]X &&<` `true>true)` describes exactly those states for which executing an action taken from the set `A` is at some point unavoidable; in our case, `A` is the set of `Response` actions with either a `Deny` or `Permit` decision, but attribute sets that match those of the `Request` action.

Property P2 *(Policy-Consistency). A set of policies is conflict-free if there is no inconsistency between policies.*

This property is important when integrating policies from different domains. Stated more formally, this property requires that executing a `Request` action (with concrete attributes) cannot lead to both a `Deny` and a `Permit` decision. This can be expressed as follows:

```
forall rs:FSet(SAtt), ro:FSet(OAtt), ra:FSet(AAtt).
[Request(rs, ro, ra)]
!(<true*.Response(rs, ro, ra, Deny)> true &&
<true*.Response(rs, ro, ra, Permit)> true)
```

Here, the subformulas shaped `<true*.A>true`, using the Kleene `*` and having the same meaning as `mu X.(<true>X||<A>true)`, describe precisely those states that, in a finite number of steps, can reach a state that can execute an action from the set `A`. Our formula thus describes that after any `Request` action, it is impossible to both reach a state that can execute a `Response` action with a `Deny` decision and a state that can execute a `Response` action with a `Permit` decision.

Property P3 *(Obligation-Safety). A concrete Request either will always yield an Obligation, or it will never yield an Obligation.*

Intuitively, this means that executing a `Request` action cannot lead to a state in which both an `Obligation` action and a non-`Obligation` action are enabled at the same time.

```
forall rs:FSet(SAtt), ro:FSet(OAtt), ra:FSet(AAtt).
[Request(rs,ro,ra)]!(<exists o:ObgID.Obligation(rs,ro,ra,o)>
true && <!exists o:ObgID.Obligation(rs, ro, ra, o)>true)
```

After translating XACML policies into mCRL2 using our *XACML2mCRL2* tool and specifying the desired properties using the modal μ-calculus, the model checker of the mCRL2 toolset can be used to do the verification as shown in Fig. 4. If the policies satisfy the desired property, a `true` will be returned as the result. However, if the property is violated, a `false` is returned, along with a counterexample illustrating the violation.

Example 1. Consider a rule that allows Doctors to Read patients' HealthData.[1]

Rule 1: $((resourceid = HealthData) \wedge (actionid = Read)$
$\wedge(subjectid = Doctor)) \Rightarrow Permit$

Analyzing the corresponding mCRL2 specification shows that the Policy-Completeness property is not held. The verification engine returns the counterexample represented in Fig. 5a showing an access request that this rule does not cover. Policy-Consistency holds because there is no other rule that can cause conflicts, and the same for Obligation-Safety as the rule has no obligation expression.

Example 2. Consider adding to the policy in Example 1 a rule that allows Doctors to Read everything and has an obligation for logging all successful accesses.

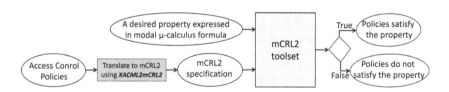

Fig. 4. Analyzing the specifications using the mCRL2 toolset

Rule 2: $((subjectid = Doctor) \wedge (actionid = Read) \Rightarrow$
$\langle Permit, Obligation(log)\rangle$

Analyzing the updated policy shows that only Policy-Consistency is held. The counterexample in Fig. 6 shows that the Obligation-Safety property is violated because there is a request that can be covered by **Rule 2** but it is possible to get a permit response for that (by **Rule 1**) without performing the log obligation.

---

[1] The XACML version of all the rules and the corresponding mCRL2 specifications generated using our XACML2mCRL2 tool are available in [4].

(a)   (b)

Fig. 5. (a) A counterexample violating the *Policy-Completeness* property in Example 1. (b) A counterexample violating the *Policy-Consistency* property in Example 3. Att = {attribute(subjectid, CareGiverA)}, {attribute(resourceid, HealthData)}, {attribute(actionid, Read)}.

Example 3. Consider adding to the policy in Example 1 another rule to deny access requests to the HealthData of patients if the requester is not a Doctor.

Rule 3: $((resourceid = HealthData) \wedge (actionid = Read)$
$\wedge \mathbf{NOT}(subjectid = Doctor)) \Rightarrow Deny$

Analyzing this updated policy shows that all our desired properties are held.

Example 4. Update the policy of Example 3 by adding a rule to allow CareGiverA (e.g., ambulance nurse) to Read the HealthData.

Rule 4: $((resourceid = HealthData) \wedge (actionid = Read)$
$\wedge (subjectid = CareGiverA)) \Rightarrow Permit$

We can verify that Policy-Completeness and Obligation-Safety hold, but for Policy-Consistency we are shown the counterexample from Fig. 5b, which demonstrates a conflict between **Rule 3** and **Rule 4**.

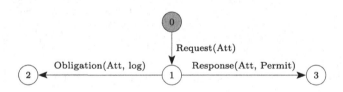

Fig. 6. A counterexample violating the *Obligation-Safety* property in Example 2. Att = {attribute(subjectid, Doctor)}, {attribute(resourceid, HealthData)}, {attribute(actionid, Read)}.

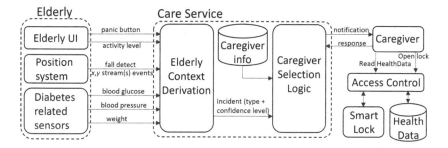

Fig. 7. Architecture of the assisted living and community care system.

4 System Behavior in Presence of XACML Policies

This section demonstrates how we can use mCRL2 to formally specify and verify also the system around the access control policies, thus allowing to perform XACML policy verification in context.

Use Case Informal Description. Our use case is taken from a pilot called Assisted Living and Community Care Systems (ALCCS) coordinated by Phillips research in a European project called SCOTT[1]. The goal of the ALCCS pilot is to develop a system for elderly home care with a simplified architecture depicted in Fig. 7. Along the way we describe its formalization in mCRL2.

Bob is an elderly person living alone in a smart home equipped with a variety of sensors, e.g., for measuring activity level or blood pressure. Important for us is the panic button, which can be used to get help when needed, and the fall detection sensors. Sensor readings are being sent to a storage and processing unit called Elderly Context Derivation (ECD), which uses these to raise emergency alerts (e.g., if Bob presses the panic button or has fallen).

When there is an emergency, a list of potential caregivers, who can be professionals or neighbors, will be notified. Once a caregiver receives the notification from the ECD (i.e., CareService) and proceeds with the case, the caregiver will be granted access to Bob's house and medical records. In this scenario, it is important that whenever Bob falls or presses the panic button, i.e., when there is an alarm, then Bob should eventually get help from a caregiver, i.e., the alarm should eventually be handled by a caregiver. Moreover, it is also important that only a caregiver who has been assigned to an elderly can open the door lock of the elderly's house in the case of an emergency.

Modeling and Verification of the ALCCS. The interacting components represented in Fig. 7 are modeled as separate mCRL2 processes running in parallel. These processes are initialized below, where we restrict the allowed actions

---

[1]EU Horizon 2020 ECSEL Joint Undertaking project SCOTT – Secure COnnected Trustable Things (https://scottproject.eu/).

to those in the list `Act` and define the synchronization pairs in the list `Com` (see the full specification in [4]). An example of a pair of synchronizing actions is `SndReply|RcvReply -> Reply`, resulting in the action `Reply`.

```
1 init allow(Act, comm(Com,
2 rename({Request->RcvACRequest, Response->SndACResponse},
3 Elderly||CareService({CG1, CG2})||Lock(false, false)||
4 AccessControl||CareGiver({attribute(subjectid, CareGiverA)},
5 {attribute(resourceid, HealthData)},
6 {attribute(actionid, Read)}))));
```

In the specification of these processes, the following data types and actions are used, where `EL` represents elderly IDs (it is assumed that there are two caregivers and two elderly patients). In the full specifications from [4] one can see that we also add in the actions and sorts used in the processes related to the access control policies from the previous section.

```
1 sort CareGivers = struct CG1 | CG2;
2 sort EL = struct EID1 | EID2;
3 act Fall, Panic, Read, Willing, Notwilling;
4 SndAlarm, RcvAlarm, Alarm:EL;
5 ...
```

We model a simplified version of the elderly patient, where an alarm is raised by the `Elderly` process when either falling or pressing the panic button. We define recursive processes, where the specified behavior continues indefinitely (unless forced to wait indefinitely for their communicating parties).

```
1 proc Elderly=(Fall + Panic).sum E:EL.SndAlarm(E).Elderly;
```

The `CareService` receives an alarm and notifies caregivers. This has been initialized above with a list of two caregivers {CG1, CG2}. The `CareService` assigns a caregiver who is willing to handle the emergencies.

```
1 CareService(L:FSet(CareGivers)) = sum E:EL.RcvAlarm(E).
2 set_emergency(E, true).sum cg:CareGivers.(cg in L) ->
3 SndNotification(E, cg).set_assignment(E, cg, true).
4 RcvFinished(E, cg).set_emergency(E, false).
5 set_assignment(E, cg, false).CareService();
```

The `CareGiver` process either accepts or rejects to be available for handling the emergencies (notice the non-deterministic choice operator + on line 6). Recall that `CareGiver` was initialized with three sets of attributes. After receiving the assignment message from the `CareService`, the caregiver is supposed to enter the elderly's house, and thus the `CareGiver` process sends an `OpenLock` message to the `Lock` process of the elderly's house.

```
1 CareGiver(RS:FSet(SAtt), RO:FSet(OAtt), RA:FSet(AAtt)) =
2 Willing.sum E:EL,CG:CareGivers.RcvNotification(E, CG).
3 SndOpenLock(E, CG).
4 ((SndACRequest(RS,RO,RA).sum D:Decision.RcvACResponse(RS,RO,RA,D).(D==
      Permit)->Read.SndFinished(E, CG).CareGiver())
5 + (SndFinished(E, CG).CareGiver()))
6 + Notwilling.CareGiver();
```

The lock can be opened only if *(i)* there is an emergency for the elderly and *(ii)* the requester is assigned as the caregiver for the elderly (notice the operator `&&` inside the condition to the deterministic conditional choice operator).

```
1 Lock(ev, av:Bool) = sum E:EL,CG:CareGivers.RcvOpenLock(E,CG).
2 ((ev && av) -> LockOpened(E,CG)<>Rejected(E,CG)).Lock(ev, av)
3 + sum E:EL. sum ev':Bool.get_emergency(E,ev').Lock(ev', av)
4 + sum E:EL, CG:CareGivers.sum av':Bool.
5 get_assignment(E, CG, av').Lock(ev, av');
```

After getting inside the elderly's house, the caregiver may try (notice again the non-deterministic choice on line 5 in the `CareGiver` process) to read the HealthData of the elderly by sending an access request (on line 4). The access request will be evaluated based on the existing access control policies through the `AccessControl` process, which is defined to make the processes related to the access control policies recursive. Here, Rule 4 from the previous section, is the only policy that we used for evaluation of access requests (the full specification in [4] contains all the policies that were introduced in Sect. 3).

```
1 AccessControl =
2 (sum RS:FSet(SAtt).sum RO:FSet(OAtt).sum RA:FSet(AAtt).
3 (RS !={} && RO !={} && RA !={}) ->
4 Request(RS,RO,RA).PolicySet_root(RS, RO, RA)).AccessControl;
5
6 PolicySet_root(RS:FSet(SAtt), RO:FSet(OAtt), RA:FSet(AAtt)) =
7 Policy_Policy1(RS, RO, RA);
8
9 Policy_Policy1(RS:FSet(SAtt), RO:FSet(OAtt), RA:FSet(AAtt)) =
10 ((attribute(resourceid, HealthData) in RO) &&
11 (attribute(actionid, Read) in RA)) ->
12 Rule_Rule4(RS, RO, RA);
13
14 Rule_Rule4(RS:FSet(SAtt), RO:FSet(OAtt), RA:FSet(AAtt)) =
15 (attribute(subjectid, CareGiverA) in RS) ->
16 Response(RS, RO, RA, Permit);
```

After handling the emergency, the `CareGiver` informs the `CareService` that the case is done, which in turn closes the emergency and unassigns the caregiver.

Specifying the System Properties. We exemplify two behavioral properties that we desire of our system above. First we are interested in a form of conditional liveness (i.e., some event will eventually happen under certain conditions), which are sometimes called *response* properties.

Property S1 *(Response). Invariantly, every alarm must eventually be handled by some caregiver.*

```
[true*]forall e:EL.
[SndAlarm(e).(!exists cg:CareGivers.Finished(e,cg))*]
<true*.exists cg:CareGivers.Finished(e,cg)>true
```

Here, the subformula of the form $[A^*]\phi$, which is shorthand for nu X. ([A]X & & ϕ), describes those states from which all states reachable by executing zero or more actions from the set A, satisfy property ϕ.

Property S2 *(Safety). Opening the door lock (LockOpened action) is not permitted, as long as there is no emergency for the elderly. Furthermore, only the assigned caregiver can open the door lock.*

This property can be split into the two following requirements:

Property S2-A. *Only a caregiver assigned to an elderly can open the lock.*

```
forall e:EL,cg:CareGivers.nu X.([!assignment(e,cg,true)]X &&
[LockOpened(e, cg)]false && [assignment(e,cg,true)] nu Y.
([!assignment(e,cg,false)]Y && [assignment(e,cg,false)]X))
```

In the above formula, the two alternating greatest fixed points are used to characterize the situation that, along a path either no **assignment** has happened, and so **LockOpened** should not be enabled, expressed by **[LockOpened(e, cg)]** *false*, *or* an **assignment** has just happened. In the latter case we descend into the fixed point Y, where any action is permitted so long as the caregiver is not unassigned. By unassigning a caregiver we again recurse to X.

Property S2-B. *An assignment for an emergency must be preceded by the emergency, and is only 'valid' for as long as the emergency is 'active'.*

```
forall e:EL.nu X.([!emergency(e, true)]X &&
[exists cg:CareGivers.assignment(e, cg, true)]false &&
[emergency(e, true)]nu Y.
([!exists cg:CareGivers.assignment(e, cg, false)]Y &&
[exists cg:CareGivers.assignment(e, cg, false)] X))
```

Analyzing the model (with 212 states and 596 transitions) based on Property S1 and Property S2 (both Property S2-A and Property S2-B) show that all the properties are held.

5   Related Work

Bryans [5] used the CSP [16] and the FDR model-checking tool for analyzing access control policies. They expressed RBAC policies in CSP and then used the FDR to analyze the CSP specifications and compare policies (to check if two policies are equivalent). However, Bryans did not consider different properties and did not model the condition part of rules nor obligations.

Kolovski et al. [19] employed the Pellet description logic reasoner to find equivalent, redundant, and incompatible XACML policies. However, Kolovski et al. also did not take into account rule conditions nor obligations.

Ahn et al. [2] used Answer Set Programming (ASP) [20,22] and ASP solvers for analyzing XACML-based RBAC policies. Ahn et al.'s approach does not handle obligations nor complex conditions and attribute functions.

Fisler et al. [9] proposed a method for analyzing XACML-based RBAC policies by representing the policies using Multi-Terminal Binary Decision Diagrams (MTBDD) [11]. However, the proposed method does not verify all the desired properties of policies and does not take into account all elements of XACML policies. Rao et al. [26] proposed an algebra, called Fine-grained Integration Algebra (FIA), for integration of XACML policies. FIA also uses MTBDDs for representing XACML policies. Policies can be integrated by mapping operations on the policies onto operations on the MTBDDs, which represent policies. After mapping operations, the resulted MRBDD can be traversed to generate an XACML policy that is the result of the integration of two or more policies. Hu et al. [17] proposed a policy-based segmentation method to detect and resolve policy anomalies (conflicts and redundancies). Hu et al.'s method first represents (parses) policies using the Binary Decision Diagram (BDD) [6], then it transfers rules into Boolean expressions. Next, it replaces Boolean expressions with Boolean variables. After that, it identifies anomalies using two proprietary algorithms. Morisset et al. [23] also employed BDDs to address the problem of missing information in ABAC. They proposed a framework for efficient extended evaluation of XACML policies, which checks all the possible outcomes of the evaluation of a given request by considering all possible values for the hidden attributes (i.e., by extending the initial request). Lin et al. [21] proposed a policy analyzer through the combination of MTBDDs (to represent/parse policies) and a SAT solver (to check if two representations are similar). The main goal was to find the similarities between XACML policies.

Turkmen et al. [28] proposed a framework based on satisfiability modulo theories (SMT) for the verification of XACML policies. The goal was to convert policies into SMT formulas and verify the desired properties using SMT solvers.

Another relevant work is the formalization of XACML in terms of multi-valued logics presented in [25]. Ramli et al. [25] provided an abstract syntax for XACML and formalized combining algorithms as operators on a partially ordered set of decisions.

In our proposed approach, mCRL2 is used for specifying all elements of XACML policies (for ABAC), including obligations, and analyzing the most important properties of access control policies. Furthermore, access control policies are also analyzed *in context*, i.e., together with the system that these policies are supposed to protect. The system surrendering access control policies is also specified and analyzed using mCRL2. The system and access control policies are combined using the parallel composition offered by mCRL2. The use of parallel composition and analysis of access control policies in context distinguish the approach presented in this paper from prior approaches and especially those based on formal methods. It would be interesting for future work to verify the soundness of our translation of XACML into mCRL2 with respect to the formal semantics for XACML provided by Rameli et al. [25].

6   Conclusion

We have presented a methodology supported by a tool for formal verification of access control policies, which is built on top of mCRL2. Our XACML2mCRL2 tool implements the mapping from XACML policies into mCRL2 specifications as described in Sect. 3. The mapping covers every element of XACML policies, i.e., policy set, policy, and rule, and allows to formally verify the completeness (Property P1) and consistency (Property P2) of the XACML policies using the first-order modal μ-calculus. Moreover, in contrast to other related approaches surveyed in Sect. 5, XACML2mCRL2 takes into account the obligation expressions; for instance, Example 2 shows a violation of our Obligation-Safety property (Property P3). The model checker provided by the mCRL2 toolset automatically generates counterexamples, such as those shown in Fig. 3 and Fig. 6, useful for detecting and resolving incomplete and inconsistent policies.

To analyze the XACML policies *in context*, i.e., together with the system that these policies are supposed to protect, we have modeled an e-Health use case represented in Fig. 7. We have integrated the mCRL2 specifications generated by XACML2mCRL2 into the use case model, including the Elderly, CareGiver, CareService, and Lock processes. We have formulated and verified liveness and safety properties, Property S1 respectively Property S2, to make sure that an elderly will always receive help in the case of an emergency, and respectively only assigned caregivers can open the door lock of the elderly person's house. Therefore, we can conclude that our methodological approach to formal verification of access control policies can potentially be used to avoid critical problems in, for example, e-Health systems. Indeed, mCRL2 verifies automatically liveness and safety properties for our use case having hundreds of states and transitions, which would be difficult to analyze manually.

Our XMLACL2mCRL2 tool translates only XACML access control policies to mCRL2 specifications. The **P*** formulas (i.e., Property P1, Property P2, and Property P3) presented in the paper are generic formulas for XACML policies. In other words, the provided formulas can be used in different environments for the same properties, i.e., *Policy-Completeness*, *Policy-Consistency*, and *Obligation-Safety*. Therefore, neither the specification of **P*** formulas needs to be automated nor the user needs to understand the generated mCRL2 specifications (and the provided formulas) for analyzing XACML access control policies.

References

1. Aceto, L., Ingólfsdóttir, A., Larsen, K.G., Srba, J.: Reactive Systems: Modelling. Cambridge University Press, Specification and Verification, Cambridge (2007)
2. Ahn, G., Hu, H., Lee, J., Meng, Y.: Representing and reasoning about web access control policies. In: Proceedings of the 34th Annual IEEE International Computer Software and Applications Conference, COMPSAC 2010, Seoul, Korea, 19–23 July 2010, pp. 137–146. IEEE Computer Society (2010). https://doi.org/10.1109/COMPSAC.2010.20
3. Al-Issa, Y., Ottom, M.A., Tamrawi, A.: eHealth cloud security challenges: a survey. J. Healthcare Eng. **2019**, 1–15 (2019). https://doi.org/10.1155/2019/7516035
4. Arshad, H., Horne, R., Johansen, C., Owe, O., Willemse, T.A.C.: GitHub repository for "Process Algebra Can Save Lives: Static Analysis of XACML Access Control Policies using mCRL2" (2022). https://github.com/haamedarshad/XACML2mCRL2

5. Bryans, J.W.: Reasoning about XACML policies using CSP. In: Proceedings of the 2nd ACM Workshop On Secure Web Services, SWS 2005, Fairfax, VA, USA, November 11, 2005, pp. 28–35. ACM (2005). https://doi.org/10.1145/1103022.1103028

6. Bryant, R.E.: Graph-based algorithms for Boolean function manipulation. IEEE Trans. Comput. **35**(8), 677–691 (1986). https://doi.org/10.1109/TC.1986.1676819

7. Bunte, O., et al.: The mCRL2 toolset for analysing concurrent systems. In: Vojnar, T., Zhang, L. (eds.) TACAS 2019. LNCS, vol. 11428, pp. 21–39. Springer, Cham (2019). https://doi.org/10.1007/978-3-030-17465-1_2

8. Cantor, S., Moreh, J., Philpott, R., Maler, E.: Metadata for the OASIS security assertion markup language (SAML) V2.0 (2005). http://docs.oasis-open.org/security/saml/v2.0/

9. Fisler, K., Krishnamurthi, S., Meyerovich, L.A., Tschantz, M.C.: Verification and change-impact analysis of access-control policies. In: 27th International Conference on Software Engineering (ICSE 2005), 15–21 May 2005, St. Louis, Missouri, USA, pp. 196–205. ACM (2005). https://doi.org/10.1145/1062455.1062502

10. Fokkink, W.: Modelling Distributed Systems. Springer, Heidelberg (2007). https://doi.org/10.1007/978-3-540-73938-8

11. Fujita, M., McGeer, P.C., Yang, J.Y.: Multi-terminal binary decision diagrams: an efficient data structure for matrix representation. Formal Methods Syst. Des. **10**(2), 149–169 (1997). https://doi.org/10.1023/A:1008647823331

12. Groote, J.F., Keiren, J.J.A.: Tutorial: designing distributed software in mCRL2. In: Peters, K., Willemse, T.A.C. (eds.) FORTE 2021. LNCS, vol. 12719, pp. 226–243. Springer, Cham (2021). https://doi.org/10.1007/978-3-030-78089-0_15

13. Groote, J.F., Keiren, J.J.A., Luttik, B., de Vink, E.P., Willemse, T.A.C.: Modelling and analysing software in mCRL2. In: Arbab, F., Jongmans, S.-S. (eds.) FACS 2019. LNCS, vol. 12018, pp. 25–48. Springer, Cham (2020). https://doi.org/10.1007/978-3-030-40914-2_2

14. Groote, J.F., Mousavi, M.R.: Modeling and Analysis of Communicating Systems. MIT Press, Cambridge (2014)

15. Hathaliya, J.J., Tanwar, S.: An exhaustive survey on security and privacy issues in Healthcare 4.0. Comput. Commun. **153**, 311–335 (2020). https://doi.org/10.1016/j.comcom.2020.02.018

16. Hoare, C.A.R.: Communicating sequential processes. Commun. ACM **21**(8), 666–677 (1978). https://doi.org/10.1145/359576.359585

17. Hu, H., Ahn, G., Kulkarni, K.: Anomaly discovery and resolution in web access control policies. In: 16th ACM Symposium on Access Control Models and Technologies, SACMAT 2011, Innsbruck, Austria, June 15–17, 2011, Proceedings, pp. 165–174. ACM (2011). https://doi.org/10.1145/1998441.1998472

18. Hu, V.C., et al.: Guide to attribute based access control (ABAC) definition and considerations. NIST Spec. Publ. (SP) **800**(162), 1–47 (2014). https://doi.org/10.6028/NIST.SP.800-162

19. Kolovski, V., Hendler, J.A., Parsia, B.: Analyzing web access control policies. In: Proceedings of the 16th International Conference on World Wide Web, WWW 2007, Banff, Alberta, Canada, May 8–12, 2007, pp. 677–686. ACM (2007). https://doi.org/10.1145/1242572.1242664

20. Lifschitz, V.: What Is Answer Set Programming? In: Proceedings of the Twenty-Third AAAI Conference on Artificial Intelligence, AAAI 2008, Chicago, Illinois, USA, July 13–17, 2008, pp. 1594–1597. AAAI Press (2008). http://www.aaai.org/Library/AAAI/2008/aaai08-270.php

21. Lin, D., Rao, P., Bertino, E., Li, N., Lobo, J.: EXAM: a comprehensive environment for the analysis of access control policies. Int. J. Inf. Sec. **9**(4), 253–273 (2010). https://doi.org/10.1007/s10207-010-0106-1

22. Marek, V.W., Truszczynski, M.: Stable models and an alternative logic programming paradigm. In: The Logic Programming Paradigm - A 25-Year Perspective, pp. 375–398. Artificial Intelligence, Springer, Cham (1999). https://doi.org/10.1007/978-3-642-60085-2_17

23. Morisset, C., Willemse, T.A.C., Zannone, N.: A framework for the extended evaluation of ABAC policies. Cybersecurity **2**(1), 1–21 (2019). https://doi.org/10.1186/s42400-019-0024-0

24. Parducci, B., Lockhart, H., Rissanen, E.: Extensible access control markup language (XACML) version 3.0. OASIS Standard, pp. 1–154 (2013)

25. Ramli, C.D.P.K., Nielson, H.R., Nielson, F.: The logic of XACML. Sci. Comput. Program. **83**, 80–105 (2014). https://doi.org/10.1016/j.scico.2013.05.003

26. Rao, P., Lin, D., Bertino, E., Li, N., Lobo, J.: An algebra for fine-grained integration of XACML policies. In: 14th ACM Symposium on Access Control Models and Technologies, SACMAT 2009, Stresa, Italy, June 3–5, 2009, Proceedings, pp. 63–72. ACM (2009). https://doi.org/10.1145/1542207.1542218

27. Ray, I., Ong, T.C., Ray, I., Kahn, M.G.: Applying attribute based access control for privacy preserving health data disclosure. In: IEEE-EMBS International Conference on Biomedical and Health Informatics (BHI), pp. 1–4. IEEE, Las Vegas, NV, USA (2016). https://doi.org/10.1109/BHI.2016.7455820

28. Turkmen, F., den Hartog, J., Ranise, S., Zannone, N.: Formal analysis of XACML policies using SMT. Comput. Secur. **66**, 185–203 (2017). https://doi.org/10.1016/j.cose.2017.01.009

The Reversible Temporal Process Language

Laura Bocchi[1]($\boxtimes$), Ivan Lanese[2]($\boxtimes$), Claudio Antares Mezzina[3]($\boxtimes$),
and Shoji Yuen[4]($\boxtimes$)

[1] School of Computing, University of Kent, Canterbury, UK
[2] Focus Team, University of Bologna/INRIA, Bologna, Italy
ivan.lanese@gmail.com
[3] Dipartimento di Scienze Pure e Applicate, Università di Urbino, Urbino, Italy
[4] Nagoya University, Nagoya, Japan

Abstract. Reversible debuggers help programmers to quickly find the causes of misbehaviours in concurrent programs. These debuggers can be founded on the well-studied theory of causal-consistent reversibility, which allows one to undo any action provided that its consequences are undone beforehand. Till now, causal-consistent reversibility never considered time, a key aspect in real world applications. Here, we study the interplay between reversibility and time in concurrent systems via a process algebra. The Temporal Process Language (TPL) by Hennessy and Regan is a well-understood extension of CCS with discrete-time and a timeout operator. We define revTPL, a reversible extension of TPL, and we show that it satisfies the properties expected from a causal-consistent reversible calculus. We show that, alternatively, revTPL can be interpreted as an extension of reversible CCS with time.

1 Introduction

Recent studies [6,30] show that reversible debuggers ease the debugging phase, and help programmers to quickly find the causes of a misbehaviour. Reversible debuggers can be built on top of a causal-consistent reversible semantics [9,12], and this is particularly suited to deal with concurrency bugs, which are hard to find using traditional debuggers. By exploiting causality information, causal-consistent reversible debuggers allow one to undo just the steps which led (are causally related) to a misbehaviour, reducing the number of steps/spurious causes and helping to understand its root cause. In the last years several reversible semantics for concurrency have been developed, see, e.g., [2,7,8,18,22]. However, none of them takes into account time[1]. Time-dependent behaviour is

---

This work has been partially supported by EPSRC project EP/T014512/1 (STARDUST), by the BehAPI project funded by the EU H2020 RISE under the Marie Sklodowska-Curie action (No: 778233), by MIUR PRIN project NiRvAna, by French ANR project DCore ANR-18-CE25-0007 and by INdAM – GNCS 2020 project *Sistemi Reversibili Concorrenti: dai Modelli ai Linguaggi*. We thank the anonymous referees for their helpful comments and suggestions.

[1] The notion of time reversibility addressed by [2] is not aimed at studying hard or soft time constraints but at performance evaluation via (time-reversible) Markov chains.

M. R. Mousavi and A. Philippou (Eds.): FORTE 2022, LNCS 13273, pp. 31–49, 2022.
https://doi.org/10.1007/978-3-031-08679-3_3

an intrinsic and important feature of real-world concurrent systems and has many applications: from the engineering of highways [21], to the manufacturing schedule [11] and to the scheduling problem for real-time operating systems [3].

Time is instrumental for the functioning of embedded systems where some events are triggered by the system clock. Embedded systems are used for both real-time and soft real-time applications, frequently in safety-critical scenarios. Hence, before being deployed or massively produced, they have to be heavily tested. The testing activity may trigger a debugging phase: if a test fails one has to track down the source(s) of the failure and fix them. Actually, debugging occurs not only upon testing, but in almost all the stages of the life-cycle of a software system: from the early stages of prototyping to the post-release maintenance (e.g., updates or security patches). Concurrency is important in embedded systems [10], and concurrency bugs frequently happen in these systems as well [14]. To debug such systems, and deal with time-dependent bugs in particular, it is crucial that debuggers can handle concurrency and time.

In this paper, we study the interplay of time and reversibility in a process algebra for concurrency. There exists a variety of timed process algebras for the analysis and specification of concurrent timed systems [27]. We build on the Temporal Process Language (TPL) [13], a CCS-like process algebra featuring an *idling* prefix (modelling a delay) and a *timeout* operator. The choice of TPL is due to its simplicity and its well-understood theory. We define revTPL, a reversible extension of TPL, and we show that it satisfies the properties expected from a causal-consistent reversible calculus. Alternatively, revTPL can be interpreted as an extension of reversible CCS (in particular CCSK [29]) with time.

A reversible semantics in a concurrent setting is frequently defined following the causal-consistent approach [8] (other approaches are also used, e.g., to model biological systems [28]). Causal-consistent reversibility states that any action can be undone, provided that its consequences are undone beforehand. Hence, it strongly relies on a notion of causality. To prove the reversible semantics of revTPL causal-consistent, we exploit the theory in [20], whereby causal-consistency follows from three key properties: any action can be undone by a corresponding backward action (Loop Lemma); concurrent actions can be executed in any order (Square Property); backward computations do not introduce new states (Parabolic Lemma).

The application of causal-consistent reversibility to timed systems is not straightforward, since time heavily changes the causal semantics of the language. In untimed systems, causal dependencies are either *structural* (e.g., via sequential composition) or determined by *synchronisations*. In timed systems further dependencies between parallel processes can be introduced by time, even when processes do not actually interact, as illustrated in Example 1.

Example 1 (Motivating example). Consider the following Erlang code.

```
1  process_A () ->              5          handleTimeout ()
2    receive                    6      end end.
3      X -> handleMsg ()
4      after 200 ->
```

```
 7  process_B(Pid) ->           10  PidA=spawn(?MODULE, process_A , [ ]) ,
 8     timer:sleep(500),        11  spawn(?MODULE, process_B , [PidA]) .
 9     Pid! Msg   end.
```

Two processes are supposed to communicate, but the timeout in process A (line 4) triggers after 200 ms, while process B will only send the message after 500 ms (lines 8–9). In this example, the timeout is ruling out an execution that would be possible in the untimed scenario (the communication between A and B) and introduces a dependency without need of actual interactions.   ◇

From a technical point of view, the semantics of TPL does not fit the formats for which a causal-consistent reversible semantics can be built automatically [15,29], and also the generalisation of the approaches developed in the literature for untimed models [7,8,18] is not straightforward. Actually, we even need to change the underlying formalisation of TPL to ensure that its reversible extension is causal consistent (see Sect. 5.1).

The rest of the paper is structured as follows. Section 2 gives an informal overview of TPL and reversibility. Section 3 introduces the syntax and semantics of the reversible Temporal Process Language (revTPL). In Sect. 4, we relate revTPL to TPL and CCSK, while Sect. 5 studies the reversibility properties of revTPL. Section 6 concludes the paper. Proofs and additional technical details are collected in the associated technical report [4].

2 Informal Overview of TPL and Reversibility

In this section we give an informal overview of Hennessy & Regan's TPL (Temporal Process Language) [13] and introduce a few basic concepts of causal-consistent reversibility [8,20].

Overview of TPL. Process $\lfloor pid.P \rfloor(Q)$ models a timeout: it can either immediately do action pid followed by P or, in case of delay, continue as Q. In (1) the timeout process is in parallel with co-party $\overline{pid}.0$ that can immediately synchronise with action pid, and hence the timeout process continues as P.

$$\overline{pid}.0 \parallel \lfloor pid.P \rfloor(Q) \xrightarrow{\tau} 0 \parallel P \tag{1}$$

In (2), $\lfloor pid.P \rfloor(Q)$ is in parallel with process $\sigma.\overline{pid}.0$ that can synchronise only after a delay of one time unit σ (σ is called a time action). Because of the delay, the timeout process continues as Q:

$$\sigma.\overline{pid}.0 \parallel \lfloor pid.P \rfloor(Q) \xrightarrow{\sigma} \overline{pid}.0 \parallel Q \tag{2}$$

The processes in (2) describe the interaction structures of the Erlang program in Example 1. More precisely, the timeout of 200 time units in process A can be encoded using nested timeouts:

$$A(0) = Q \quad A(n+1) = \lfloor pid.P \rfloor(A(n)) \quad (n \in \mathbb{N})$$

while process B can be modelled as the sequential composition of 500 actions σ followed by action $\overline{pid}$, as follows:

$$B(0) = \overline{pid} \quad B(n+1) = \sigma.B(n) \quad (n \in \mathbb{N})$$

Using the definition above, $\lfloor pid.P \rfloor(A(200))$ models a process that executes pid and continues as P if a co-party is able to synchronise within 200 time units, otherwise executes Q. Hence, Example 1 is rendered as follows:

$$\lfloor pid.P \rfloor(A(200)) \parallel B(500)$$

The design of TPL is based on (and enjoys) three properties [13]: time-determinism, patience, and maximal progress. *Time-determinism* means that time actions from one state can never reach distinct states, formally: if $P \xrightarrow{\sigma} Q$ and $P \xrightarrow{\sigma} Q'$ then $Q = Q'$. A consequence of time-determinism is that choices can only be decided via communication actions and not by time actions, for example $\alpha.P + \beta.Q$ can change state by action α or β, but not by time action σ. Process $\alpha.P + \beta.Q$ can make an action σ, by a property called patience, but this action would not change the state, as shown in (3).

$$\alpha.P + \beta.Q \xrightarrow{\sigma} \alpha.P + \beta.Q \tag{3}$$

Patience ensures that communication processes $\alpha.P$ can indefinitely delay communication α with σ actions (without changing state) until a co-party is available. *Maximal progress* states that (internal/synchronisation) τ actions cannot be delayed, formally: if $P \xrightarrow{\tau} Q$ then $P \xrightarrow{\sigma} Q'$ for no Q'. Namely, a delay can only be attained via explicit σ prefixes or because synchronisation is not possible. Basically, patience allows for time actions when communication is not possible, and maximal progress disallows time actions when communication is possible:

$$\alpha.P \xrightarrow{\sigma} \qquad \qquad \text{(by patience)}$$
$$\alpha.P \parallel \overline{\alpha}.Q \xrightarrow{\sigma}\!\!\!\!/ \;\; \text{because } \alpha.P \parallel \overline{\alpha}.Q \xrightarrow{\tau} \;\; \text{(by maximal progress)}$$

Overview of Causal-Consistent Reversibility. Before presenting `revTPL`, we discuss the *reversing technique* we adopt. In the literature, two approaches to define a causal-consistent extension of a given calculus or language have been proposed: dynamic and static [16]. The dynamic approach (as in [7,8,18]) makes explicit use of memories to keep track of past events and causality relations, while the static approach (originally proposed in [29]) is based on two ideas: making all the operators of the language static so that no information is lost and using communication keys to keep track of which events have been executed. In the dynamic approach, constructors of processes disappear upon reduction (as in standard calculi).

For example, in the following CCS reduction:

$$a.P \xrightarrow{a} P$$

the action a disappears as effect of the reduction. The dynamic approach prescribes to use a memory to keep track of the discarded items. In static approaches, such as [29], actions are syntactically maintained, and process $a.P$ reduces as follows

$$a.P \xrightarrow{a[i]} a[i].P$$

where P is decorated with the executed action a and a unique key i. The term $a[i].P$ acts like P in forward reductions, while the coloured part decorating P is used to define backward reductions, e.g.,

$$a[i].P \xrightarrow{a[i]} a.P$$

Keys are important to correctly revert synchronisations. Consider the process below. It can take two forward synchronisations with keys i and j, respectively:

$$a.P_1 \parallel \overline{a}.P_2 \parallel a.Q_1 \parallel \overline{a}.Q_2 \xrightarrow{\tau[i],\,\tau[j]} a[i].P_1 \parallel \overline{a}[i].P_2 \parallel a[j].Q_1 \parallel \overline{a}[j].Q_2$$

From the reached state, there are two possible backward actions: $\tau[i]$ and $\tau[j]$. The keys are used to ensure that a backward action, say $\tau[i]$, only involves parallel components that have previously synchronised and not, for instance, $a[i].P_1$ and $\overline{a}[j].Q_2$. When looking at the choice operator, in the following CCS reduction:

$$a.P + b.Q \xrightarrow{a} P$$

both the choice operator "+" and the discarded branch $b.Q$ disappear as effect of the reduction. In static approaches, the choice operator and the discarded branch are syntactically maintained, and process $a.P + b.Q$ reduces as follows:

$$a.P + b.Q \xrightarrow{a[i]} a[i].P + b.Q$$

where $a[i].P + b.Q$ acts like P in forward reductions, while the coloured part allows one to undo $a[i]$ and then possibly proceed forward with an action $b[j]$.

In this paper, we adopt the static approach since it is simpler, while the dynamic approach is more suitable to complex languages such as the π-calculus, see the discussion in [16, 19].

3   Reversible Temporal Process Language

In this section we define revTPL, an extension of TPL [13] with reversibility following the static approach in the style of [29].

Syntax of revTPL. We denote with $\mathcal{X}$ the set of all the processes generated by the grammar in Fig. 1.

Programs $(P, Q, \ldots)$ describe timed interactions following [13]. We let $\mathcal{A}$ be the set of action names a, $\overline{\mathcal{A}}$ the set of action conames $\overline{a}$. We use α to range over a, $\overline{a}$ and internal actions τ. We assume $\overline{\overline{a}} = a$. In program $\pi.P$, prefix π can be a

$$P = \pi.P \mid \lfloor P \rfloor(Q) \mid P + Q \mid P \parallel Q \mid P \setminus a \mid A \mid \mathbf{0} \qquad (\pi = \alpha \mid \sigma)$$

$$X = \pi[i].X \mid \lfloor X \rfloor[\,\underrightarrow{i}\,](Y) \mid \lfloor X \rfloor[\,\underleftarrow{i}\,](Y) \mid X + Y \mid X \parallel Y \mid X \setminus a \mid P$$

Fig. 1. Syntax of revTPL

communication action α or a time action σ, and P is the continuation. Timeout $\lfloor P \rfloor(Q)$ executes either P (if possible) or Q (in case of timeout). $P + Q$, $P \parallel Q$, $P \setminus a$, A, and $\mathbf{0}$ are the usual choice, parallel composition, name restriction, recursive call, and terminated program from CCS. For each recursive call A we assume a recursive definition $A \stackrel{def}{=} P$.

Processes $(X, Y, \ldots)$ describe states via annotation of executed actions with keys following the static approach. We let $\mathcal{K}$ be the set of all keys $(k, i, j, \ldots)$. Processes are programs with (possibly) some computational history (i.e., prefixes marked with keys): $\pi[i].X$ is the process that has already executed π, and the execution of such π is identified by key i. Process $\lfloor X \rfloor[\,\underrightarrow{i}\,](Y)$ is executing the main branch X whereas $\lfloor X \rfloor[\,\underleftarrow{i}\,](Y)$ is executing Y.

A process can be thought of as a context with actions that have already been executed, each associated to a key, containing a program P, with actions yet to execute and hence with no keys. Notably, keys are distinct but for actions happening together: an action and a co-action that synchronise, or the same timed action traced by different processes, e.g., by two parallel delays. A program P can be thought of as the initial state of a computation, where no action has been executed yet. We call such processes *standard*. Definition 1 formalises this notion via function $\mathtt{keys}(X)$ that returns the set of keys of a process.

Definition 1 (Standard process). *The set of keys of a process X, written $\mathtt{keys}(X)$, is inductively defined as follows:*

$$\mathtt{keys}(P) = \emptyset \quad \mathtt{keys}(\pi[i].X) = \{i\} \cup \mathtt{keys}(X) \quad \mathtt{keys}(X \setminus a) = \mathtt{keys}(X)$$
$$\mathtt{keys}(\lfloor Y \rfloor[\,\underleftarrow{i}\,](X)) = \mathtt{keys}(\lfloor X \rfloor[\,\underrightarrow{i}\,](Y)) = \{i\} \cup \mathtt{keys}(X)$$
$$\mathtt{keys}(X + Y) = \mathtt{keys}(X \parallel Y) = \mathtt{keys}(X) \cup \mathtt{keys}(Y)$$

A process X is standard, *written* $\mathtt{std}(X)$, *if* $\mathtt{keys}(X) = \emptyset$.

Basically, a standard process is a program. To handle the delicate interplay between time-determinism and reversibility of time actions, it is useful to distinguish the class of processes that have not executed any *communication* action (but may have executed time actions). We call these processes *not-acted* and characterise them formally using the predicate $\mathtt{nact}(\cdot)$ below.

Definition 2 (Not-acted process). *The not-acted predicate $\mathtt{nact}(\cdot)$ is inductively defined as:*

$$\mathtt{nact}(\mathbf{0}) = \mathtt{nact}(A) = \mathtt{nact}(\lfloor X \rfloor(Y)) = \mathtt{nact}(\pi.X) = \mathtt{tt}$$
$$\mathtt{nact}(\alpha[i].X) = \mathtt{nact}(\lfloor X \rfloor[\,\underleftarrow{i}\,](Y)) = \mathtt{ff}$$
$$\mathtt{nact}(\sigma[i].X) = \mathtt{nact}(X \setminus a) = \mathtt{nact}(\lfloor Y \rfloor[\,\underrightarrow{i}\,](X)) = \mathtt{nact}(X)$$
$$\mathtt{nact}(X \parallel Y) = \mathtt{nact}(X + Y) = \mathtt{nact}(X) \wedge \mathtt{nact}(Y)$$

A process X is not-acted *(resp.* acted*) if* $\text{nact}(X) = \text{tt}$ *(resp.* $\text{nact}(X) = \text{ff}$ *).*

Basic standard processes are always not-acted (first line of Definition 2). Indeed, it is not possible to reach a process $\pi.X$ where X is acted. In the second line, a process that has executed communication actions is acted. In particular, we will see that $\lfloor X \rfloor [\_i\_](Y)$ is only reachable via a communication action. The processes in the third line are not-acted if their continuations are not-acted. For parallel composition and choice, $\text{nact}(\cdot)$ is defined as a conjunction. For example $\text{nact}(\alpha[i].P \parallel \beta.Q) = \text{ff}$ and $\text{nact}(\alpha[i].P + \beta.Q) = \text{ff}$. Note that in a choice process $X_1 + X_2$, at most one between X_1 and X_2 can be not-acted. Whereas $\text{std}(X)$ implies $\text{nact}(X)$, the opposite implication does not hold. For example, $\text{std}(\sigma[i].\mathbf{0}) = \text{ff}$ but $\text{nact}(\sigma[i].\mathbf{0}) = \text{tt}$.

Semantics of revTPL. We denote with $\mathcal{A}^t$ the set $\mathcal{A} \cup \overline{\mathcal{A}} \cup \{\tau, \sigma\}$ of actions and let π to range over the set $\mathcal{A}^t$. We define the set of all the labels $\mathcal{L} = \mathcal{A}^t \times (\mathcal{K} \cup \{\star\})$. The labels associate each $\pi \in \mathcal{A}^t$ to either a key i or a wildcard $\star$. The key is used to associate the forward occurrence of an action with its corresponding reversal. Also, instances of actions occurring together (synchronising action and co-action or the effect of time passing in different components of a process) have the same key, otherwise keys are distinct. We introduce a wildcard $\star$ to label time transitions that leave the state unchanged. We call transitions with key $i \in \mathcal{K}$ *recorded* and transitions with $\star$ *patient*. We let $u, v, w, \ldots$ to range over $\mathcal{K} \cup \{\star\}$.

Definition 3 (Semantics). *The operational semantics of* revTPL *is given by two LTSs defined on the same set of all processes $\mathcal{X}$, and the set of all labels $\mathcal{L}$: a forward LTS $(\mathcal{X}, \mathcal{L}, \rightarrow)$ and a backward LTS $(\mathcal{X}, \mathcal{L}, \hookrightarrow)$. We define $\mapsto = \rightarrow \cup \hookrightarrow$, where $\rightarrow$ and $\hookrightarrow$ are the least transition relations induced by the rules in Fig. 2 and Fig. 3, respectively.*

Given a relation $\mathcal{R}$, we indicate with $\mathcal{R}^*$ its transitive and reflexive closure. We use notation $X \not\rightarrow$ (resp. $X \not\hookrightarrow$) for $X \xrightarrow{\tau[i]} X'$ (resp. $X \xhookrightarrow{\tau[i]} X'$) for any process X' and key i.

We now discuss the rules of the forward semantics (Fig. 2). Rule [PAct] describes patient actions: program $\alpha.P$ can make a time step to itself. This kind of actions allows a process to wait indefinitely until it can communicate (by patience [13]). Since [PAct] does not change the state of $\alpha.P$, we do not track this action by associating it to wildcard $\star$ rather than to a key. [RAct] executes recorded actions $\alpha[i]$ or $\sigma[i]$ on a prefix program. Observe that, unlike patient time actions on $\alpha.P$ (which may or may not happen depending on the context), a time action on $\sigma.P$ corresponds to a deliberate and planned time consuming action and is, therefore, recorded so that it may be later reversed. [Act] lifts actions of the continuation X on processes where prefix $\pi[i]$ has already been executed. [STout] and [SWait] model timeouts. In [STout], if X is not able to make τ actions then Y is executed; this rule models a timeout that triggers only if the main process X is stuck. The negative premise on [STout] can be encoded into a decidable positive one as shown in the associated technical

$$\text{ACT } \frac{X \xrightarrow{\pi'[u]} X' \qquad u \neq i}{\pi[i].X \xrightarrow{\pi'[u]} \pi[i].X'}$$

$$\text{PACT } \alpha.P \xrightarrow{\sigma[\star]} \alpha.P \qquad \text{RACT } \pi.P \xrightarrow{\pi[i]} \pi[i].P$$

$$\text{STOUT } \frac{X \not\xrightarrow{?} \quad \text{std}(X) \quad \text{std}(Y)}{\lfloor X \rfloor(Y) \xrightarrow{\sigma[i]} \lfloor X \rfloor \lfloor \underset{\rightarrow}{i} \rfloor(Y)} \qquad \text{SWAIT } \frac{Y \xrightarrow{\pi[u]} Y' \qquad u \neq i}{\lfloor X \rfloor \lfloor \underset{\rightarrow}{i} \rfloor(Y) \xrightarrow{\pi[u]} \lfloor X \rfloor \lfloor \underset{\rightarrow}{i} \rfloor(Y')}$$

$$\text{TOUT } \frac{X \xrightarrow{\alpha[i]} X' \quad \text{std}(Y)}{\lfloor X \rfloor(Y) \xrightarrow{\alpha[i]} \lfloor X' \rfloor \lfloor \underset{\leftarrow}{i} \rfloor(Y)} \qquad \text{WAIT } \frac{X \xrightarrow{\pi[u]} X' \qquad u \neq i}{\lfloor X \rfloor \lfloor \underset{\leftarrow}{i} \rfloor(Y) \xrightarrow{\pi[u]} \lfloor X' \rfloor \lfloor \underset{\leftarrow}{i} \rfloor(Y)}$$

$$\text{SYNW } \frac{X \xrightarrow{\sigma[u]} X' \quad Y \xrightarrow{\sigma[v]} Y' \quad (X \parallel Y) \not\xrightarrow{?} \quad \delta(u,v) = w}{X \parallel Y \xrightarrow{\sigma[w]} X' \parallel Y'}$$

$$\text{PAR } \frac{X \xrightarrow{\alpha[i]} X' \quad i \notin \text{keys}(Y)}{X \parallel Y \xrightarrow{\alpha[i]} X' \parallel Y} \qquad \text{SYN } \frac{X \xrightarrow{\alpha[i]} X' \quad Y \xrightarrow{\overline{\alpha}[i]} Y'}{X \parallel Y \xrightarrow{\tau[i]} X' \parallel Y'}$$

$$\text{CHOW1 } \frac{X_1 \xrightarrow{\sigma[u]} X_1' \quad X_2 \xrightarrow{\sigma[v]} X_2' \quad \delta(u,v) = w \quad \text{nact}(X_1 + X_2)}{X_1 + X_2 \xrightarrow{\sigma[w]} X_1' + X_2'}$$

$$\text{CHOW2 } \frac{X_1 \xrightarrow{\sigma[u]} X_1' \quad \text{nact}(X_2) \wedge \neg \text{nact}(X_1)}{X_1 + X_2 \xrightarrow{\sigma[u]} X_1' + X_2} \qquad \text{CHO } \frac{X_1 \xrightarrow{\alpha[i]} X_1' \quad \text{nact}(X_2)}{X_1 + X_2 \xrightarrow{\alpha[i]} X_1' + X_2}$$

$$\text{IDLE } \mathbf{0} \xrightarrow{\sigma[\star]} \mathbf{0} \qquad \text{HIDE } \frac{X \xrightarrow{\pi[u]} X' \quad \pi \notin \{a, \overline{a}\}}{X \setminus a \xrightarrow{\pi[u]} X' \setminus a} \qquad \text{CONST } \frac{A \overset{def}{=} P \quad P \xrightarrow{\pi[u]} X}{A \xrightarrow{\pi[u]} X}$$

The set of rules also includes symmetric versions of rules [PAR], [CHOW2] and [CHO].

Fig. 2. revTPL forward LTS

report [4]. In rule [TOUT] instead the main process can execute and the timeout does not trigger. Rule [SWAIT] (resp. [WAIT]) models transitions inside a timeout process where the Y (resp. X) branch has been previously taken. The semantics of timeout construct becomes clearer in the larger context of parallel processes, when looking at rule [SYNW]. Rule [SYNW] models time passing for parallel processes. The negative premise ensures that, in case X or Y is a timeout process, timeout can trigger only if no synchronisation may occur, that is if the processes are stuck. [SYNW] requires time to pass in the same way (an action σ is taken by both components) for the whole system. Note that u and v may or may not be wildcards, depending on the form of X and Y. To determine w we use a synchronisation function $\delta : (\mathcal{K} \cup \{\star\} \times \mathcal{K} \cup \{\star\}) \mapsto \mathcal{K} \cup \{\star\}$ defined as follows, assuming $i, j \in \mathcal{K}$:

$$\delta(i, i) = i \qquad \delta(i, \star) = \delta(\star, i) = i \qquad \delta(\star, \star) = \star \qquad \delta(i, j) = \perp \; (i \neq j)$$

Basically, in rule [SYNW], if either u or v needs to be recorded then w also needs to be recorded, and if both u and v need to be recorded then we require $u = v$. Rules [PAR] (and symmetric) and [SYN] are as usual for communication actions and allow parallel processes to either proceed independently or to synchronise. Defining the semantics of choice process $X_1 + X_2$ requires special care to ensure time-determinism (recall, choices are only decided via communication actions). Also, we need to record time actions (unless they have a wildcard) to be able to reverse them correctly (cfr. Loop Lemma, discussed later on in Lemma 1). Rule [CHOW1] is for time actions when no choice between X_1 and X_2 has been made yet (as enforced by premise $\mathtt{nact}(X_1 + X_2)$), and a time action happens in both branches. As in rule [SYNW], w is determined by the synchronisation function $\delta(u, v)$. Rule [CHOW2] models a time action when branch X_1 has already been chosen, as enforced by premise $\neg\mathtt{nact}(X_1)$; the time action only affects the 'active' branch X_1. For example, in the process below, the premise $\mathtt{nact}(\beta.Q) \wedge \neg\mathtt{nact}(\alpha[i].\sigma.P)$ allows us to apply [CHOW2] obtaining:

$$\alpha[i].\sigma.P + \beta.Q \xrightarrow{\sigma[j]} \alpha[i].\sigma[j].P + \beta.Q$$

Having rule [CHOW2], besides [CHOW1], for time actions on a chosen branch, is justified by scenarios as the following:

$$\alpha[i].\sigma.P + \lfloor Q \rfloor(R)$$

If we would model time transitions of the process above using [CHOW1] we would obtain

$$\alpha[i].\sigma.P + \lfloor Q \rfloor(R) \xrightarrow{\sigma[j]} \alpha[i].\sigma[j].P + \lfloor Q \rfloor [\underset{\rightarrow}{j}](R)$$

wrongly suggesting that the timeout on the right branch has evolved. Rule [CHO] allows one to take one branch, or continue executing a previously taken branch. The choice construct is syntactically preserved, to allow for reversibility, but the one branch that is not taken remains non-acted (i.e., $\mathtt{nact}(X_2)$). This ensures that choices can be decided by a communication action only. Rules [IDLE], [HIDE], and [CONST] are standard, except that [IDLE] only does patient actions using wildcards, and [HIDE] and [CONST] may or may not use wildcards depending on the form of X.

The rules of the backward semantics, in Fig. 3, undo actions previously recorded via the forward semantics, and they allow for timed actions with wildcard. Backward rules are symmetric to the forward ones.

Definition 4 (Initial and reachable processes). *A process X is initial if* $\mathtt{std}(X)$. *A process X is reachable if it can be derived by an initial process.*

Basically, a process is initial if it has no computational history, and reachable if it can be obtained via forward and backward actions from an initial process.

$$\text{ACT } \frac{X \xLeftarrow{\pi'[u]} X' \quad u \neq i}{\pi[i].X \xLeftarrow{\pi'[u]} \pi[i].X'}$$

$$\text{PACT } \alpha.P \xLeftarrow{\sigma[*]} \alpha.P \qquad \text{RACT } \pi[i].P \xLeftarrow{\pi[i]} \pi.P$$

$$\text{STOUT } \frac{X \not\xLeftarrow{\mathcal{I}} \quad \mathbf{std}(X) \quad \mathbf{std}(Y)}{\lfloor X \rfloor [\underleftarrow{i}](Y) \xLeftarrow{\sigma[i]} \lfloor X \rfloor(Y)} \qquad \text{SWAIT } \frac{Y \xLeftarrow{\pi[u]} Y' \quad u \neq i}{\lfloor X \rfloor [\underleftarrow{i}](Y) \xLeftarrow{\pi[u]} \lfloor X \rfloor [\underleftarrow{i}](Y')}$$

$$\text{TOUT } \frac{X \xLeftarrow{\alpha[i]} X' \quad \mathbf{std}(Y)}{\lfloor X \rfloor [\underleftarrow{i}](Y) \xLeftarrow{\alpha[i]} \lfloor X' \rfloor(Y)} \qquad \text{WAIT } \frac{X \xLeftarrow{\pi[u]} X' \quad u \neq i}{\lfloor X \rfloor [\underleftarrow{i}](Y) \xLeftarrow{\pi[u]} \lfloor X' \rfloor [\underleftarrow{i}](Y)}$$

$$\text{SYNW } \frac{X \xLeftarrow{\sigma[u]} X' \quad Y \xLeftarrow{\sigma[v]} Y' \quad (X \parallel Y) \not\xLeftarrow{\mathcal{I}} \quad \delta(u,v) = w}{X \parallel Y \xLeftarrow{\sigma[w]} X' \parallel Y'}$$

$$\text{PAR } \frac{X \xLeftarrow{\alpha[i]} X' \quad i \notin \mathbf{keys}(Y)}{X \parallel Y \xLeftarrow{\alpha[i]} X' \parallel Y} \qquad \text{SYN } \frac{X \xLeftarrow{\alpha[i]} X' \quad Y \xLeftarrow{\bar\alpha[i]} Y'}{X \parallel Y \xLeftarrow{\tau[i]} X' \parallel Y'}$$

$$\text{CHOW1 } \frac{X_1 \xLeftarrow{\sigma[u]} X_1' \quad X_2 \xLeftarrow{\sigma[v]} X_2' \quad \delta(u,v) = w \quad \mathbf{nact}(X_1 + X_2)}{X_1 + X_2 \xLeftarrow{\sigma[w]} X_1' + X_2'}$$

$$\text{CHOW2 } \frac{X_1 \xLeftarrow{\sigma[u]} X_1' \quad \mathbf{nact}(X_2) \wedge \neg\mathbf{nact}(X_1)}{X_1 + X_2 \xLeftarrow{\sigma[u]} X_1' + X_2} \qquad \text{CHO } \frac{X_1 \xLeftarrow{\alpha[i]} X_1' \quad \mathbf{nact}(X_2)}{X_1 + X_2 \xLeftarrow{\alpha[i]} X_1' + X_2}$$

$$\text{IDLE } \mathbf{0} \xLeftarrow{\sigma[*]} \mathbf{0} \qquad \text{HIDE } \frac{X \xLeftarrow{\pi[u]} X' \quad \pi \notin \{a, \bar{a}\}}{X \setminus a \xLeftarrow{\pi[u]} X' \setminus a} \qquad \text{CONST } \frac{A \overset{def}{=} P \quad X \xLeftarrow{\pi[u]} P}{X \xLeftarrow{\pi[u]} A}$$

The set of rules also includes symmetric versions of rules [PAR], [CHOW2] and [CHO].

Fig. 3. revTPL backward LTS

4 Properties

We now give some properties of revTPL. In Sect. 4.1 we introduce a syntactic characterisation of the class of processes that can delay without changing state. In Sect. 4.2 we show that revTPL extends both (non reversible) TPL and (untimed) reversible CCS.

4.1 Idempatience and Properties of $\star$

We introduce a class of processes, which we call *idempatient*, that can make state-preserving patient actions. This class is key to define the causal-consistent reversible semantics of revTPL (see Sect. 5.1).

Definition 5 (Idempatience). *We say that X is* idempatient *if* $\text{IP}(X)$ *where:*

$\text{IP}(0) = \text{IP}(\alpha.P) = \texttt{tt} \qquad \text{IP}(\lfloor P \rfloor(Q)) = \text{IP}(\sigma.P) = \texttt{ff}$

$\text{IP}(X_1 \parallel X_2) = \text{IP}(X_1) \wedge \text{IP}(X_2) \wedge X_1 \parallel X_2 \overset{\tau}{\nrightarrow}$

$\text{IP}(X_1 + X_2) = \text{IP}(X_1) \wedge \text{IP}(X_2)$

$\text{IP}(\pi[i].X) = \text{IP}(\lfloor Y \rfloor[\underrightarrow{i}](X)) = \text{IP}(\lfloor X \rfloor[\underleftarrow{i}](Y)) = \text{IP}(X \setminus a) = \text{IP}(X)$

Proposition 1 shows that idempatience is a sound and complete characterisation of processes that can make state-preserving patient actions.

Proposition 1 (Idempatience). $\text{IP}(X) \Leftrightarrow X \overset{\sigma[*]}{\longmapsto} X$.

Next, we give a property of time actions, and show that patient actions are state preserving.

Proposition 2 (Patient actions). $X \overset{\sigma[*]}{\longrightarrow}$ *implies* $X \overset{g[i]}{\nrightarrow}$, *and* $X \overset{\sigma[i]}{\longrightarrow}$ *implies* $X \overset{g[*]}{\nrightarrow}$. *Moreover, if* $X \overset{\sigma[*]}{\longrightarrow} Y$ *then* $X = Y$. *The same for* $\longmapsto$.

4.2   Relations with TPL and Reversible CCS

We can consider `revTPL` as a reversible extension of TPL, but also as an extension of reversible CCS (in particular CCSK [29]) with time. First, if we consider the forward semantics only, then we have a tight correspondence with TPL. To show this we define a forgetful map which discards the history information of a process.

Definition 6 (History forgetting map). *The history forgetting map* ϕ^{h} : $\mathcal{X} \to \mathcal{P}$ *is inductively defined as follows:*

$$\phi^{\text{h}}(P) = P \qquad\qquad \phi^{\text{h}}(\pi[i].X) = \phi^{\text{h}}(X)$$

$$\phi^{\text{h}}(\lfloor X \rfloor[\underleftarrow{i}](Y)) = \phi^{\text{h}}(X) \qquad \phi^{\text{h}}(\lfloor X \rfloor[\underrightarrow{i}](Y)) = \phi^{\text{h}}(Y)$$

$$\phi^{\text{h}}(X \parallel Y) = \phi^{\text{h}}(X) \parallel \phi^{\text{h}}(Y) \quad \phi^{\text{h}}(X \setminus a) = \phi^{\text{h}}(X) \setminus a$$

$$\phi^{\text{h}}(X_1 + X_2) = \begin{cases} \phi^{\text{h}}(X_1) & \text{if } \neg\texttt{nact}(X_1) \wedge \texttt{nact}(X_2) \\ \phi^{\text{h}}(X_2) & \text{if } \neg\texttt{nact}(X_2) \wedge \texttt{nact}(X_1) \\ \phi^{\text{h}}(X_1) + \phi^{\text{h}}(X_2) & \text{otherwise} \end{cases}$$

In TPL time cannot decide choices. This is reflected into the definition of $\phi^{\text{h}}(X_1 + X_2)$, where a branch disappears only if the other did an untimed action.

Notably, the restriction of ϕ^{h} to untimed processes is a map from CCSK to CCS. In the following we will indicate with $\rightarrow_{\text{t}}$ the semantics of TPL [13] and with $\mapsto_{\text{k}}$ the semantics of CCSK [29].

Proposition 3 (Embedding of TPL). *Let X be a reachable `revTPL` process:*

1. *if $X \overset{\pi[u]}{\longrightarrow} Y$ then $\phi^{\text{h}}(X) \overset{\pi}{\rightarrow}_{\text{t}} \phi^{\text{h}}(Y)$;*
2. *if $\phi^{\text{h}}(X) \overset{\pi}{\rightarrow}_{\text{t}} Q$ then*

- *either for any $i \in \mathcal{K} \setminus \mathbf{keys}(X)$ there is Y such that $X \xrightarrow{\pi[i]} Y$ or*
- *$\pi = \sigma$ and there is Y such that $X \xrightarrow{\pi[*]} Y$*

In both the cases $\phi^h(Y) = Q$.

Also, TPL is a conservative extension of CCS. This is stated in [13], even if not formally proved. Hence, we can define a *forgetful* map which discards all the temporal operators of a TPL term and get a CCS one. We can obtain a stronger result and relate revTPL with CCSK [29]. That is, if we consider the untimed part of revTPL what we get is a reversible CCS which is exactly CCSK. To this end, we define a time forgetting map ϕ^t. We denote with $\mathcal{X}^-$ the set of untimed reversible processes of revTPL. The set inclusion $\mathcal{X}^- \subset \mathcal{X}$ holds.

Definition 7 (Time forgetting map). *The time forgetting map $\phi^t : \mathcal{X} \to \mathcal{X}^-$ is inductively defined as follows:*

$$
\begin{aligned}
&\phi^t(0) = 0 && \phi^t(A) = A \\
&\phi^t(\alpha.P) = \alpha.\phi^t(P) && \phi^t(\alpha[i].X) = \alpha[i].\phi^t(X) \\
&\phi^t(X + Y) = \phi^t(X) + \phi^t(Y) && \phi^t(X \parallel Y) = \phi^t(X) \parallel \phi^t(Y) \\
&\phi^t(X \setminus a) = \phi^t(X) \setminus a && \phi^t(\lfloor X \rfloor(Y)) = \phi^t(X) + \phi^t(Y) \\
&\phi^t(\sigma.P) = \phi^t(P) && \phi^t(\sigma[i].X) = \phi^t(X) \\
&\phi^t(\lfloor X \rfloor [\underleftarrow{i}](Y)) = \phi^t(X) + \phi^t(Y) && \phi^t(\lfloor X \rfloor [\underrightarrow{i}](Y)) = \phi^t(X) + \phi^t(Y)
\end{aligned}
$$

Notably, the restriction of ϕ^t to standard processes is a map from TPL to CCS.

The most interesting aspect in the definition above is that the temporal operator $\lfloor X \rfloor(Y)$ is rendered as a sum. This also happens for the decorated processes $\lfloor X \rfloor [\underleftarrow{i}](Y)$ and $\lfloor X \rfloor [\underrightarrow{i}](Y)$. Also, since we are relating a temporal semantics with an untimed one (CCSK), the σ actions performed by the timed semantics are not reflected in CCSK.

Proposition 4 (Embedding of CCSK [29]). *Let X be a reachable revTPL process. We have:*

1. *if $X \xrightarrow{\alpha[i]} Y$ then $\phi^t(X) \xrightarrow{\alpha[i]}_k \phi^t(Y)$;*
2. *if $X \xrightarrow{\sigma[u]} Y$ then $\phi^t(X) = \phi^t(Y)$;*

Notably, it is not always the case that transitions of the underlying untimed process can be matched in a timed setting, think, e.g., to the process in Example 1 (and its formalisation in Sect. 2) for a counterexample.

Figure 4 summarises our results: if we remove the timed behaviour from a revTPL process we get a CCSK term, thanks to Proposition 4. On the other side, if from revTPL we remove reversibility we get a TPL term (thanks to Proposition 3). Note that the same forgetful maps (and properties) justify the arrows in the bottom part of the diagram, as discussed above. This is in line with Theorem 5.21 of [29], showing that by removing reversibility and history information from CCSK we get CCS.

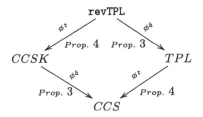

Fig. 4. Forgetting maps.

5   Reversibility in revTPL

In a fully reversible calculus any computation can be undone. This is a fundamental property of reversibility [8,20], and revTPL enjoys it. Formally:

Lemma 1 (Loop Lemma). *If X is a reachable process, then $X \xrightarrow{\pi[u]} X' \iff X' \xrightarrow{\pi[u]} X$*

Another fundamental property of causal-consistent reversibility is causal-consitency [8,20], which essentially states that we store the correct amount of causal information. In order to discuss it, we now borrow some definitions from [8]. We use t, t', s, s' to range over transitions. In a transition $t : X \xrightarrow{\pi[u]} Y$ we call X the *source* of the transition, and Y the *target* of the transition. Two transitions are said to be *coinitial* if they have the same source, and *cofinal* if they have the same target. Given a transition t, we indicate with $\underline{t}$ its opposite, that is if $t : X \xrightarrow{\pi[u]} Y$ (resp., $t : X \xleftarrow{\pi[u]} Y$) then $\underline{t} : Y \xleftarrow{\pi[u]} X$ (resp., $\underline{t} : Y \xrightarrow{\pi[u]} X$). We let ρ, ω to range over sequences of transitions, which we call *paths*, and with ϵ_X we indicate the empty sequence starting and ending in X.

Definition 8 (Causal Equivalence). *Let $\asymp$ be the smallest equivalence on paths closed under composition and satisfying:*

1. *if $t : X \xrightarrow{\pi_1[u]} Y_1$ and $s : X \xrightarrow{\pi_2[v]} Y_2$ are independent, and $s' : Y_1 \xrightarrow{\pi_2[v]} Z$, $t' : Y_2 \xrightarrow{\pi_1[u]} Z$ then $ts' \asymp st'$;*
2. *$t\underline{t} \asymp \epsilon$ and $\underline{t}t \asymp \epsilon$*

Intuitively, paths are causal equivalent if they differ only for swapping independent transitions (we will discuss independence below) and for adding do-undo or undo-redo pairs of transitions.

Definition 9 (Causal Consistency (CC)). *If ρ and ω are coinitial and cofinal paths then $\rho \asymp \omega$.*

Intuitively, if coinitial paths are cofinal then they have the same causal information and can reverse in the same ways: we want only causal equivalent paths to reverse in the same ways.

Unfortunately, causal consistency does not hold in `revTPL` as defined in the previous sections (and this is not related to a specific definition of independence). This is due to actions with label $\sigma[\star]$.

Example 2 (CC does not hold with $\sigma[\star]$). Consider the path $\rho : \alpha.P \xrightarrow{\sigma[\star]} \alpha.P$. Trivially, ρ and $\epsilon_{\alpha.P}$ are coinitial and cofinal, but not causal equivalent. Indeed, the number of forward transitions minus the number of backward transitions is invariant under causal equivalence, and this is not the same for the two paths.◇

This leaves us two possibilities to enforce the property: either we change the definition of causal equivalence (e.g., allowing one to freely add and remove transitions with label $\sigma[\star]$), or we change the semantics. We opt for the latter, since it allows us to stay in the framework studied in [20] and exploit the theory developped there to prove our results.

5.1   Revised Semantics

We change the semantics simply dropping all transitions with label $\sigma[\star]$. Technically, this ensures that causal consistency (as well as other relevant properties) holds. Conceptually, those transitions do not amount to actual actions of the process (as shown in Proposition 2, they do not change the process) and are mainly used to simplify a compositional definition of the semantics, see, e.g., rule [SYNW]. A compositional semantics could be defined by replacing premises of the form $X \xrightarrow{\sigma[\star]} X$ with $\mathrm{IP}(X)$ thanks to Proposition 1. This option is discussed in more detail in the companion technical report [4].

For simplicity, from now on we consider the semantics given by the labelled transition system obtained by dropping all transitions with label $\sigma[\star]$:

Definition 10 (Semantics with no self-loops). *The operational semantics with no self-loops of* `revTPL` *is given by the forward LTS* $(\mathcal{X}, \mathcal{L}, \rightarrow_n)$ *and the backward LTS* $(\mathcal{X}, \mathcal{L}, \rightsquigarrow_n)$, *on the same sets* $\mathcal{X}$ *of processes and* $\mathcal{L}$ *of labels. Transition relations* $\rightarrow_n$ *and* $\rightsquigarrow_n$ *are obtained by dropping from, respectively,* $\rightarrow$ *and* $\rightsquigarrow$ *the transitions with label* $\sigma[\star]$.

Notably, the Loop Lemma holds also for the new semantics. Concerning embeddings, the embedding of TPL does not hold any more (a new operational correspondence taking care of dropped transitions can be defined), while the one of CCSK is unaffected.

We discuss below reversibility in `revTPL` using the semantics with no self-loops. We first need to discuss the notion of independence.

5.2   Independence

We now define a notion of independence between `revTPL` transitions, based on a causality preorder (inspired by [19]) on keys. Independence is useful to show that reversibility never breaks causal links between actions.

Definition 11 (Partial order on keys). *The function* $\mathsf{po}(\cdot)$, *that computes the set of causal relations among the keys in a process, is inductively defined as:*

$$\mathsf{po}(P) = \emptyset \qquad \mathsf{po}(X \setminus a) = \mathsf{po}(X)$$
$$\mathsf{po}(X \parallel Y) = \mathsf{po}(X + Y) = \mathsf{po}(\lfloor X \rfloor(Y)) = \mathsf{po}(X) \cup \mathsf{po}(Y)$$
$$\mathsf{po}(\pi[i].X) = \mathsf{po}(\lfloor X \rfloor[\,\underset{\rightarrow}{i}\,](Y)) = \mathsf{po}(\lfloor Y \rfloor[\,\underset{\leftarrow}{i}\,](X)) = \{i < j \mid j \in \mathsf{keys}(X)\} \cup \mathsf{po}(X)$$

The partial order $\leq_X$ *on* $\mathsf{keys}(X)$ *is the reflexive and transitive closure of* $\mathsf{po}(X)$.

Let us note that function po computes a partial order relation, namely a set of pairs (i, j), denoted $i < j$ to stress that they form a partial order.

Definition 12 (Choice context). *A choice context* **C** *is a process with a hole*
• *defined by the following grammar (we omit symmetric cases for* $+$ *and* $\parallel$):

$$\mathbf{C} = \bullet \mid \pi[i].\mathbf{C} \mid \lfloor \mathbf{C} \rfloor(Y) \mid \lfloor X \rfloor[\,\underset{\rightarrow}{i}\,](\mathbf{C}) \mid \lfloor \mathbf{C} \rfloor[\,\underset{\leftarrow}{i}\,](Y) \mid X + \mathbf{C} \mid X \parallel \mathbf{C} \mid \mathbf{C} \setminus a$$

Intuitively, a choice context may enclose an enabled (forward) choice. We now define a notion of conflict, and independence as its negation. For simplicity of formalisation, we assume that generation of fresh keys in forward transitions is deterministic: the same redex in the same process cannot generate different keys.

Definition 13 (Conflict and independence). *Given a reachable process* X, *two coinititial transitions* $t : X \xmapsto{\pi_1[i]}_n Y$ *and* $s : X \xmapsto{\pi_2[j]}_n Z$ *are conflicting, written* $t \# s$, *if and only if one of the following conditions holds:*

1. $X \xrightarrow{\sigma[i]}_n Y$ *and* $X \xrightarrow{\alpha[j]}_n Z$;
2. $X \xrightarrow{\pi_1[i]}_n Y$ *and* $X \xleftarrow{\pi_2[j]}_n Z$ *with* $j \leq_Y i$;
3. $X = \mathbf{C}[Y' + Z']$, $Y' \xrightarrow{\pi_1[i]}_n Y''$ *and* $Z' \xrightarrow{\pi_2[j]}_n Z''$.

Transitions t *and* s *are* independent, *written* $t \mathcal{I} s$, *if* $t \neq s$ *and they are not conflicting.*

The first clause tells us that a delay cannot be swapped with a communication action. Consider process $\lfloor b.0 \rfloor(0)$:

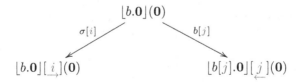

Transitions $\sigma[i]$ and $b[j]$ are in conflict: they cannot be swapped since action b is no longer possible after action σ, and vice versa. The second clause dictates that two transitions are in conflict when a reverse step eliminates some causes of a forward step. E.g., process $a[i].b.0$ can do a forward step with label $b[j]$ or a backward one with label $a[i]$. Undoing $a[i]$ disables the action on b. The last case is the most intuitive: processes in different branches of a choice operator are in conflict, e.g., $a.\mathbf{0} + b.\mathbf{0}$ can do actions on a and b, but they can not be swapped.

The Square Property tells that two coinitial independent transitions commute, thus closing a diamond. Formally:

Property 1 (Square Property - SP) *Given a reachable process X and two coinititial transitions $t : X \xmapsto{\pi_1[i]}_n Y$ and $s : X \xmapsto{\pi_2[j]}_n Z$ with $t \mathcal{I} s$ there exist two cofinal transitions $t' : Y \xmapsto{\pi_2[j]}_n W$ and $s' : Z \xmapsto{\pi_1[i]}_n W$.*

5.3   Causal Consistency

We can now prove causal consistency, using the theory in [20]. It ensures that causal consistency follows from SP, already discussed, and two other properties, stated below. BTI (Backward Transitions are Independent) generalises the concept of backward determinism used for reversible sequential languages [31]. It specifies that two backward transitions from a same process are always independent.

Property 2 (Backward transition are independent - BTI) *Given a reachable process X, any two distinct coinitial backward transitions $t : X \xhookleftarrow{\pi_1[i]}_n Y$ and $s : X \xhookleftarrow{\pi_2[j]}_n Z$ are independent.*

The property trivially holds since by looking at the definition on conflicting and independent transitions (Definition 13) there are no cases in which two backward transitions are deemed as conflicting, hence two backward transitions are always independent.

We now show that reachable processes have a finite past.

Property 3 (Well-Foundedness - WF) *Let X_0 be a reachable process. Then there is no infinite sequence such that $X_i \xhookleftarrow{\pi_n[j_n]}_n X_{i+1}$ for all $i = 0, 1, \ldots$.*

WF follows since each backward transition removes a key.

The following lemma tells us that any path is causally equivalent to a path made by only backward steps, followed by only forward steps. In other words, up to causal equivalence, paths can be rearranged so as to first reach the maximum freedom of choice, going only backwards, and then continuing only forwards.

Definition 14 (Parabolic Lemma). *For any path ρ, there exist two forward-only paths ω, ω' such that $\rho \asymp \underline{\omega}\omega'$ and $|\omega| + |\omega'| \leq |\rho|$.*

We can now prove our main results thanks to the proof schema of [20].

Theorem 1 (From [20]). *Suppose BTI and SP hold, then PL holds. Suppose WF and PL hold, then CC holds.*

6   Conclusions

The main contribution of this paper is the study of the interplay between time and causal-consistent reversibility. A reversible semantics for TPL cannot be automatically derived using well-established frameworks [15,29], since some operator acts differently depending on whether the label is a communication or a time action. For example, in TPL a choice cannot be decided by the passage of time, making the $+$ operator both static and dynamic, and the approach in [29] not applicable. To faithfully capture patient actions in a reversible semantics we introduced wildcards. However, as $\sigma[\star]$ actions violate causal consistency, to recover it we had to refine the formalisation of the semantics. Another peculiarity of TPL is the timeout operator $\lfloor P \rfloor(Q)$, which can be seen as a choice operator whose left branch has priority over the right one. Although we have been able to use the static approach to reversibility [29], adapting it to our setting has been challenging for the aforementioned reasons. Notably, our results have a double interpretation: as an extension of CCSK [29] with time, and as a reversible extension of TPL [13]. As a side result, by focusing on the two fragments, we derive notions of independence and conflict for CCSK and TPL, which were not available in the literature. We have just started to study the relations among revTPL, CCSK and TPL. We leave as future work a further investigation in terms of behavioural equivalences or simulations among the three calculi.

Maximal progress of TPL (as well as revTPL) has connections with Markov chains [5], e.g., $\tau.P + (\lambda).Q$ (where λ is a rate) will not be delayed since τ is instantaneously enabled. This resembles maximal progress for the timeout operator. A deep comparison between deterministic time, used by TPL, and stochastic time used by stochastic process algebras can be found in [1]. Further investigation on the relation between our work and [2], studying reversibility in Markov chains, is left for future work. The treatment of passage of time shares some similarities with broadcast [24]: time actions affect parallel components in the same way, and idempatience can be seen as unavailability of top-level receivers.

We have just started our research quest towards a reversible timed semantics. A further improvement would be to add an explicit rollback operator, as in [17], that could be triggered, e.g., in reaction to a timeout. Also, asynchronous communications (like in Erlang) could be taken into account. TPL is a conservative timed extension of CCS. Due to its simplicity, it has a very clear behavioural theory [13]. A further step could be to adapt such behavioural theory to account for reversibility. Also, we could consider studying more complex temporal operators [27]. Timed Petri nets are a valid tool for analysing real-time systems. A step towards the analysis of real-time systems would be to encode revTPL into (reversible) timed Petri nets [32], by extending the encoding of reversible CCS into reversible Petri nets [23]. Another possibility would be to study the extension of a monitored timed semantics for multiparty session types, as the one of [26], with reversibility [25].

References

1. Bernardo, M., Corradini, F., Tesei, L.: Timed process calculi with deterministic or stochastic delays: commuting between durational and durationless actions. Theor. Comput. Sci. **629**, 2–39 (2016)
2. Bernardo, M., Mezzina, C.A.: Towards bridging time and causal reversibility. In: Gotsman, A., Sokolova, A. (eds.) FORTE 2020. LNCS, vol. 12136, pp. 22–38. Springer, Cham (2020). https://doi.org/10.1007/978-3-030-50086-3_2
3. Bertolotti, I.C.: Real-time embedded operating systems. In: Zurawski, R. (ed.) Embedded Systems Handbook. CRC Press, Boca Raton (2005)
4. Bocchi, L., Lanese, I., Mezzina, C.A., Yuen, S.: The reversible temporal process language (technical report). Technical report (2022). http://www.cs.unibo.it/~lanese/work/TR/forte2022-tr.pdf
5. Brinksma, E., Hermanns, H.: Process algebra and Markov Chains. In: Brinksma, E., Hermanns, H., Katoen, J.-P. (eds.) EEF School 2000. LNCS, vol. 2090, pp. 183–231. Springer, Heidelberg (2001). https://doi.org/10.1007/3-540-44667-2_5
6. Britton, T., Jeng, L., Carver, G., Cheak, P.: Reversible debugging software "quantify the time and cost saved using reversible debuggers" (2013)
7. Cristescu, I., Krivine, J., Varacca, D.: A compositional semantics for the reversible π-calculus. In: 28th Annual ACM/IEEE Symposium on Logic in Computer Science, LICS, pp. 388–397. IEEE Computer Society (2013)
8. Danos, V., Krivine, J.: Reversible communicating systems. In: Gardner, P., Yoshida, N. (eds.) CONCUR 2004. LNCS, vol. 3170, pp. 292–307. Springer, Heidelberg (2004). https://doi.org/10.1007/978-3-540-28644-8_19
9. Fabbretti, G., Lanese, I., Stefani, J.-B.: Causal-consistent debugging of distributed Erlang programs. In: Yamashita, S., Yokoyama, T. (eds.) RC 2021. LNCS, vol. 12805, pp. 79–95. Springer, Cham (2021). https://doi.org/10.1007/978-3-030-79837-6_5
10. Fant, J.S., Gomaa, H., Pettit, R.G. IV.: A comparison of executable model based approaches for embedded systems. In: Zhang, H., Zhu, L., Kuz, I., (eds.), Second International Workshop on Software Engineering for Embedded Systems, SEES 2012, pp. 16–22. IEEE (2012)
11. Ghaleb, M., Zolfagharinia, H., Taghipour, S.: Real-time production scheduling in the industry-4.0 context: addressing uncertainties in job arrivals and machine breakdowns. Comput. Oper. Res. **123**, 105031 (2020)
12. Giachino, E., Lanese, I., Mezzina, C.A.: Causal-consistent reversible debugging. In: Gnesi, S., Rensink, A. (eds.) FASE 2014. LNCS, vol. 8411, pp. 370–384. Springer, Heidelberg (2014). https://doi.org/10.1007/978-3-642-54804-8_26
13. Hennessy, M., Regan, T.: A process algebra for timed systems. Inf. Comput. **117**(2), 221–239 (1995)
14. Koopman, P.: Better Embedded System Software. Drumnadrochit Press, Drumnadrochit (2010)
15. Lanese, I., Medic, D.: A general approach to derive uncontrolled reversible semantics. In: Konnov, I., Kovács, L. (eds.), 31st International Conference on Concurrency Theory, CONCUR 2020, vol. 171 of LIPIcs, pp. 33:1–33:24. Schloss Dagstuhl - Leibniz-Zentrum für Informatik (2020)
16. Lanese, I., Medić, D., Mezzina, C.A.: Static versus dynamic reversibility in CCS. Acta Informatica 1–34 (2019). https://doi.org/10.1007/s00236-019-00346-6

17. Lanese, I., Mezzina, C.A., Schmitt, A., Stefani, J.-B.: Controlling reversibility in higher-order pi. In: Katoen, J.-P., König, B. (eds.) CONCUR 2011. LNCS, vol. 6901, pp. 297–311. Springer, Heidelberg (2011). https://doi.org/10.1007/978-3-642-23217-6_20

18. Lanese, I., Mezzina, C.A., Stefani, J.-B.: Reversibility in the higher-order π-calculus. Theor. Comput. Sci. **625**, 25–84 (2016)

19. Lanese, I., Phillips, I.: Forward-reverse observational equivalences in CCSK. In: Yamashita, S., Yokoyama, T. (eds.) RC 2021. LNCS, vol. 12805, pp. 126–143. Springer, Cham (2021). https://doi.org/10.1007/978-3-030-79837-6_8

20. Lanese, I., Phillips, I., Ulidowski, I.: An axiomatic approach to reversible computation. In: FoSSaCS 2020. LNCS, vol. 12077, pp. 442–461. Springer, Cham (2020). https://doi.org/10.1007/978-3-030-45231-5_23

21. Mauro, R., Pompigna, A.: State of the art and computational aspects of time-dependent waiting models for non-signalised intersections. J. Traffic Transp. Eng. **7**(6), 808–831 (2020). English Edition

22. Medic, D., Mezzina, C.A., Phillips, I., Yoshida, N.: A parametric framework for reversible π-calculi. Inf. Comput. **275**, 104644 (2020)

23. Melgratti, H., Mezzina, C.A., Pinna, G.M.: Towards a truly concurrent semantics for reversible CCS. In: Yamashita, S., Yokoyama, T. (eds.) RC 2021. LNCS, vol. 12805, pp. 109–125. Springer, Cham (2021). https://doi.org/10.1007/978-3-030-79837-6_7

24. Mezzina, C.A.: On reversibility and broadcast. In: Kari, J., Ulidowski, I. (eds.) RC 2018. LNCS, vol. 11106, pp. 67–83. Springer, Cham (2018). https://doi.org/10.1007/978-3-319-99498-7_5

25. Mezzina, C.A., Pèrez, J.A.: Causal consistency for reversible multiparty protocols. Logical Methods Comput. Sci. 17(4), (2021)

26. Neykova, R., Bocchi, L., Yoshida, N.: Timed runtime monitoring for multiparty conversations. Formal Aspects Comput. **29**(5), 877–910 (2017). https://doi.org/10.1007/s00165-017-0420-8

27. Nicollin, X., Sifakis, J.: An overview and synthesis on timed process algebras. In: de Bakker, J.W., Huizing, C., de Roever, W.P., Rozenberg, G. (eds.) REX 1991. LNCS, vol. 600, pp. 526–548. Springer, Heidelberg (1992). https://doi.org/10.1007/BFb0032006

28. Phillips, I., Ulidowski, I., Yuen, S.: A reversible process calculus and the modelling of the ERK signalling pathway. In: Glück, R., Yokoyama, T. (eds.) RC 2012. LNCS, vol. 7581, pp. 218–232. Springer, Heidelberg (2013). https://doi.org/10.1007/978-3-642-36315-3_18

29. Phillips, I.C.C., Ulidowski, I.: Reversing algebraic process calculi. J. Log. Algebraic Methods Program. **73**(1–2), 70–96 (2007)

30. Vizard, M.: Report: Debugging efforts cost companies $61b annually (2020)

31. Yokoyama, T., Glück, R.: A reversible programming language and its invertible self-interpreter. In: Ramalingam, G., Visser, E. (eds.), Proceedings of the 2007 ACM SIGPLAN Workshop on Partial Evaluation and Semantics-based Program Manipulation, pp. 144–153. ACM (2007)

32. Zimmermann, A., Freiheit, J., Hommel, G.: Discrete time stochastic Petri nets for the modeling and evaluation of real-time systems. In: Proceedings of the 15th International Parallel & Distributed Processing Symposium (IPDPS-01), p. 100. IEEE Computer Society (2001)

Branch-Well-Structured Transition Systems and Extensions

Benedikt Bollig[1], Alain Finkel[1,2], and Amrita Suresh[1(✉)]

[1] Université Paris-Saclay, ENS Paris-Saclay, CNRS, LMF, Gif-sur-Yvette, France
amrita.suresh@ens-paris-saclay.fr
[2] Institut Universitaire de France, Paris, France

Abstract. We propose a relaxation to the definition of a well-structured transition systems (WSTS) while retaining the decidability of boundedness and termination. In this class, we ease the well-quasi-ordered (wqo) condition to be applicable only between states that are reachable one from another. Furthermore, we also relax the monotony condition in the same way. While this retains the decidability of termination and boundedness, it appears that the coverability problem is undecidable. To this end, we define a new notion of monotony, called cover-monotony, which is strictly more general than the usual monotony and still allows to decide a restricted form of the coverability problem.

Keywords: Verification · Decidability · Coverability · Termination · Well-quasi-ordering

1 Introduction

Well-structured transition systems (WSTS) (initially called structured transition systems in [10]) have decidable termination and boundedness problems. They capture properties common to a wide range of formal models used in model-checking, system verification and concurrent programming [13].

A WSTS is an infinite set X (of states) with a transition relation $\rightarrow \subseteq X \times X$. The set X is quasi-ordered by $\leq$, and $\rightarrow$ fulfills one of various possible monotonies with respect to $\leq$. The quasi-ordering of X is further assumed to be well, i.e. well-founded and with no infinite antichains (see Sect. 2 for precise formal definitions). These two properties lead to a general framework in which it is possible to algorithmically decide verification problems like coverability, termination and boundedness.

This class of systems includes Lossy Channel Systems, Petri Nets and their extensions, among others [1,13]. More recently, the theory of WSTS has been applied to study computational models resulting from a combination of different types of systems like asynchronous systems defined by extending pushdown systems with an external memory [5], cryptographic protocols [7], and others.

Various strengthenings and weakenings of the notion of monotony (of $\rightarrow$ with respect to $\leq$) were introduced, to allow WSTS to capture more models [1,13].

© IFIP International Federation for Information Processing 2022
Published by Springer Nature Switzerland AG 2022
M. R. Mousavi and A. Philippou (Eds.): FORTE 2022, LNCS 13273, pp. 50–66, 2022.
https://doi.org/10.1007/978-3-031-08679-3_4

More recently, [3] showed that the wellness assumption in the definition of WSTS can be relaxed while some decidabilities are retained (notably, the coverability problem is decidable).

Our main contribution is to prove that the monotony and well-quasi-order (wqo) assumptions can further be weakened while some problems remain decidable. More precisely, we introduce a notion of well-structured transition systems, called branch-well-structured transition systems, where the monotony is only applicable to states reachable one from another. Furthermore, we also relax the wqo condition to such states. With this relaxation, it is still possible to retain the decidability of termination and boundedness. Furthermore, for the coverability problem, we introduce a notion of monotony, called cover-monotony, which still allows deciding the coverability problem, even in the absence of strong (or strict or transitive or reflexive) monotony. Indeed, while the usual backward algorithm for coverability relies on well-foundedness, the forward algorithm described in [3] does not require that property.

Outline. Sect. 2 introduces terminology and some well-known results concerning well-quasi-orderings and well-structured transition systems. Section 3 defines branch-WSTS, and shows that both the boundedness and the termination problems are decidable for such systems. Section 4 investigates the coverability problem for WSTS with relaxed conditions. We conclude in Sect. 5. Due to space constraints, some proofs are omitted.

2   Preliminaries

Quasi-Orderings. Let X be a set and $\leq \subseteq X \times X$ be a binary relation over X, which we also write as $(X, \leq)$. We call $\leq$ a *quasi-ordering (qo)* if it is reflexive and transitive. As usual, we call $\leq$ a *partial ordering* if it is a qo and anti-symmetric (if $x \leq y$ and $y \leq x$, then $x = y$).

For the following definitions, we also use the terminology qo for the ordering $\leq$ and its associated set X, i.e. $(X, \leq)$.

We write $x < y$ if $x \leq y$ and $y \not\leq x$. If $\leq$ is a partial ordering, $x < y$ is then equivalent to $x \leq y$ and $x \neq y$.

To any $x \in X$, we associate the sets $\uparrow x \stackrel{\text{def}}{=} \{y \mid x \leq y\}$ and $\downarrow x \stackrel{\text{def}}{=} \{y \mid y \leq x\}$. Moreover, for $A \subseteq X$, we let $\uparrow A \stackrel{\text{def}}{=} \bigcup_{x \in A} \uparrow x$ and $\downarrow A \stackrel{\text{def}}{=} \bigcup_{x \in A} \downarrow x$. We say that A is *upward-closed* if $A = \uparrow A$. Similarly, A is *downward-closed* if $A = \downarrow A$. A *basis* of an upward-closed set A is a set $B \subseteq X$ such that $A = \uparrow B$.

We call $(X, \leq)$ *well-founded* if there is no infinite strictly decreasing sequence $x_0 > x_1 > \ldots$ of elements of X. An *antichain* is a subset $A \subseteq X$ of pairwise incomparable elements, i.e., for every distinct $x, y \in A$, we have $x \not\leq y$ and $y \not\leq x$. For example, consider the alphabet $\Sigma = \{a, b\}$. There exists an infinite antichain $\{b, ab, aab, \ldots\}$ with respect to the prefix ordering over Σ^*.

An *ideal* is a downward-closed set $I \subseteq X$ that is also *directed*, i.e., it is nonempty and, for every $x, y \in I$, there exists $z \in I$ such that $x \leq z$ and $y \leq z$. The set of ideals is denoted by $\mathsf{Ideals}(X)$.

Well-Quasi-Orderings. When a qo satisfies some additional property, we deal with a well-quasi-ordering:

Definition 1. *A* well-quasi-ordering (wqo) *is a qo* $(X, \leq)$ *such that every infinite sequence* $x_0, x_1, x_2, \ldots$ *over* X *contains an* increasing pair, *i.e., there are* $i < j$ *such that* $x_i \leq x_j$.

For example, the set of natural numbers $\mathbb{N}$, along with the standard ordering $\leq$ is a wqo. Moreover, $(\mathbb{N}^k, \leq)$, i.e. the set of vectors of $k \geq 1$ natural numbers with component-wise ordering, is a wqo [6]. On the other hand, the prefix ordering of words over an alphabet Σ, denoted by $\preceq$, is not a wqo since, in the infinite sequence $b, ab, a^2b, a^3b, \ldots a^nb, \ldots$, we have $a^ib \not\preceq a^jb$ for all $i < j$.

In general, for qo, upward-closed sets do not necessarily have a *finite* basis. However, from [14], we know that every upward-closed set in a wqo has a finite basis.

We have the following equivalent characterization of wqos.

Proposition 1 ([9]). *A qo* $(X, \leq)$ *is a wqo iff every infinite sequence in* X *has an infinite increasing subsequence.*

Moreover, one can prove that a qo is a wqo iff it is well-founded and contains no infinite antichain.

The following proposition is useful to design the forward coverability algorithm that enumerates finite subsets of ideals composing inductive invariants. It shows that the wqo hypothesis is not necessary to decide coverability.

Proposition 2 ([9]). *A qo* $(X, \leq)$ *contains no infinite antichain iff every downward-closed set decomposes into a finite union of ideals.*

Transition Systems. A *transition system* is a pair $\mathcal{S} = \langle X, \rightarrow \rangle$ where X is the set of states and $\rightarrow \subseteq X \times X$ is the transition relation. We write $x \rightarrow y$ for $(x, y) \in \rightarrow$. Moreover, we let $\xrightarrow{*}$ be the transitive and reflexive closure of the relation $\rightarrow$, and $\xrightarrow{+}$ be the transitive closure of $\rightarrow$.

Given a state $x \in X$, we write $Post_{\mathcal{S}}(x) = \{y \in X \mid x \rightarrow y\}$ for the set of immediate successors of x. Similarly, $Pre_{\mathcal{S}}(x) = \{y \in X \mid y \rightarrow x\}$ denotes the set of its immediate predecessors.

We call $\mathcal{S}$ *finitely branching* if, for all $x \in X$, the set $Post_{\mathcal{S}}(x)$ is finite. The *reachability set* of $\mathcal{S}$ from $x \in X$ is defined as $Post^*_{\mathcal{S}}(x) = \{y \in X \mid x \xrightarrow{*} y\}$. Note that, when $\mathcal{S}$ is clear from the context, we may drop the subscript and write, e.g., $Post^*(x)$. We say that a state y is reachable from x if $y \in Post^*(x)$ (resp. $y \in \downarrow Post^*(x)$).

A *(well-)ordered transition system* is a triple $\mathcal{S} = (X, \rightarrow, \leq)$ consisting of a transition system $\langle X, \rightarrow \rangle$ equipped with a qo (resp., wqo) $(X, \leq)$. An ordered transition system $\mathcal{S} = (X, \rightarrow, \leq)$ is *effective* if $\leq$ and $\rightarrow$ are decidable. We say that a state y is coverable from x if $y \in \downarrow Post^*(x)$.

Definition 2 ([10]). *A* well-structured transition system (WSTS) *is a well-ordered transition system* $S = (X, \rightarrow, \leq)$ *that satisfies (general)* monotony: *for all* $x, y, x' \in X$, *we have:* $x \leq y \wedge x \rightarrow x' \implies \exists y' \in X : x' \leq y' \wedge y \xrightarrow{*} y'$.

We define other types of monotony. We say that a well-ordered transition system $S = (X, \rightarrow, \leq)$ satisfies *strong monotony* (resp., *transitive monotony*) if, for all $x, y, x' \in X$ such that $x \leq y$ and $x \rightarrow x'$, there is $y' \in X$ such that $x' \leq y'$ and $y \rightarrow y'$ (resp., $y \xrightarrow{+} y'$). The transition system S satisfies *strict monotony* if, for all $x, y, x' \in X$ such that $x < y$ and $x \rightarrow x'$, there is $y' \in X$ such that $x' < y'$ and $y \rightarrow y'$.

Definition 3. *We define the following decision problems. Given an ordered transition system* $S = (X, \rightarrow, \leq)$ *and an initial state* $x_0 \in X$:

- The non-termination problem: *Is there an infinite sequence of states* $x_1, x_2, \ldots$ *such that* $x_0 \rightarrow x_1 \rightarrow x_2 \rightarrow \ldots$?
- The boundedness problem: *Is* $Post_S^*(x_0)$ *finite?*
- The coverability problem: *Given states* $x, y \in X$, *is* y *coverable from* x?

It is folklore [10,13] that termination is decidable for finitely branching WSTS with transitive monotony and that boundedness is decidable for finitely branching WSTS $S = (X, \rightarrow, \leq)$ where $\leq$ is a partial ordering and $\rightarrow$ is strictly monotone; in both cases, we suppose that the WSTS are effective and that $Post(x)$ is computable, for all $x \in X$.

Recall that, in a wqo $(X, \leq)$, upward-closed sets have a finite basis. Coverability is decidable for a large class of WSTS:

Theorem 1 ([1,13]). *The coverability problem is decidable for effective WSTS* $S = (X, \rightarrow, \leq)$ *equipped with an algorithm that, for all finite sets* $I \subseteq X$, *computes a finite basis* $pb(I)$ *of* $\uparrow Pre(\uparrow I)$.

Assume $S = (X, \rightarrow, \leq)$ is a WSTS and $x \in X$ is a state. The *backward coverability algorithm* involves computing (a finite basis of) $Pre^*(\uparrow x)$ as the limit of the infinite increasing sequence $\uparrow I_0 \subseteq \uparrow I_1 \subseteq \ldots$ where $I_0 = \{x\}$ and $I_{n+1} \stackrel{\text{def}}{=} I_n \cup pb(I_n)$. Since there exists an integer k such that $\uparrow I_{k+1} = \uparrow I_k$, the finite set I_k is computable (one may test, for all n, whether $\uparrow I_{n+1} = \uparrow I_n$) and I_k is then a finite basis of $Pre^*(\uparrow x)$ so one deduces that coverability is decidable.

Coverability can be also decided by using the *forward coverability algorithm* that relies on two semi-decision procedures (as described below). It applies to the class of well-behaved transition systems, which are more general than WSTS. A *well-behaved transition system (WBTS)* is an ordered transition system $S = (X, \rightarrow, \leq)$ with monotony such that $(X, \leq)$ contains no infinite antichain. We describe effectiveness hypotheses that allow manipulating downward-closed sets in WBTS.

Definition 4 ([3, **Definition 3.4**]). *A class C of WBTS is* ideally effective *if, given* $S = (X, \rightarrow, \leq) \in C$,

- the set of encodings of Ideals(X) is recursive,
- the function mapping the encoding of a state $x \in X$ to the encoding of the ideal $\downarrow x \in$ Ideals(X) is computable;
- inclusion of ideals of X is decidable;
- the downward closure $\downarrow Post(I)$ expressed as a finite union of ideals is computable from the ideal $I \in$ Ideals(X).

Theorem 2 ([3]). *The coverability problem is decidable for ideally effective WBTS.*

The proof is done by two semi-decision procedures where downward-closed sets are represented by their finite decomposition in ideals and this is effective. Procedure 1 checks for coverability of y from x_0, by recursively computing $\downarrow x_0$, $\downarrow(\downarrow x_0 \cup Post(\downarrow x_0))$ and so on. This procedure terminates only if y belongs to one of these sets, hence it terminates if y is coverable. Hence, we deduce:

Proposition 3 ([3]). *For an ideally effective WBTS $\mathcal{S} = (X, \rightarrow, \leq)$, an initial state x_0, and a state y, Procedure 1 terminates iff y is coverable from x_0.*

Procedure 1 : Checks for a coverability certificate of y from x_0

---

input: $\mathcal{S} = (X, \rightarrow, \leq)$ and x_0, y

$\quad D := \downarrow x_0$
$\quad$**while** $y \notin D$ **do**
$\quad\quad D := \downarrow(D \cup Post_{\mathcal{S}}(D))$
$\quad$**end while**
$\quad$**return** *"y is coverable from x_0"*

Procedure 2 enumerates all downward-closed subsets (by means of their finite decomposition in ideals) in some fixed order $D_1, D_2, \ldots$ such that for all i, $D_i \subseteq X$ and $\downarrow Post(D_i) \subseteq D_i$. This enumeration is effective since $\mathcal{S}$ is ideally effective. If such a set D_i contains x_0, it is an over-approximation of $Post^*(x_0)$. Hence, if there is such a set D_i such that $x_0 \in D_i$ but $y \notin D_i$, it is a certificate of non-coverability. Moreover, this procedure terminates if y is non-coverable because $\downarrow Post^*(x_0)$ is such a set, and hence, will eventually be found.

Proposition 4 ([3]). *For a WBTS $\mathcal{S} = (X, \rightarrow, \leq)$, an initial state x_0 and a state y, Procedure 2 terminates iff y is not coverable from x_0.*

3   Termination and Boundedness

In this section, we generalize wqo and monotony such that these properties only consider states along a branch in the reachability tree. To define these notions, we use labels on the transitions, hence, we consider labeled transition systems.

Procedure 2 : Checks for non-coverability

---

input: $\mathcal{S} = (X, \rightarrow, \leq)$ and x_0, y

    enumerate $D_1, D_2, \ldots$
    $i := 1$
    while $\neg(\downarrow Post(D_i) \subseteq D_i$ **and** $x_0 \in D_i$ **and** $y \notin D_i)$ **do**
      $i := i + 1$
    end while
    return false

Labeled Transition Systems. A *labeled transition system (LTS)* is a tuple $\mathcal{S} = (X, \Sigma, \rightarrow, x_0)$ where X is the set of states, Σ is the finite action alphabet, $\rightarrow \subseteq X \times \Sigma \times X$ is the transition relation, and $x_0 \in X$ is the initial state.

Definition 5. *An* (quasi-)ordered labeled transition system (OLTS) *is defined as a tuple* $\mathcal{S} = (X, \Sigma, \rightarrow, \leq, x_0)$ *where* $(X, \Sigma, \rightarrow, x_0)$ *is an LTS and* $(X, \leq)$ *is a qo.*

In the case of an LTS or OLTS, we write $x \xrightarrow{a} x'$ instead of $(x, a, x') \in \rightarrow$. For $\sigma \in \Sigma^*$, $x \xrightarrow{\sigma} x'$ is defined as expected. We also let $x \rightarrow x'$ if $(x, a, x') \in \rightarrow$ for some $a \in \Sigma$, with closures $\xrightarrow{*}$ and $\xrightarrow{+}$.

We call an OLTS $\mathcal{S}$ *effective* if $\leq$ and, for all $a \in \Sigma$, $\xrightarrow{a}$ are decidable.

Remark 1. We can similarly define a labeled WSTS as an OLTS such that the ordering is well and it satisfies the general monotony condition (canonically adapted to take care of the transition labels). Moreover, we lift the decision problems from Definition 3 to OLTS in the obvious way.

Branch-WSTS. Consider an OLTS $\mathcal{S} = (X, \Sigma, \rightarrow, \leq, x_0)$. A *run* (or *branch*) of $\mathcal{S}$ is a finite or infinite sequence $\rho = (x_0 \rightarrow x_1)(x_1 \rightarrow x_2)...$ simply written $\rho = x_0 \rightarrow x_1 \rightarrow x_2 \ldots$. We say that ρ is *branch-wqo* if the set of states $\{x_0, x_1, x_2, \ldots\}$ visited along ρ is wqo w.r.t. $\leq$.

Definition 6. *An OLTS* $\mathcal{S} = (X, \Sigma, \rightarrow, \leq, x_0)$ *is branch-wqo if every run of* $\mathcal{S}$ *is branch-wqo.*

Example 1. Consider the FIFO machine (formally defined in Definition 10) $\mathcal{M}_1$ in Fig. 1 with one FIFO channel. In control-state q_0, it makes a loop by sending letter a to the channel. Then, we may go, non-deterministically, to control-state q_1 by sending letter b once, and then we stop. Let us consider the set of states $X_1 = \{q_0, q_1\} \times \{a, b\}^*$ together with the ordering $\leq_p$ defined by $(q, u) \leq_p (q', u')$ if $q = q'$ and u is a prefix of u', i.e., $u \preceq u'$. The reachability set of $\mathcal{M}_1$ from (q_0, ε) is equal to $\{(q_0, w), (q_1, w) \mid w \in a^*, w' \in a^*b\}$. Note that $\leq_p$ is not a wqo since elements of the set $\{(q_1, w) \mid w \in a^*b\}$ form an infinite antichain for $\leq_p$. However, the reachability tree of $\mathcal{M}_1$ is branch-wqo for the initial state (q_0, ε). Hence, there exist branch-wqo OLTS $\mathcal{S} = (X, \Sigma, \rightarrow, \leq, x_0)$ such that $(X, \leq)$ is not a wqo.

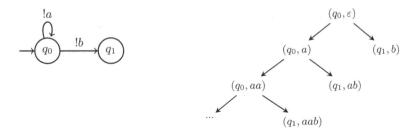

Fig. 1. The FIFO machine $\mathcal{M}_1$ (left), and its corresponding (incomplete) infinite reachability tree (right).

Remark 2. There exist a system $\mathcal{S} = (X, \Sigma, \rightarrow, \leq, x_0)$ and $x_0' \in X$ such that $\mathcal{S}$ is branch-wqo but $(X, \Sigma, \rightarrow, \leq, x_0')$ is not branch-wqo (cf. Figure 2).

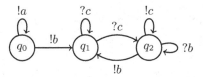

Fig. 2. The FIFO machine shown is branch-wqo if the initial control-state is q_0. If the initial control-state is q_2, then it is not branch-wqo as the states in the set $\{(q_1, w) \mid w \in c^+ b\}$, which form an infinite antichain, are reachable from (q_2, ε).

We now look at a generalization of *strong monotony*, which we will refer to as branch-monotony.

Definition 7 (Branch-monotony). *An OLTS* $\mathcal{S} = (X, \Sigma, \rightarrow, \leq, x_0)$ *is branch-monotone if, for all* $x, x' \in X$, $\sigma \in \Sigma^*$ *such that* $x \xrightarrow{\sigma} x'$ *and* $x \leq x'$, *there exists a state* y *such that* $x' \xrightarrow{\sigma} y$ *and* $x' \leq y$.

Remark 3. Let $\mathcal{S}$ be a branch-monotone OLTS and let there be states x, x' such that $x \xrightarrow{\sigma} x'$ and $x \leq x'$, with $\sigma \in \Sigma^*$. Then, for any $n \geq 1$, there exists $y_n \in X$ such that $x \xrightarrow{\sigma^n} y_n$ with $x \leq y_n$.

As in the case of general monotony, *strict* branch-monotony is defined using strict inequalities in both cases.

Example 2. Consider $\mathcal{M}_1$ from Example 1 once again. Note $\mathcal{M}_1$ induces an OLTS by considering the actions on the edges to be the labels. Moreover, $\mathcal{M}_1$ is branch-monotone. For every $x \xrightarrow{\sigma} x'$ such that $x \leq x'$ and $\sigma \in \Sigma^*$, it is necessary that $x = (q_0, a^n)$, $x' = (q_0, a^{n+k})$, for some $n, k \in \mathbb{N}$. Moreover, there always exists a transition from x' such that $x' \xrightarrow{\sigma} y = (q_0, a^{n+k+k})$. Hence, $x' \leq y$. We deduce that $\mathcal{M}_1$ is branch-monotone.

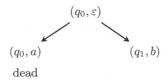

Fig. 3. The reduced reachability tree of $\mathcal{M}_1$ from (q_0, ε). Note that (q_0, a) is dead because it is subsumed by state (q_0, ε). As a matter of fact, we have $(q_0, \varepsilon) \overset{*}{\rightarrow} (q_0, a)$ and $(q_0, \varepsilon) \leq_p (q_0, a)$. State (q_1, b) is also dead but it is not subsumed.

We are now ready to extend the definition of WSTS.

Definition 8 (Branch-WSTS). *A* branch-WSTS *is an OLTS* $S = (X, \Sigma, \rightarrow, \leq, x_0)$ *that is finitely branching, branch-monotone, and branch-wqo.*

When we say, without ambiguity, that a machine $\mathcal{M}$ is branch-wqo, WSTS, or branch-WSTS, we mean that the ordered transition system $S_{\mathcal{M}}$, associated with machine $\mathcal{M}$, is branch-wqo, WSTS, or branch-WSTS, resp.

Remark 4. Branch-WSTS is a strict superclass of labeled WSTS. For example, machine $\mathcal{M}_1$ is branch-WSTS for the ordering $\leq_p$ but $\mathcal{M}_1$ is not WSTS for $\leq_p$ since $\leq_p$ is not a wqo on $\{q_0, q_1\} \times \{a, b\}^*$ or on the subset $\{(q_1, w) \mid w \in a^*b\}$.

Let us recall the *Reduced Reachability Tree (RRT)*, which was defined as Finite Reachability Tree in [10,13]. Suppose that $S = (X, \Sigma, \rightarrow, \leq, x_0)$ is an OLTS. Then, the *Reduced Reachability Tree* from x_0, denoted by $RRT(S, x_0)$, is a tree where nodes are labeled by states of X, and $n(x)$ denotes that node n is labeled by state x. Nodes are either *dead* or *live*. The root node $n_0(x_0)$ is live. A dead node has no child node. A live node $n(y)$ has one child $n'(y')$ for each successor $y' \in Post_S(y)$. If there is a path in the tree $n_0(x_0) \overset{*}{\rightarrow} n'(y') \overset{+}{\rightarrow} n(y)$ such that $n' \neq n$ and $y' \leq y$, we say that n' *subsumes* n, and then n is dead. Otherwise n is live. See Fig. 3 for the RRT of $\mathcal{M}_1$.

Proposition 5. *Let* $S = (X, \Sigma, \rightarrow, \leq, x_0)$ *be an OLTS that is finitely branching and branch-wqo. Then, $RRT(S, x_0)$ is finite.*

Proposition 6. *Let* $S = (X, \Sigma, \rightarrow, \leq, x_0)$ *be a branch-WSTS, equipped with strict branch-monotony and such that $\leq$ is a partial ordering. The reachability set $Post_S^*(x_0)$ is infinite iff there exists a branch $n_0(x_0) \overset{*}{\rightarrow} n_1(x_1) \overset{+}{\rightarrow} n_2(x_2)$ in $RRT(S, x_0)$ such that $x_1 < x_2$.*

We now need a notion of effectivity adapted to branch-WSTS.

Definition 9. *A branch-WSTS* $S = (X, \Sigma, \rightarrow, \leq, x_0)$ *is* branch-effective *if S is effective and $Post_S(x)$ is a (finite) computable set, for all $x \in X$.*

Theorem 3. *Boundedness is decidable for branch-effective branch-WSTS $S = (X, \Sigma, \rightarrow, \leq, x_0)$ with strict branch-monotony such that $\leq$ is a partial ordering.*

Proof. Suppose $\mathcal{S} = (X, \Sigma, \rightarrow, \leq, x_0)$ satisfies the above conditions. From Proposition 5, we obtain that $RRT(\mathcal{S}, x_0)$ is finite. By hypothesis, $\mathcal{S}$ is finitely branching and branch-effective. In particular, for all x, $Post_{\mathcal{S}}(x)$ is a finite computable set. As $\leq$ is decidable, we deduce that $RRT(\mathcal{S}, x_0)$ is effectively computable. From Proposition 6, we know that $Post^*_{\mathcal{S}}(x_0)$ is infinite iff there exists a finite branch $n_0(x_0) \xrightarrow{*} n_1(x_1) \xrightarrow{+} n_2(x_2)$ such that $x_1 < x_2$. This last property can be decided on $RRT(\mathcal{S}, x_0)$, and so the boundedness property can be decided, too. □

We also generalize the decidability of termination for WSTS [13] to branch-WSTS.

Proposition 7. *A branch-WSTS $\mathcal{S} = (X, \Sigma, \rightarrow, \leq, x_0)$ does not terminate from state x_0 iff there exists a subsumed node in $RRT(\mathcal{S}, x_0)$.*

Theorem 4. *Termination is decidable for branch-effective branch-WSTS.*

Proof. Given a branch-WSTS $\mathcal{S} = (X, \Sigma, \rightarrow, \leq, x_0)$, we apply Proposition 7 so that it is sufficient to build $RRT(\mathcal{S}, x_0)$ and check if there exists a subsumed node. Since $\mathcal{S}$ is branch-effective, we can effectively construct $RRT(\mathcal{S}, x_0)$ and verify the existence of a subsumed node. □

Note that we can thus solve the termination and boundedness problems for the example machine $\mathcal{M}_1$, and since there exists nodes $n_0(x_0)$ and $n_1(x_1)$ in the RRT such that $x_0 = (q_0, \varepsilon)$ and $x_1 = (q_0, a)$ such that $x_0 < x_1$ and $x_0 \xrightarrow{+} x_1$, the machine $\mathcal{M}_1$ is unbounded. Moreover, since $n_1(x_1)$ is also a subsumed node, it is non-terminating.

On the other hand, boundedness becomes undecidable if we relax the strict monotony condition to general monotony (even when we strengthen the order to be wqo). This is because boundedness is undecidable for Reset Petri nets [8]. Reset Petri nets are effective WSTS $\mathcal{S} = (X, \Sigma, \rightarrow, \leq, x_0)$, hence branch-effective WSTS, where $\leq$ is the wqo on vectors of integers. Hence, we deduce:

Proposition 8. *Boundedness is undecidable for branch-effective branch-WSTS $\mathcal{S} = (X, \Sigma, \rightarrow, \leq, x_0)$ where $\leq$ is a wqo.*

Counter Machines with Restricted Zero Tests. Now, we show an example of a class that is branch-WSTS. We study counter machines with restricted zero tests. In [4], it was shown that termination and boundedness (and moreover, reachability) are decidable for this class of systems. However, using the alternative approach of branch-WSTS, we can verify that termination and boundedness are decidable for this class without reducing these problems to reachability.

We recall that a *counter machine* (with zero tests) is a tuple $\mathcal{C} = (Q, V, T, q_0)$. Here, Q is the finite set of *control states* and $q_0 \in Q$ is the *initial control state*. Moreover, V is a finite set of *counters* and $T \subseteq Q \times A_{\mathcal{C}} \times Q$ is the transition relation where $A_{\mathcal{C}} = \{\mathsf{inc}(v), \mathsf{dec}(v) \mid v \in V\} \times 2^V$ (an element of 2^V will indicate the set of counters to be tested to 0).

The counter machine $\mathcal{C}$ induces an LTS $\mathcal{S}_\mathcal{C} = (X_\mathcal{C}, A_\mathcal{C}, \rightarrow_\mathcal{C}, x_0)$ with set of states $X_\mathcal{C} = Q \times \mathbb{N}^V$. In $(q, \ell) \in X_\mathcal{C}$, the first component q is the current control state and $\ell = (\ell_v)_{v \in V}$ represents the counter values. The initial state is then $x_0 = (q_0, \ell)$ with all ℓ_v equal to 0.

For $op \in \{\mathsf{inc}, \mathsf{dec}\}$, $v \in V$, and $Z \subseteq V$ (the counters tested for zero), there is a transition $(q, \ell) \xrightarrow{op(v), Z}_\mathcal{C} (q', m)$ if $(q, (op(v), Z), q') \in T$, $\ell_{v'} = 0$ for all $v' \in Z$ (applies the zero tests), $m_v = \ell_v + 1$ if $op = \mathsf{inc}$ and $m_v = \ell_v - 1$ if $op = \mathsf{dec}$, and $m_{v'} = \ell_{v'}$ for all $v' \in V \setminus \{v\}$.

We define *counter machines with restricted zero tests (CMRZ)* imposing the following requirement: Once a counter has been tested for zero, it cannot be incremented or decremented anymore. Formally, we require that, for all valid transition sequences $(q_1, \ell_1) \xrightarrow{op(v_1), Z_1}_\mathcal{C} (q_2, \ell_2) \xrightarrow{op(v_2), Z_2}_\mathcal{C} \cdots \xrightarrow{op(v_n), Z_n}_\mathcal{C} (q_{n+1}, \ell_{n+1})$ and every two positions $1 \le i \le j \le n$, we have $v_j \notin Z_i$.

Let us consider the wqo $\le$ on $Q \times \mathbb{N}^V$ where $(q, \ell) \le (q', m)$ if $q = q'$ and $\ell \le m$. Note that this ordering is a partial ordering.

Proposition 9. *CMRZs are branch-monotone and strictly branch-monotone for the wqo $\le$.*

Therefore, since $\le$ is a wqo:

Theorem 5. *CMRZs are branch-WSTS.*

Furthermore, since $\le$ and $\rightarrow_\mathcal{C}$ are decidable, and $Post_{\mathcal{S}_\mathcal{C}}(x)$ is a finite, computable set for all $x \in X_\mathcal{C}$, we have:

Proposition 10. *CMRZs are branch-effective.*

Hence, we deduce:

Theorem 6. *Termination and boundedness are decidable for counter machines with restricted zero tests.*

Restrictions on FIFO Machines. Next, we consider FIFO machines.

Definition 10. *A FIFO machine $\mathcal{M}$ with a unique channel over the finite message alphabet A is a tuple $\mathcal{M} = (Q, A, T, q_0)$ where Q is a finite set of control states and $q_0 \in Q$ is an initial control state. Moreover, $T \subseteq Q \times \{!, ?\} \times A \times Q$ is the transition relation, where $\{!\} \times A$ and $\{?\} \times A$ are the set of send and receive actions, respectively.*

The FIFO machine $\mathcal{M}$ induces the LTS $\mathcal{S}_\mathcal{M} = (X_\mathcal{M}, \Sigma_\mathcal{M}, \rightarrow_\mathcal{M}, x_0)$. Its set of states is $X_\mathcal{M} = Q \times A^*$. In $(q, w) \in X_\mathcal{M}$, the first component q denotes the current control state and $w \in A^*$ denotes the contents of the channel. The initial state is $x_0 = (q_0, \varepsilon)$, where ε denotes the empty channel. Moreover, $\Sigma_\mathcal{M} = \{!, ?\} \times A$. The transitions are given as follows:

- $(q, w) \xrightarrow{!a}_\mathcal{M} (q', w')$ if $(q, !a, q') \in T$ and $w' = w \cdot a$.

– $(q, w) \xrightarrow{?a}_{\mathcal{M}} (q', w')$ if $(q, ?a, q') \in T$ and $w = a \cdot w'$.

The index $\mathcal{M}$ may be omitted whenever $\mathcal{M}$ is clear from the context. When there is no ambiguity, we confuse machines and their associated LTS.

The FIFO machine $\mathcal{M}_1$ from Fig. 1 is an example of a system that is branch-WSTS but the underlying set of states is not well-quasi-ordered. We first try to generalize a class of systems which are branch-wqo, and which includes $\mathcal{M}_1$.

Branch-Wqo FIFO Machines. We consider a restriction that has been studied in [4], which we go on to prove is branch-wqo. These systems are known as input-bounded FIFO machines, which we formally define below. First, we recall the definition of a bounded language.

Let $w_1, \ldots, w_n \in A^+$ be non-empty words where $n \geq 1$. A *bounded language* over $(w_1, \ldots, w_n)$ is a language $L \subseteq w_1^* \ldots w_n^*$. We let $\mathsf{proj}_! : \Sigma_{\mathcal{M}}^* \to A^*$ be the homomorphism defined by $\mathsf{proj}_!(!a) = a$ for all $a \in A$ and $\mathsf{proj}_!(\beta) = \varepsilon$ if β is not of the form $!a$ for some $a \in A$. We define $\mathsf{proj}_?$ the same way. Using these notions, the input language of $\mathcal{M}$ is defined as $L_{\mathrm{input}}(\mathcal{M}) = \{\mathsf{proj}_!(\sigma) \mid x_0 \xrightarrow{\sigma}_{\mathcal{M}} x$ for some $x \in X_{\mathcal{M}}\}$. Note that the input language is prefix-closed. Moreover, the prefix language of a bounded language is a bounded language.

Definition 11. *A FIFO machine* $\mathcal{M} = (Q, A, T, q_0)$ *is* input-bounded *if its input language* $L_{\mathrm{input}}(\mathcal{M})$ *is bounded.*

Let us recall the extended prefix ordering on the states of a FIFO machine: we let $(q, w) \leq_p (q', w')$ if $q = q'$ and $w \preceq w'$.

Proposition 11. *Input-bounded FIFO machines are branch-wqo for the prefix-ordering* $\leq_p$.

It is clear that $\mathcal{M}_1$ belongs to this class of FIFO systems. But, we see that this subclass is not branch-WSTS (cf. Figure 4). We have $(q_1, \varepsilon) \xrightarrow{\sigma} (q_1, a)$, where $\sigma = !b?b!a$. Moreover, $(q_1, \varepsilon) \leq_p (q_1, a)$. However, there exists no (q_1, w) such that $(q_1, a) \xrightarrow{\sigma} (q_1, w)$, and $(q_1, a) \leq_p (q_1, w)$. In fact, σ cannot be executed from (q_1, a). Therefore, the machine is not branch-monotone under the prefix ordering.

Proposition 12. *Input-bounded FIFO machines are, in general, not branch-monotone for the prefix-ordering.*

However, when we consider *the normal form of input-bounded FIFO machines,* as defined in [4], we conjecture that they are branch-monotone for the prefix-ordering. Furthermore, since they are input-bounded, this would imply that they are branch-WSTS. Moreover, it was also shown in [4], that for every input-bounded FIFO machine, one can construct an equivalent normal form with an exponential blow-up. This would give us another method to verify if a given machine is bounded or has a terminating run, which bypasses checking the reachability of a state.

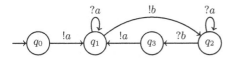

Fig. 5. The FIFO machine $\mathcal{M}_3$.

Fig. 4. The FIFO machine $\mathcal{M}_2$

Branch-Monotone FIFO Machines. We now modify the prefix-ordering further, in order to construct another subclass of FIFO systems which are branch-WSTS. This relation has been previously studied, notably in [12].

Definition 12. *For two states* (q, w) *and* (q', w') *of a FIFO machine* $\mathcal{M}$*, we say that* $(q, w)\ R\ (q', w')$ *if* $q = q'$ *and there exists a sequence* $\sigma \in \Sigma_{\mathcal{M}}^*$ *such that* $(q, w) \xrightarrow{\sigma} (q', w')$ *and*

- $\mathsf{proj}_?(\sigma) = \varepsilon$*, or*
- $w \preceq w'$ *and* $(\mathsf{proj}_?(\sigma))^\omega = w.(\mathsf{proj}_!(\sigma))^\omega$*.*

In fact, R is not a qo. It is reflexive, but not transitive:

Example 3. Consider the FIFO machine $\mathcal{M}_3$ in Fig. 5. Consider states $x_1 = (q, a)$, $x_2 = (q, ab)$, and $x_3 = (q, abab)$. We represent the sequence of actions $!a!b!a!b$ by a single transition $!abab$ in the figure, and omit the intermediate control-states for simplicity (and similarly, for $?ab$). It is easy to see that $x_1\ R\ x_2$ and $x_2\ R\ x_3$. When we consider $x_1 \leq_p x_3$, we have $x_1 \xrightarrow{\sigma} x_3$, where $\sigma = !b(!abab)(?ab)$. However, $(ab)^\omega \neq a.(babab)^\omega$, hence, $x_1 \not{R} x_3$, and thus, the relation is not transitive.

Earlier, we defined branch-monotony for transition systems equipped with a quasi-ordering. We now extend the notion for transition systems with a relation.

Proposition 13. *FIFO machines are branch-monotone for the relation* R*.*

Remark 5. This monotony relation is equivalent to the one described in [15], for FIFO systems. However, we have generalized the notion, and included it in the framework. Hence, we can extend this notion to prove the decidability of termination, something which was not shown earlier.

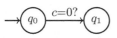

Fig. 6. System $\mathcal{M}_4$ is branch-WSTS.

Fig. 7. System $\mathcal{M}_5$ is branch-WSTS.

4 Decidability of Coverability

Coverability Algorithms for Branch-WSTS. We show that the two existing coverability algorithms for WSTS do not allow one to decide coverability for branch-WSTS. Remark that, contrary to WSTS, $Pre^*(\uparrow x)$ is not necessarily upward-closed. In fact, even with a single zero-test, this property is not satisfied.

In Fig. 6, let us consider the counter machine $\mathcal{M}_4$ with a single counter c. Let $x = (q_1, 0)$. We see that $Pre^*(\uparrow x) = \{(q_1, n) \mid n \geq 0\} \cup \{(q_0, 0)\}$. However, $\uparrow Pre^*(\uparrow x) = Pre^*(\uparrow x) \cup \{(q_0, n) \mid n \geq 1\}$. Thus, we get:

Proposition 14. *Given a branch-effective branch-WSTS $\mathcal{S} = (X, \Sigma, \rightarrow, \leq, x_0)$ and a state $x \in X$, the set $Pre^*(\uparrow x)$ is not necessarily upward-closed. Hence, we cannot use the backward algorithm.*

Let us consider using the forward algorithm instead. The second procedure computes all sets X which satisfy the property $\downarrow Post^*(X) \subseteq X$. This is because for WSTS, the set $\downarrow Post^*(x)$ satisfies this property. However, we now show a counter-example of a branch-WSTS which does not satisfy this property.

Consider the counter machine $\mathcal{M}_5$ from Fig. 7, with $x_0 = (q_0, 0)$. We compute $\downarrow Post^*(x_0)$. We see that $Post^*(x_0) = \{(q_0, 0), (q_1, 1)\}$, hence, $Y = \downarrow Post^*(x_0) = \{(q_0, 0), (q_1, 1), (q_1, 0)\}$. However, $\downarrow Post^*(Y) \not\subseteq Y$, as $\downarrow Post^*(Y) = \{(q_0, 0), (q_1, 1), (q_1, 0), (q_2, 0)\}$, which is strictly larger than Y. Hence:

Proposition 15. *For branch-effective, branch-WSTS $\mathcal{S} = (X, \Sigma, \rightarrow, \leq, x_0)$ such that $\downarrow Post(\downarrow x)$ is computable for all $x \in X$, the set $Y = \downarrow Post^*(x_0)$ does not necessarily satisfy the property $\downarrow Post^*(Y) \subseteq Y$. Hence, the forward coverability algorithm may not terminate.*

We can deduce:

Proposition 16. *For branch-WSTS, both the backward coverability algorithm and the forward coverability algorithm do not terminate, in general.*

Not only the two coverability algorithms do not terminate but we may prove that coverability is undecidable.

Theorem 7. *The coverability problem is undecidable for branch-effective branch-WSTS $\mathcal{S} = (X, \Sigma, \rightarrow, \leq, x_0)$ (even if $\mathcal{S}$ is strongly monotone and $\leq$ is wqo).*

Proof. We use the family of systems given in the proof of Theorem 4.3 [11]. Let us denote by TM_j the jth Turing Machine in some enumeration. Consider the family of functions $f_j : \mathbb{N}^2 \rightarrow \mathbb{N}^2$ defined by $f_j(n, k) = (n, 0)$ if $k = 0$ and TM_j runs for more than n steps, else $f_j(n, k) = (n, n + k)$. Let $g : \mathbb{N}^2 \rightarrow \mathbb{N}^2$ be the function defined by $g(n, k) = (n + 1, k)$. The transition system $\mathcal{S}_j$ induced by the two functions f_j and g is strongly monotone hence it is also branch-monotone. Moreover, system $\mathcal{S}_j$ is branch-effective and we observe that $Post$ is computable and $\leq$ is wqo. Now, we have $(1, 1)$ is coverable from $(0, 0)$ in $\mathcal{S}_j$ iff TM_j halts. This proves that coverability is undecidable. □

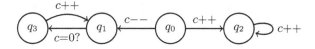

Fig. 8. Machine $\mathcal{M}_6$ is cover-monotone. However, if we modify the system such that the initial state $(q_0, 1)$, then it is not cover-monotone.

Decidability of Coverability. We show that coverability is decidable for a class of systems with a wqo but with a restricted notion of monotony. We define $Cover_{\mathcal{S}}(x) = \downarrow Post_{\mathcal{S}}^*(x)$. Let us consider the following monotony condition.

Definition 13 (cover-monotony). *Let $\mathcal{S} = (X, \Sigma, \rightarrow, \leq, x_0)$ be a system. We say that $\mathcal{S}$ is* cover-monotone *(resp. strongly cover-monotone) if, for all $y_1 \in Cover_{\mathcal{S}}(x_0)$ and for all $x_1, x_2 \in X$ such that $x_1 \leq y_1$ and $x_1 \rightarrow x_2$, there exists a state $y_2 \in X$ such that $y_1 \overset{*}{\rightarrow} y_2$ (resp. $y_1 \rightarrow y_2$) and $x_2 \leq y_2$.*

Let us emphasize that cover-monotony of a system $\mathcal{S} = (X, \Sigma, \rightarrow, \leq, x_0)$ is a property that depends on the initial state x_0 while the usual monotony does not depend on any initial state (see Fig. 8).

Remark 6. The strong cover-monotony property is not trivially decidable for general models while (usual) strong-monotony is decidable for many powerful models like FIFO machines and counter machines. However, this notion is still of theoretical interest, as it shows that we can relax the general monotony condition.

However, there is a link between general monotony and cover-monotony.

Proposition 17. *A system $\mathcal{S} = (X, \Sigma, \rightarrow, \leq)$ is monotone iff for all $x_0 \in X$, $(X, \Sigma, \rightarrow, \leq, x_0)$ is cover-monotone.*

We may now define cover-WSTS as follows.

Definition 14 (Cover-WSTS). *A* cover-WSTS *is a finitely branching cover-monotone system $\mathcal{S} = (X, \Sigma, \rightarrow, \leq, x_0)$ such that $(X, \leq)$ is wqo.*

For cover-WSTS, the backward algorithm fails. This is once again because the presence of a single zero test removes the property of the set being upward-closed. But we will now show that the forward coverability approach is possible.

Proposition 18. *Given a system $\mathcal{S} = (X, \Sigma, \rightarrow, \leq, x_0)$ and a downward-closed set $D \subseteq X$ such that $\downarrow Post(D) \subseteq D$, then we have the inclusion $\downarrow Post^*(D) \subseteq D$.*

Let us define a particular instance of the coverability problem in which we verify if a state is coverable from the initial state.

Definition 15. *Given a system $\mathcal{S} = (X, \Sigma, \rightarrow, \leq, x_0)$. The x_0-coverability problem is: Given a state $y \in X$, do we have $y \in \downarrow Post_{\mathcal{S}}^*(x_0)$?*

We show that x_0-coverability is decidable for cover-WSTS:

Theorem 8. *Let $S = (X, \Sigma, \rightarrow, \leq, x_0)$ be an ideally effective cover-WSTS such that Post is computable. Then, the x_0-coverability problem is decidable.*

Proof. Consider a system $S = (X, \Sigma, \rightarrow, \leq, x_0)$ that is cover-WSTS, and let us consider a state $y \in X$. To find a certificate of coverability (if it exists), we cannot use Procedure 1 since general monotony is not satisfied and then, in general, $\downarrow Post^*(x_0) \neq \downarrow Post^*(\downarrow x_0)$ but we can use a variation of Procedure 1, where we iteratively compute x_0, $Post(x_0)$, $Post(Post(x_0))$, and so on, and at each step check if $y \leq x$ for some x in the computed set. This can be done because S is finitely branching and the sets $Post^k(x_0)$ are computable for all $k \geq 0$. Hence, if there exists a state that can cover y reachable from x_0, it will eventually be found.

Now, let us prove that Procedure 2 terminates for input y iff y is not coverable from x_0. If Procedure 2 terminates, then at some point, the while condition is not satisfied and there exists a set D such that $y \notin D$ and $x_0 \in D$ and $\downarrow Post(D) \subseteq D$. Moreover, $\downarrow Post^*(I) \subseteq I$ for every inductive invariant I (see Proposition 18). Hence, $Cover_S(x_0) \subseteq D$, therefore, since $y \notin D$, we deduce that $y \notin Cover_S(x_0)$ and then y is not coverable from x_0.

Note that every downward-closed subset of X decomposes into finitely many ideals since $(X, \leq)$ is wqo. Moreover, since S is ideally effective, ideals of X may be effectively enumerated. By [2] and [3], for ideally effective systems, testing of inclusion of downward-closed sets, and checking the membership of a state in a downward-closed set, are both decidable.

To show the opposite direction, let us prove that if y is not coverable from x_0, the procedure terminates. It suffices to prove that $Cover_S(x_0)$ is an inductive invariant. Indeed, this implies that $Cover_S(x_0)$ is eventually computed by Procedure 2 when y is not coverable from x_0.

Let us show $\downarrow Post(Cover_S(x_0)) \subseteq Cover_S(x_0)$. Let $b \in \downarrow Post(Cover_S(x_0))$. Then, there exists a', a', b' such that $x_0 \xrightarrow{*} a'$, $a' \geq a$, $a \rightarrow b'$ and $b' \geq b$. Furthermore, $a', a \in Cover(x_0)$. Hence, by cover-monotony, there exists $b'' \geq b'$ such that $a' \xrightarrow{*} b''$. Therefore, $x_0 \xrightarrow{*} b''$ and $b'' \geq b' \geq b$, hence, $b \in Cover_S(x_0)$. Hence, the x_0-coverability problem is decidable. □

Theorem 9. *The coverability problem is undecidable for cover-WSTS.*

Proof. Given any counter machine $C = (Q, V, T, q_0)$, let $S_C = (X, A_C, \rightarrow, \leq, x_0)$ be its transition system equipped with the natural order on counters. We can construct a system $S' = (X', A_C, \rightarrow', \leq, x'_0)$ such that S' is cover-monotone, and any state $x \in X$ is coverable iff it is also coverable in X'. The construction is as follows. We add a new control state q from the initial state in the counter machine (q_0) reachable via an empty transition, therefore, $X' = X \cup \{(q, 0)\}$. This new control state is a sink state, i.e. there are no transitions from q to any other control state (except itself). Moreover, we let $x'_0 = (q, 0)$. Note that S' is cover-monotone, because there is no state reachable from x'_0, hence, the property is vacuously satisfied. However, for all other states, as we leave the system unchanged, we see that a state x is coverable in S by a state y iff it is coverable in

$\mathcal{S}'$. Hence, coverability for counter machines reduces to the coverability problem for cover-WSTS, and coverability is therefore, undecidable for cover-WSTS. $\square$

5 Conclusion

We have tried to relax the notions of monotony and of the wellness of the quasi-ordering which were traditionally used to define a WSTS. We observed that we do not need the wellness of the quasi-ordering or monotony between all states. By relaxing the conditions to only states reachable from one another, thus defining what we call *branch-WSTS*, we are still able to decide termination and boundedness. Furthermore, some systems that have been studied recently have been shown to belong to this class, which adds interest to this relaxation.

However, as coverability is undecidable for branch-WSTS, the notion of coverability seems to require a stricter condition than what we define for branch-WSTS. This leads us to introduce a different class of systems, incomparable to branch-WSTS, which we call *cover-WSTS*. These systems relax the condition of monotony to only states within the coverability set, while still retaining the decidability of a restricted form of coverability.

As future work, other systems that belong to these classes can be studied. It would also be interesting to see if the branch-WSTS relaxation translates to better hope for usability of WSTS and relaxations as a verification technique.

Acknowledgements. The work reported was carried out in the framework of ReLaX, UMI2000 (ENS Paris-Saclay, CNRS, Univ. Bordeaux, CMI, IMSc). It is partly supported by ANR FREDDA (ANR-17-CE40-0013) and ANR BRAVAS (ANR-17-CE40-0028).

References

1. Abdulla, P.A., Cerans, K., Jonsson, B., Tsay, Y.: Algorithmic analysis of programs with well quasi-ordered domains. Inf. Comput. **160**(1-2), 109–127 (2000). https://doi.org/10.1006/inco.1999.2843
2. Blondin, M., Finkel, A., McKenzie, P.: Handling infinitely branching WSTS. In: Esparza, J., Fraigniaud, P., Husfeldt, T., Koutsoupias, E. (eds.) ICALP 2014. LNCS, vol. 8573, pp. 13–25. Springer, Heidelberg (2014). https://doi.org/10.1007/978-3-662-43951-7_2
3. Blondin, M., Finkel, A., McKenzie, P.: Well behaved transition systems. Log. Methods Comput. Sci. **13**(3) (2017). https://doi.org/10.23638/LMCS-13(3:24)2017
4. Bollig, B., Finkel, A., Suresh, A.: Bounded reachability problems are decidable in FIFO machines. In: Konnov, I., Kovács, L. (eds.) 31st International Conference on Concurrency Theory, CONCUR 2020, September 1–4, 2020, Vienna, Austria (Virtual Conference). LIPIcs, vol. 171, pp. 49:1–49:17. Schloss Dagstuhl - Leibniz-Zentrum für Informatik (2020). https://doi.org/10.4230/LIPIcs.CONCUR.2020.49
5. Chadha, R., Viswanathan, M.: Deciding branching time properties for asynchronous programs. Theor. Comput. Sci. **410**(42), 4169–4179 (2009). https://doi.org/10.1016/j.tcs.2009.01.021

6. Dickson, L.E.: Finiteness of the odd perfect and primitive abundant numbers with n distinct prime factors. Am. J. Math. **35**(4), 413–422 (1913)

7. D'Osualdo, E., Stutz, F.: Decidable inductive invariants for verification of cryptographic protocols with unbounded sessions. In: Konnov, I., Kovács, L. (eds.) 31st International Conference on Concurrency Theory, CONCUR 2020, September 1–4, 2020, Vienna, Austria (Virtual Conference). LIPIcs, vol. 171, pp. 31:1–31:23. Schloss Dagstuhl - Leibniz-Zentrum für Informatik (2020). https://doi.org/10.4230/LIPIcs.CONCUR.2020.31

8. Dufourd, C., Finkel, A., Schnoebelen, P.: Reset nets between decidability and undecidability. In: Larsen, K.G., Skyum, S., Winskel, G. (eds.) ICALP 1998. LNCS, vol. 1443, pp. 103–115. Springer, Heidelberg (1998). https://doi.org/10.1007/BFb0055044

9. Erdős, P., Rado, R.: A partition calculus in set theory. Bull. Amer. Math. Soc. **62**(5), 427–489 (1956)

10. Finkel, A.: Reduction and covering of infinite reachability trees. Inf. Comput. **89**(2), 144–179 (1990). https://doi.org/10.1016/0890-5401(90)90009-7

11. Finkel, A., McKenzie, P., Picaronny, C.: A well-structured framework for analysing petri net extensions. Inf. Comput. **195**(1-2), 1–29 (2004). https://doi.org/10.1016/j.ic.2004.01.005, http://www.lsv.ens-cachan.fr/Publis/PAPERS/PS/FMP-wstsPN-icomp.ps

12. Finkel, A., Praveen, M.: Verification of flat fifo systems. In: Fokkink, W., van Glabbeek, R. (eds.) Proceedings of the 30th International Conference on Concurrency Theory (CONCUR 2019), Leibniz International Proceedings in Informatics, Leibniz-Zentrum für Informatik, Amsterdam, The Netherlands, August 2019

13. Finkel, A., Schnoebelen, P.: Well-structured transition systems everywhere! Theor. Comput. Sci. **256**(1–2), 63–92 (2001). https://doi.org/10.1016/S0304-3975(00)00102-X

14. Higman, G.: Ordering by divisibility in abstract algebras. In: Proceedings of The London Mathematical Society, pp. 326–336 (1952)

15. Jéron, T., Jard, C.: Testing for unboundedness of fifo channels. Theor. Comput. Sci. **113**, 93–117 (1993)

Offline and Online Monitoring of Scattered Uncertain Logs Using Uncertain Linear Dynamical Systems

Bineet Ghosh[1]([✉])[iD] and Étienne André[2][iD]

[1] The University of North Carolina at Chapel Hill, Chapel Hill, NC, USA
bineet@cs.unc.edu
[2] Université de Lorraine, CNRS, Inria, LORIA, 54000 Nancy, France

Abstract. Monitoring the correctness of distributed cyber-physical systems is essential. We address the analysis of the log of a black-box cyber-physical system. Detecting possible safety violations can be hard when some samples are uncertain or missing. In this work, the log is made of values known with some uncertainty; in addition, we make use of an over-approximated yet expressive model, given by a non-linear extension of dynamical systems. Given an offline log, our approach is able to monitor the log against safety specifications with a limited number of false alarms. As a second contribution, we show that our approach can be used online to minimize the number of sample triggers, with the aim at energetic efficiency. We apply our approach to two benchmarks, an anesthesia model and an adaptive cruise controller.

Keywords: Energy-aware monitoring · Cyber-physical systems · Formal methods

1 Introduction

The pervasiveness of distributed cyber-physical systems is highly increasing, accompanied by associated safety concerns. Formal verification techniques usually require a (white-box) model, which is not often available, because some components are black-box, or because the entire system has no formal model. In addition, formal verification techniques for cyber-physical systems are often subject to state space explosion, often preventing a satisfactory scalability. Therefore, *monitoring*, as a lightweight yet feasible verification technique, can bring practical results of high importance for larger models.

Monitoring aims at analyzing the log of a concrete system, so as to deduce whether a specification (e.g., a safety property) is violated. Monitoring can be done *offline* (i.e., after the system execution, assuming the knowledge of the

This work is partially supported by the ANR-NRF French-Singaporean research program ProMiS (ANR-19-CE25-0015), and the National Science Foundation (NSF) of the United States of America under grant number 2038960.

M. R. Mousavi and A. Philippou (Eds.): FORTE 2022, LNCS 13273, pp. 67–87, 2022.
https://doi.org/10.1007/978-3-031-08679-3_5

entire log), or *online* (at runtime, assuming a partial log). When the log is an aperiodic timed sequence of valuations of continuous variables, with a logging *not* occurring at every discrete time step, and when the system under monitoring is a black box, a major issue is: how to be certain that, in between two discrete valuations, the specification was not violated at another discrete time step at which no logging was performed? For example, consider a system for which a logging at every discrete time step would yield the log depicted in Fig. 1a. Assume the logging was done at only *some* time steps, given in Fig. 1b, due to some sensor faults, or to save energy with only a sparse, scattered logging. How to be certain that, in between two discrete samples, another discrete sample (not recorded) did not violate the specification? For example, by just looking at the discrete samples in Fig. 1b, there is no way to formally guarantee that the unsafe zone (i.e., above the red, dashed line) was never reached by another discrete sample which was not recorded. In many practical cases, a piecewise-constant or linear approximation (see, e.g., Figs. 1c and 1d, where the large blue dots denote actual samples, while the small green dots denote reconstructed samples using some extrapolation) is arbitrary and not appropriate; even worse, it can yield a "safe" answer, while the actual system could actually have been unsafe at some of the missing time steps. On the contrary, assuming a completely arbitrary dynamics will always yield "potentially unsafe"—thus removing the interest of monitoring. For example, from the samples in Fig. 1b, without any knowledge of the model, one can always envision the situation in Fig. 1e, which shows the variable x crossing the unsafe region (dashed) at some unlogged discrete time step—even though this is unlikely if the dynamics is known to vary "not very fast".

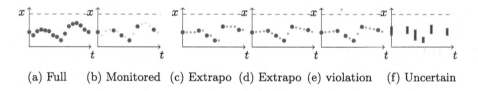

(a) Full   (b) Monitored   (c) Extrapo   (d) Extrapo   (e) violation   (f) Uncertain

Fig. 1. Monitoring at discrete time steps

Contributions. In this work, we address the problem of performing monitoring over a set of scattered and *uncertain* samples. First, we cope with uncertainties from the sensors by allowing for *uncertain* samples, given by zonotopes over the continuous variables; that is, at each logged timestamp, the log gives not a constant value for the continuous variables, but a *zonotope*. A simple case of an uncertain log over a single variable x is depicted in Fig. 1f in the form of simple intervals. The timestamp at each discrete sample of the log is however supposed to be constant (i.e., a single point). Second, to over-approximate the system behavior, and in the spirit of the "model-bounded monitoring" proposed in [34], we use an extension of *linear dynamical systems*, extended with uncertainty, i.e., allowing *uncertainty* in the dynamics matrix [22]. Having some over-approximated knowledge of the system is a natural assumption in practice: when monitoring a car, one generally knows an upper-bound on its maximum speed, or on its maximum acceleration (perhaps depending on its current speed). To cope with the liberal dynamics of our extension of linear dynamical systems, we use a recent technique [18], that performs an efficient reachability analysis for such uncertain linear dynamical systems. The use of such an over-approximation of the actual system is the crux of our approach, allowing us to discard unlikely behaviors, such as the unlikely safety violation depicted in Fig. 1e.

Our first main contribution is to propose a new rigorous analysis technique for offline monitoring of safety properties over scattered *uncertain* samples, using uncertain linear systems as an over-approximation of the system. This over-approximation allows us to extrapolate the behavior since the latest known sample, and to rule out safety violations at some missing discrete samples. Note that our approach uses some discrete analysis as underlying reachability computation technique, and will not however guarantee the absence of safety violations at arbitrary (continuous) timestamps; its main advantage is to offer formal guarantees in the context of missing discrete samples for a given logging granularity.

Our second main contribution focuses on *energy-efficient online monitoring*. For each recorded sample, we run a reachability analysis, and we derive the smallest next discrete time step t in the future at which the safety property may be violated depending on the latest known sample and the over-approximated model dynamics. In a context in which monitoring simply observes the behavior and does not lead to corrective actions, any sample before t is useless because we *know* from the over-approximated model dynamics that no safety violation can happen before t. Therefore, we can schedule the next sample at time t, which reduces the number of discrete samples, and therefore the energy consumption and bandwidth use. We show that our method is correct, i.e., we can safely discard discrete samples without missing any unsafe behavior. We show the practical applicability of our approach on two benchmarks: an anesthesia model, and an adaptive cruise controler.

Outline. We review related works in Sect. 2. We recall uncertain linear dynamical systems in Sect. 3. We introduce our (offline and online) monitoring frameworks in Sect. 4, and run experiments in Sect. 5.

2   Related Works

Monitoring Monitoring complex systems, and notably cyber-physical systems, drew a lot of attention in the last decades, e.g., [5,6,23,24,34]. In parallel to monitoring specifications using signal temporal logics (see e.g., [13,20,29]), monitoring using automata-based specifications drew recent attention. Complex, quantitative extensions of automata were studied in the recent years: after timed pattern matching on timed regular expressions [31] was proposed by Ulus *et al.*, Waga *et al.* proposed a technique for timed pattern matching [32] (with an additional work by Bakhirkin *et al.* [4]) and then for parametric timed pattern matching [3,33,35], with application to offline monitoring.

In [34], we proposed *model-bounded monitoring*: instead of monitoring a black-box system against a sole specification, we use in addition a (limited, over-approximated) knowledge of the system, to eliminate false positives. This over-approximated knowledge is given in [34] in the form of a *linear hybrid automaton* (LHA) [19], an extension of finite-state automata with continuous variables; their flow in each location ("mode") is given as a linear constraint over derivatives; location invariants and transition guards are given by linear constraints over the system variables. We use in [34] both an *ad-hoc* implementation, and another one based on PHAVerLite [7]. In this work, we share with [34] the principle of using an over-approximation of the model to rule out some violation of the specification. However, we consider here a different formalism, and we work on discrete samples. In terms of expressiveness of the over-approximated model: *i*) our approach can be seen as less expressive than [34], in the sense that we have a single (uncertain) dynamics, as opposed to LHAs, where a different dynamics can be defined in each mode; this also allows us to propose a simpler (therefore more efficient) analysis, as each new sample allows us to restart from an exact basis, while in [34] at each new sample, the system (from an algorithmic point of view) can be in "different modes at the same time"; *ii*) conversely, our dynamics is also significantly more expressive than the LHA dynamics of [34]; we consider not only the class of linear dynamical systems, but even fit into a special case of non-linear systems, by allowing *uncertainy* in the model dynamics—this is what makes our model an over-approximation of the actual behavior. In addition, we also allow for *uncertain* logs, coping with sensor uncertainties—not considered in [34]. We also propose a new *ad-hoc* implementation based on [18].

In [25,26], a monitor is constructed from a system model in differential dynamic logic [28]. The main difference between [25,26] and our approach relies in the system model: in [25,26], the compliance between the model and the behavior is checked at runtime, while our model is assumed to be an over-approximation of the behavior—which is by assumption compliant with the model.

Reachability in Linear Dynamical Systems. In [2], given a continuous time linear system with input, the system is discretized and reachable sets for consecutive time intervals are computed. At each step, the *state transition matrix* is expressed using the *Peano-Baker* series. The series is then numerically approximated iteratively using *Riemann sums*. Then a zonotope-based convex hull is computed over-approximating the result of all possible matrices in the uncertain matrix. In [11], Combastel and Raka extend an existing algorithm based on zonotopes so that it can efficiently propagate structured parametric uncertainties. As a result, they provide an algorithm for computation of envelopes enclosing the possible states and/or outputs of a class of uncertain linear dynamical systems. In [22], given an uncertain linear dynamical system $\dot{x} = \Lambda_u x$, Lal *et al.* provide a sampling interval $\delta > 0$, given an $\epsilon > 0$, s.t. the piecewise bilinear function, approximating the solution by interpolating at these sample values, is within ϵ

of the original trajectory. [16] identifies a class of uncertainties by a set of sufficient conditions on the structure of the dynamics matrix Λ_u. For such classes of uncertainties, the exact reachable set of the linear dynamical system can be computed very efficiently. But this method is not applicable for arbitrary classes of uncertainties. In [18], given an uncertain linear dynamical system, we provide two algorithms to compute reachable sets. The first method is based on perturbation theory, and the second method leverages a property of linear systems with inputs by representing them as Minkowski sums. In [17], given an uncertain linear dynamical system, we provide an algorithm to compute statistically correct over-approximate reachable sets using *Jeffries Bayes Factor*. Note that uncertain linear dynamical systems are a special subset of non-linear systems. Thus, uncertain linear dynamical systems can also be modelled as a non-linear system. Some additional works that deal with computing reachable sets of non-linear systems are [1,8–10,14,21,30].

3   Preliminaries

Formal analysis of safety critical systems requires a precise mathematical model of the system, such as linear dynamical systems. But in reality, the precise, exact model is almost never available—parameter variations, sensor and measurement errors, unaccounted parameters are few such causes that make the availability of a precise model impossible. Presence of such uncertainties in the model makes the safety analysis of these systems, using traditional methods, useless. Thus, for the analysis to be indeed useful, the safety analysis must consider all possible uncertainties. In [22], the authors provide a model, known as *uncertain linear dynamical systems*, to capture such uncertainties. Consider the following example of an uncertain linear dynamical system.

Example 1 ([16, Example 1.1]). Let a discrete linear dynamical system $x^+ = \Lambda x$, where $\Lambda = \begin{bmatrix} 1 & \alpha \\ 0 & 2 \end{bmatrix}$ and α represents either the modeling uncertainty or a parameter, assuming $2 \leq \alpha \leq 3$. Note that any safety analysis assuming a *fixed* value of α will render the analysis useless—for the safety analysis to be indeed sound, it must consider *all* possible values of α, and they cannot be enumerated.

Intuitively, uncertain linear dynamical systems model the uncertainties in the system by representing all possible dynamics matrices of the system—clearly, this forms a special class of non-linear dynamical systems. To perform safety analysis of uncertain linear dynamical systems, these works provide reachable set computation techniques that account for all possible uncertainties.

Definition 1 (Uncertain linear dynamical systems ([16, Definition 2.4])). *An* uncertain linear dynamical system *is denoted as*

$$x^+ = \Lambda x \tag{1}$$

where $\Lambda \subset \mathbb{R}^{n \times n}$ is the uncertain dynamics matrix.

Definition 2 (Reachable set of an uncertain linear dynamical systems ([16, Definitions 2.3 and 2.4])). *Given an initial set θ_0 and time step $t \in \mathbb{Z}$, the reachable set of an uncertain linear dynamical system is defined as:*

$$RS(\Lambda, \theta_0, t) = \theta_t = \{ \theta \mid \theta = \xi_A(\theta_0, t), A \in \Lambda \}. \tag{2}$$

where $\xi_A(\theta_0, t) = A^t \theta_0$. An alternative definition is:

$$RS(\Lambda, \theta_0, t) = \theta_t = \bigcup_{A \in \Lambda} \xi_A(\theta_0, t). \tag{3}$$

Note that uncertain linear dynamical systems are capable of modelling systems with parameters or when the system dynamics is not perfectly known—the system has modelling uncertainties. [16–18,22] propose various algorithms to compute reachable sets of these systems that account for uncertainties. In this work, we leverage a recently proposed reachable set computation technique, given in [18], to propose our offline and online monitoring algorithm, primarily due to its efficiency vis-à-vis our setting.

Given an initial set $\theta_0 \subset \mathbb{R}^n$ and given a time step t, we denote by $\theta_t \subset \mathbb{R}^n$ the reachable set of the system (given by Eq. (1)) at time step t. Next, we define a log of the system with uncertainties.

Definition 3 (Log). *Given an uncertain linear dynamical system as in Eq. (1), a finite length (uncertain) log of the system is defined as follows: $\ell = \{(\hat{\theta}_t, t) \mid \theta_t \subseteq \hat{\theta}_t, t \leq H\}$ where H is a given time bound.*

Each tuple $(\hat{\theta}_t, t)$ is called a *sample*. Observe that our samples are not necessarily reduced to a *point*. The length of log ℓ—number of samples in ℓ—is given by $|\ell|$. Given a log ℓ, the k-*th* sample of ℓ is given as $\ell_k = (\hat{\theta}_{t_k}, t_k)$, where $\hat{\theta}_{t_k}$ is an over-approximation of the system at time step t_k. Note that the length of a log is not necessarily equal to H, but $|\ell| \leq H$: therefore, our logs are *scattered*, in the sense that they do not necessarily contain a sample for each $t \in \{1, \ldots, H\}$. We further note that the uncertainties in the logs, arising from the sensor uncertainties of the logging system, are independent of the uncertainties in the system modelling (Definition 1). We assume that each sample of the log contains the true state of the system at a given time step. Note that this generally holds in practice: the physical sensors (such as used in medical devices, cars, etc.) record values within an error tolerance, thus giving a range of values containing the actual value.

We call a log ℓ *accurate* if it satisfies the following condition: $\forall 1 \leq k \leq |\ell| : \hat{\theta}_{t_k} = \theta_{t_k}$. Given an uncertain linear dynamical system, $x^+ = \Lambda x$ with an initial set $\theta_0 \subset \mathbb{R}^n$, an *over-approximate reachable set* of x^+ at time step t is $\texttt{overReach}(\Lambda, \theta_0, t)$, such that $\theta_t \subseteq \texttt{overReach}(\Lambda, \theta_0, t)$. We use the technique proposed in [18] to compute $\texttt{overReach}(\Lambda, \theta_0, t)$ in this work.

4 Monitoring Using Uncertain Linear Dynamical Systems as Bounding Model

In this section, we propose the two main contributions of this work: 1) *Offline monitoring*: Given a log with uncertainties, we propose an algorithm to infer the safety of a system as given in Eq. (1). We prove our method's soundness. 2) *Online monitoring*: We propose a framework to infer safety of a system, as in Eq. (1), that triggers the logging system to sample only when needed. Note that, as we only consider the system at *discrete* time steps, the method cannot be sound nor complete, i.e., there always exists a small possibility that the system might violate the safety specification in between two concrete samples (this will be discussed in Sect. 6). However, our online method *is* both *sound* and *complete at the discrete time stamps*, and under the assumption that the samples are free from uncertainties. That is, our method infers the system to be *safe* if and only if the actual behavior of the system is safe at any discrete time stamp, when the logging system can generate accurate samples of the system. Put it differently, we guarantee that skipping some logging in the future using our method will not remove any sample where a violation could have been observed.

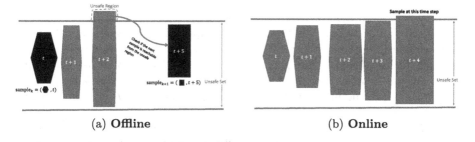

(a) **Offline**   (b) **Online**

Fig. 2. (2a): **Offline Monitoring**. Black: Two consecutive samples, k and $k + 1$, at time steps t and $t+5$ respectively. Blue: The over-approximate reachable set computed from sample k using overReach(.). (2b): **Online Monitoring**. Blue: Over-approximate reachable set computed, at each step, using overReach(.).

4.1 Offline Monitoring

Our first contribution addresses offline monitoring: in this setting, we assume full knowledge of the uncertain log, usually after an execution is completely over. Before we propose our offline algorithm, we illustrate the approach in Fig. 2a. Consider two consecutive samples k and $k + 1$, marked in black, at time steps t and $t+5$ respectively. The reachable sets, in blue, represent the over-approximate behaviors possible by the system between time steps t and $t + 5$. Consider the case where at time step $t + 2$ the over-approximate reachable set intersects with the unsafe region. Once our algorithm detects a possible unsafe behavior, it

---

Algorithm 1: Offline monitoring

---

input : An uncertain log ℓ of a system $x^+ = \Lambda x$, and an unsafe set $\mathcal{U}$.
output : Return *safe* (resp. *unsafe*) if the actual system behavior is safe (resp.
           potentially unsafe).

1 **for** $k \in \{1, \ldots, |\ell| - 1\}$ **do**
2 $\quad$ $(\hat{\theta}_{t_k}, t_k) \leftarrow \ell_k$;   // current sample
3 $\quad$ $(\hat{\theta}_{t_{k+1}}, t_{k+1}) \leftarrow \ell_{k+1}$;   // next sample
4 $\quad$ $t_\Delta = t_{k+1} - t_k - 1$;   // time gap between two samples
5 $\quad$ **for** $p \in \{1, \ldots, t_\Delta - 1\}$ **do**
6 $\quad\quad$ **if** $\hat{\theta}_{t_k+p} \cap \mathcal{U} \neq \emptyset$ **then**
7 $\quad\quad\quad$ $\psi \leftarrow \hat{\theta}_{t_k+p} \cap \mathcal{U}$;   // compute the unsafe region of the system
8 $\quad\quad\quad$ $t_d = t_{k+1} - (t_k + p)$;
9 $\quad\quad\quad$ $\vartheta \leftarrow \text{overReach}(\Lambda, \psi, t_d)$;
   $\quad\quad\quad$ /* Check if next sample is reachable from unsafe   */
10 $\quad\quad\quad$ **if** $\vartheta \cap \hat{\theta}_{t_{k+1}} \neq \emptyset$ **then**
11 $\quad\quad\quad\quad$ **return** *unsafe* ;   // next sample is reachable from unsafe
12 $\quad\quad$ $\hat{\theta}_{t_k+p+1} \leftarrow \text{overReach}(\Lambda, \hat{\theta}_{t_k+p}, 1)$;

13 **return** *safe* ;

---

computes the intersection between the over-approximate reachable set (here, the reachable set at time-step $t + 2$) and the unsafe set. Then it checks whether the reachable set, given in the next sample $(k + 1)$, is reachable from the unsafe region—if yes, it infers *unsafe*; if not, it infers *safe*. Now, we formally propose our offline monitoring method in Algorithm 1 for a given log ℓ with uncertainty.

Description. The **for** loop, starting in line 1, traverses through each sample, and checks if the system can reach a possibly unsafe behavior between two consecutive samples (computed in lines 2 and 3), using over-approximate reachable set computation. If the over-approximate reachable set between two consecutive samples intersect with the unsafe set (line 6), we perform a refinement as follows (line 7–line 11): We compute the unsafe region (intersection between unsafe set and over-approximate reachable set) in line 7, then check if we can reach the next sample from the unsafe region (line 9–line 11). If the next sample is reachable from the unsafe behavior, we conclude the system is unsafe (line 10–line 11).

Soundness and Incompleteness. Our proposed offline monitoring approach is *sound* at discrete time steps, but not *complete*—there might be cases where our algorithm returns *unsafe* even though the actual system is *safe*. The primary reason for its incompleteness is due to the fact that overReach(.) computes an over-approximate reachable set. Formally:

Theorem 1 (soundness at discrete time steps). *If the actual system is unsafe at some discrete time step, then Algorithm 1 returns unsafe. Equivalently, if Algorithm 1 returns safe, then the actual system is safe at every discrete step.*

Proof. Let the actual trajectory τ, between two samples k and $k + 1$, become unsafe at time step t_{un}. Therefore, the over-approximate reachable set, computed by overReach($\cdot$) at time step t_{un}, will also intersect with the unsafe set (due to soundness of overReach($\cdot$)). Note that the actual trajectory τ, originating from the sample k, intersects the unsafe region at time step t_{un}, and reaches the sample $k + 1$. The refinement module (Algorithm 1, line 7–line 11), using over-approximate reachable sets will therefore infer the same, concluding the system behavior to be unsafe.

4.2 Online Monitoring

Algorithm 2: Online monitoring

---

    input : An uncertain system $x^+ = \Lambda x$, an unsafe set $\mathcal{U}$, time bound H.
    output : Return *safe iff* the actual system behavior is safe.
1 $\hat{\theta}_0 \leftarrow$ Sampling at time step 0 ;   // initial behavior of the system.
    /* Check whether the initial behavior is safe   */
2 **if** $\hat{\theta}_0 \cap \mathcal{U} \neq \emptyset$ **then return** *unsafe* ;
3 **for** $t \in \{1, 2, \ldots, H - 1\}$ **do**
4 $\hat{\theta}_{t+1} \leftarrow$ overReach($\Lambda, \hat{\theta}_t, 1$) ;   // over-approximate reachable set
        /* Check whether the over-approximate reachable set is unsafe */
5   **if** $\hat{\theta}_{t+1} \cap \mathcal{U} \neq \emptyset$ **then**
6 $\ell_{t+1} \leftarrow$ Sample at time step $t + 1$;
            /* Check whether the actual reachable set is unsafe   */
7   **if** $\ell_{t+1} \cap \mathcal{U} \neq \emptyset$ **then**
8   **return** *unsafe* ;
9 $\hat{\theta}_{t+1} = \ell_{t+1}$;   // reset to actual behavior
10 **return** *safe*;

Given a time bound H, we propose our online monitoring method in Algorithm 2. The online monitoring algorithm begins by sampling the system at the initial time step, say 0, in line 1. As a sanity check, we confirm if the initial behavior of the system is safe in line 2. The **for** loop starting in line 2—where each iteration corresponds to the set of actions for a time step t—performs the following: At a given time step t, we compute the over-approximate reachable set at the next time step $t + 1$ (line 6). If the computed over-approximate reachable set intersects with the unsafe set, we sample the system at time step $t + 1$ to check if the actual behavior is also unsafe (line 5–line 9). If safe, we reset the behavior (line 9); if unsafe, we return *unsafe* (line 8). Intuitively, this method samples the actual system only when the over-approximate reachable set, computed by overReach(.), intersects the unsafe set. This process is illustrated in Fig. 2b.

Soundness and Completeness. Our online monitoring algorithm is correct (safe and complete) at discrete time steps, *provided* the samples are accurate—it returns safe if and only if the actual behavior of the system is safe at all discrete time steps, when accurate samples are obtained. Intuitively, we get the completeness from the fact that it returns unsafe if and only if the (accurate) sample is unsafe. Formally:

Theorem 2 (correctness at discrete time steps). *Algorithm 2 returns safe iff the actual behavior at all discrete time steps is safe.*

Proof. The soundness proof—if the actual behavior is unsafe, Algorithm 2 infers unsafe—is straightforward. Hence, we now argue the completeness—if the actual behavior is safe, Algorithm 2 infers *safe*. Note that, Algorithm 2 infers the system behavior as *unsafe* only when a sampled log (actual behavior) becomes unsafe: therefore, if the samples are free from uncertainties (i.e., exact), Algorithm 2 is complete.

Remark 1. While our aim is to consider continuous systems, note that, for *discrete-time systems*, our approach is entirely correct (sound and complete), without the restriction to "discrete time steps", since we can find a granularity small enough for the discrete-time evolution. This is notably the case for systems where the behavior does not change faster than a given frequency (e.g., the processor clock).

5   Case Studies

We demonstrate the applicability and usability of our approach on two examples, a medical device and an adaptive cruise control. We implemented our online and offline monitoring algorithms in a Python-based prototype tool MoULDyS. Tool, models and raw results are available through a GitHub repository[1]. All our experiments were performed on a Lenovo ThinkPad Mobile Workstation with i7-8750H CPU with 2.20 GHz and 32 GiB memory on Ubuntu 20.04 LTS (64 bit). Our tool uses numpy, scipy, mpmath for matrix multiplications, [18] to compute overReach(.), and the Gurobi engine for visualization of the reachable sets.

Implementation details vis-à-vis Algorithms 1 and 2. The intersection checking between two sets in Algorithms 1 and 2 has been implemented as an optimization formulation in Gurobi. That is, given two sets, our implementation of intersection check returns true iff the two sets intersect. In other words, our intersection check is *exact*. In contrast, *computing* the result of the intersection between two sets adds an over-approximation in our implementation—given two sets, we compute a box hull of the two sets and then compute intersection of the two box hulls. Therefore, the only over-approximate operation we perform in Algorithm 1 and 2—apart from overReach($\cdot$)—is Algorithm 1 line 7.

---

[1] https://github.com/bineet-coderep/MoULDyS.

Generating Scattered Uncertain Logs for Offline Monitoring. At each time step, the logging system may take a snapshot of the system evolution at that time step; the logging occurs with a probability p (given). In other words, at each time step, it records the evolution of the system with probability p. Clearly, due to the probabilistic logging, this logger is not guaranteed to generate periodic samples. We also do not assume that the samples logged by the logging system, at each time step, are accurate—the logging system, due to sensor uncertainties, logs an over-approximate sample of the system at that time step. In our experiments, each log was generated statically from our bounding model (the uncertain linear dynamical system) by simulating its evolution from an uncertain initial set (i.e., not reduced to a point). In the end, we get an uncertain log (as in Definition 3).

Logging System for Online Monitoring. When the logging system is triggered, at a time step, to generate a sample, the logging system records the evolution of the system and sends it to the online monitoring algorithm. Similar to the offline logging system, we do not assume that the samples logged by the logging system are perfectly accurate. Here, all the generated logs are *safe*.

Research Questions. We consider the following research questions:

1. Effect of logging probability (number of log samples) on the rate of false alarms raised by the offline monitoring—inferring a behavior as "potentially unsafe" when the actual behavior is "safe".
2. For offline monitoring, does the size of the samples (in other words, volume of the set obtained as sample), gathered at each step, have an impact on the rate of false alarms? Put it differently, what is the effect, *vis-à-vis* false alarms, of the amount of the uncertainty in the log?
3. For online monitoring, how frequent is the logging system triggered to generate a sample?
4. For the same execution, how do the outcome (in terms of verdict on safety by the monitoring algorithms) and the efficiency (in terms of number of samples needed) of the offline and online monitoring algorithms compare?

5.1 First Benchmark: Anesthesia

We first demonstrate our approach on an automated anesthesia delivery model [15]. The anesthetic drug considered in this model is propofol. Such safety critical systems are extremely important to be verified formally before they are deployed, as under or overdose of the anesthetic drug can be fatal to the patient.

Model: The model as in [15] has two components: 1) Pharmacokinetics (PK): models the change in concentration of the drug as the body metabolizes it. 2) Pharmacodynamics (PD): models the effect of drug on the body. The PK component is further divided into three compartments: *i*) first peripheral compartment c_1, *ii*) second peripheral compartment c_2, *iii*) plasma compartment c_p. The PD component has one compartment, called c_e. The set of state variables

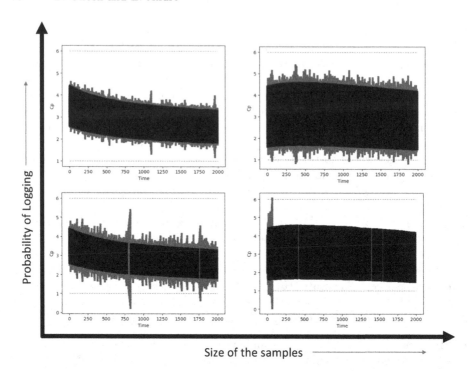

Fig. 3. *Offline monitoring*: We plot the change in concentration level of c_p with time. The volume of the samples increase from left to right, and the probability of logging increases from bottom to top. The blue regions are the reachable sets showing the over-approximate reachable sets as computed by the offline monitoring, the black regions are the samples from the log given to the offline monitoring algorithm, and the red dotted line represents safe distance level. Note that although the top-row plots and the bottom left plots' reachable sets seem to intersect with the red line (unsafe set), the refinement module infers them to be *unreachable*, therefore concluding the system behavior as *safe*—unlike the bottom-right plot.

of this system is $\begin{bmatrix} c_p & c_1 & c_2 & c_e \end{bmatrix}^\top$. The input to the system is the infusion rate of the drug (propofol) u. The complete state-space model of this system in given in [15, Equation 5].

Model Parameters: The evolution of states—c_p, c_1, c_2—is dependent on several parameters, such as: the weight of the patient (*weight*), the first order rate constants between the compartments k_{10}, k_{12}, k_{13}, k_{21} and k_{31}. The evolution of the state c_e is dependent on the parameter k_d, the rate constant between plasma and effect site.

Safety: The system is considered safe if the following concentration levels are maintained at all time steps: $c_p \in [1, 6]$, $c_1 \in [1, 10]$, $c_2 \in [1, 10]$, $c_e \in [1, 8]$.

In this case study, we focus our attention on the effect of perturbation, in the weight of the patient (*weight*), on the concentration level of plasma compart-

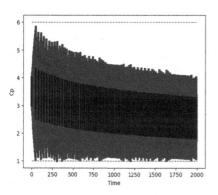
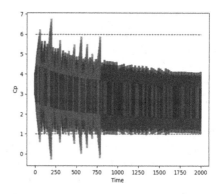

Fig. 4. *Online monitoring*: We plot the change in concentration level of c_p with time. The blue regions are the reachable sets showing the over-approximate reachable sets as computed by the online monitoring, the black regions are the samples generated when the logging system was triggered by the online monitoring algorithm, and the red dotted line represents safe concentration levels. *Left*: We apply our online monitoring to the anesthesia model. *Right*: We compare our online and offline algorithms. The green regions are the reachable sets showing the over-approximate reachable sets between two consecutive samples from the offline logs, the magenta regions are the offline logs, given as an input to the offline monitoring algorithm, generated by the logging system, and the red dotted line represents safe concentration levels. The blue regions are the reachable sets showing the over-approximate reachable sets as computed by the online monitoring, the black regions are the samples generated when the logging system was triggered by the online monitoring algorithm, and the red dotted line represents safe concentration levels.

ment c_p. We assume that the weight of the patient has an additive perturbation of ± 0.8 kg in this case study—at each time step, the weight of the patient is $weight + \delta_w$, $\delta_w \in [0, 0.8]$. With perturbation in the weight, we want to infer safety of this system using monitoring.

We now answer questions (1)–(4), using Figs. 3 and 4. In Fig. 3: *i*) the plots in the bottom row have logging probability of 20%, and the plots in top row have a logging probability of 40%; *ii*) the plots in left column and the right column have been simulated with an initial set of $[\,[3,4]\ [3,4]\ [4,5]\ [3,4]\,]^{\top}$, $u \in [2,5]$ and $[\,[2,4]\ [3,6]\ [3,6]\ [2,4]\,]^{\top}$, $u \in [2,10]$ respectively. That is, the volume of the samples increases from left to right. In Fig. 4, we simulated the trajectory with an initial set $[\,[3,4]\ [3,4]\ [4,5]\ [3,4]\,]^{\top}$, $u \in [2,5]$.

Answer to Question 1. We answer this question by comparing two sets figures in the left column and the right column of Fig. 3. *For the left column, i.e., with smaller sample size*: the bottom-left plot took 51.40 s and concluded the system to be safe. The analysis in this plot invoked the refinement module of the offline algorithm. But increasing the probability of logging, i.e., more number of samples, as in the top-left plot, resulted in not invoking the refinement module at all, thus taking 32.92 s. *For the right column, i.e., with larger sample size:*

this analysis, as shown in the bottom-right column, took 1.73 s to complete, and concluded the system behavior to be unsafe. The behavior of the system, shown in top-right plot with 40% probability of logging, results in inferring the behavior of the system as safe, by invoking the refinement module several times. Overall, this analysis, as shown in the top-right plot, took 35.93 s to complete, and concluded the system behavior to be safe.

Answer to Question 2. We answer this question by comparing two sets figures in the top row and the bottom row of Fig. 3. *For the bottom row, i.e., with smaller logging probability*: Increasing the volume of the samples results in inferring the behavior from safe (bottom-left plot) to unsafe (bottom-right plot), as per the offline monitoring algorithm. *For the top row, i.e., with higher logging probability*: Increasing the volume of the samples results in not invoking the refinement module (top-left plot) to invoking the refinement module several times (top-right plot), as per the offline monitoring algorithm.

Answer to Question 3. The result is given in Fig. 4 (left). Using our online algorithm, we were able to prove safety of the system in 109.04 s. The online algorithm triggered the logging system to generate samples for 83 time steps— this is less than 5% of total time steps. We observe, as shown in Fig. 4 (left), that the logging system is triggered more when the trajectory is closer to the unsafe region.

Answer to Question 4. We compare our offline and online algorithms, for 2 000 time steps, on the same trajectory. The result is given in Fig. 4 (right). Note that, using our online algorithm, we were able to prove safety of the system in 107.99 s. The online algorithm triggered the logging system to generate samples only 84 times. In contrast, the offline algorithm, with a log size of 115 (5% logging probability) stopped at the 35th sample, (wrongly) inferring the system as unsafe, taking 71.37 s.

5.2   Second Benchmark: Adaptive Cruise Control

We now apply our algorithms to an adaptive cruise control (ACC) [27]. An ACC behaves like an ordinary cruise control when there is no car in the sight of its sensor, and when there is a car in its sight, it maintains a safe distance.

Model: The model as in [27] has the following state variables: *i*) velocity of the vehicle v, *ii*) distance between the two vehicles h, and *iii*) velocity of the lead vehicle v_L. The state space of the system is given in [27, Equation 3]. The set of state variables of this system is $\left[\, v\; h\; v_L \,\right]^\top$.

Model Parameters: The model is dependent on two parameters: *i*) acceleration of the lead vehicle a_L, and *ii*) breaking force and torque applied to the wheels as a lumped net force F. Note that the model is dependent of acceleration of the vehicle a_L, which is very hard to accurately measure due to sensor uncertainties. Similarly the torque F applied to the wheels is also dependent of the coefficient of

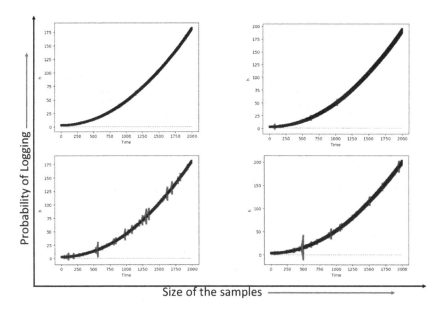

Size of the samples

Fig. 5. *Offline monitoring*: We plot the change in distance h between the vehicles with time. The volume of the samples increase from left to right, and the probability of logging increases from bottom to top.

friction of the ground. To reflect such uncertainties, we consider $a_L \in [-0.9, 0.6]$ and $F \in [-0.6, 2.46]$.

Safety: The system is safe if the distance between vehicles $h > 0.5$.

Consider an event of a car crash, where the log stored by the car before the crash, is the only data available to analyze the crash; such an analysis might benefit police, insurance companies, vehicle manufacturers, etc. Using our offline algorithm one can figure out if the car might have shown unsafe behavior or not. Similarly, consider a vehicle on a highway with a lead vehicle in its sight. The ACC in such a case needs to continuously read sensor values to track several parameters, such as acceleration of the lead vehicle, braking force, etc.—this results in wastage of energy. Using our online monitoring algorithm, the car reads sensor values only when there is a potential unsafe behavior. This intermittent behavior will result in saving energy without compromising safety of the system.

Next, we answer questions (1)–(4), using Figs. 5 and 6. In Fig. 5: *i*) the plots in the bottom row have logging probability of 20%, and the plots in top row have a logging probability of 40%; *ii*) the plots in left column and the right column have been simulated with an initial set of $[\,[15,15.01]\,[3,3.03]\,[14.9,15]\,]^\top$ and $[\,[15,15.1]\,[3,3.5]\,[14.9,15.1]\,]^\top$ respectively. In Fig. 4, we simulated the trajectory with an initial set $[\,[15,15.01]\,[3,3.03]\,[14.9,15]\,]^\top$, $u \in [2,5]$.

Answer to Question 1. We answer this question by comparing two sets figures in the left column and the right column of Fig. 5. *For the left column, i.e.,*

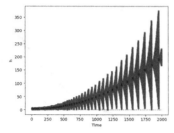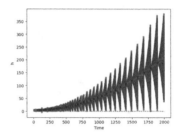

Fig. 6. *Online monitoring*: We plot the change in distance between two vehicle h with time. The color coding is same as Fig. 4. *Left*: We apply our online monitoring to the ACC model. *Right*: We compare our online and offline algorithms.

with smaller sample size: the bottom-left plot took 19.08 s and concluded the system to be safe. This analysis in this plot invoked the refinement module of the offline algorithm. But increasing the probability of logging, i.e., more number of samples, as in the top-left plot, resulted in not invoking the refinement module at all, thus taking 16.5 s. *For the right column, i.e., with larger sample size*: The analysis is similar to that of the left column. The bottom-right plot invoked the refinement module several times, thus taking 20.84 s, while the top-right plot took 17.5 s, as it invoked the refinement module a smaller number of times.

Answer to Question 2. We answer this question by comparing two sets figures in the top row and the bottom row of Fig. 5. *For the bottom row, i.e., with smaller logging probability*: Comparing the bottom-left and bottom-right shows that increasing sample volume results in invoking the refinement module more frequently. A very similar behavior is seen by comparing the top row (i.e., with higher logging probability).

Answer to Question 3. Using our online algorithm, we were able to prove safety of the system in 104.58 s. The online algorithm triggered the logging system to generate samples for 53 time steps—this is less than 3% of total time steps. This is shown in Fig. 6 (left).

Answer to Question 4. We compare our offline and online algorithm, for 2 000 time steps, on the same trajectory. The result is given in Fig. 6 (right). Note that, using our online algorithm, we were able to prove safety of the system in 124.46 s. The online algorithm triggered the logging system to generate samples only 50 times. In contrast, the offline algorithm, with a log size of 281 (14% logging probability) took 28.54 s to infer that the system is safe.

5.3   General Observations

In this section, we provide general answers to questions (1)–(4):

Answer to Question 1. Increasing the probability of logging reduces the chances of inclusion of spurious behaviors due to over-approximate reachable set computation over longer time horizon. Therefore, it has a reduced chance of spuriously inferring the system unsafe, also fewer chance of invoking the refinement module (as there are less spurious behaviors).

Answer to Question 2. Increasing the size of samples (due to uncertainties or inherent nature of the system) results in increasing chances of invoking the refinement module more frequently. It also increases the chance of (wrongly) inferring the system to be unsafe, as the refinement module can in itself add to the over-approximation.

Answer to Question 3. We observed that our online algorithm is able to prove the system's safety very efficiently with very few samples.

Answer to Question 4. We observed that for a given random log, the offline algorithm was unable to prove safety of the system, whereas our online algorithm was able to prove safety of the system, using fewer samples, by intelligently sampling the system only when needed. We also note that, though here we just demonstrated the result for one random log, but our internal experiments showed that the online algorithm always needed fewer samples to prove safety—which is unsurprising, as it is designed to sample the system only when needed. This can also result in energy saving, as sampling usually requires energy and bandwidth.

Reachable Sets Computation Using Flow*.* As uncertain linear dynamical systems are a special type of non-linear systems, Flow* [8] would have been a natural candidate to benchmark our offline and online monitoring implementation by comparing various methods to compute overReach($\cdot$). However, we ran into the following issues: *i)* To the best of our understanding, Flow* expects the model of the continuous dynamics to be given as input, along with a discretization parameter. Therefore, trying to encode the time-varying uncertainties in the system as state variables will lead to discretization of the variables encoding uncertainties; such discretization leads to undesired behavior, as those uncertain variables will fail to capture the actual range of values that are possible at any time step. *ii)* However, Flow* does allow time varying uncertainties, but only additive[2]. Unfortunately, our benchmark requires *multiplicative* uncertainties. Still, we believe Flow* could be compared with our implementation when the bounding model has a simpler dynamics than our uncertain linear dynamical systems.

6   Conclusion

We presented a new approach for monitoring cyber-physical systems against safety specifications, using the additional knowledge of an over-approximation

---

[2] See example at https://flowstar.org/benchmarks/2-dimensional-ltv-system/.

of the system expressed using an uncertain linear dynamic system. Our approach assumes as first input a log with exact (but scattered) timestamps and uncertain variable samplings (in the form of zonotopes), and as second input an over-approximated model, bounding the possible behaviors. The over-approximation is modeled by *uncertainty* in the variables of the dynamics. In the offline setting, we are thus able to detect possible violations of safety properties, by extrapolating the known samples with the over-approximated dynamics, and if needed using a second reachability analysis to check whether the next sample is "compatible" with the possible unsafe behavior, i.e., can be reached from the unsafe zone. In the online setting, we are capable of *decreasing* the number of samples, triggering a sample only when there might be a safety violation in a near future, based on the latest known sample and on the over-approximated model dynamics—increasing the energetic efficiency. Our method is sound in the sense that an absence of detection of violation by our method indeed guarantees the absence of an actual violation at any discrete time step. In the online method, provided the samples are accurate, our method is in addition complete, i.e., the method outputs *safe* iff the actual system is safe at all discrete time steps. Put it differently, we guarantee that *not* triggering a sample at some time steps is harmless and will not lead to missing a safety violation.

Future Works. On the log side, we considered fixed timestamps, but uncertain values for the continuous variables; in fact, the timestamps could also be uncertain. This makes sense when the samples are triggered by sensors distributed over a network, which can create delays and therefore timed uncertainty. This was not considered in our approach, and is on our agenda.

A possible threat to validity remains the *enumeration* of time steps in both our algorithms (line 5 in Algorithm 1 and line 3 in Algorithm 2), which could slow down the analysis for very sparse logs—even though this did not seem critical in our experiments. Using skipping methods could help improving the efficiency of our approach.

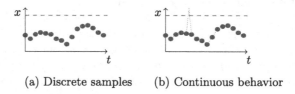

(a) Discrete samples   (b) Continuous behavior

Fig. 7. Incompleteness

Another future work consists in increasing our guarantees, notably due to the *continuous* nature of cyber-physical systems under monitoring. Indeed, even with a rather fine-grained sampling showing no specification violation (e.g., in Fig. 7a), it can always happen that the actual *continuous* behavior violated the specification (e.g., in Fig. 7b). While setting discrete time steps at a sufficiently fine-grained scale will help to increase the confidence in the results of our approach, no absolutely formal guarantee can be derived. Therefore, one of our future works is to propose some additional conditions for extrapolating (continuous) behaviors between consecutive discrete samples. Also, improving the scope of our guarantees (in the line of, e.g., [12]) is on our agenda.

References

1. Althoff, M.: An introduction to CORA 2015. In: ARCH@CPSWeek. EPiC Series in Computing, vol. 34, pp. 120–151. EasyChair (2015). https://doi.org/10.29007/zbkv

2. Althoff, M., Le Guernic, C., Krogh, B.H.: Reachable set computation for uncertain time-varying linear systems. In: HSCC, pp. 93–102. ACM (2011). https://doi.org/10.1145/1967701.1967717

3. André, É., Hasuo, I., Waga, M.: Offline timed pattern matching under uncertainty. In: ICECCS, pp. 10–20. IEEE Computer Society (2018). https://doi.org/10.1109/ICECCS2018.2018.00010

4. Bakhirkin, A., Ferrère, T., Nickovic, D., Maler, O., Asarin, E.: Online timed pattern matching using automata. In: Jansen, D.N., Prabhakar, P. (eds.) FORMATS 2018. LNCS, vol. 11022, pp. 215–232. Springer, Cham (2018). https://doi.org/10.1007/978-3-030-00151-3_13

5. Bartocci, E., et al.: Specification-based monitoring of cyber-physical systems: a survey on theory, tools and applications. In: Bartocci, E., Falcone, Y. (eds.) Lectures on Runtime Verification. LNCS, vol. 10457, pp. 135–175. Springer, Cham (2018). https://doi.org/10.1007/978-3-319-75632-5_5

6. Basin, D.A., Klaedtke, F., Zalinescu, E.: The MonPoly monitoring tool. In: RV-CuBES. Kalpa Publications in Computing, vol. 3, pp. 19–28. EasyChair (2017)

7. Becchi, A., Zaffanella, E.: Revisiting polyhedral analysis for hybrid systems. In: Chang, B.-Y.E. (ed.) SAS 2019. LNCS, vol. 11822, pp. 183–202. Springer, Cham (2019). https://doi.org/10.1007/978-3-030-32304-2_10

8. Chen, X., Ábrahám, E., Sankaranarayanan, S.: Flow*: an analyzer for non-linear hybrid systems. In: Sharygina, N., Veith, H. (eds.) CAV 2013. LNCS, vol. 8044, pp. 258–263. Springer, Heidelberg (2013). https://doi.org/10.1007/978-3-642-39799-8_18

9. Chen, X., Sankaranarayanan, S.: Decomposed reachability analysis for nonlinear systems. In: RTSS, pp. 13–24. IEEE Computer Society (2016). https://doi.org/10.1109/RTSS.2016.011

10. Chen, X., Sankaranarayanan, S., Ábrahám, E.: Under-approximate flowpipes for non-linear continuous systems. In: FMCAD, pp. 59–66. IEEE (2014). https://doi.org/10.1109/FMCAD.2014.6987596

11. Combastel, C., Raka, S.A.: On computing envelopes for discrete-time linear systems with affine parametric uncertainties and bounded inputs. IFAC Proc. Volumes 44(1), 4525–4533 (2011). https://doi.org/10.3182/20110828-6-IT-1002.02585

12. Dauer, J.C., Finkbeiner, B., Schirmer, S.: Monitoring with verified guarantees. In: Feng, L., Fisman, D. (eds.) RV 2021. LNCS, vol. 12974, pp. 62–80. Springer, Cham (2021). https://doi.org/10.1007/978-3-030-88494-9_4

13. Donzé, A., Ferrère, T., Maler, O.: Efficient robust monitoring for STL. In: Sharygina, N., Veith, H. (eds.) CAV 2013. LNCS, vol. 8044, pp. 264–279. Springer, Heidelberg (2013). https://doi.org/10.1007/978-3-642-39799-8_19

14. Duggirala, P.S., Mitra, S., Viswanathan, M., Potok, M.: C2E2: a verification tool for stateflow models. In: Baier, C., Tinelli, C. (eds.) TACAS 2015. LNCS, vol. 9035, pp. 68–82. Springer, Heidelberg (2015). https://doi.org/10.1007/978-3-662-46681-0_5

15. Gan, V., Dumont, G.A., Mitchell, I.: Benchmark problem: a PK/PD model and safety constraints for anesthesia delivery. In: ARCH@CPSWeek. EPiC Series in Computing, vol. 34, pp. 1–8. EasyChair (2014). https://doi.org/10.29007/8drm

16. Ghosh, B., Duggirala, P.S.: Robust reachable set: accounting for uncertainties in linear dynamical systems. ACM Trans. Embed. Comput. Syst. **18**(5s), 97:1–97:22 (2019). https://doi.org/10.1145/3358229

17. Ghosh, B., Duggirala, P.S.: Reachability of linear uncertain systems: sampling based approaches. Technical Report 2109.07638, arXiv (2021). https://arxiv.org/abs/2109.07638

18. Ghosh, B., Duggirala, P.S.: Robustness of safety for linear dynamical systems: symbolic and numerical approaches. Technical Report 2109.07632, arXiv (2021). https://arxiv.org/abs/2109.07632

19. Halbwachs, N., Proy, Y.-E., Raymond, P.: Verification of linear hybrid systems by means of convex approximations. In: Le Charlier, B. (ed.) SAS 1994. LNCS, vol. 864, pp. 223–237. Springer, Heidelberg (1994). https://doi.org/10.1007/3-540-58485-4_43

20. Jakšić, S., Bartocci, E., Grosu, R., Nguyen, T., Ničković, D.: Quantitative monitoring of STL with edit distance. Formal Methods Syst. Des. **53**(1), 83–112 (2018). https://doi.org/10.1007/s10703-018-0319-x

21. Kong, S., Gao, S., Chen, W., Clarke, E.: dReach: δ-reachability analysis for hybrid systems. In: Baier, C., Tinelli, C. (eds.) TACAS 2015. LNCS, vol. 9035, pp. 200–205. Springer, Heidelberg (2015). https://doi.org/10.1007/978-3-662-46681-0_15

22. Lal, R., Prabhakar, P.: Bounded error flowpipe computation of parameterized linear systems. In: EMSOFT, pp. 237–246. IEEE (2015). https://doi.org/10.1109/EMSOFT.2015.7318279

23. Maler, O., Nickovic, D.: Monitoring temporal properties of continuous signals. In: Lakhnech, Y., Yovine, S. (eds.) FORMATS/FTRTFT -2004. LNCS, vol. 3253, pp. 152–166. Springer, Heidelberg (2004). https://doi.org/10.1007/978-3-540-30206-3_12

24. Mamouras, K., Chattopadhyay, A., Wang, Z.: A compositional framework for quantitative online monitoring over continuous-time signals. In: Feng, L., Fisman, D. (eds.) RV 2021. LNCS, vol. 12974, pp. 142–163. Springer, Cham (2021). https://doi.org/10.1007/978-3-030-88494-9_8

25. Mitsch, S., Platzer, A.: ModelPlex: verified runtime validation of verified cyber-physical system models. FMSD **49**(1-2), 33–74 (2016). https://doi.org/10.1007/s10703-016-0241-z

26. Mitsch, S., Platzer, A.: Verified runtime validation for partially observable hybrid systems. Technical Report (2018). http://arxiv.org/abs/1811.06502

27. Nilsson, P., et al.: Correct-by-construction adaptive cruise control: two approaches. IEEE Trans. Control Syst. Technol. **24**(4), 1294–1307 (2016). https://doi.org/10.1109/TCST.2015.2501351

28. Platzer, A.: The complete proof theory of hybrid systems. In: LICS, pp. 541–550. IEEE Computer Society (2012). https://doi.org/10.1109/LICS.2012.64

29. Qin, X., Deshmukh, J.V.: Clairvoyant monitoring for signal temporal logic. In: Bertrand, N., Jansen, N. (eds.) FORMATS 2020. LNCS, vol. 12288, pp. 178–195. Springer, Cham (2020). https://doi.org/10.1007/978-3-030-57628-8_11

30. Testylier, R., Dang, T.: NLTOOLBOX: a library for reachability computation of nonlinear dynamical systems. In: Van Hung, D., Ogawa, M. (eds.) ATVA 2013. LNCS, vol. 8172, pp. 469–473. Springer, Cham (2013). https://doi.org/10.1007/978-3-319-02444-8_37

31. Ulus, D., Ferrère, T., Asarin, E., Maler, O.: Timed pattern matching. In: Legay, A., Bozga, M. (eds.) FORMATS 2014. LNCS, vol. 8711, pp. 222–236. Springer, Cham (2014). https://doi.org/10.1007/978-3-319-10512-3_16

32. Waga, M., Akazaki, T., Hasuo, I.: A Boyer-Moore type algorithm for timed pattern matching. In: Fränzle, M., Markey, N. (eds.) FORMATS 2016. LNCS, vol. 9884, pp. 121–139. Springer, Cham (2016). https://doi.org/10.1007/978-3-319-44878-7_8

33. Waga, M., André, É.: Online parametric timed pattern matching with automata-based skipping. In: Badger, J.M., Rozier, K.Y. (eds.) NFM 2019. LNCS, vol. 11460, pp. 371–389. Springer, Cham (2019). https://doi.org/10.1007/978-3-030-20652-9_26

34. Waga, M., André, É., Hasuo, I.: Model-bounded monitoring of hybrid systems. ACM Trans. Cyber-Phys. Syst. (2022). https://doi.org/10.1145/3529095

35. Waga, M., André, É., Hasuo, I.: Parametric timed pattern matching. ACM Trans. Softw. Eng. Methodol. (2022). https://doi.org/10.1145/3517194

Co-engineering Safety-Security Using Statistical Model Checking

Rajesh Kumar[(✉)], Siddhant Singh, Bhavesh Narra, and Rohan Kela

Department of Computer Science and Information Systems, Birla Institute of
Technology and Science, Pilani, India
`rajesh.k@pilani.bits-pilani.ac.in`

Abstract. In this journal-first paper, we present an overview of our
novel formalism of Attack-Fault-Maintenance Trees (AFMTs). Detailed
version of work is available in [3]. AFMTs enable practitioners to quantify the disruption scenarios by answering several safety-security metrics.
Alongside, it provides an informed decision on optimal maintenance policies by suggesting preventive component repairs and inspection frequen-
cies. We answer the aforementioned metrics through "what-if" and "scenario analysis". The models are supported by a graphical friendly tool
of PASST. The tool's front-end is a drawing canvas that provides the
different syntactic elements used to design a well-formed AFMT model.
The back-end of the tool is based on the statistical-model checking techniques. From the practitioner perspective, once the AFMT is designed
and input parameters on component failure, detection rates, inspection
rates are provided, the entire analysis can be then done as push-button
technology using model-checking techniques

1 Context and Motivation

Broadly current risk analysis methods for critical infrastructures exclusively
focus either on safety/availability (ISO 262262, IEC 61508) or on information
security (ISO 27001, SA/IEC 62443). As a result, sub-optimal solutions are
implemented, or money is wasted, for instance, because proposed security measures interfere with safety. Increasingly, researchers have recognized the importance of threat analysis and quantitative scenario analysis to ensure safety and
security-by-design. Following, a number of papers, propose independent quantitative modelling and analysis techniques, for example, fault trees in safety, attack
trees in security etc.

In this paper, we propose the Attack-Fault-Maintenance trees (AFMTs, [3]);
a model-based risk analysis to perform an integral safety-security risk analysis.
AFMTs take into account component deterioration, attack events, inspection and
complex maintenance policies. The output of the framework is an optimal main-
tenance/inspection frequency that balances repair/re-storage/inspection costs
against the disruption costs. Note, the disruption can be due to accidental loss
of component, attack-event or both attack event and accidental events occurring

© IFIP International Federation for Information Processing 2022
Published by Springer Nature Switzerland AG 2022
M. R. Mousavi and A. Philippou (Eds.): FORTE 2022, LNCS 13273, pp. 88–92, 2022.
https://doi.org/10.1007/978-3-031-08679-3_6

in tandem. Syntactically, AFMTs combine two popular graphical formalisms of Attack-Fault trees (AFTs, [4]) and Fault-Maintenance trees [6]. Technically, each AFMT element is translated into a stochastic timed automaton (STA) while the metrics of interest are encoded in a variant of temporal logic. The usage of STAs allows to formally capture the different system attributes of soft time constraints, hard time constraints, probabilistic choice and different cost structures. The mathematical engine of AFMTs is based on the well-established technique of Statistical Model-Checking (SMC, [5]). The model-checker of Uppaal SMC [1] is used to answer the different metrics. AFMTs are supported with PASST, a practitioner-friendly tool. The tool is available via a web-interface[1] and as a standalone collection of Uppaal models and scripts. To use the standalone collection of Uppaal models, one needs to maintain a working Uppaal tool available at Uppaal's webpage[2], which is free to use with an academic license.

2   AFMTs and Informal Semantics

AFMTs extend AFTs with predictive and reactive maintenance strategies. The underlying model of AFTs has been discussed in the doctoral thesis of Kumar et al. [2]. To familiarize the reader with the AFMTs, we discuss them with an illustrative example.

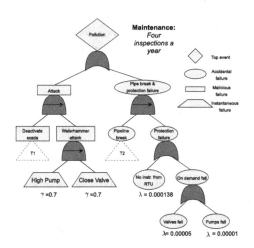

Fig. 1. An example AFMT. Here, T1 and T2 are subtrees, which can be refined.

Figure 1 is an excerpt from [4]. The original model is extended with inspection and maintenance strategies. It models a disruption scenario of an industrial pipeline carrying a toxic pollutant. The top event in the tree is Pollution. It

---

[1] http://afmt-simulator.com.
[2] https://uppaal.org/downloads/.

represents the undesirable system state. This event can occur as a result of an attack Attack or via Pipeline_break_&_protection_failure, hence the top event is refined using an OR gate. An attack can execute the event Attack by executing both the attack steps of Deactivate_SCADA and Waterhammer_attack, however, it needs to be performed in order, where the execution of the rightmost event Waterhammer_attack can only be started after the successful disruption of its previous left event of Deactivate_SCADA. Hence, the event Attack is refined using the SAND gate. Similarly, other subsystems are refined until we reach to the leaf nodes, that indicate atomic events. Here, *rectangular boxes*, termed as **Extended Basic Attacker Actions (EBAS)**, represent attacker actions. Accidental events, **Extended basic component failures (EBCF)** are represented by *oval boxes*. *Trapezoid boxes* are special form of EBCF that represent component disruption at start. Here, we assume the inspection frequency is of four times/year.

An EBAS models attacker actions over time, put as exponential distribution. Owning to preventive and deterrent measures, an attacker may caught by placing preventive countermeasures. We model this uncertainty using a discrete probability distribution. We also assume that as the attack is underway, an inspection may be carried out. The inspection acts as a check that may halt the attacker's progress if the ongoing attack-specific patches are placed during the inspections. However, these inspections remain oblivious to the attacker, who may continue with the ongoing attacks. Once the attacker has successfully compromised the atomic step, its disruption is signalled to a repair box. Thereafter, the EBAS may be repaired to its original "new" state, or no corrective action is taken, depending on the criticality of the compromised component.

An EBCF model shows the component's deterioration over time. We model the component degradation behaviour as a hypoexponential distribution. In our model, the degradation phenomenon is divided over n phases. After a component reaches a threshold degradation phase, it sends out an inspection signal to its corresponding inspection module. After a component is degraded over all its n phases, it transitions to a disrupted state. Repairs and replacements restore the component to its original, undamaged state.

AFT Gates. Gates are logical constructs that dictate how disruptions propagate through the system. It also prescribes the operations on system attributes, for example, how costs are to be computed from the children of a gate to their parent node. AFMTs adopt all the gate behavior, namely AND, OR, FDEP and SAND gates from both ATs and FTs. To keep the paper self-contained, its behaviour is as described: we activate the AFMT by sending an `activate` signal that propagates from the root of the tree to the leaf nodes adhering to the gate semantics. For example, in an AND gate with two children, both are activated simultaneously, while in the SAND gate, which is used to model temporal dependencies between the children, the leftmost child is activated first, with the activation of the subsequent child depending on whether the previous one is disrupted/not disrupted. The disrupt signal propagates from leaf nodes to the root node of the AFMT, again adhering to the gate semantics. If the root node receives the disrupt signal, it implies that the disruption event described by the root of AFMT has occurred.

Maintenance Models. We consider two types of maintenance activities: preventive maintenance and corrective maintenance. a) Preventive maintenance aims at restoring the component to its original unwearied state through periodic inspections and repairs before its complete loss. b) Corrective maintenance aims at restoring the componentâĂŹs functionality after the component has failed through replacement and reactive repairs.

Preventive maintenance in AFMTs. An inspection module (IM) enforces preventive maintenance in EBAS and EBCF. The IM is programmed with an inspection frequency, such as four times per year in our example. We allow the component to be repaired for an extended BCF by signalling its degradation phase. When a component reaches a certain level of deterioration, it is repaired in the next inspection cycle. In the case of the EBAS, if the attack is in progress while an inspection is taking place, the attacker may be forced to abort the attack or restart it after the inspection.

Corrective maintenance in AFMTs. In EBAS and EBCF, corrective maintenance is modelled by signalling their degradation behavior/attack success to a repair box. The repair box initiates a component repair for EBCF when it reaches its final phase. In the case of an EBAS, a decision on corrective maintenance is made based on the extent of damage caused by an attack. In many practical scenarios, for example, if the attacker is careful not to disrupt/tamper with component functionality, no repairs are required. In other cases, information about a successful compromise may not be widely disseminated or known right away. We model the uncertainty associated with such contextual cases as a uniform distribution, after which the disruption of the EBAS is communicated to the repair box, which invokes its replacement. From the perspective of the repair box, it is opaque to where the disruption signals have originated. Based on a repair policy, the repair box restores the component to its completely "as-good-as-new" state.

Model checking of AFMTs using Uppaal SMC. To answer the safety-security metrics through statistical model checking, we translate each AFMT construct, i.e. EBAS, EBCF, and gates, to a stochastic timed automaton (STA) template. Additionally, we constructed an STA template of an inspection module and a repair box. These templates are then parameterized according to the AFMT structure. The security metrics are encoded in the Uppaal SMC language. For example, to obtain the probability of reaching the top node of the AFMT within a mission time of 1 year (8800 h hours), we encode the property as Pr [t<=8800] (<> top event.goal), where goal is a location in the STA top event, indicating that the root node of the AFMT is reached. Here "t" is the global clock. We use the popular toolbox of Uppaal SMC to derive the results.

3   Conclusion

In this paper, we positioned AFMTs as an instrument to perform model based safety-security risk analysis taking complex maintenance and repair policies into account. Supported by PASST tool, it uses statistical model-checking (SMC) techniques at its back-end. In future, we plan to extend our work with complex cybernetics policies, realistic attackers personas and ways to work with categorical input data.

References

1. David, A., Larsen, K.G., Legay, A., Mikucionis, M., Poulsen, D.B.: Uppaal SMC tutorial. Int. J. Softw. Tools Technol. Transf. **17**(4), 397–415 (2015)
2. Kumar, R.: Truth or dare: quantitative security risk analysis via attack trees. Ph.D. thesis (2018)
3. Kumar, R., Narra, B., Kela, R., Singh, S.: Afmt: maintaining the safety-security of industrial control systems. Comput. Ind. **136**, 103584 (2022)
4. Kumar, R., Stoelinga, M.: Quantitative security and safety analysis with attack-fault trees. In: 2017 IEEE 18th International Symposium on High Assurance Systems Engineering (HASE), pp. 25–32 (2017)
5. Legay, A., Lukina, A., Traonouez, L.M., Yang, J., Smolka, S.A., Grosu, R.: Statistical model checking. In: Steffen, B., Woeginger, G. (eds.) Computing and Software Science. LNCS, vol. 10000, pp. 478–504. Springer, Cham (2019). https://doi.org/10.1007/978-3-319-91908-9_23
6. Ruijters, E., Guck, D., Drolenga, P., Stoelinga, M.: Fault maintenance trees: reliability centered maintenance via statistical model checking. In: 2016 Annual Reliability and Maintainability Symposium (RAMS), pp. 1–6 (2016)

Fault-Tolerant Multiparty Session Types

Kirstin Peters[1]([✉])[ID], Uwe Nestmann[2][ID], and Christoph Wagner[3]

[1] TU Darmstadt, Darmstadt, Germany
kirstin.peters@uni-a.de
[2] TU Berlin, Berlin, Germany
[3] Siemens Mobility, Braunschweig, Germany

Abstract. Multiparty session types are designed to abstractly capture the structure of communication protocols and verify behavioural properties. One important such property is progress, i.e., the absence of deadlock. Distributed algorithms often resemble multiparty communication protocols. But proving their properties, in particular termination that is closely related to progress, can be elaborate. Since distributed algorithms are often designed to cope with faults, a first step towards using session types to verify distributed algorithms is to integrate fault-tolerance.

We extend multiparty session types to cope with system failures such as unreliable communication and process crashes. Moreover, we augment the semantics of processes by failure patterns that can be used to represent system requirements (as, e.g., failure detectors). To illustrate our approach we analyse a variant of the well-known rotating coordinator algorithm by Chandra and Toueg.

1 Introduction

Multi-Party Session Types (MPST) are used to statically ensure correctly coordinated behaviour in systems without global control [13,22]. One important such property is progress, i.e., the absence of deadlock. Like with every other static typing approach, the main advantage is their efficiency, i.e., they avoid the problem of state space explosion. MPST are designed to abstractly capture the structure of communication protocols. They describe global behaviours as *sessions*, i.e., units of conversations [3,4,22]. The participants of such sessions are called *roles*. *Global types* specify protocols from a global point of view. These types are used to reason about processes formulated in a *session calculus*.

Distributed algorithms (DA) very much resemble multiparty communication protocols. An essential behavioural property of DA is termination [26,33], despite failures, but it is often elaborate to prove. It turns out that progress (as provided by MPST) and termination (as required by DA) are closely related.

Many DA were designed in a fault-tolerant way, in order to work in environments, where they have to cope with system failures—be it links dropping messages or processes crashing. Gärtner [19] suggested four different forms of fault-tolerance, depending on whether the safety and liveness requirements are

© IFIP International Federation for Information Processing 2022
Published by Springer Nature Switzerland AG 2022
M. R. Mousavi and A. Philippou (Eds.): FORTE 2022, LNCS 13273, pp. 93–113, 2022.
https://doi.org/10.1007/978-3-031-08679-3_7

met, or not. An algorithm is called *masking* in the (best) case that both properties hold while tolerating faults transparently, i.e., without further intervention by the programmer. It is called *non-masking*, however, if faults are dealt with explicitly in order to cope with unsafe states, while still guaranteeing liveness. The *fail-safe* case then captures algorithms that remain safe, but not live. (The fourth form is just there for completeness; here neither safety nor liveness is guaranteed.) We focus on masking fault-tolerant algorithms.

While the detection of conceptual design errors is a standard property of type systems, proving correctness of algorithms despite the occurrence of system failures is not. Likewise, traditional MPST do not cover fault tolerance or failure handling. There are several approaches to integrate explicit failure handling in MPST (e.g. [1,6,7,12,16,34]). These approaches are sometimes enhanced with recovery mechanisms such as [8] or even provide algorithms to help find safe states to recover from as in [29]. Many of these approaches introduce nested TRY-and-CATCH-blocks and a challenge is to ensure that all participants are consistently informed about concurrent THROWS of exceptions. Therefore, exceptions are propagated within the system. Though explicit failure handling makes sense for high-level applications, the required message overhead is too inefficient for many low-level algorithms. Instead these low-level algorithms are often designed to tolerate a certain amount of failures. Since we focus on the communication structure of systems, additional messages as reaction to faults (e.g. to propagate faults) are considered *non-masking* failure handling. In contrast, we expect masking fault-tolerant algorithms to cope without messages triggered by faults. We study how much unhandled failures a well-typed system can tolerate, while maintaining the typical properties of MPST.

We propose a variant of MPST with unreliable interactions and augment the semantics to also represent failures such as message loss and crashing processes, as well as more abstract concepts of fault-tolerant algorithms such as the possibility to suspect a process to be faulty. To guide the behaviour of unreliable communication, the semantics of processes uses failure patterns that are not defined but *could* be instantiated by an application. This allows us to cover requirements on the system—as, e.g., a bound on the number of faulty processes—as well as more abstract concepts like failure detectors. It is beyond the scope of this paper to discuss *how* failure patterns could be implemented.

Related Work. Type systems are usually designed for failure-free scenarios. An exception is [23] that introduces unreliable broadcast, where a transmission can be received by multiple receivers but not necessarily all available receivers. In the latter case, the receiver is deadlocked. In contrast, we consider fault-tolerant interactions, where in the case of a failure the receiver is *not* deadlocked.

The already mentioned systems in [6,7,12,16,34] extend session types with exceptions thrown by processes within TRY-and-CATCH-blocks, interrupts, or similar syntax. They structurally and semantically encapsulate an unreliable part of a protocol and provide some means to 'detect' a failure and 'react' to it. For example [34] proposes a variant of MPST with the explicit handling of crash failures. Therefore they coordinate asynchronous messages for run-time crash notifications using a coordinator. Processes in [34] have access to local failure detectors which eventually detect all failed peers and do not falsely suspect peers. In contrast we augment the semantics of the session calculus with failure patterns that e.g. allow to implement failure detectors but may also be used to implement system requirements. Exceptions may also describe, why a failure occurred. Here we deliberately do not model causes of failures or how to 'detect' a failure. Different system architectures might provide different mechanisms to do so, for example, by means of time-outs. As is standard for the analysis of DA, our approach allows us to port the verified algorithms on different system architectures that satisfy the necessary system requirements.

Another essential difference is how systems react to faults. In [6], THROW-messages are propagated among nested TRY-and-CATCH-blocks to ensure that all participants are *consistently* informed about concurrent THROWS of exceptions. Fault-tolerant DA, however, have to deal with the problem of inconsistency that some part of a system may consider a process/link as crashed, while at the same time the same process/link is regarded as correct by another part. (This is one of the most challenging problems in the design and verification of *fault-tolerant* DA.) The reason is that *distributed* processes usually cannot reliably observe an error on another system part, unless they are informed by some system "device" (like the "coordinator" of [34] or the "oracle" of [6]). Therefore, abstractions like unreliable failure detectors are used to model this restricted observability which can, for example, be implemented by time-outs. Failure detectors are often considered to be local (see previous paragraph), but they cannot ensure global consistency. Various degrees of consistency, or [un]reliability, of failure detectors are often defined via constraints that are expressed as global temporal properties [10] (see also Sect. 6). Abstract properties, like the communication predicates in the Heard-Of model [11], can also be used to specify minimum requirements on system behaviours at a global level of abstraction in order to be able to guarantee correctness properties.

In previous work, we used the above-mentioned failure detector abstractions in the context of (untyped) process calculi [27] to verify properties of several algorithms for Distributed Consensus [24,28]. Key for the respective proofs was the intricate reconstruction of global state information from process calculus terms, as we later on formalized in [35]. We conjecture that MPST could provide proof support in this context, for example, for the methods that apply to these global states. The work by Francalanza and Hennessy [17] also uses a process calculus for the analysis of DA, but employs bisimulation proof techniques. In order to do so, however, the intended properties need to be formulated via some global wrapper code, which provides a level of indirection to proofs. This approach suffers from the absence of clear global state information. In contrast, MPST supply useful global (session type) information from scratch.

The missing proofs and some additional material can be found in [30].

2   Fault-Tolerance in Distributed Algorithms

We consider three sources of failure in an unreliable communication (Fig. 1(a)): (1) the sender may crash before it releases the message, (2) the receiver may crash before it can consume the message, or (3) the communication medium may lose the message. The design of a DA may allow it to handle some kinds of failures better than others. Failures are unpredictable events that occur at runtime. Since types consider only static and predictable information, we do not distinguish between different kinds of failure or model their source in types. Instead we allow types, i.e., the specifications of systems, to distinguish between potentially faulty and reliable interactions.

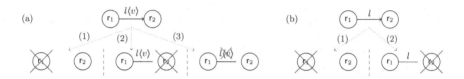

Fig. 1. Unreliable communication (a) and Weakly Reliable branching (b).

A fault-tolerant algorithm has to solve its task despite such failures. Remember that MPST analyse the communication structure. Accordingly, we need a mechanism to tolerate faults in the communication structure. We want our type system to ensure that a faulty interaction neither blocks the overall protocol nor influences the communication structure of the system after this fault. We consider an unreliable communication as fault-tolerant if a failure does not influence the guarantees for the overall communication structure except for this particular communication. Moreover, if a potentially unreliable communication is executed successfully, then our type system ensures the same guarantees as for reliable communication such as e.g. the absence of communication mismatches.

To ensure that a failure does not block the algorithm, both the receiver and the sender need to be allowed to proceed without their unreliable communication partner. Therefore, the receiver of an unreliable communication is required to specify a default value that, in the case of failure, is used instead of the value the process was supposed to receive. The type system ensures the existence of such default values and checks their sort. Moreover, we augment unreliable communication with labels that help us to avoid communication mismatches.

Branching in the context of failures is more difficult, because a branch marks a decision point in a specification, i.e., the participants of the session are supposed to behave differently w.r.t. this decision. In an unreliable setting it is difficult to ensure that all participants are informed consistently about such a decision.

Consider a reliable branching that is decided by a process r_1 and transmitted to r_2. If we try to execute such a branching despite failures, we observe that there are again three ways in that this branching can go wrong (Fig. 1(b)): (1) The sender may crash before it releases its decision. This will block r_2, because it is missing the information about the branch it should move to. (2) The receiver might crash. (3) The message of r_1 is lost. Then again r_2 is blocked.

Case (2) can be dealt with similar to unreliable communication, i.e., by marking the branching as potentially faulty and by ensuring that a crash of r_2 will not block another process. To deal with Case (1), we declare one of the offered branches as default. If r_1 has crashed, r_2 moves to the default branch. Then r_2 will not necessarily move to the branch that r_1 had in mind before it crashed, but to a valid/specified branch and, since r_1 is crashed, no two processes move to different branches. The main problem is in Case (3). Let r_1 move to a non-default branch and transmit its decision to r_2, this message gets lost, and r_2 moves to the default branch. Now both processes did move to branches that are described by their types; but they are in different branches. This case violates the specification in the type and we want to reject it. More precisely, we consider three levels of failures in interactions:

Strongly Reliable (r): Neither the sender nor the receiver can crash as long as they are involved in this interaction. The message cannot be lost by the communication medium. This form corresponds to reliable communication as it was described in [2] in the context of distributed algorithms. This is the standard, failure-free case.

Weakly Reliable (w): Both the sender and the receiver might crash at every possible point during this interaction. But the communication medium cannot lose the message.

Unreliable (u): Both the sender and the receiver might crash at every possible point during this interaction and the communication medium might lose the message. There are no guarantees that this interaction—or any part of it—takes place. Here, it is difficult to ensure interesting properties in branching.

3 Fault-Tolerant Types and Processes

We assume that the sets $\mathcal{N}$ of names $a, s, x \ldots$; $\mathcal{R}$ of roles $n, r, \ldots$; $\mathcal{L}$ of labels $l, l_d, \ldots$; $\mathcal{V}_T$ of type variables t; and $\mathcal{V}_P$ of process variables X are pairwise distinct. To simplify the reduction semantics of our session calculus, we use natural numbers as roles (compare to [22]). Sorts S range over $\mathbb{B}, \mathbb{N}, \ldots$. The set $\mathcal{E}$ of expressions $e, v, b, \ldots$ is constructed from the standard Boolean operations, natural numbers, names, and (in)equalities.

Global types specify the desired communication structure from a global point of view. In local types this global view is projected to the specification of a single role/participant. We use standard MPST [21,22] extended by unreliable communication and weakly reliable branching (highlighted in blue) in Fig. 2.

A new session s with n roles is initialised with $\overline{a}[n](s).P$ and $a[r](s).P$ via the shared channel a. We identify sessions with their unique session channel.

The type $r_1 \rightarrow_r r_2 : \langle S \rangle . G$ specifies a strongly reliable communication from role r_1 to role r_2 to transmit a value of the sort S and then continues with G. A system with this type will be guaranteed to perform a corresponding action. In a session s this communication is implemented by the sender $s[r_1, r_2]!_r \langle e \rangle . P_1$ (specified as

Global Types	Local Types	Processes
		$P ::= \overline{a}[n](s).P$
		$\mid\ a[r](s).P$
	$T ::= [r_2]!_r\langle S\rangle.T$	$\mid\ s[r_1, r_2]!_r\langle e\rangle.P$
$G ::= r_1 \to_r r_2{:}\langle S\rangle.G$	$\mid\ [r_1]?_r\langle S\rangle.T$	$\mid\ s[r_2, r_1]?_r(x).P$
	$\mid\ [r_2]!_u l\langle S\rangle.T$	$\mid\ s[r_1, r_2]!_u l\langle e\rangle.P$
$\mid\ r_1 \to_u r_2{:}l\langle S\rangle.G$	$\mid\ [r_1]?_u l\langle S\rangle.T$	$\mid\ s[r_2, r_1]?_u l\langle v\rangle(x).P$
	$\mid\ [r_2]!_r\{l_i.T_i\}_{i\in I}$	$\mid\ s[r_1, r_2]!_r l.P$
$\mid\ r_1 \to_r r_2{:}\{l_i.G_i\}_{i\in I}$	$\mid\ [r_1]?_r\{l_i.T_i\}_{i\in I}$	$\mid\ s[r_2, r_1]?_r\{l_i.P_i\}_{i\in I}$
	$\mid\ [R]!_w\{l_i.T_i\}_{i\in I}$	$\mid\ s[r, R]!_w l.P$
$\mid\ r \to_w R{:}\{l_i.G_i\}_{i\in I, l_d}$	$\mid\ [r]?_w\{l_i.T_i\}_{i\in I, l_d}$	$\mid\ s[r_j, r]?_w\{l_i.P_i\}_{i\in I, l_d}$
$\mid\ G_1 \parallel G_2$		$\mid\ P_1 \mid P_2$
$\mid\ (\mu t)G \mid t \mid \mathbf{end}$	$\mid\ (\mu t)T \mid t \mid \mathbf{end}$	$\mid\ (\mu X)P \mid X \mid \mathbf{0}$
		$\mid\ \mathbf{if}\ b\ \mathbf{then}\ P_1\ \mathbf{else}\ P_2$
		$\mid\ (\nu x)P \mid \perp$
	$\mid\ [r_2]!\langle s'[r]{:}T\rangle.T'$	$\mid\ s[r_1, r_2]!\langle\!\langle s'[r]\rangle\!\rangle.P$
$\mid\ r_1 \to r_2{:}\langle s'[r]{:}T\rangle.G$	$\mid\ [r_1]?\langle s'[r]{:}T\rangle.T'$	$\mid\ s[r_2, r_1]?(\!(s'[r])\!).P$
		$\mid\ s_{r_1 \to r_2}{:}M$

Message Types	Messages
$\mathsf{mt} ::= \langle S\rangle^r \mid l\langle S\rangle^u \mid l^r \mid l^w \mid s[r]$	$\mathsf{m} ::= \langle v\rangle^r \mid l\langle v\rangle^u \mid l^r$
	$\mid\ l^w \mid s[r]$

Fig. 2. Syntax of fault-tolerant MPST

$[r_2]!_r\langle S\rangle.T_1)$ and the receiver $s[r_2, r_1]?_r(x).P_2$ (specified as $[r_1]?_r\langle S\rangle.T_2$). As result, the receiver instantiates x in its continuation P_2 with the received value.

The type $r_1 \to_u r_2{:}l\langle S\rangle.G$ specifies an unreliable communication from r_1 to r_2 transmitting (if successful) a label l and a value of type S and then continues (regardless of the success of this communication) with G. The unreliable counterparts of senders and receivers are $s[r_1, r_2]!_u l\langle e\rangle.P_1$ (specified as $[r_2]!_u l\langle S\rangle.T_1$) and $s[r_2, r_1]?_u l\langle v\rangle(x).P_2$ (specified as $[r_1]?_u l\langle S\rangle.T_2$). The receiver $s[r_2, r_1]?_u l\langle v\rangle(x).P_2$ declares a default value v that is used instead of a received value to instantiate x after a failure. Moreover, a label is communicated that helps us to ensure that a faulty unreliable communication has no influence on later actions.

The strongly reliable branching $r_1 \to_r r_2{:}\{l_i.G_i\}_{i\in I}$ allows r_1 to pick one of the branches offered by r_2. We identify the branches with their respective label. Selection of a branch is by $s[r_1, r_2]!_r l.P$ (specified as $[r_2]!_r\{l_i.T_i\}_{i\in I}$). Upon receiving l_j, $s[r_2, r_1]?_r\{l_i.P_i\}_{i\in I}$ (specified as $[r_1]?_r\{l_i.T_i\}_{i\in I}$) continues with P_j.

As discussed in the end of Sect. 1, the counterpart of branching is weakly reliable and not unreliable. It is implemented by $r \to_w R{:}\{l_i.G_i\}_{i\in I, l_d}$, where $R \subseteq \mathcal{R}$ and l_d with $d \in I$ is the default branch. We use a broadcast from r to all roles in R to ensure that the sender can influence several participants consistently. Splitting this action to inform the roles in R separately does not work, because we cannot ensure consistency if the sender crashes while performing these subsequent actions. The type system will ensure that no message is lost. Because of that, all processes that are not crashed will move to the same branch. We often abbreviate branching w.r.t. to a small set of branches by omitting the set brackets and instead separating the branches by $\oplus$, where the last branch is always the default branch. In contrast to the strongly reliable cases, $s[\mathsf{r}, \mathsf{R}]!_\mathsf{w}l.P$ (specified as $[\mathsf{R}]!_\mathsf{w}\{l_i.T_i\}_{i \in \mathsf{I}}$) allows to broadcast its decision to R and $s[\mathsf{r}_j, \mathsf{r}]?_\mathsf{w}\{l_i.P_i\}_{i \in \mathsf{I}, l_\mathsf{d}}$ (specified as $[\mathsf{r}]?_\mathsf{w}\{l_i.T_i\}_{i \in \mathsf{I}, l_\mathsf{d}}$) defines a default label l_d.

The $\perp$ denotes a process that crashed. Similar to [22], we use message queues to implement asynchrony in sessions. Therefore, session initialisation introduces a directed and initially empty message queue $s_{\mathsf{r}_1 \to \mathsf{r}_2}:[\,]$ for each pair of roles $\mathsf{r}_1 \neq \mathsf{r}_2$ of the session s. The separate message queues ensure that messages with different sources or destinations are not ordered, but each message queue is FIFO. Since the different forms of interaction might be implemented differently (e.g. by TCP or UDP), it make sense to further split the message queues into three message queues for each pair $\mathsf{r}_1 \neq \mathsf{r}_2$ such that different kinds of messages do not need to be ordered. To simplify the presentation of examples in this paper and not to blow up the number of message queues, we stick to a single message queue for each pair $\mathsf{r}_1 \neq \mathsf{r}_2$, but the correctness of our type system does not depend on this decision. We have five kinds of messages m and corresponding message types mt in Fig. 2—one for each kind of interaction. In strongly reliable communication a value v (of sort S) is transmitted in a message $\langle v \rangle^\mathsf{r}$ of type $\langle \mathsf{S} \rangle^\mathsf{r}$. In unreliable communication the message $l \langle v \rangle^\mathsf{u}$ (of type $l \langle \mathsf{S} \rangle^\mathsf{u}$) additionally carries a label l. For branching only the picked label l is transmitted and we add the kind of branching as superscript, i.e., message/type l^r is for strongly reliable branching and message/type l^w for weakly reliable branching. Finally, message/type $s[\mathsf{r}]$ is for session delegation. A message queue M is a queue of messages m and MT is a queue of message types mt.

The remaining operators for independence $G \parallel G'$; parallel composition $P \mid P'$; recursion $(\mu t)G$, $(\mu X)P$; inaction $\mathbf{end}$, $\mathbf{0}$; conditionals $\mathbf{if}\ b\ \mathbf{then}\ P_1\ \mathbf{else}\ P_2$; session delegation $\mathsf{r}_1 \to \mathsf{r}_2 : \langle s'[\mathsf{r}]{:}T \rangle.G$, $s[\mathsf{r}_1, \mathsf{r}_2]!\langle\!\langle s'[\mathsf{r}] \rangle\!\rangle.P$, $s[\mathsf{r}_2, \mathsf{r}_1]?(\!(s'[\mathsf{r}])\!).P$; and restriction $(\nu x)P$ are all standard. As usual, we assume that recursion variables are guarded and do not occur free in types or processes.

Local types are used as a mediator between the global specification and the respective local end points. To ensure that the local types correspond to the global type, they are *projected* from global types. We use a standard variant of projection as introduced in [9,20,36], where the new unreliable and weakly reliable cases are straightforwardly obtained from their strongly reliable counterparts.

A session channel and a role together uniquely identify a participant of a session, called an *actor*. A process has an actor $s[\mathsf{r}]$ if it has an action prefix on s that mentions r as its first role. Let $\mathsf{A}(P)$ be the set of actors of P.

Labels. We use labels for two purposes: they allow us to distinguish between different branches, as usual in MPST-frameworks, and we assume that they may carry additional runtime information such as timestamps. Of course, the presented type system remains valid if we use labels without additional information. In contrast to standard MPST and to support unreliable communication, our MPST variant will ensure that all occurrences of the same label are associated with the same sort. We assume a predicate $\doteq$ that compares two labels and is satisfied if the parts of the labels that do not refer to runtime information correspond. If labels do not contain runtime information, $\doteq$ can be instantiated with equality. We require that $\doteq$ is unambiguous on labels used in types, i.e., given two labels of processes l_P, l'_P and two labels of types l_T, l'_T then $l_P \doteq l'_P \wedge l_P \doteq l_T \Rightarrow l'_P \doteq l_T$ and $l_P \doteq l_T \wedge l_T \neq l'_T \Rightarrow l_P \neq l'_T$.

One of the properties that our type system has to ensure even in the case of failures is the absence of communication mismatches, i.e., the type of a transmitted value has to be the type that the receiver expects. The global type $1 \rightarrow_u 2{:}l_1\langle\mathbb{N}\rangle.1 \rightarrow_u 2{:}l_2\langle\mathbb{B}\rangle.\mathbf{end}$ specifies two subsequent unreliable communications in that values of different sorts are transmitted. If the first message with its natural number is lost but the second message containing a Boolean value is transmitted, 2 could wrongly receive a Boolean value although it still waits for a natural number. To avoid this mismatch, we add a label to unreliable communication and ensure (by the typing rules) that the same label is never associated with different types. Similarly, labels are used in [5] to avoid communication errors. Since the type system ensures $l_1 \neq l_2$ and the reduction rules in Fig. 3 compare labels of messages and reception-prefixes, the Boolean message cannot be consumed before 2 has reduced its first prefix.

We do that because we think of labels not only as identifiers for branching, but also as some kind of meta data of messages as they can be often found in communication media or as they are assumed by many distributed algorithms. Our unreliable communication mechanism exploits such meta data to guarantee strong properties about the communication structure including the described absence of communication mismatches.

Examples. Consider the specification $G_{\text{dice},r}$ of a simple dice game in a bar

$$(\mu t)3 \rightarrow_r 1{:}\langle\mathbb{N}\rangle.3 \rightarrow_r 2{:}\langle\mathbb{N}\rangle.3 \rightarrow_r 1{:}\{roll.3 \rightarrow_r 2{:}roll.t, exit.3 \rightarrow_r 2{:}exit.\mathbf{end}\}$$

where the dealer Role 3 continues to *roll* a dice and tell its value to player 1 and then to *roll* another time for player 2 until the dealer decides to *exit* the game.

We can combine strongly reliable communication/branching and unreliable communication, e.g. by ordering a drink before each round in $G_{\text{dice},r}$.

$$(\mu t)3 \rightarrow_u 4{:}drink\langle\mathbb{N}\rangle.3 \rightarrow_r 1{:}\langle\mathbb{N}\rangle.3 \rightarrow_r 2{:}\langle\mathbb{N}\rangle.$$
$$3 \rightarrow_r 1{:}\{roll.3 \rightarrow_r 2{:}roll.t, \quad exit.3 \rightarrow_r 2{:}exit.\mathbf{end}\}$$

where role 4 represents the bar tender and the noise of the bar may swallow these orders. Moreover, we can remove the branching and specify a variant of the dice game in that 3 keeps on rolling the dice forever, but, e.g. due to a bar fight, one of our three players might get knocked out at some point or the noise of this fight might swallow the announcements of role 3:

$$G_{\text{dice},u} = (\mu t)3 \rightarrow_u 1{:}roll\langle\mathbb{N}\rangle.3 \rightarrow_u 2{:}roll\langle\mathbb{N}\rangle.t$$

To restore the branching despite the bar fight that causes failures, we need the weakly reliable branching mechanism.

$$G_{\text{dice}} = (\mu t)3 \to_{\text{w}} \{1,2\} : play.3 \to_{\text{u}} 1:roll\langle\mathbb{N}\rangle.3 \to_{\text{u}} 2:roll\langle\mathbb{N}\rangle.t,$$
$$\oplus \ end.3 \to_{\text{u}} 1:win\langle\mathbb{B}\rangle.3 \to_{\text{u}} 2:win\langle\mathbb{B}\rangle.\text{end}$$

If 3 is knocked out by the fight, i.e., crashes, the game cannot continue. Then 1 and 2 move to the default branch end, have to skip the respective unreliable communications, and terminate. But the game can continue as long as 3 and at least one of the players $1, 2$ participate.

(Init)	$\overline{a}[n](s).P_n \mid \prod_{1\leq i\leq n-1} a[i](s).P_i \longmapsto (\nu s)\left(\prod_{1\leq i\leq n} P_i \mid \prod_{1\leq i,j\leq n, i\neq j} s_{i\to j}:[\,]\right)$	
		if $a \neq s$
(RSend)	$s[r_1,r_2]!_r\langle y\rangle.P \mid s_{r_1\to r_2}:M \longmapsto P \mid s_{r_1\to r_2}:M\#\langle v\rangle^r$	if $\text{eval}(y) = v$
(RGet)	$s[r_1,r_2]?_r(x).P \mid s_{r_2\to r_1}:\langle v\rangle^r\#M \longmapsto P\{v/x\} \mid s_{r_2\to r_1}:M$	
(USend)	$s[r_1,r_2]!_u l\langle y\rangle.P \mid s_{r_1\to r_2}:M \longmapsto P \mid s_{r_1\to r_2}:M\#l\langle v\rangle^u$	if $\text{eval}(y) = v$
(UGet)	$s[r_1,r_2]?_u l\langle dv\rangle(x).P \mid s_{r_2\to r_1}:l'\langle v\rangle^u\#M \longmapsto P\{v/x\} \mid s_{r_2\to r_1}:M$	
		if $l \ \not\stackrel{\cdot}{\downarrow} \ \text{FP}_{\text{uget}}(s, r_1, r_2, l')$
(USkip)	$s[r_1,r_2]?_u l\langle dv\rangle(x).P \longmapsto P\{dv/x\}$	if $\text{FP}_{\text{uskip}}(s, r_1, r_2, l)$
(ML)	$s_{r_1\to r_2}:l\langle v\rangle^u\#M \longmapsto s_{r_1\to r_2}:M$	if $\text{FP}_{\text{ml}}(s, r_1, r_2, l)$
(RSel)	$s[r_1,r_2]!_r l.P \mid s_{r_1\to r_2}:M \longmapsto P \mid s_{r_1\to r_2}:M\#l^r$	
(RBran)	$s[r_1,r_2]?_r\{l_i.P_i\}_{i\in I} \mid s_{r_2\to r_1}:l^r\#M \longmapsto P_j \mid s_{r_2\to r_1}:M$	if $l \ \stackrel{\cdot}{\downarrow} \ j\in I$
(WSel)	$s[r,R]!_w l.P \mid \prod_{r_i\in R} s_{r\to r_i}:M_i \longmapsto P \mid \prod_{r_i\in R} s_{r\to r_i}:M_i\#l^w$	
(WBran)	$s[r_1,r_2]?_w\{l_i.P_i\}_{i\in I, l_d} \mid s_{r_2\to r_1}:l^w\#M \longmapsto P_j \mid s_{r_2\to r_1}:M$	if $l \ \stackrel{\cdot}{\downarrow} \ j\in I$
(WSkip)	$s[r_1,r_2]?_w\{l_i.P_i\}_{i\in I, l_d} \longmapsto P_d$	if $\text{FP}_{\text{wskip}}(s, r_1, r_2)$
(Crash)	$P \longmapsto \bot$	if $\text{FP}_{\text{crash}}(P)$

Fig. 3. Selected reduction rules ($\longmapsto$) of fault-tolerant processes.

An implementation of G_{dice} is $P_{\text{dice}} = P_3 \mid P_1 \mid P_2$, where for $i \in \{1,2\}$:

$P_3 = \overline{a}[3](s).(\mu X)\text{if } x_1 \leq 21 \wedge x_2 \leq 21$

       $\text{then } s[3,\{1,2\}]!_w play.s[3,1]!_u roll\langle roll(x_1)\rangle.s[3,2]!_u roll\langle roll(x_2)\rangle.X$

       $\text{else } s[3,\{1,2\}]!_w end.s[3,1]!_u win\langle x_1 \leq 21\rangle.s[3,2]!_u win\langle x_2 \leq 21\rangle.0$

$P_i = a[i](s).(\mu X)s[i,3]?_w play.s[i,3]?_u roll\langle x\rangle(x).X \oplus end.s[i,3]?_u win\langle\mathbf{f}\rangle(w).0$

Role 3 stores the sums of former dice rolls for the two players in its local variables x_1 and x_2, and $roll(x_i)$ rolls a dice and adds its value to the respective x_i. Role 3 keeps rolling dice until the sum x_i for one of the players exceeds 21. If both sums x_1 and x_2 exceed 21 in the same round, then 3 wins, i.e., both players receive $\mathbf{f}$; else, the player that stayed below 21 wins and receives $\mathbf{t}$. The players 1 and 2 use their respective last known sum that is stored in x as default value for the unreliable communication in the branch $play$ and $\mathbf{f}$ as default value in the branch end. The last branch, i.e., end, is the default branch.

4   A Semantics with Failure Patterns

The application of a substitution $\{y/x\}$ on a term A, denoted as $A\{y/x\}$, is defined as the result of replacing all free occurrences of x in A by y, possibly applying alpha-conversion to avoid capture or name clashes. For all names $n \in \mathcal{N} \setminus \{x\}$ the substitution behaves as the identity mapping. We use substitution on types as well as processes and naturally extend substitution to the substitution of variables by terms (to unfold recursions) and names by expressions (to instantiate a bound name with a received value). We assume an evaluation function $\mathrm{eval}(\cdot)$ that evaluates expressions to values.

The reduction semantics of the session calculus is defined in Fig. 3 (the remaining rules are given in [30]), where we follow [22]: session initialisation is synchronous and communication within a session is asynchronous using message queues. The rules are standard except for the five failure pattern and two rules for system failures: (Crash) for *crash failures* and (ML) for *message loss*. *Failure patterns* are predicates that we deliberately choose not to define here (see below). They allow us to provide information about the underlying communication medium and the reliability of processes: FP_{uget} could, e.g., be used to reject messages that are too old. FP_{uskip} tells us whether a reception can be skipped (e.g. via failure detector). FP_{wskip} allows a process to move to its default branch. FP_{crash} can e.g. model immortal processes or global bounds on the number of crashes. FP_{ml} allows, e.g., to implement safe channels that never lose messages or a global bound on the number of lost messages.

We deliberately do not specify failure pattern, although we usually assume that the failure patterns FP_{uget}, FP_{uskip}, and FP_{wskip} use only local information, whereas FP_{ml} and FP_{crash} may use global information of the system in the current run. We provide these predicates to allow for the implementation of system requirements or abstractions like failure detectors that are typical for distributed algorithms. Directly including them in the semantics has the advantage that all traces satisfy the corresponding requirements, i.e., all traces are valid w.r.t. the assumed system requirements. An example for the instantiation of these patterns is given implicitly via the Condition 1.1–1.6 in Sect. 5 and explicitly in Sect. 6. If we instantiate the patterns FP_{uget} with true and the patterns FP_{uskip}, FP_{wskip}, FP_{crash}, FP_{ml} with false, then we obtain a system without failures. In contrast, the instantiation of all five patterns with true results in a system where failures can happen completely non-deterministically at any time.

Note that we keep the failure patterns abstract and do not model how to check them in producing runs. Indeed system requirements such as bounds on the number of processes that can crash usually cannot be checked, but result from observations, i.e., system designers ensure that a violation of this bound is very unlikely and algorithm designers are willing to ignore these unlikely events. In particular, FP_{ml} and FP_{crash} are thus often implemented as oracles for verification, whereas e.g. FP_{uskip} and FP_{wskip} are often implemented by system specific time-outs. Note that we are talking about implementing these failure patterns and not formalising them. Failure patterns are abstractions of real world system requirements or software. We implement them by conditions providing the necessary guarantees that we need in general (i.e., for subject reduction and progress) or for the verification of concrete algorithms. In practice, we expect that the systems on which the verified algorithms are running satisfy the respective conditions. Accordingly, the session channels, roles, labels, and processes mentioned in Fig. 3 are not parameters of the failure patterns, but just a vehicle to more formally specify the conditions on failure patterns in Sect. 5.

Similarly, strongly reliable and weakly reliable interactions in potentially faulty systems are abstractions. They are usually implemented by handshakes and redundancy; replicated servers against crash failures and retransmission of late messages against message loss. Algorithm designers have to be aware of the additional costs of these interactions.

(RSend) $\Gamma \vdash s[r_1, r_2]!_r\langle y\rangle.P \triangleright \Delta \cdot s[r_1]:[r_2]!_r\langle S\rangle.T$ if $\Gamma \Vdash y{:}S,\ \Gamma \vdash P \triangleright \Delta \cdot s[r_1]{:}T$

(USend) $\Gamma \vdash s[r_1, r_2]!_u l\langle y\rangle.P \triangleright \Delta \cdot s[r_1]:[r_2]!_u l'\langle S\rangle.T$
  if $\Gamma \Vdash y{:}S,\ l \ \dot{}\ \not\equiv,\ l'{:}S \in \Gamma,\ \Gamma \vdash P \triangleright \Delta \cdot s[r_1]{:}T$

(RGet) $\Gamma \vdash s[r_1, r_2]?_r(x).P \triangleright \Delta \cdot s[r_1]:[r_2]?_r\langle S\rangle.T$
  if $x\sharp(\Gamma, \Delta, s),\ \Gamma \cdot x{:}S \vdash P \triangleright \Delta \cdot s[r_1]{:}T$

(UGet) $\Gamma \vdash s[r_1, r_2]?_u l(v)(x).P \triangleright \Delta \cdot s[r_1]:[r_2]?_u l'\langle S\rangle.T$
  if $x\sharp(\Gamma, \Delta, s),\ \Gamma \Vdash v{:}S,\ l \ \dot{}\ \not\equiv,\ l'{:}S \in \Gamma,\ \Gamma \cdot x{:}S \vdash P \triangleright \Delta \cdot s[r_1]{:}T$

(RSel) $\Gamma \vdash s[r_1, r_2]!_r l.P \triangleright \Delta \cdot s[r_1]:[r_2]!_r\{l_i.T_i\}_{i\in I}$
  if $j \in I,\ l \ \dot{}\ \not\equiv,\ \Gamma \vdash P \triangleright \Delta \cdot s[r_1]{:}T_j$

(WSel) $\Gamma \vdash s[r, R]!_w l.P \triangleright \Delta \cdot s[r]:[R]!_w\{l_i.T_i\}_{i\in I}$ if $j \in I,\ l \ \dot{}\ \not\equiv,\ \Gamma \vdash P \triangleright \Delta \cdot s[r]{:}T_j$

(RBran) $\Gamma \vdash s[r_1, r_2]?_r\{l_i.P_i\}_{i\in I_1} \triangleright \Delta \cdot s[r_1]:[r_2]?_r\{l_i.T_i\}_{i\in I_2}$
  if $\forall j \in I_2.\ \exists i \in I_1.\ l_i \ \dot{}\ \not\equiv \wedge \Gamma \vdash P_i \triangleright \Delta \cdot s[r_1]{:}T_j$

(WBran) $\Gamma \vdash s[r_1, r_2]?_w\{l_i.P_i\}_{i\in I_1, l_d} \triangleright \Delta \cdot s[r_1]:[r_2]?_w\{l_i.T_i\}_{i\in I_2, l'_d}$
  if $l_d \ \dot{}\ \not\equiv,\ \forall j \in I_2.\ \exists i \in I_1.\ l_i \ \dot{}\ \not\equiv \wedge \Gamma \vdash P_i \triangleright \Delta \cdot s[r_1]{:}T_j$

(Crash) $\Gamma \vdash \bot \triangleright \Delta$ if $\mathrm{nsr}(\Delta)$

Fig. 4. Selected typing rules.

5 Typing Fault-Tolerant Processes

A *typed judgment* is a triple $\Gamma \vdash P \triangleright \Delta$, where $\Delta ::= \emptyset \mid \Delta \cdot s[r]{:}T \mid \Delta \cdot s_{r_1 \to r_2}{:}\mathrm{MT}^*$ and $\Gamma ::= \emptyset \mid \Gamma \cdot x{:}S \mid \Gamma \cdot a{:}G \mid \Gamma \cdot l{:}S$. Global environments Γ relate variables to their sort, shared channels to the type of the session they introduce, and connect labels with a sort. Session environments Δ collect the local types of actors and the list of message types MT^* of queues.

We write $x\sharp\Gamma$ and $x\sharp\Delta$ if the name x does not occur in Γ and Δ, respectively. We use $\cdot$ to add an assignment provided that the new assignment is not in conflict with the type environment, i.e., $\Gamma \cdot A$ implies that the respective name/variable/label in A is not contained in Γ and $\Delta \cdot A$ implies that the respective actor/queue in A is not contained in Δ. These conditions on $\cdot$ for global and session environments are referred to as *linearity*. We restrict in the following our attention to linear environments.

We write nsr(Δ) if none of the prefixes in T is strongly reliable or for delegation for all local types T in Δ and if Δ does not contain message queues. With $\Gamma \Vdash y{:}S$ we check that y is an expression of the sort S if all names x in y are replaced by arbitrary values of sort S_x for $x{:}S_x \in \Gamma$. A complete set of typing rules can be found in [30]. In Fig. 4 we concentrate on the interaction cases, where we observe that all new cases are quite similar to their strongly reliable counterparts. The unreliable and weakly reliable cases additionally check the sorts assigned to labels in Γ, the sorts of default values, and the relation between default labels of processes and their types. Figure 4 also gives the Rule (Crash) for crashed processes. It only checks that nsr(Δ).

We have to prove that our extended type system satisfies the standard properties of MPST, i.e., subject reduction and progress. Because of the failure pattern in the reduction semantics in Fig. 3, subject reduction and progress do not hold in general. Instead we have to fix conditions on failure patterns that ensure these properties. Subject reduction needs one condition on crashed processes and progress requires that no part of the system is blocked. In fact, different instantiations of these failure patterns may allow for progress. We leave it for future work to determine what kind of conditions on failure patterns or requirements on their interactions are necessary. Here, we consider only one such set.

Condition 1 (Failure Pattern)

1. *If* $\mathrm{FP_{crash}}(P)$, *then* nsr(P).
2. *The failure pattern* $\mathrm{FP_{uget}}(s, r_1, r_2, l)$ *is always valid.*
3. *The pattern* $\mathrm{FP_{ml}}(s, r_1, r_2, l)$ *is valid iff* $\mathrm{FP_{uskip}}(s, r_2, r_1, l)$ *is valid.*
4. *If* $\mathrm{FP_{crash}}(P)$ *and* $s[r] \in \mathrm{A}(P)$ *then eventually* $\mathrm{FP_{uskip}}(s, r_2, r, l)$ *and also* $\mathrm{FP_{wskip}}(s, r_2, r, l)$ *for all* r_2, l.
5. *If* $\mathrm{FP_{crash}}(P)$ *and* $s[r] \in \mathrm{A}(P)$ *then eventually* $\mathrm{FP_{ml}}(s, r_1, r, l)$ *for all* r_1, l.
6. *If* $\mathrm{FP_{wskip}}(s, r_1, r_2)$ *then* $s[r_2]$ *is crashed, i.e., the system does no longer contain an actor* $s[r_2]$ *and the message queue* $s_{r_2 \to r_1}$ *is empty.*

The crash of a process should not block strongly reliable actions, i.e., only processes with nsr(P) can crash (Condition 1.1). Condition 1.2 requires that no process can refuse to consume a message on its queue to prevent deadlocks that may arise from refusing a message that is never dropped. Condition 1.3 requires that if a message can be dropped from a message queue then the corresponding receiver has to be able to skip this message and vice versa. Similarly, processes that wait for messages from a crashed process have to be able to skip (Condition 1.4) and all messages of a queue towards a crashed receiver can be dropped (Condition 1.5). Finally, weakly reliable branching requests should not be lost. To ensure that the receiver of such a branching request can proceed if the sender is crashed but is not allowed to skip the reception of the branching request before the sender crashed, we require that $\mathrm{FP_{wskip}}(s, r_1, r_2)$ is false as long as $s[r_2]$ is alive or messages on the respective queue are still in transit (Condition 1.6).

The combination of these 6 conditions might appear quite restrictive on a first glance. It is important to remember that they are minimal assumptions on the system requirements and that system requirements are abstractions. Parts of them may be realised by actual software-code (which then allows to check them), whereas other parts of the system requirements may not be realised at all but rather observed (which then does not allow to verify them). Because of that, it is an established method to verify the correctness of algorithms w.r.t. given system requirements (e.g. in [10,25,32]), even if these system requirements are not verified and often do not hold in all (but only nearly all) cases.

Coherence intuitively describes that a session environment captures all local endpoints of a collection of global types. Since we capture all relevant global types in the global environment, we define coherence on pairs of global and session environments.

Definition 1 (Coherence). *The type environments Γ, Δ are coherent if, for all session channels s in Δ, there exists a global type G in Γ such that the restriction of Δ on assignments with s is the set Δ' such that $\{s[r]:G\restriction_r \mid r \in R(G)\} \cdot \{s_{r\to r'}:[] \mid r, r' \in R(G)\} \overset{s}{\mapsto} \Delta'$.*

The relation $\overset{s}{\mapsto}$ describes how a session environment evolves alongside reductions of the system, i.e., it emulates the reduction steps of processes. As an example consider the rule $\Delta \cdot s[r_1]:[r_2]!_r\langle S\rangle.T \cdot s_{r_1\to r_2}:MT \overset{s}{\mapsto} \Delta \cdot s[r_1]:T \cdot s_{r_1\to r_2}:MT\#\langle S\rangle^r$ that emulates (RSend). Let $\overset{s}{\Mapsto}$ denote the reflexive and transitive closure of $\overset{s}{\mapsto}$. We use $\overset{s}{\Mapsto}$ in the above definition to define coherence for systems that already performed some steps. We can now prove subject reduction.

Theorem 1 (Subject Reduction). *If $\Gamma \vdash P \triangleright \Delta$, Γ, Δ are coherent, and $P \longmapsto P'$, then there is some Δ' such that $\Gamma \vdash P' \triangleright \Delta'$.*

The proof is by induction on the derivation of $P \longmapsto P'$ (see [30]). In every case, we use the information about the structure of the processes to generate partial proof trees for the respective typing judgement. Additionally, we use Condition 1.1 to ensure that the type environment of a crashed process cannot contain the types of reliable communication prefixes.

Progress states that no part of a well-typed system can block other parts, that eventually all matching communication partners of strongly reliable and weakly reliable communications (that are not crashed) are unguarded, and that there are no communication mismatches. Subject reduction and progress together then imply *session fidelity*, i.e., that processes behave as specified in their global types.

To ensure that the interleaving of sessions and session delegation cannot introduce deadlocks, we assume an interaction type system as introduced in [3,22]. For this type system it does not matter whether the considered actions are strongly reliable, weakly reliable, or unreliable. More precisely, we can adapt the interaction type system of [3] in a straightforward way to the above session calculus, where unreliable communication and weakly reliable branching is treated in exactly the same way as strongly reliable communication/branching. We say that *P is free of cyclic dependencies between sessions* if this interaction type system does not detect any cyclic dependencies. In this sense fault-tolerance is more flexible than explicit failure handling, which requires a more substantial revision of the interaction type system to cover the additional dependencies that are introduced e.g. by the propagation of faults.

In the literature there are different formulations of progress. We are interested in a rather strict definition of progress that ensures that well-typed systems cannot block. Therefore, we need an additional assumption on session requests and acceptances. Coherence ensures the existence of communication partners within sessions only. If we want to avoid blocking, we need to be sure, that no participant of a session is missing during its initialisation. Note that without action prefixes all participants either terminated or crashed.

Theorem 2 (Progress/Session Fidelity). *Let $\Gamma \vdash P \triangleright \Delta$, Γ, Δ be coherent, and let P be free of cyclic dependencies between sessions. Assume that in the derivation of $\Gamma \vdash P \triangleright \Delta$, whenever $\overline{a}[\mathsf{n}](s).Q$ or $a[\mathsf{r}](s).Q$ in P, then $a{:}G \in \Gamma$, $|\mathrm{R}(G)| = \mathsf{n}$, and there are $\overline{a}[\mathsf{n}](s).Q_n$ as well as $a[\mathsf{r}_i](s).Q_i$ in P for all $1 \le \mathsf{r}_i < \mathsf{n}$.*

1. *Then either P does not contain any action prefixes or $P \longmapsto P'$.*
2. *If P does not contain recursion, then there exists P' such that $P \longmapsto^* P'$ and P' does not contain any action prefixes.*

The proof of progress relies on the Condition 1.2–1.6 to ensure that failures cannot block the system: in the failure-free case unreliable messages are eventually received (1.2), the receiver of a lost message can skip (1.3), no receiver is blocked by a crashed sender (1.4), messages towards receivers that crashed or skipped can be dropped (1.5 + 1.3), and branching requests cannot be ignored (1.6).

6   The Rotating Coordinator Algorithm

To illustrate our approach we study a Consensus algorithm by Chandra and Toueg (cf. [10,18]). This algorithm is small but not trivial. It was designed for systems with crash failures, but the majority of the algorithm can be implemented with unreliable communication.

As this algorithm models consensus, the goal is that every agent i eventually decides on a proposed belief value, where no two agents decide on different values. It is a round based algorithm, where each round consists of four phases. In each round, one process acts as a coordinator decided by round robin, denoted by c.

In Phase 1 every agent i sends its current belief to the coordinator c.

In Phase 2 the coordinator waits until it has received at least half of the messages of the current round and then sends the best belief to all other agents.

In Phase 3 the agents either receive the message of the coordinator or suspect the coordinator to have crashed and reply with ack or nack accordingly. Suspicion can yield false positives.

In Phase 4 the coordinator waits, as in Phase 2, until it has received at least half of the messages of the current round and then sends a weakly reliable broadcast if at least half of the messages contained ack.

It is possible for agents to skip rounds by suspecting the coordinator of the current round and by proceeding to the next round. There are also no synchronisation fences thus it is possible for the agents to be in different rounds and have messages of different rounds in the system. Having agents in different rounds makes proving correctness much more difficult.

Let $\left(\bigodot_{1 \leq i \leq n} \pi_i\right).G$ abbreviate the sequence $\pi_1.\ldots.\pi_n.G$ to simplify the presentation, where $G \in \mathcal{G}$ is a global type and $\pi_1,\ldots,\pi_n$ are sequences of prefixes. More precisely, each π_i is of the form $\pi_{i,1}.\ldots.\pi_{i,m}$ and each $\pi_{i,j}$ is a type prefix of the form $r_1 \rightarrow_u r_2{:}l\langle S\rangle$ or $r \rightarrow_w R{:}l_1.T_1 \oplus \ldots \oplus l_n.T_n \oplus l_d$, where the latter case represents a weakly reliable branching prefix with the branches $l_1,\ldots,l_n,l_d$, the default branch l_d, and where the next global type provides the missing specification for the default case. We assume the sorts $S_{\text{belief}} = \{0,1\}$ and $S_{\text{ack}} = \{t,f\}$. Let n be the number of agents. We start with the specification as a global type.

$$G_{rc}(n) \triangleq (\mu t) \bigodot_{1 \leq c \leq n} \left(\left(\bigodot_{1 \leq i \leq n, i \neq c} i \rightarrow_u c{:}p_1\langle S_{\text{belief}}\rangle\right).\right.$$
$$\left(\bigodot_{1 \leq i \leq n, i \neq c} c \rightarrow_u i{:}p_2\langle S_{\text{belief}}\rangle\right).\left(\bigodot_{1 \leq i \leq n, i \neq c} i \rightarrow_u c{:}p_3\langle S_{\text{ack}}\rangle\right).$$
$$\left. c \rightarrow_w \{i | 1 \leq i \leq n, i \neq c\}{:}Zero.\text{end} \oplus One.\text{end} \oplus l_d\right).t$$

It specifies a loop containing a collection of n rounds, where each process functions as a coordinator once. This collection of n rounds is specified with the first $\bigodot$, i.e., the continuation of l_d in the end of the description is the specification of round $r + 1$ for all rounds $r < n$ whereas in the last round n we have $l_d.t$. By unfolding the recursion on t, $G_{rc}(n)$ starts the next n rounds. The following three $\bigodot$ specify the Phases 1–3 of the algorithm within one round. Phase 4 is specified by a weakly reliable branching that does not need a $\bigodot$, since it is a broadcast.

In Phase 1 all processes except the coordinator c transmit a belief to c using label p_1. In Phase 2 c transmits a belief to all other processes using label p_2. Then all processes transmit a value of type S_{ack} to the coordinator using label p_3 in Phase 3. Finally, in Phase 4 the coordinator broadcasts one of the labels $Zero$, One, or l_d, where the first two labels represent a decision and terminate the protocol, whereas the default label l_d specifies the need for another round. All interactions in the specification are unreliable or weakly reliable.

Let $\left(\bigodot_{1 \leq i \leq n} \pi_i\right).P$ abbreviate the sequence $\pi_1.\ldots.\pi_n.P$, where $P \in \mathcal{P}$ is a process and $\pi_1,\ldots,\pi_n$ are sequences of prefixes.

$$Sys\left(n, \vec{V^0}\right) \triangleq \overline{a}[n](s).P\left(n, n, \vec{V_n^0}\right) \mid \prod_{1 \leq i < n} a[i](s).P\left(i, n, \vec{V_i^0}\right)$$
$$P\left(i, n, \vec{V}\right) \triangleq (\mu X)\left(\bigodot_{1 \leq c \leq n} \text{if } i = c \text{ then } P_1^C\left(i, n, \vec{V}\right) \text{ else } P_1^{NC}\left(i, n, c, \vec{V}\right)\right).X$$

$Sys\left(\mathsf{n}, \vec{V}^0\right)$ describes the session initialisation of a system with n participants and the initial knowledge $\vec{V}^0$, where $\vec{V}_i^0$ is a vector that contains only the initial knowledge of role i. Let $\left|\vec{V}\right| \triangleq |\{i \mid v_i \neq \bot\}|$ return the number of non-empty entries. $P\left(\mathsf{i}, \mathsf{n}, \vec{V}\right)$ describes a process i in a set of n processes. Each process then runs for at most n rounds and then loops.

$$P_1^C\left(\mathsf{c}, \mathsf{n}, \vec{V}\right) \triangleq \left(\bigodot_{1 \leq i \leq n, i \neq c} s[\mathsf{c}, \mathsf{i}]?_u p_1 \langle \bot \rangle (v_i)\right).\mathtt{if}\ \left|\vec{V}\right| \geq \left\lceil \frac{\mathsf{n}-1}{2} \right\rceil$$
$$\mathtt{then}\ P_2^C\left(\mathsf{c}, \mathsf{n}, \mathrm{best}(\vec{V})\right)\ \mathtt{else}\ P_2^C\left(\mathsf{c}, \mathsf{n}, \vec{V}_c^0\right)$$
$$P_1^{NC}\left(\mathsf{i}, \mathsf{n}, \mathsf{c}, \vec{V}\right) \triangleq s[\mathsf{i}, \mathsf{c}]!_u p_1 \langle v_i \rangle.P_2^{NC}\left(\mathsf{i}, \mathsf{n}, \mathsf{c}, \vec{V}\right)$$

Every non-coordinator $P_1^{NC}\left(\mathsf{i}, \mathsf{n}, \mathsf{c}, \vec{V}\right)$ sends its own belief via unreliable communication to the coordinator and proceeds to Phase 2. The coordinator receives (some of) these messages and proceeds to Phase 2. If the reception of at least half of the messages was successful, it is updating its belief using the function best() that replaces all belief values with the best one. Otherwise, it discards all beliefs except its own. We are using $\left\lceil \frac{\mathsf{n}-1}{2} \right\rceil$ to check for a majority, since in our implementation processes do not transmit to themselves.

$$P_2^C\left(\mathsf{c}, \mathsf{n}, \vec{V}\right) \triangleq \left(\bigodot_{1 \leq i \leq n, i \neq c} s[\mathsf{c}, \mathsf{i}]!_u p_2 \langle v_i \rangle\right).P_3^C\left(\mathsf{c}, \mathsf{n}, \vec{V}\right)$$
$$P_2^{NC}\left(\mathsf{i}, \mathsf{n}, \mathsf{c}, \vec{V}\right) \triangleq s[\mathsf{i}, \mathsf{c}]?_u p_2 \langle \bot \rangle (x).\mathtt{if}\ x = \bot\ \mathtt{then}\ P_3^{NC}\left(\mathsf{i}, \mathsf{n}, \mathsf{c}, \vec{V}, \mathtt{f}\right)$$
$$\mathtt{else}\ P_3^{NC}\left(\mathsf{i}, \mathsf{n}, \mathsf{c}, \mathrm{update}(\vec{V}, \mathsf{i}, x), \mathtt{t}\right)$$

In Phase 2, the coordinator sends its updated belief to all other processes via unreliable communication and proceeds. Note that, v_i is either $\bot$ for all $i \neq \mathsf{c}$ or the best belief identified in Phase 1. If a non-coordinator process successfully receives a belief other than $\bot$, it updates its own belief with the received value and proceeds to Phase 3, where we use the Boolean value $\mathtt{t}$ for the acknowledgement. If the coordinator is suspected to have crashed or $\bot$ was received, the process proceeds to Phase 3 with the Boolean value $\mathtt{f}$, signalling nack.

$$P_3^C\left(\mathsf{c}, \mathsf{n}, \vec{V}\right) \triangleq \left(\bigodot_{1 \leq i \leq n, i \neq c} s[\mathsf{c}, \mathsf{i}]?_u p_3 \langle \bot \rangle (v_i)\right).P_4^C\left(\mathsf{c}, \mathsf{n}, \vec{V}\right)$$
$$P_3^{NC}\left(\mathsf{i}, \mathsf{n}, \mathsf{c}, \vec{V}, b\right) \triangleq s[\mathsf{i}, \mathsf{c}]!_u p_3 \langle b \rangle.P_4^{NC}\left(\mathsf{i}, \mathsf{n}, \mathsf{c}, \vec{V}\right)$$

In Phase 3, every non-coordinator sends either ack or nack to the coordinator. If the coordinator successfully receives the message, it writes the Boolean value at the index of the sender into its knowledge vector. In case of failure, $\bot$ is used as default. After that the processes continue with Phase 4. Let

$\mathcal{I} = \{i \mid 1 \leq i \leq n, i \neq c\}.$

$$P_4^C\left(c, n, \vec{V}\right) \triangleq \text{if } \text{ack}(\vec{V}) \geq \left\lceil \frac{n-1}{2} \right\rceil \text{ then (if } v_c = 0 \text{ then } s[c, \mathcal{I}]!_w \text{Zero.}0$$

$$\text{else } s[c, \mathcal{I}]!_w \text{One.}0) \text{ else } s[c, \mathcal{I}]!_w l_d$$

$$P_4^{NC}\left(i, n, c, \vec{V}\right) \triangleq s[i, n]?_w \text{Zero.}0 \oplus \text{One.}0 \oplus l_d$$

In Phase 4 the coordinator checks if at least half of the non-coordinator roles signalled acknowledgement, utilising the function ack to count. If it received enough acknowledgements it transmits the decision via *Zero* or *One* and causes all participants to terminate. Otherwise, the coordinator sends the default label and continues with the next round. Remember that the missing continuation after the default label l_d for coordinators and non-coordinators is implemented by the next round.

We use a weakly reliable branching mechanism in conjunction with unreliable communication. The algorithm was modelled for systems with crash failures but without message loss. However, as long as the branching mechanism (i.e., the specified broadcast of decisions) is weakly reliable, we can relax the system requirements for the remainder of the algorithm. To ensure termination, however, we have to further restrict the number of lost messages.

Failure Patterns. Chandra and Toueg introduce in [10] also the failure detector $\Diamond \mathcal{S}$. The failure detector $\Diamond \mathcal{S}$ is called *eventually strong*, meaning that (1) eventually every process that crashes is permanently suspected by every correct process and (2) there is a time after which some correct process is never suspected by any other process. We observe that the suspicion of senders is only possible in Phase 3, where processes may suspect the coordinator of the round. Accordingly, the failure pattern FP_{uskip} implements this failure detector to allow processes to suspect unreliable coordinators in Phase 2, i.e., with label p_2. In Phase 1 and Phase 3 FP_{uskip} may allow to suspect processes that are not crashed after the coordinator received enough messages. In all other cases these two patterns eventually return true iff the respective sender is crashed. FP_{uget} can be used to reject outdated messages, since this is not important for this algorithm we implement it with the constant true. To ensure that messages of wrongly suspected coordinators in Phase 2 do not block the system, FP_{ml} is eventually true for messages with label p_2 that were suspected using $\Diamond \mathcal{S}$ or skipped p_1/p_3-messages and otherwise returns false. By the system requirements in [10], no messages get lost, but it is realistic to assume that receivers can drop messages of skipped receptions on their incoming message queues. As there are at least half of the processes required to be correct for this algorithm, we implement FP_{crash} by false if only half of the processes are alive and true otherwise. For the weakly reliable broadcast, FP_{wskip} returns true if and only if the respective coordinator is crashed, i.e., not suspected but indeed crashed. In [10] this broadcast, which is called just reliable in [10], is used to announce the decision. Since we use it for branching even before a decision was reached, our implementation is less efficient compared to [10]. We briefly discuss in the conclusions how to regain the original algorithm. These failure patterns satisfy the Condition 1.1–1.6.

Termination, Agreement, and Validity. Following [26,33], a network of processes solves Consensus if **Termination:** all non-failing participants eventually decide, **Agreement:** all decision values are the same, and **Validity:** each decision value is an initial value of some participant. By [18] the Rotating Coordinator algorithm solves Consensus in the presence of crash-failures.

In the proof of termination well-typedness of the implementation and progress in Theorem 2 are the main ingredients. Well-typedness ensures that the implementation follows its specification and progress ensures that it cannot get stuck. Apart from that, we only need to deduce from the system requirements, i.e., the used failure detector, that the implementation will eventually exit the loop. Validity can be checked by analysing the code of a single process and check whether it uses (to decide and to transmit) only its own initial belief or the belief it received from others. Session fidelity in Theorem 2 then ensures that there are no communication mismatches and all steps preserve this property. Agreement follows from the weakly reliable broadcast, because the decision is broadcasted.

Theorem 3. *The algorithm satisfies termination, validity, and agreement.*

7   Conclusions

We present a fault-tolerant variant of MPST for systems that may suffer from message loss or crash failures. We implemented unreliable communication and weakly reliable branching. The failure patterns in the semantics allow to verify algorithms modulo system requirements. We prove subject reduction and progress and present a small but relevant case study.

An open question is how to conveniently type unreliable recursive parts of protocols. Distributed algorithms are often recursive and exit this recursion if a result was successfully computed. We present a first attempt to solve this problem using a weakly reliable branching. In further research we want to analyse, whether or in how far branching can be extended to the case of message loss.

Indeed our implementation of the rotating coordinator algorithm is not ideal. It implements the decision making procedure correctly and also allows processes to be in different rounds at the same time. So, it represents a non-trivial variant of the rotating coordinator algorithm. But it does not allow the processes to diverge in their rounds as freely as the original rotating coordinator algorithm, because the weakly reliable branching implementation implies that the coordinator has always to be the first process to leave a round. We can solve this problem by wrapping each round in an unreliable sub-session (e.g. an unreliable variant of the sub-sessions introduced in [14,15]). If we allow processes to skip such an unreliable sub-session altogether, we obtain the intended behaviour.

We considered strongly reliable session delegation. Next we want to study whether and in how far we can introduce weakly reliable or unreliable session delegation. Similarly, we want to study unreliable variants of session initialisation including process crashes and lost messages during session initialisation.

In Sect. 5 we fix one set of conditions on failure patterns to prove subject reduction, session fidelity, and progress. We can also think of other sets of conditions. The failure pattern FP_{uget} can be used to reject the reception of outdated messages. Therefore, we drop Condition 1.2 and instead require for each message m whose reception is refused that FP_{ml} ensures that m is eventually dropped from the respective queue and that FP_{uskip} allows to skip the reception of these messages. An interesting question is to find minimal requirements and minimal sets of conditions that allow to prove correctness in general.

It would be nice to also fully automate the remaining proofs for the distributed algorithm in Sect. 6. The approach in [31] sequentialises well-typed systems and gives the much simpler remaining verification problem to a model checker. Interestingly, the main challenges to adopt this approach are not the unreliable or weakly reliable prefixes but the failure patterns.

References

1. Adameit, M., Peters, K., Nestmann, U.: Session types for link failures. In: Bouajjani, A., Silva, A. (eds.) FORTE 2017. LNCS, vol. 10321, pp. 1–16. Springer, Cham (2017). https://doi.org/10.1007/978-3-319-60225-7_1
2. Kawazoe Aguilera, M., Chen, W., Toueg, S.: Heartbeat: a timeout-free failure detector for quiescent reliable communication. In: Mavronicolas, M., Tsigas, P. (eds.) WDAG 1997. LNCS, vol. 1320, pp. 126–140. Springer, Heidelberg (1997). https://doi.org/10.1007/BFb0030680
3. Bettini, L., Coppo, M., D'Antoni, L., De Luca, M., Dezani-Ciancaglini, M., Yoshida, N.: Global progress in dynamically interleaved multiparty sessions. In: van Breugel, F., Chechik, M. (eds.) CONCUR 2008. LNCS, vol. 5201, pp. 418–433. Springer, Heidelberg (2008). https://doi.org/10.1007/978-3-540-85361-9_33
4. Bocchi, L., Honda, K., Tuosto, E., Yoshida, N.: A theory of design-by-contract for distributed multiparty interactions. In: Gastin, P., Laroussinie, F. (eds.) CONCUR 2010. LNCS, vol. 6269, pp. 162–176. Springer, Heidelberg (2010). https://doi.org/10.1007/978-3-642-15375-4_12
5. Caires, L., Vieira, H.T.: Conversation types. Theoret. Comput. Sci. **411**(51–52), 4399–4440 (2010). https://doi.org/10.1016/j.tcs.2010.09.010
6. Capecchi, S., Giachino, E., Yoshida, N.: Global escape in multiparty sessions. Math. Struct. Comput. Sci. **26**(2), 156–205 (2016). https://doi.org/10.1017/S0960129514000164
7. Carbone, M., Honda, K., Yoshida, N.: Structured interactional exceptions in session types. In: van Breugel, F., Chechik, M. (eds.) CONCUR 2008. LNCS, vol. 5201, pp. 402–417. Springer, Heidelberg (2008). https://doi.org/10.1007/978-3-540-85361-9_32
8. Castellani, I., Dezani-Ciancaglini, M., Giannini, P.: Concurrent reversible sessions. In: Proceedings of CONCUR. LIPIcs, vol. 85, pp. 30:1–30:17 (2017). https://doi.org/10.4230/LIPIcs.CONCUR.2017.30
9. Castellani, I., Dezani-Ciancaglini, M., Giannini, P., Horne, R.: Global types with internal delegation. Theoret. Comput. Sci. **807**, 128–153 (2020). https://doi.org/10.1016/j.tcs.2019.09.027

10. Chandra, T.D., Toueg, S.: Unreliable failure detectors for reliable distributed systems. J. ACM **43**(2), 225–267 (1996). https://doi.org/10.1145/226643.226647

11. Charron-Bost, B., Schiper, A.: The heard-of model: computing in distributed systems with benign faults. Distrib. Comput. **22**(1), 49–71 (2009). https://doi.org/10.1007/s00446-009-0084-6

12. Chen, T.-C., Viering, M., Bejleri, A., Ziarek, L., Eugster, P.: A type theory for robust failure handling in distributed systems. In: Albert, E., Lanese, I. (eds.) FORTE 2016. LNCS, vol. 9688, pp. 96–113. Springer, Cham (2016). https://doi.org/10.1007/978-3-319-39570-8_7

13. Coppo, M., Dezani-Ciancaglini, M., Padovani, L., Yoshida, N.: A gentle introduction to multiparty asynchronous session types. In: Bernardo, M., Johnsen, E.B. (eds.) SFM 2015. LNCS, vol. 9104, pp. 146–178. Springer, Cham (2015). https://doi.org/10.1007/978-3-319-18941-3_4

14. Demangeon, R.: Nested Protocols in Session Types (2015), personal communication about an extended version of [15] that is currently prepared by R. Demangeon

15. Demangeon, R., Honda, K.: Nested protocols in session types. In: Koutny, M., Ulidowski, I. (eds.) CONCUR 2012. LNCS, vol. 7454, pp. 272–286. Springer, Heidelberg (2012). https://doi.org/10.1007/978-3-642-32940-1_20

16. Demangeon, R., Honda, K., Hu, R., Neykova, R., Yoshida, N.: Practical interruptible conversations: distributed dynamic verification with multiparty session types and Python. Formal Methods Syst. Des. **46**(3), 197–225 (2014). https://doi.org/10.1007/s10703-014-0218-8

17. Francalanza, A., Hennessy, M.: A fault tolerance bisimulation proof for consensus (extended abstract). In: De Nicola, R. (ed.) ESOP 2007. LNCS, vol. 4421, pp. 395–410. Springer, Heidelberg (2007). https://doi.org/10.1007/978-3-540-71316-6_27

18. Fuzzati, R., Merro, M., Nestmann, U.: Distributed Consensus, revisited. Acta Informatica, 377–425 (2007). https://doi.org/10.1007/s00236-007-0052-1

19. Gärtner, F.C.: Fundamentals of fault-tolerant distributed computing in asynchronous environments. ACM Comput. Surv. **31**(1), 1–26 (1999). https://doi.org/10.1145/311531.311532

20. van Glabbeek, R., Höfner, P., Horne, R.: Assuming just enough fairness to make session types complete for lock-freedom. In: Proceedings of LICS, pp. 1–13. IEEE (2021)

21. Honda, K., Yoshida, N., Carbone, M.: Multiparty asynchronous session types. In: Proceedings of POPL, vol. 43, pp. 273–284. ACM (2008). https://doi.org/10.1145/1328438.1328472

22. Honda, K., Yoshida, N., Carbone, M.: Multiparty asynchronous session types. J. ACM **63**(1) (2016). https://doi.org/10.1145/2827695

23. Kouzapas, D., Gutkovas, R., Gay, S.J.: Session types for broadcasting. In: Proceedings of PLACES. EPTCS, vol. 155, pp. 25–31 (2014). https://doi.org/10.4204/EPTCS.155.4

24. Kühnrich, M., Nestmann, U.: On process-algebraic proof methods for fault tolerant distributed systems. In: Lee, D., Lopes, A., Poetzsch-Heffter, A. (eds.) FMOODS/FORTE -2009. LNCS, vol. 5522, pp. 198–212. Springer, Heidelberg (2009). https://doi.org/10.1007/978-3-642-02138-1_13

25. Lamport, L.: Paxos made simple. ACM SIGACT News **32**(4), 18–25 (2001)

26. Lynch, N.A.: Distributed Algorithms. Morgan Kaufmann (1996)

27. Nestmann, U., Fuzzati, R.: Unreliable failure detectors via operational semantics. In: Saraswat, V.A. (ed.) ASIAN 2003. LNCS, vol. 2896, pp. 54–71. Springer, Heidelberg (2003). https://doi.org/10.1007/978-3-540-40965-6_5

28. Nestmann, U., Fuzzati, R., Merro, M.: Modeling consensus in a process calculus. In: Amadio, R., Lugiez, D. (eds.) CONCUR 2003. LNCS, vol. 2761, pp. 399–414. Springer, Heidelberg (2003). https://doi.org/10.1007/978-3-540-45187-7_26

29. Neykova, R., Yoshida, N.: Let it recover: multiparty protocol-induced recovery. In: Proceedings of CC, pp. 98–108. ACM (2017). https://doi.org/10.1145/3033019.3033031

30. Peters, K., Nestmann, U., Wagner, C.: Fault-tolerant multiparty session types (Technical Report). Technical report (2022). https://doi.org/10.48550/arXiv.2204.07728

31. Peters, K., Wagner, C., Nestmann, U.: Taming concurrency for verification using multiparty session types. In: Hierons, R.M., Mosbah, M. (eds.) ICTAC 2019. LNCS, vol. 11884, pp. 196–215. Springer, Cham (2019). https://doi.org/10.1007/978-3-030-32505-3_12

32. van Steen, M., Tanenbaum, A.S.: Distributed Systems. Maarten van Steen (2017)

33. Tel, G.: Introduction to Distributed Algorithms. Cambridge University Press, Cambridge (1994)

34. Viering, M., Chen, T.-C., Eugster, P., Hu, R., Ziarek, L.: A typing discipline for statically verified crash failure handling in distributed systems. In: Ahmed, A. (ed.) ESOP 2018. LNCS, vol. 10801, pp. 799–826. Springer, Cham (2018). https://doi.org/10.1007/978-3-319-89884-1_28

35. Wagner, C., Nestmann, U.: States in process calculi. In: Proceedings of EXPRESS/SOS. EPTCS, vol. 160, pp. 48–62 (2014). https://doi.org/10.4204/EPTCS.160.6

36. Yoshida, N., Deniélou, P.-M., Bejleri, A., Hu, R.: Parameterised multiparty session types. In: Ong, L. (ed.) FoSSaCS 2010. LNCS, vol. 6014, pp. 128–145. Springer, Heidelberg (2010). https://doi.org/10.1007/978-3-642-12032-9_10

Effective Reductions of Mealy Machines

Florian Renkin[(✉)] [ID], Philipp Schlehuber-Caissier[ID], Alexandre Duret-Lutz[ID],
and Adrien Pommellet[ID]

LRDE, EPITA, Kremlin-Bicêtre, France
{frenkin,philipp,adl,adrien}@lrde.epita.fr

Abstract. We revisit the problem of reducing incompletely specified
Mealy machines with reactive synthesis in mind. We propose two techniques: the former is inspired by the tool MEMIN [1] and solves the minimization problem, the latter is a novel approach derived from simulation-
based reductions but may not guarantee a minimized machine. However,
we argue that it offers a good enough compromise between the size of
the resulting Mealy machine and performance. The proposed methods
are benchmarked against MEMIN on a large collection of test cases made
of well-known instances as well as new ones.

1 Introduction

Program synthesis is a well-established formal method: given a logical specification of a system, it allows one to automatically generate a provably correct
implementation. It can be applied to reactive controllers (Fig. 1a): circuits that
produce for an input stream of Boolean valuations (here, over Boolean variables
a and b) a matching output stream (here, over x and y).

The techniques used to translate a specification (say, a Linear Time Logic
formula that relates input and output Boolean variables) into a circuit often
rely on automata-theoretic intermediate models such as Mealy machines. These
transducers are labeled graphs whose edges associate input valuations to a choice
of one or more output valuations, as shown in Fig. 1b.

Since Mealy machines with fewer states result in smaller circuits, reducing
and minimizing the size of Mealy machines are well-studied problems [2,12].

However, vague specifications may cause incompletely specified machines: for
some states (i.e., nodes of the graph) and inputs, there may not exist a unique,
explicitly defined output, but a set of valid outputs. Resolving those choices to
a single output (among those allowed) will produce a fully specified machine
that satisfies the initial specification, however those different choices may have
an impact on the minimization of the machine. While minimizing fully specified
machines is efficiently solvable [8], the problem is NP-complete for incompletely
specified machines [14]. Hence, it may also be worth exploring faster algorithms
that seek to reduce the number of states without achieving the optimal result.

Consider Fig. 1b: this machine is incompletely specified, as for instance state
0 allows multiple outputs for input ab (i.e., when both input variables a and b

© IFIP International Federation for Information Processing 2022
Published by Springer Nature Switzerland AG 2022
M. R. Mousavi and A. Philippou (Eds.): FORTE 2022, LNCS 13273, pp. 114–130, 2022.
https://doi.org/10.1007/978-3-031-08679-3_8

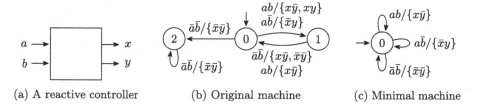

Fig. 1. Minimizing a Mealy machine that models a reactive controller

are true) and implicitly allows any output for input $\bar{a}b$ (i.e., only b is true) as it isn't constrained in any way by the specification. We can benefit from this flexibility in unspecified outputs to help reduce the automaton. For instance if we constrain state 2 to behave exactly as state 0 for inputs ab and $a\bar{b}$, then these two states can be merged. Adding further constraints can lead to the single-state machine shown in Fig. 1c. These smaller machines are not *equivalent*, but they are *compatible*: for any input stream, they can only produce output streams that could also have been produced by the original machine.

We properly define *Incompletely specified Generalized Mealy Machines* in Sect. 2 and provide a SAT-based minimization algorithm in Sect. 3. Since the minimization of incompletely specified Mealy machines is desirable but not crucial for reactive synthesis, we propose a faster reduction technique yielding "small enough" machines in Sect. 4. Finally, in Sect. 5 we benchmark these techniques against the state-of-the-art tool MeMin [1].

2   Definitions

Given a set of propositions (i.e., Boolean variables) X, let $\mathbb{B}^X$ be the set of all possible valuations on X, and let $2^{\mathbb{B}^X}$ be its set of subsets. Any element of $2^{\mathbb{B}^X}$ can be expressed as a Boolean formula over X. The negation of proposition p is denoted $\bar{p}$. We use $\top$ to denote the Boolean formula that is always true, or equivalently the set $\mathbb{B}^X$, and assume that X is clear from the context. A *cube* is a conjunction of propositions or their negations (i.e., literals). As an example, given three propositions a, b and c, the cube $a \wedge \bar{b}$, written $a\bar{b}$, stands for the set of all valuations such that a is true and b is false, i.e. $\{abc, ab\bar{c}\}$. Let $\mathbb{K}^X$ stand for the set of all cubes over X. $\mathbb{K}^X$ contains the cube $\top$, that stands for the set of all possible valuations over X. Note that any set of valuations can be represented as a disjunction of disjoint cubes (i.e., not sharing a common valuation).

Definition 1. *An* Incompletely specified Generalized Mealy Machine *(IGMM) is a tuple* $M = (I, O, Q, q_{init}, \delta, \lambda)$, *where* I *is a set of* input *propositions,* O *a set of* output *propositions,* Q *a finite set of* states, q_{init} *an* initial *state,* $\delta\colon (Q, \mathbb{B}^I) \to Q$ *a partial transition function, and* $\lambda\colon (Q, \mathbb{B}^I) \to 2^{\mathbb{B}^O} \setminus \{\emptyset\}$ *an output function such that* $\lambda(q, i) = \top$ *when* $\delta(q, i)$ *is undefined. If* δ *is a total function, we then say that* M *is input-complete.*

It is worth noting that the transition function is input-deterministic but not complete with regards to Q as $\delta(q, i)$ could be undefined. Furthermore, the output function may return many valuations for a given input valuation and state. This is not an unexpected definition from a reactive synthesis point of view, as a given specification may yield multiple compatible output valuations for a given input.

Definition 2 (Semantics of IGMMs). *Let $M = (I, O, Q, q_{init}, \delta, \lambda)$ be an IGMM. For all $u \in \mathbb{B}^I$ and $q \in Q$, if $\delta(q, u)$ is defined, we write that $q \xrightarrow{u/v} \delta(q, u)$ for all $v \in \lambda(q, u)$. Given two infinite sequences of valuations $\iota = i_0 \cdot i_1 \cdot i_2 \cdots \in (\mathbb{B}^I)^\omega$ and $o = o_0 \cdot o_1 \cdot o_2 \cdots \in (\mathbb{B}^O)^\omega$, $(\iota, o) \models M_q$ if and only if:*

- *either there is an infinite sequence of states $(q_j)_{j \geq 0} \in Q^\omega$ such that $q = q_0$ and $q_0 \xrightarrow{i_0/o_0} q_1 \xrightarrow{i_1/o_1} q_2 \xrightarrow{i_2/o_2} \cdots$;*
- *or there is a finite sequence of states $(q_j)_{0 \leq j \leq k} \in Q^{k+1}$ such that $q = q_0$, $\delta(q_k, i_k)$ is undefined, and $q_0 \xrightarrow{i_0/o_0} q_1 \xrightarrow{i_1/o_1} \cdots q_k$.*

We then say that starting from state q, M produces output o given the input ι.

Note that if $\delta(q_k, i_k)$ is undefined, the machine is allowed to produce an arbitrary output from then on. Furthermore, given an input word ι, there may be several output words o such that $(\iota, o) \models M_q$ (in accordance with a lax specification).

As an example, consider the input sequence $\iota = ab \cdot \bar{a}\bar{b} \cdot ab \cdot \bar{a}\bar{b} \cdots$ applied to the initial state 0 of the machine shown in Fig. 1b. We have $(\iota, o) \models M_0$ if and only if for all $j \in \mathbb{N}$, $o_{2j} \in x$ and $o_{2j+1} \in \bar{y}$, where x and $\bar{y}$ are cubes that respectively represent $\{xy, x\bar{y}\}$ and $\{x\bar{y}, \bar{x}\bar{y}\}$.

Definition 3 (Variation and specialization). *Let $M = (I, O, Q, q_{init}, \delta, \lambda)$ and $M' = (I, O, Q', q'_{init}, \delta', \lambda')$ be two IGMMs. Given two states $q \in Q$, $q' \in Q'$, we say that q' is a:*

- *variation of q if $\forall \iota \in (\mathbb{B}^I)^\omega$, $\{o \mid (\iota, o) \models M'_{q'}\} \cap \{o \mid (\iota, o) \models M_q\} \neq \emptyset$;*
- *specialization of q if $\forall \iota \in (\mathbb{B}^I)^\omega$, $\{o \mid (\iota, o) \models M'_{q'}\} \subseteq \{o \mid (\iota, o) \models M_q\}$.*

We say that M' is a variation (resp. specialization) of M if q'_{init} is a variation (resp. specialization) of q_{init}.

Intuitively, all the input-output pairs accepted by a specialization q' in M' are also accepted by q in M. Therefore, if all the outputs produced by state q in M comply with the original specification, then so do the outputs produced by state q' in M'. In order for two states to be a variation of one another, for all possible inputs they must be able to agree on a common output behaviour.

We write $q' \approx q$ (resp. $q' \sqsubseteq q$) if q' is a variation (resp. specialization) of q. Note that $\approx$ is a symmetric but non-transitive relation, while $\sqsubseteq$ is transitive ($\sqsubseteq$ is a preorder).

Our goal in this article is to solve the following problems:

Reducing an IGMM M**:** finding a specialization of M having at most the same number of states, preferably fewer.

Minimizing an IGMM M**:** finding a specialization of M having the least number of states.

Consider again the IGMM shown in Fig. 1b. The IGMM shown in Fig. 1c is a specialization of this machine and has a minimal number of states.

Generalizing Inputs and Outputs. Note that the output function of an IGMM returns a set of valuations, but it can be rewritten equivalently to output a set of cubes as $\lambda\colon (Q, \mathbb{B}^I) \to 2^{\mathbb{K}^O}$. As an example, consider $I = \{a\}$ and $O = \{x, y, z\}$; the set of valuations $v = \{\bar{x}yz, \bar{x}y\bar{z}, x\bar{y}z, x\bar{y}\bar{z}\} \in 2^{\mathbb{B}^O}$ is equivalent to the set of cubes $v_c = \{\bar{x}y, x\bar{y}\} \in 2^{\mathbb{K}^O}$.

In the literature, a Mealy machine commonly maps a single input valuation to a single output valuation: its output function is therefore of the form $\lambda\colon (Q, \mathbb{B}^I) \to \mathbb{B}^O$. The tool MEMIN [1] uses a slight generalization by allowing a single output cube, hence $\lambda\colon (Q, \mathbb{B}^I) \to \mathbb{K}^O$. Thus, unlike our model, neither the common definition nor the tool MEMIN can feature an edge outputting the aforementioned set v (or equivalently v_c), as it cannot be represented by a single cube or valuation. Our model is therefore *strictly more expressive*, although it comes at a price for minimization.

Note that, in practice, edges with identical source state, output valuations, and destination state can be merged into a single transition labeled by the set of allowed inputs. Both our tool and MEMIN feature this optimization. While it does not change the expressiveness of the underlying model, this more succinct representation of the machines does improve the efficiency of the algorithms detailed in the next section, as they depend on the total number of transitions.

3   SAT-Based Minimization of IGMM

This section builds upon the approach presented by Abel and Reineke [1] for machines with outputs constrained to cubes, and generalizes it to the IGMM model (with more expressive outputs).

3.1   General Approach

Definition 4. *Given an IGMM* $M = (I, O, Q, q_{init}, \delta, \lambda)$, *a variation class* $C \subseteq Q$ *is a set of states such that all elements are pairwise variations, i.e.* $\forall q, q' \in C$, $q' \approx q$. *For any input* $i \in \mathbb{B}^I$, *we define:*

- *the* successor function $\mathrm{Succ}(C, i) = \bigcup_{q \in C} \{\delta(q, i) \mid \delta(q, i) \text{ is defined}\}$;
- *the* output function $\mathrm{Out}(C, i) = \bigcap_{q \in C} \lambda(q, i)$.

Intuitively, the successor function returns the set of all states reachable from a given class under a given input symbol. The output function returns the set of all shared output valuations between the various states in the class.

In the remainder of this section we will call a variation class simply a class, as there is no ambiguity. We consider three important notions concerning classes, or rather sets thereof, of the form $S = \{C_0, \ldots, C_{n-1}\}$.

Definition 5 (Cover condition). *We say that a set of classes S covers the machine M if every state of M appears in at least one of the classes.*

Definition 6 (Closure condition). *We say that a set of classes S is closed if for all $C_j \in S$ and for all inputs $i \in \mathbb{B}^I$ there exists a $C_k \in S$ such that $\mathrm{Succ}(C_j, i) \subseteq C_k$.*

Definition 7 (Nonemptiness condition). *We say that a class C has a nonempty output if $\mathrm{Out}(C, i) \neq \emptyset$ for all inputs $i \in \mathbb{B}^I$.*

The astute reader might have observed that the nonempty output condition is strictly stronger than the condition that all elements in a class have to be pairwise variations of one another. We will see that this distinction is however important, as it gives rise to a different set of clauses in the SAT problem, reducing the total runtime.

Combining these conditions yields the main theorem for this approach. This extends a similar theorem by Abel and Reineke [1, Thm 1] by adding the nonemptiness condition to support the more expressive IGMM model.

Theorem 1. *Let $M = (I, O, Q, q_{init}, \delta, \lambda)$ be an IGMM and $S = \{C_0, \ldots, C_{n-1}\}$ be a minimal (in terms of size) set of classes such that (1) S is closed, (2) S covers every state of the machine M and (3) each of the classes C_j has a nonempty output. Then the IGMM $M' = (I, O, S, q'_{init}, \delta', \lambda')$ where:*

- $q'_{init} = C$ *for some $C \in S$ such that $q_{init} \in C$;*
- $\delta'(C_j, i) = \begin{cases} C_k \text{ for some } k \text{ s.t. } \mathrm{Succ}(C_j, i) \subseteq C_k & \text{if } \mathrm{Succ}(C_j, i) \neq \emptyset \\ \text{undefined} & \text{else;} \end{cases}$
- $\lambda'(C_j, i) = \begin{cases} \mathrm{Out}(C_j, i) & \text{if } \mathrm{Succ}(C_j, i) \neq \emptyset \\ \top & \text{else;} \end{cases}$

is a specialization of minimal size (in terms of states) of M.

Figure 2a illustrates this construction on an example with a single input proposition $I = \{a\}$ (hence two input valuations $\mathbb{B}^I = \{a, \bar{a}\}$), and three output propositions $O = \{x, y, z\}$. To simplify notations, elements of $2^{\mathbb{B}^O}$ are represented as Boolean functions (happening to be cubes in this example) rather than sets.

States have been colored to indicate their possible membership to one of the three variational classes. The SAT solver needs to associate each state to at least one of them in order to satisfy the cover condition (5), while simultaneously respecting Conditions (6)–(7). A possible choice would be: $C_0 = \{0\}$, $C_1 = \{1, 3, 6\}$, and $C_2 = \{2, 4, 5\}$. For this choice, the *violet* class C_0 has only a single state, so the closure Condition (6) is trivially satisfied. All transitions of the

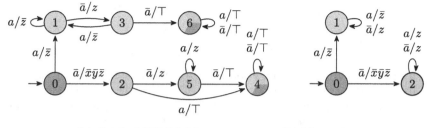

(a) Original IGMM M (b) Minimal specialization of M

Fig. 2. Minimization example (Color figure online)

states in the *orange* class C_1 go to states in C_1, also satisfying the condition. The same can be said of the *green* class C_2.

Finally, we need to check the nonempty output Condition (7). Once again, it is trivially satisfied for the *violet* class C_0. For the *orange* and *green* classes, we need to compute their respective output. We get $\mathrm{Out}(C_1, a) = \bar{z}$, $\mathrm{Out}(C_1, \bar{a}) = z$, $\mathrm{Out}(C_2, a) = \bar{z}$ and $\mathrm{Out}(C_2, \bar{a}) = z$. None of the output sets is empty, thus Condition (7) is satisfied as well. Note that, since the outgoing transitions of states 4 and 6 are self-loops compatible with all possible output valuations, another valid choice is: $C_0 = \{0, 4, 6\}$, $C_1 = \{1, 3, 4, 6\}$, and $C_2 = \{2, 4, 5, 6\}$.

The corresponding specialization, constructed as described in Theorem 1, is shown in Fig. 2b. Note that this machine is input-complete, so the incompleteness of the specification only stems from the possible choices in the outputs.

3.2   Proposed SAT Encoding

We want to design an algorithm that finds a minimal specialization of a given IGMM M. To do so, we will use the following approach, starting from $n = 1$:

- Posit that there are n classes, hence, n states in the minimal machine.
- Design SAT clauses ensuring cover, closure and nonempty outputs.
- Check if the resulting SAT problem is satisfiable.
- If so, construct the minimal machine described in Theorem 1.
- If not, increment n by one and apply the whole process again, unless $n = |Q| - 1$, which serves as a proof that the original machine is already minimal.

Encoding the Cover and Closure Conditions. In order to guarantee that the set of classes $S = \{C_0, \ldots, C_{n-1}\}$ satisfies both the cover and closure conditions and that each class C_j is a variation class, we need two types of literals:

- $s_{q,j}$ should be true if and only if state q belongs to the class C_j;
- $z_{i,k,j}$ should be true if $\mathrm{Succ}(C_k, i) \subseteq C_j$ for $i \in \mathbb{B}^I$.

The cover condition, encoded by Equation (1), guarantees that each state belongs to at least one class.

$$\bigwedge_{q \in Q} \bigvee_{0 \leq j < n} s_{q,j} \quad (1) \qquad\qquad \bigwedge_{0 \leq j < n} \bigwedge_{\substack{q,q' \in Q \\ q \not\approx q'}} \overline{s_{q,j}} \vee \overline{s_{q',j}} \quad (2)$$

Equation (2) ensures that each class is a variational class: two states q and q' that are not variations of each other cannot belong to the same class.

The closure condition must ensure that for every class C_i and every input symbol $i \in \mathbb{B}^I$, there exists at least one class that contains all the successor states: $\forall k, \forall i, \exists j, \; Succ(C_k, i) \subseteq C_j$. This is expressed by the constraints (3) and (4).

$$\bigwedge_{0 \leq k < n} \bigwedge_{i \in \mathbb{B}^I} \bigvee_{0 \leq j < n} z_{i,k,j} \quad (3) \qquad \bigwedge_{0 \leq j,k < n} \bigwedge_{\substack{q,q' \in Q, i \in \mathbb{B}^I \\ q' = \delta(q,i)}} (z_{i,k,j} \wedge s_{q,k}) \rightarrow s_{q',j} \quad (4)$$

The constraint (3) ensures that at least one C_j contains $Succ(C_k, i)$, while (4) ensures this mapping of classes matches the transitions of M.

Encoding the Nonempty Output Condition. Each class in S being a variation class is necessary but not sufficient to satisfy the nonempty output condition. We indeed want to guarantee that for any input i, all states in a given class can agree on at least one common output valuation.

However it is possible to have three or more states (like $\textcircled{0} \rightsquigarrow a/\{xy, x\bar{y}\}$, $\textcircled{1} \rightsquigarrow a/\{\bar{x}y, x\bar{y}\}$, and $\textcircled{2} \rightsquigarrow a/\{xy, \bar{x}y\}$) that are all variations of one another, but still cannot agree on a common output.

This situation cannot occur in MEMIN since their model uses *cubes* as outputs rather than arbitrary sets of valuations as in our model. A useful property of cubes is that if the pairwise intersections of all cubes in a set are nonempty, then the intersection of all cubes in the set is necessarily nonempty as well.

Since *cubes* are not expressive enough for our model, we will therefore generalize the output as discussed earlier in Sect. 2: we represent the arbitrary set of valuations produced by the output function λ as a set of cubes whose disjunction yields the original set. For $q \in Q$ and $i \in \mathbb{B}^I$, we partition the set of valuations $\lambda(q, i)$ into cubes, relying on the Minato [11] algorithm, and denote the obtained set of cubes as $CS(\lambda(q, i))$.

Our approach for ensuring that there exists a common output is to search for disjoint cubes and exclude them from the possible outputs by selectively deactivating them if necessary; an active cube is a set in which we will be looking for an output valuation that the whole class can agree on. To express this, we need two new types of literals:

- $a_{c,q,i}$ should be true iff the particular instance of the cube $c \in CS(\lambda(q, i))$ used in the output of state q when reading i is *active*;
- $sc_{q,q'}$ should be true iff $\exists C_j \in S$ such that $q \in C_j$ and $q' \in C_j$

The selective deactivation of a cube can then be expressed by the following:

$$\bigwedge_{\substack{q,q'\in Q \\ 0\le j<n}} (s_{q,j} \wedge s_{q',j}) \rightarrow sc_{q,q'} \quad (5) \qquad \bigwedge_{\substack{q\in Q,\, i\in\mathbb{B}^I \\ \delta(q,i) \text{ is defined}}} \bigvee_{c\in CS(\lambda(q,i))} a_{c,q,i} \quad (6)$$

$$\bigwedge_{\substack{q,q'\in Q,\, i\in\mathbb{B}^I \\ \delta(q,i) \text{ is defined} \\ \delta(q',i) \text{ is defined}}} \bigwedge_{\substack{c\in CS(\lambda(q,i)) \\ c'\in CS(\lambda(q',i)) \\ c\cap c'=\emptyset}} (a_{c,q,i} \wedge a_{c',q',i}) \rightarrow \overline{sc_{q,q'}}. \quad (7)$$

Constraint (5) ensures that $sc_{q,q'}$ is true if there exists a class containing both q and q', in accordance with the expected definition.

Constraint (6) guarantees that at least one of the cubes in the output $\lambda(q,i)$ is active, causing the restricted output to be nonempty.

Constraint (7) expresses selective deactivation and only needs to be added for a given $q,q' \in Q$ and $i \in \mathbb{B}^I$ if $\delta(q,i)$ and $\delta(q',i)$ are properly defined. This formula guarantees that if there exists a class to which q and q' belong to (i.e., $sc_{q,q'}$ is true) but there also exist disjoint cubes in the partition of their respective outputs, then we deactivate at least one of these: only cubes that intersect can be both activated. Thus, this constraint guarantees the nonempty output condition.

Since encoding an output set requires a number of cubes exponential in $|O|$, the above encoding uses $O(|Q|(2^{|I|+|O|} + |Q|) + n^2 \cdot 2^{|I|})$ variables as well as $O(Q^2(n+2^{2|O|})+n^2\cdot 2^{|I|}+|\delta|(2^{|O|}+n^2))$ clauses. We use additional optimizations to limit the number of clauses, and make the algorithm more practical despite its frightening worst case. In particular the CEGAR approach of Sect. 3.3 strives to avoid introducing constraints (5)–(7).

3.3 Adjustment of Prior Optimizations

Constructing the SAT problem iteratively starting from $n = 1$ would be grossly inefficient. We can instead notice that two states that are not variations of each other can never be in the same class. Thus, assuming we can find k states that are not pairwise variations of one another, we can infer that we need at least as many classes as there are states in this set, providing a lower bound for n. This idea was first introduced in [1]; however, performing a more careful inspection of the constraints with respect to this "partial solution" allows us to reduce the number of constraints and literals needed.

The nonemptiness condition involves the creation of many literals and clauses and necessitates an expensive preprocessing step to decompose the arbitrary output sets returned by output function ($\lambda\colon (Q,\mathbb{B}^I) \rightarrow 2^{\mathbb{B}^O} \setminus \{\emptyset\}$) into disjunctions of cubes ($\lambda\colon (Q,\mathbb{B}^I) \rightarrow 2^{\mathbb{K}^O} \setminus \{\emptyset\}$). We avoid adding unnecessary nonempty output clauses in a counter-example guided fashion. Violation of these conditions can easily be detected before constructing the minimized machine. If detected, a small set of these constraints is added to SAT problem excluding this particular violation. In many cases, this optimization greatly reduces the number of literals and constraints needed, to the extent we can often avoid their use altogether.

From now on, we consider an IGMM with N states $Q = \{q_0, q_1, \ldots, q_{N-1}\}$.

Variation Matrix. We first need to determine which states are not pairwise variations of one another in order to extract a partial solution and perform simplifications on the constraints. We will compute a square matrix of size $N \times N$ called mat such that $\text{mat}[k][\ell] = 1$ if and only if $q_k \not\approx q_\ell$ in the following fashion:

1. Initialize all entries of mat to 0.
2. Iterate over all pairs (k, ℓ) with $0 \leq k < \ell < N$. If the entry $\text{mat}[k][\ell]$ is 0, check if $\exists i \in \mathbb{B}^I$ such that $\lambda(q_k, i) \cap \lambda(q_l, i) = \emptyset$. If it exists, $\text{mat}[k][\ell] \leftarrow 1$.
3. For all pairs (k, ℓ) whose associated value $\text{mat}[k][\ell]$ changed from 0 to 1, set all existing predecessor pairs (m, n) with $m < n$ under the same input to 1 as well, that is, $\exists i \in \mathbb{B}^I$ such that $\delta(q_m, i) = q_k$ and $\delta(q_n, n) = q_l$. Note that we may need to propagate these changes to the predecessors of (m, n).

As "being a variation of" is a symmetric, reflexive relation, we only compute the elements above the main diagonal of the matrix. The intuition behind this algorithm is that two states q and q' are not variations of one another if either:

- There exists an input symbol for which the output sets are disjoint.
- There exists a pair of states which are not variations of one another and that can be reached from q and q' under the same input sequence.

The complexity of this algorithm is $O(|Q|^2 \cdot 2^{|I|})$ if we assume that the disjointness of the output sets can be checked in constant time; see [1]. This assumption is not correct in general: testing disjointness for cubes has a complexity linear in the number of input propositions. On the other hand, testing disjointness for generalized Mealy machines that use arbitrary sets of valuations has a complexity exponential in the number of input propositions. This increased complexity is however counterbalanced by the succinctness the use of arbitrary sets allows.

As an example, given $2m$ output propositions $o_0, \ldots, o_{2m-1}$, consider the set of output valuations expressed as a disjunction of cubes $\bigvee_{0 \leq k < m} o_{2k} \overline{o_{2k+1}} \vee \overline{o_{2k}} o_{2k+1}$. Exponentially many *disjoint* cubes are needed to represent this set. Thus, a non-deterministic Mealy machine labeled by output cubes will incur an exponential number of computations performed in linear time, whereas a generalized Mealy machine will only perform a single test with exponential runtime.

Computing a Partial Solution. The partial solution corresponds to a set of states such that none of them is a variation of any other state in the set. Thus, none of these states can belong to the same (variation) class. The size of this set is therefore a lower bound for the number of states in the minimal machine.

Finding the largest partial solution is an NP-hard problem; we therefore use the greedy heuristic described in [1]. For each state q of M, we count the number of states q' such that q is not a variation of q'; call this number nvc_q. We then successively add to the partial solution the states that have the highest nvc_q but are not variations of any state already inserted.

CEGAR Approach to Ensure the Nonempty Output Condition. Assuming a solution satisfying the cover and closure constraints has already

Data: a machine $M = (I, O, Q, q_{init}, \delta, \lambda)$
Result: a minimal specialization M'
/* Computing the variation matrix   */
bool[][] mat ← isNotVariationOf(M);
/* Looking for a partial solution P   */
set P ← extractPartialSol(mat);
clauses ← empty list;
/* Using the lower bound inferred from P   */
for $n \leftarrow |P|$ to $|Q| - 1$ do
  addCoverCondition(clauses, M, P, mat, n);
  addClosureCondition(clauses, M, P, mat, n);
  /* Solving the cover and closure conditions   */
  (sat, solution) ← satSolver(clauses);
  while *sat* **do**
    if *verifyNonEmpty(M, solution)* **then**
    $\quad$ ⌊ **return** buildMachine(M, solution);
    /* Adding the relevant nonemptiness clauses   */
    addNonemptinessCondition(clauses, M, solution);
    (sat, solution) ← satSolver(clauses);

/* If no solution has been found, return M   */
return copyMachine(M);

Algorithm 1: SAT-based minimization

been found, we then need to check if said solution satisfies the nonempty output condition. If this is indeed the case, we can then construct and return a minimal machine.

If the condition is not satisfied, we look for one or more combinations of classes and input symbols such that $\text{Succ}(C_k, i) = \emptyset$. We add for the states in C_k and the input symbol i the constraints described in Sect. 3.2, and for these states and input symbols only. Then we check if the problem is still satisfiable.

If it is not, then we need to increase the number of classes to find a valid solution. If it is, the solution either respects Condition (7) and we can return a minimal machine, or it does not and the process of selectively adding constraints is repeated. Either way, this *counter-example guided abstraction refinement* (CEGAR) scheme ensures termination, as the problem is either shown to be unsatisfiable or solved through iterative exclusion of all violations of Condition (7).

3.4 Algorithm

The optimizations described previously yield Algorithm 1.

Further Optimizations and Comparison to MeMin. The proposed algorithm relies on the general approach outline in [1], as well as the SAT encoding for the cover and closure conditions. We find a partial solution by using a similar heuristic and adapt some optimizations found in their source code, which are neither detailed in their paper nor here due to a lack of space.

The main difference lies in the increased expressiveness of the input and output symbols that causes some significant changes. In particular, we added the nonemptiness condition to guarantee correctness, as well as a CEGAR-based implementation to maintain performance. Other improvements mainly stem from a better usage of the partial solution.

For instance, each state q of the partial solution is associated to "its own" class C_j. Since the matching literal $s_{q,j}$ is trivially true, it can be omitted by replacing all its occurrences by true. States belonging to the partial solution have other peculiarities that can be leveraged to reduce the number of possible successor classes, further reducing the amount of literals and clauses needed.

We therefore require fewer literals and clauses, trading a more complex construction of the SAT problem for a reduced memory footprint. The impact of these improvements is detailed in Sect. 5.

The Mealy machine described by [1] come in two flavors: One with an explicit initial state and a second one where all states are considered to be possible initial states. While our approach does explicit an initial state, it does not further influence the resulting minimal machine when all original states are reachable.

4   Bisimulation with Output Assignment

We introduce in this section another approach tailored to our primary use case, that is, efficient reduction of control strategies in the context of reactive synthesis. This technique, based on the $\sqsubseteq$ specialization relation, yields non-minimal but "relatively small" machines at significantly reduced runtimes.

Given two states q and q' such that $q' \sqsubseteq q$, one idea is to restrict the possible outputs of q to match those of q'. Concretely, for all inputs $i \in \mathbb{B}^I$, we restrict $\lambda(q, i)$ to its subset $\lambda(q', i)$; q and q' thus become bisimilar, allowing us to merge them. In practice, rather than restricting the output first then reducing bisimilar states to their quotient, we instead directly build a machine that is minimal with respect to $\sqsubseteq$ where all transitions going to q are redirected to q'.

Note that if two states q and q' are bisimilar, then necessarily $q' \sqsubseteq q$ and $q \sqsubseteq q'$: therefore, both states will be merged by our approach. As a consequence, the resulting machine is always smaller than the bisimulation quotient of the original machine (as shown in Sect. 5).

4.1   Reducing Machines with $\sqsubseteq$

Our algorithm builds upon the following theorem:

Theorem 2. *Let $M = (I, O, Q, q_{init}, \delta, \lambda)$ be an IGMM, and $r : Q \to Q$ be a mapping satisfying $r(q) \sqsubseteq q$. Define $M' = (I, O, Q', q'_{init}, \delta', \lambda)$ as an IGMM where $Q' = r(Q)$, $q'_{init} = r(q_{init})$ and $\delta'(q, i) = r(\delta(q, i))$ for all states q and input i. Then M' is a specialization of M.*

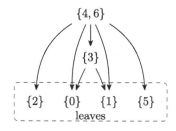

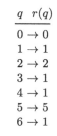

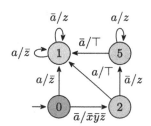

Fig. 3. Specialization graph of the IGMM of Fig. 2a

Fig. 4. Chosen representative mapping.

Fig. 5. IGMM obtained by reducing that of Fig. 2a

Intuitively, if a state q is remapped to a state $q' \sqsubseteq q$, then the set of words w that can be output for an input i is simply reduced to a subset of the original output. The smaller the image $r(Q)$, the more significant the reduction performed on the machine. Thus, to find a suitable function r, we map each state q to one of the *minimal elements* of the $\sqsubseteq$ preorder, also called the *representative states*.

Definition 8 (Specialization graph). *A* specialization graph *of an IGMM* $M = (I, O, Q, q_{init}, \delta, \lambda)$ *is the* condensation graph *of the directed graph representing the relation* $\sqsubseteq$*: the vertices of the specialization graph are sets that form a partition of Q such that two states q and q' belong to the same vertex if $q \sqsubseteq q'$ and $q' \sqsubseteq q$; there is an edge* $\{q_1, q_2, ...\} \longrightarrow \{q'_1, q'_2, ...\}$ *if and only if $q'_i \sqsubseteq q_j$ for some (or equivalently all) i, j. Note that this graph is necessarily acyclic.*

Figure 3 shows the specialization graph associated to the machine of Fig. 2a.

Definition 9 (Representative of a state). *Given two states q and q' of an IGMM, q' is a* representative *of q if, in the specialization graph of M, q' belongs to a leaf that can be reached from the vertex containing q. In other words, q' is a representative of q if $q' \sqsubseteq q$ and q' is a minimal element of the $\sqsubseteq$ preorder.*

Note that any state has at least one representative. In Fig. 3 we see that 0 represents 0, 3, 4, and 6. States 3, 4, and 6 can be represented by 0 or 1.

By picking one state in each leaf, we obtain a set of representative states that cover all states of the IGMM. We then apply Theorem 2 to a function r that maps each state to its representative in this cover. In Fig. 3, all leaves are singletons, so the set $\{0, 1, 2, 5\}$ contains representatives for all states. Applying Theorem 2 using r from Fig. 4 yields the machine shown in Fig. 5. Note that while this machine is smaller than the original, it is still bigger than the minimal machine of Fig. 2b, as this approach does not appraise the variation relation $\approx$.

4.2 Implementing $\sqsubseteq$

We now introduce an effective decision procedure for $q \sqsubseteq q'$. Note that $\sqsubseteq$ can be defined recursively like a simulation relation. Assuming, without loss of generality, that the IGMM is input-complete, $\sqsubseteq$ is the coarsest relation satisfying:

$$q' \sqsubseteq q \implies \forall i \in \mathbb{B}^I, \begin{cases} \lambda(q', i) \subseteq \lambda(q, i) \\ \delta(q', i) \sqsubseteq \delta(q, i) \end{cases}$$

As a consequence, $\sqsubseteq$ can be decided using any technique that is suitable for computing simulation relations [6,7]. Our implementation relies on a straightforward adaptation of the technique of signatures described by Babiak et al. [4, Sec. 4.2]: for each state q, we compute its *signature* $\mathrm{sig}(q)$, that is, a Boolean formula (represented as a BDD) encoding the outgoing transitions of that state such that $\mathrm{sig}(q) \Rightarrow \mathrm{sig}(q')$ if and only if $q \sqsubseteq q'$. Using these signatures, it becomes easy to build the *specialization graph* and derive a remapping function r.

Note that, even if $\sqsubseteq$ can be computed like a simulation, we do not use it to build a bisimulation quotient. The remapping applied in Thorem 2 does not correspond to the quotient of M by the equivalence relation induced by $\sqsubseteq$.

5 Benchmarks

The two approaches described in Sects. 3 and 4 have been implemented within Spot 2.10 [5], a toolbox for ω-automata manipulation, and used in our Synt-Comp'21 submission [15]. The following benchmarks are based on a development version of Spot[1] that features efficient variation checks (verifying whether $q \approx q'$) thanks to an improved representation of cubes.

We benchmark the two proposed approaches against MeMin, against a simple bisimulation-based approach, and against one another. The MeMin tool has already been shown [1] to be superior to existing tools like Bica [13], Stamina [16], and Cosme [3]; we are not aware of more recent contenders. For this reason, we only compare our approaches to MeMin.

In a similar manner to Abel and Reineke [1], we use the ISM benchmarks [10] as well as the MCNC benchmark suite [17]. These benchmarks share a severe drawback: they only feature very small instances. MeMin is able to solve any of these instances in less than a second. We therefore extend the set of benchmarks with our main use-cases: Mealy machines corresponding to control strategies obtained from SYNTCOMP LTL specifications [9].

As mentioned in Sect. 2, MeMin processes Mealy machines, encoded using the KISS2 input format [17], whose output can be chosen from a cube. However, the IGMM formalism we promote allows an arbitrary set of output valuations instead. This is particularly relevant for the SYNTCOMP benchmark, as the LTL specifications from which the sample's Mealy machines are derived often fail to fully specify the output. In order to (1) show the benefits of the generalized

---

[1] For instructions to reproduce, see https://www.lrde.epita.fr/~philipp/forte22/.

formalism while (2) still allowing comparisons with MEMIN, we prepared two versions of each SYNTCOMP input: the "full" version features arbitrary sets of output valuations that cannot be processed by MEMIN, while in the "cube" version said sets have been replaced by the first cube produced by the Minato algorithm [11] on the original output set. The ACM and MCNC benchmarks, on the other hand, already use a single output cube in the first place.

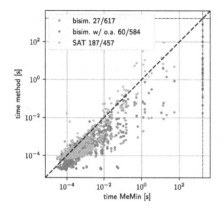

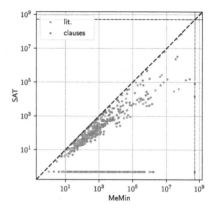

Fig. 6. Log-log plot of runtimes. The legend a/b stands for a cases above diagonal, and b below.

Fig. 7. Comparison of the number of literals and clauses in the encodings.

Figure 6 displays a log-log plot comparing our different methods to MEMIN, using only the "cube" instances.[2] The label "*bisim. w/ o.a.*" refers to the approach outlined in Sect. 4, "*bisim.*", to a simple bisimulation quotient, and "*SAT*", to the approach of Sect. 3. Points on the black diagonal stand for cases where MEMIN and the method being tested had equal runtime; cases above this line favor MEMIN, while cases below favor the aforementioned methods. Points on the dotted line at the edges of the figure represent timeouts. Only MEMIN fails this way, on 10 instances. Figure 7 compares the maximal number of literals and clauses used to perform the SAT-based minimization by MEMIN or by our implementation. These two figures only describe "cube" instances, as MEMIN needs to be able to process the sample machines.

To study the benefits of our IGMM model's generic outputs, Table 1 compares the relative reduction ratios achieved by the various methods w.r.t. other methods as well as the original and minimal size of the sample machines. We use the "full" inputs everywhere with the exception of MEMIN.

Interpretation. Reduction via bisimulation solves all instances and has been proven to be by far the fastest method (Fig. 6), but also the coarsest, with a mere

---

[2] A 30 min timeout was enforced for all instances. The benchmarks were run on an Asus G14 with a Ryzen 4800HS CPU with 16GB of RAM and no swap.

Table 1. Statistics about our three reduction algorithms. The leftmost pane counts the number of instances where algorithm (y) yields a smaller result than algorithm (x); as an example, bisimulation with output assignment (2) outperforms standard bisimulation (1) in 249 cases. The middle pane presents mean (avg.) and median (md.) size ratios relative to the original size and the minimal size of the sample machines. The rightmost pane presents similar statistics while ignoring all instances that were already minimal in the first place.

	>(1)	>(2)	>(3)	>(4)	$\frac{size}{orig}$ avg. md.	$\frac{size}{min}$ avg. md.	$\frac{size}{orig}$ avg. md.	$\frac{size}{min}$ avg. md.
original	114	304	271	314	1.00 1.0	6.56 1.0	1.00 1.00	12.23 1.77
(1) bisim (full)		249	214	275	0.94 1.0	1.85 1.0	0.88 1.00	2.72 1.50
(2) bisim w/ o.a. (full)	0		68	84	0.83 1.0	1.55 1.0	0.66 0.67	2.10 1.00
(3) MEMIN (minimal cube)	74	0		77	0.81 1.0	1.13 1.0	0.63 0.69	1.27 1.00
(4) SAT (full)	0	0	0	0	0.77 1.0	1.00 1.0	0.54 0.56	1.00 1.00

all 634 instances without timeout | 314 non-minimal instances without timeout

0.94 reduction ratio (Table 1). Bisimulation with output assignment achieves a better reduction ratio of 0.83, very close to MEMIN's 0.81.

In most cases, the proposed SAT-based approaches remain significantly slower than approaches based on bisimulation (Fig. 6). Our SAT-based algorithm is sometimes slower than MEMIN's, as the model's increased expressiveness requires a more complex method. However, improving the use of partial solutions and increasing the expressiveness of the input symbols significantly reduce the size of the encoding of the intermediate SAT problems featured in our method (Fig. 7), hence, achieve a lower memory footprint. Points on the horizontal line at the bottom of Fig. 7 correspond to instances that have already been proven minimal, since the partial solution is equal to the entire set of states: in these cases, no further reduction is required.

Finally, the increased expressiveness of our model results in significantly smaller minimal machines, as shown by the 1.27 reduction ratio of MEMIN's cube-based machines compared to the minimisation of generic IGMMs derived from the same specification. There are also 74 cases where this superior expressiveness allows the bisimulation with output assignment to beat MEMIN.

6   Conclusion

We introduced a generalized model for incompletely specified Mealy machines, whose output is an arbitrary choice between multiple possible valuations. We have presented two reduction techniques on this model, and compared them against the state-of-the-art minimization tool MEMIN (where the output choices are restricted to a cube).

The first technique is a SAT-based approach inspired by MeMin [1] that yields a minimal machine. Thanks to this generalized model and an improved use of the partial solution, we use substantially fewer clauses and literals.

The second technique yields a reduced yet not necessarily minimal machine by relying on the notion of state specialization. Compared to the SAT-based approach, this technique offers a good compromise between the time spent performing the reduction, and the actual state-space reduction, especially for the cases derived from SYNTCOMP from which our initial motivation originated.

Both techniques are implemented in Spot 2.10. They have been used in our entry to the 2021 Synthesis Competition [15]. Spot comes with Python bindings that make it possible to experiment with these techniques and compare their respective effects[3].

References

1. Abel, A., Reineke, J.: MeMin: SAT-based exact minimization of incompletely specified Mealy machines. In: ICCAD 2015, pp. 94–101. IEEE Press (2015)
2. Alberto, A., Simao, A.: Minimization of incompletely specified finite state machines based on distinction graphs. In: LATW 2009, pp. 1–6. IEEE (2009)
3. Alberto, A., Simao, A.: Iterative minimization of partial finite state machines. Open Comput. Sci. 3(2), 91–103 (2013). https://doi.org/10.2478/s13537-013-0106-0
4. Babiak, T., Badie, T., Duret-Lutz, A., Křetínský, M., Strejček, J.: Compositional approach to suspension and other improvements to LTL translation. In: Bartocci, E., Ramakrishnan, C.R. (eds.) SPIN 2013. LNCS, vol. 7976, pp. 81–98. Springer, Heidelberg (2013). https://doi.org/10.1007/978-3-642-39176-7_6
5. Duret-Lutz, A., Lewkowicz, A., Fauchille, A., Michaud, T., Renault, É., Xu, L.: Spot 2.0 — a framework for LTL and ω-automata manipulation. In: Artho, C., Legay, A., Peled, D. (eds.) ATVA 2016. LNCS, vol. 9938, pp. 122–129. Springer, Cham (2016). https://doi.org/10.1007/978-3-319-46520-3_8
6. Etessami, K., Holzmann, G.J.: Optimizing Büchi Automata. In: Palamidessi, C. (ed.) CONCUR 2000. LNCS, vol. 1877, pp. 153–168. Springer, Heidelberg (2000). https://doi.org/10.1007/3-540-44618-4_13
7. Henzinger, M., Henzinger, T., Kopke, P.: Computing simulations on finite and infinite graphs. In: Proceedings of the 36th Symposium on Foundations of Computer Science, pp. 453–462 (1995)
8. Hopcroft, J.: An $n \log n$ algorithm for minimizing states in a finite automaton. In: Proceedings of an International Symposium on the Theory of Machines and Computations, pp. 189–196. Academic Press (1971)
9. Jacobs, S., Bloem, R.: The 5th reactive synthesis competition-SYNTCOMP 2018 (2020)
10. Kam, T., Villa, T., Brayton, R., Sangiovanni-Vincentelli, A.: A fully implicit algorithm for exact state minimization. In: 31st Design Automation Conference, pp. 684–690. IEEE (1994)
11. Minato, S.: Fast generation of irredundant sum-of-products forms from binary decision diagrams. In: SASIMI 1992, pp. 64–73 (1992)

---

[3] See: https://spot.lrde.epita.fr/ipynb/synthesis.html.

12. Paull, M.C., Unger, S.H.: Minimizing the number of states in incompletely specified sequential switching functions. IRE Trans. Electron. Comput. **EC-8**(3), 356–367 (1959)
13. Pena, J., Oliveira, A.: A new algorithm for exact reduction of incompletely specified finite state machines. IEEE Trans. Comput. Aided Des. Integr. Circuits Syst. **18**(11), 1619–1632 (1999)
14. Pfleeger, C.P.: State reduction in incompletely specified finite-state machines. IEEE Trans. Comput. **C-22**(12), 1099–1102 (1973)
15. Renkin, F., Schlehuber, P., Duret-Lutz, A., Pommellet, A.: Improvements to ltlsynt. Presented at the SYNT 2021 Workshop, without Proceedings, July 2021. https://www.lrde.epita.fr/~adl/dl/adl/renkin.21.synt.pdf
16. Rho, J.-K., Hachtel, G., Somenzi, F., Jacoby, R.: Exact and heuristic algorithms for the minimization of incompletely specified state machines. IEEE Trans. Comput. Aided Des. Integr. Circuits Syst. **13**(2), 167–177 (1994)
17. Yang, S.: Logic synthesis and optimization benchmarks user guide: version 3.0. Citeseer (1991)

Traits: Correctness-by-Construction for Free

Tobias Runge[1,2]([⊠]), Alex Potanin[3]([⊠]), Thomas Thüm[4]([⊠]), and Ina Schaefer[1,2]([⊠])

[1] TU Braunschweig, Braunschweig, Germany
[2] Karlsruhe Institute of Technology, Karlsruhe, Germany
`{tobias.runge,ina.schaefer}@kit.edu`
[3] Australian National University, Canberra, Australia
`alex.potanin@anu.edu.au`
[4] University of Ulm, Ulm, Germany
`thomas.thuem@uni-ulm.de`

Abstract. We demonstrate that traits are a natural way to support correctness-by-construction (CbC) in an existing programming language in the presence of traditional post-hoc verification (PhV). With Correctness-by-Construction, programs are constructed incrementally along with a specification that is inherently guaranteed to be satisfied. CbC is complex to use without specialized tool support, since it needs a set of refinement rules of fixed granularity which are additional rules on top of the programming language.

In this work, we propose TraitCbC, an incremental program construction procedure that implements correctness-by-construction on the basis of PhV by using traits. TraitCbC enables program construction by trait composition instead of refinement rules. It provides a programming guideline, which similar to CbC should lead to well-structured programs, and allows flexible reuse of verified program building blocks. We introduce TraitCbC formally and prove the soundness of our verification strategy. Additionally, we implement TraitCbC as a proof of concept.

1 Introduction

Correctness-by-Construction (CbC) [19,22,30,37] is a methodology that incrementally constructs correct programs guided by a pre-/postcondition specification.[1] CbC uses small tractable refinement rules where in each refinement step, an abstract statement (i.e., a hole in the program) is refined to a more concrete implementation that can still contain some nested abstract statements. While

---

[1] The approach should not be confused with other CbC approaches such as CbyC of Hall and Chapman [24]. CbyC is a software development process that uses formal modeling techniques and analysis for various stages of development (architectural design, detailed design, code) to detect and eliminate defects as early as possible [13]. We also exclude data refinement from abstract data types to concrete ones during code generation as for example in Isabelle/HOL [23].

M. R. Mousavi and A. Philippou (Eds.): FORTE 2022, LNCS 13273, pp. 131–150, 2022.
https://doi.org/10.1007/978-3-031-08679-3_9

refining the program, the correctness of the whole program is guaranteed through the check of conditions in the refinement rules. The construction ends when no abstract statement is left. Through the structured reasoning discipline that is enforced by the refinement rules, it is claimed that program quality increases and verification effort is reduced [30,50].

Despite these benefits, CbC has a drawback: the refinement rules extend the programming language (i.e., refinements are an additional linguistic construct to transform programs). Special tool support [42] is necessary to introduce the CbC refinement process to a programming language. Additionally, the predefined rules have a fine granularity such that for every new statement the programmer adds to the program, an application of a refinement rule is necessary. Consequently, the concepts of CbC (e.g., abstract statements and refinement rules) increase the effort and necessary knowledge of the developer to construct programs.

Post-hoc verification (PhV) is another approach to develop correct programs. A method is verified against its pre- and postconditions after implementation. In practice, it often happens that a program is constructed first, with the objective of verifying it later [50]. This can lead to tedious verification work if the program is not well-structured. An example is the difficult search for the many reasons preventing the verification of a method to be completed: an incorrect specification, an incorrect method, or inadequate tool support. Therefore, a structured programming approach is desirable to construct programs which are amenable to software verification.

In this work, we use *traits* [20] to overcome the drawbacks of CbC (complex programming style using external refinement rules) and introduce a programming guideline for an incremental trait-based program construction approach that guarantees that the resulting trait-based program is correct-by-construction. TraitCbC is based on PhV. With TraitCbC, the same programs can be verified as with PhV, but in addition, TraitCbC introduces an explicit program construction approach. It utilizes the flexibility of traits, which is beneficial for scenarios as incremental development [18] and the development of software product lines [10,15].

Traits [20] are a flexible object-oriented language construct supporting a rich form of modular code reuse orthogonal to inheritance. A trait contains a set of *concrete* or *abstract* methods (i.e., the method has either a body or has no body), independent of any class or inheritance hierarchy.[2] Traits are independent modules that can be composed into larger traits or classes. When traits are composed, the resulting code contains all methods of all composed traits. To verify traits, Damiani et al. [18] proposed a modular and incremental *post-hoc verification* process. Each method in every trait is verified in isolation by showing that the method satisfies its *contract* [35]. Then, during the composition of traits, it has to be checked whether a method implemented in one trait is compatible with the abstract method with the same signature in another trait. That means,

---

[2] The term trait has been used by many programming languages: Java interfaces with default methods are a good approximation for what has been called trait in the literature, while Scala traits are mixins [21], and Rust traits are type classes [46].

a concrete method has to satisfy the specification of the abstract method. A concrete method with a weaker precondition and a stronger postcondition fulfills the contract of the abstract method (cf. Liskov substitution principle [34]).

A developer using TraitCbC starts by implementing a method (e.g., a method a) in a first trait. Similar to CbC, the method can contain holes that are refined in subsequent steps. A hole in TraitCbC is an abstract method (e.g., an abstract method b) that is called in method a; that is, a call to an abstract method corresponds to an abstract statement in CbC. In the next step, one of these new abstract methods (e.g., b) is implemented in a second trait, again more abstract methods can be declared for the implementation. Similar to PhV, it must be proven that the implemented methods satisfy their specifications. Afterwards, the traits are composed; the composition operation checks that the contract of the concrete method b in the second trait fulfills the contract of the abstract method b in the first trait. This incremental process stops when the last abstract method is implemented, and all traits are composed.

The main result of our work is the discovery that traits intrinsically enable correctness-by-construction. This work is not about pushing verification forward in the sense of adding more expressive power. TraitCbC realizes a refinement-based program development approach using pre-/postcondition contracts and method calls instead of refinement rules and abstract statements as in CbC. Refinement rules in the form of trait composition exist as a direct concept of the programming language instead of being a program transformation concept. Additionally, each method implemented in the refinement process can be reused by composing traits in different contexts (i.e., already proven methods can be called by new methods under construction). This is advantageous compared to the limited reuse potential of methods in class-based inheritance. Finally, TraitCbC is parametric w.r.t. the specification logic. Thus, a language with traits can adopt the proposed CbC methodology.

2 Motivating Example

In this section, we go through an example of how our development process enables CbC using traits.

Incremental Construction of MaxElement. We use a sample object-oriented language in the code examples. We construct a method `maxElement` that finds the maximum element in a list of numbers. A list has a head and a tail. Only non-empty lists have a maximum element. This is explicit in the precondition of our specification, where we require that the list has at least one element. In the postcondition, we specify that the result is in the list and larger than or equal to every other element. A method `contains` checks that the result is a member of the list. In the first step, we create a trait `MaxETrait1` that defines the abstract method `maxElement`. The method `maxElement` is abstract, i.e., equivalent to an abstract statement in CbC.

```
1   trait MaxETrait1 {
2     @Pre: list.size() > 0
3     @Post: list.contains(result) &
4       (forall Num n: list.contains(n) ==> result >= n)
5     abstract Num maxElement(List list);
6   }
```

In the second step in trait `MaxETrait2`, we implement the method `maxElement` using two abstract methods. We introduce an `if-elseif-else`-expression where the branches invoke abstract methods. The guards check whether the list has only one element or whether the current element is larger than or equal to the maximum of the rest of the list. The abstract method `accessHead` returns the current element, and the abstract method `maxTail` returns the maximum in the remaining list. So, we recursively search the list for the largest element by comparing the maximum element of the list tail with the current element until we reach the end of the list.

```
1   trait MaxETrait2 {
2     @Pre: list.size() > 0
3     @Post: list.contains(result) &
4       (forall Num n: list.contains(n) ==> result >= n)
5     Num maxElement(List list) =
6       if (list.size() == 1) {accessHead(list)}
7       elseif (accessHead(list) >= maxTail(list))
8         {accessHead(list)}
9       else {maxTail(list)}
10
11    @Pre: list.size() > 0
12    @Post: result == list.element()
13    abstract Num accessHead(List list);
14
15    @Pre: list.size() > 1
16    @Post: list.tail().contains(result) &
17      (forall Num n: list.tail().contains(n) ==> result >= n)
18    abstract Num maxTail(List list);
19  }
```

The correct implementation of the method `maxElement` can be guaranteed under the assumptions that all introduced abstract methods are correctly implemented. Similar to PhV, a program verifier conducts a proof of method `maxElement` and uses the introduced specifications of the methods `accessHead` and `maxTail`. When the proof succeeds, we know that the first method is correctly implemented. In our incremental CbCTrait process, we verify each method implementation directly after construction; and so we are able to reuse each implemented method in the following steps (e.g., by calling the method in the body of other methods).

We now compose the developed traits to complete the first refinement step. To perform the composition `MaxETrait1 + MaxETrait2`, we check that the specification of the method `maxElement` fulfills the specification of the abstract method in the first trait (cf. Liskov substitution principle [34]). In this case, this means checking that:
`MaxETrait1.maxElement(..).pre ==> MaxETrait2.maxElement(..).pre` as well as:
`MaxETrait2.maxElement(..).post ==> MaxETrait1.maxElement(..).post`.
When the composition of two verified traits is successful, the result is also a verified trait. Note that the composed trait does not need to be verified directly by a program verifier in TraitCbC because it is correct by construction. In this example, the specifications are the same, thus checking for a successful composition is trivial, but this is

not generally the case. In particular, the logic needs to take into account ill-founded specifications and recursion in the specification. We discuss the difficulties of handling those cases in the technical report [41].

The methods `accessHead` and `maxTail` are implemented in the next two refinement steps in traits `MaxETrait3` and `MaxETrait4`[3]. As we implement a recursive method, the method `maxTail` calls the `maxElement` method, thus `maxElement` is introduced as an abstract method in this trait. We have to verify that the method `accessHead` satisfies its specification using a program verifier. Similarly, we have to verify the correctness of the method `maxTail`.

```
1   trait MaxETrait3 {
2     @Pre: list.size() > 0
3     @Post: result == list.element()
4     Num accessHead(List list) = list.element()
5   }
```

```
1    trait MaxETrait4 {
2      @Pre: list.size() > 1
3      @Post: list.tail().contains(result) &
4        (forall Num n: list.tail().contains(n) ==> result >= n)
5      Num maxTail(List list) = maxElement(list.tail())
6
7      @Pre: list.size() > 0
8      @Post: list.contains(result) &
9        (forall Num n: list.contains(n) ==> result >= n)
10     abstract Num maxElement(List list);
11   }
```

As before, all traits are composed, and it is checked that the specifications of the concrete methods fulfill the specifications of the abstract ones. As we have no contradicting specifications for the same methods, the composition is well-formed. The final program `MaxE` is as follows.

```
1    class MaxE = MaxETrait1 + MaxETrait2 + MaxETrait3 + MaxETrait4
```

Advantages of TraitCbC. As shown in the example, TraitCbC enables the CbC programming style without the need of external refinement rules. In classical CbC, when designing a unit of code, the programmer has to proceed with atomic steps of a predefined granularity. In contrast, in TraitCbC the programmer is free to divide a unit of code in any granularity, by including as many auxiliary methods as needed to bring the verification to an appropriate granularity. TraitCbC helps to construct code in fine-grained steps which are more amenable for verification than single more complex methods. If the programmer chooses to not include any auxiliary methods at all, this is essentially the same as the traditional post-hoc verification style. In the example above, we could implement the method `maxElement` in one step without the intermediate step that introduces the two abstract methods `accessHead` and `maxTail`.

Additionally, the already proven auxiliary methods in traits can be reused. For example, if we want to implement a `minElement` method, we could reuse already implemented traits to reduce the programming and verification effort. The method `minElement` is implemented in the following in trait `MinE` with one abstract method.

---

[3] The methods could also be implemented in one trait.

The specification of the method `accessHead` is the same as for the method `accessHead` above, so `MaxETrait3` can be reused. In this example, we show the flexible granularity of TraitCbC by directly implementing the else branch, instead of introducing an auxiliary method as for `maxElement`.

```
1   trait MinE {
2       @Pre: list.size() > 0
3       @Post: list.contains(result) &
4           (forall Num n: list.contains(n) ==> result <= n)
5       Num minElement(List list) =
6           if (list.size() == 1) {accessHead(list)}
7           elseif (accessHead(list) <= minElement(list.tail()))
8               {accessHead(list)}
9           else {minElement(list.tail())}
10
11      @Pre: list.size() > 0
12      @Post: result == list.element()
13      abstract Num accessHead(List list);
14  }
```

The correctness of `minElement` is verified with the specifications of the method `accessHead`. By composing `MinE` with `MaxETrait3`, we get a correct implementation of `minElement`. Note how this verification process supports abstraction: as long as the contracts are compatible, methods can be implemented in different styles by different programmers to best meet non-functional requirements while preserving the specified observable behavior [9]. A completely different implementation of `maxElement` can be used if it fulfills the specification of the abstract method `maxElement` in trait `MaxETrait1`. This decoupling of specification and corresponding satisfying implementations facilitates an incremental development process where a specified code base is extended with suitable implementations [18].

3   Object-Oriented Trait-Based Language

In this section, we formally introduce the syntax, type system, and flattening semantics of a minimal core calculus for TraitCbC. We keep this calculus for TraitCbC parametric in the specification logic so that it can be used with a suitable program verifier and associated logic. The presented rules to compose traits are conventional. The focus of our work is to enable a CbC approach using traits that programmers can easily adopt. Therefore, we present the calculus to prove soundness of TraitCbC, but focus on the presentation of the advantages of incremental trait-based programming in this paper. Indeed, languages with traits and with a suitable specification language intrinsically enable incremental program construction. For the sake of completeness, reduction rules of TraitCbC are presented in the technical report [41].

3.1   Syntax

The concrete syntax of our core calculus for TraitCbC is shown in Fig. 1, where nonterminals ending with 's' are implicitly defined as a sequence of non-terminals, i.e., $vs ::= v_1 \ldots v_n$. We use the metavariables t for trait names, C for class names and m for method names. A program consists of trait and class definitions. Each definition has a name and a trait expression E. The trait expression can be a *Body*, a trait name, a composition of two trait expressions E, or a trait expression E where a method is made abstract, written as $E[\texttt{makeAbstract } m]$. A *Body* has a flag $\texttt{interface}$ to define an interface, a set of implemented interfaces Cs and a list of methods Ms. Methods have a method header MH consisting of a specification S, the return type, a method name, and a list of parameters. Methods have an optional method body. In the method body, we have standard expressions, such as variable references, method calls, and object initializations. For simplicity, we exclude updatable state. Field declarations are emulated by method declarations, and field accesses are emulated by method calls.

The specification S in each method header is used to verify that methods are correctly implemented. The specification is written in some logic. In our examples, we will use first-order logic (cf. the example in Sect. 2). A well-formed program respects the following conditions:

Every *Name* in Ds must be unique so that Ds can be seen as a map from names to trait expressions. Trait expressions E can refer to trait names t. A well-formed Ds does not have any circular trait definitions like $t = t$ or $t_1 = t_2$ and $t_2 = t_1$. In a *Body*, all names of implemented interfaces must be unique and all method names must be unique, so that *Body* is a map from method names to method definitions. In a method header, parameters must have unique names, and no explicit parameter can be called $\texttt{this}$.

3.2   Typing Rules

In our type system, we have a typing context $\Gamma ::= x_1 : C_1 \ldots x_n : C_n$ which assigns types C_i to variables x_i. We define typing rules for our three kinds of expressions: x, method calls, and object initialization. We combine typing and verification in our type checking $\Gamma \vdash e : C \dashv P_0 \models P_1$. This judgment can be read as: under typing context Γ, the expression e has type C, where under the knowledge P_0 we need to prove P_1. The knowledge P_0 is our collected information that we use to prove a method correct. That means, in our typing rules, we collect the knowledge about the parameters and expressions in a method body to verify that this method body fulfills the specification defined in the method header. The verification obligation P_1 should follow from the knowledge P_0.

We check if methods are well-typed with judgments of form $Ds; Name \vdash M : OK$. This judgment can be read as: in the definition table, the method M defined under the definition *Name* is correct. The typing rules of Fig. 2 are explained in the technical report [41] in detail. The first four rules type different expressions and collect the information of these expressions to prove with rule MOK that a method fulfills its specification. In the rule MOK with keyword **verify**, we call a verifier to prove each method once. Abstract methods (ABSOK) are always correct. Rule BODYOK ensures that all methods in a body are correctly typed.

3.3   Flattening Semantics

When we implement methods in several traits, we have to check that these traits are compatible when they are composed. This process to derive a complete class from a set of traits is called flattening. We follow the traditional flattening semantics [20]. A class that is defined by composing several traits is obtained by flattening rules. All methods are direct members of the class [20]. Overall, our flattening process works as

$$
\begin{array}{lll}
Prog & ::= & Ds\ e \\
D & ::= & TD \mid CD \\
Name & ::= & t \mid C \\
TD & ::= & t = E \\
CD & ::= & C = E \\
E & ::= & Body \mid t \mid E + E \mid E[\texttt{makeAbstract}\ m] \\
Body & ::= & \{\texttt{interface?}\ [Cs]\ Ms\} \\
M & ::= & MH\ e?; \\
MH & ::= & S\ \texttt{method}\ C\ m(C_1\ x_1 \ldots C_n\ x_n) \\
e & ::= & x \mid e.m(es) \mid \texttt{new}\ C(es) \\
\mathcal{E}_v & ::= & [].m(es) \mid v.m(vs\ []\ es) \mid \texttt{new}\ C(vs\ []\ es) \\
v & ::= & \texttt{new}\ C(vs) \\
\Gamma & ::= & x_1 : C_1 \ldots x_n : C_n \\
S & ::= & \ldots e.g.\ \textbf{Pre} : P\ \textbf{Post} : P \\
P & ::= & \ldots e.g.\ \text{First order logic}
\end{array}
$$

Fig. 1. Syntax of the trait system

a big step reduction arrow, where we reduce a trait expression into a well-typed and verified body.

To introduce our flattening rules in Fig. 3, we first define the helper functions. The function *allMeth* collects all method headers with the same name as m in all input bodies (Definition 1). When two *Body*s are composed (Definition 2), the implemented interfaces are united and the methods are composed. The composition of methods (Definition 3) collects methods that are only defined in one of the input sets. If a method is in both sets, it is composed (Definition 4). Here, we distinguish four cases. If one method is abstract and the other is concrete, we have to show that the precondition of the abstract method implies the precondition of the concrete method. Additionally, the postcondition of the concrete one has to imply the postcondition of the abstract one. This is similar to Liskov's substitution principle [34]. The second case is the symmetric variant of the first case. In the third and fourth case, two abstract methods are composed. Here, the specification of one abstract method has to imply the specification of the other abstract method such that an implementation can still satisfy all specifications of abstract methods. If both method are concrete, the composition is correctly left undefined. This composition error can be resolved by making one method m abstract in the *Body*, as defined in Definition 5. The resulting *Body* is similar with the difference that the implementation of the method m is omitted. The flattening rules in Fig. 3 are explained in the following in detail. In these rules, a set of traits is flattened to a declaration containing all methods. If abstract and concrete methods with the same name are composed, Definitions 2–4 are used to guarantee correctness of the composition.

Definition 1 (All Methods). *allMeth*$(m,\ Bodys) =$
$\{MH;\ \mid\ Body\ \in\ Bodys,\ Body(m) = MH;\ \}$

Definition 2 (Body Composition). $Body_1 + Body_2 = Body$
$\{\texttt{interface?}\ [Cs_1]\ Ms_1\} + \{\texttt{interface?}\ [Cs_1]\ Ms_1\} =$
$\{\texttt{interface?}\ [Cs_1\ \cup\ Cs_2]\ Ms_1 + Ms_2\}$

$$\frac{}{\Gamma \vdash x : \Gamma(x) \dashv \texttt{result} : \Gamma(x) \ \& \ \texttt{result} = x \models \mathit{true}} \quad (\text{x})$$

$$\frac{\begin{array}{c} S \ \texttt{method} \ C \ m(C_1 \ x_1 \ldots C_n \ x_n)_{\text{-}}; \ \in \ methods(C_0) \\ \Gamma \vdash e_0 : C_0 \dashv P_0 \models P_0' \ \ldots \ \Gamma \vdash e_n : C_n \dashv P_n \models P_n' \\ x_0' \ldots x_n' \ fresh \qquad S' = S[\texttt{this} := x_0', \ x_1 := x_1', \ \ldots, \ x_n := x_n'] \\ P = (\texttt{result} : C \ \& \ P_0[\texttt{result} := x_0'] \ \& \ \ldots \ \& \ P_n[\texttt{result} := x_n'] \\ \& \ (Pre(S') \implies Post(S'))) \end{array}}{\Gamma \vdash e_0.m(e_1 \ldots e_n) : C \dashv P \models P_0' \ \& \ \ldots \ \& \ P_n' \ \& \ Pre(S')} \quad (\text{METHOD})$$

$$\frac{\begin{array}{c} \Gamma \vdash e_1 : C_1 \dashv P_1 \models P_1' \ \ldots \ \Gamma \vdash e_n : C_n \dashv P_n \models P_n' \\ getters(C) = S_1 \ \texttt{method} \ C_1 \ x_1(); \ \ldots \ S_n \ \texttt{method} \ C_n \ x_n(); \qquad x_1' \ldots x_n' \ fresh \\ S_i' = S_i[\texttt{this} := \texttt{result}] \qquad P_i'' = (P_i[\texttt{result} := x_i'] \ \& \ (Pre(S_i') \implies \texttt{result}.x_i() = x_i')) \\ P = (\texttt{result} : C \ \& \ P_1'' \ \& \ \ldots \ \& \ P_n'') \end{array}}{\Gamma \vdash \texttt{new} \ C(e_1 \ldots e_n) : C \dashv P \models P_1' \ \& \ \ldots \ \& \ P_n' \ \& \ Pre(S_1') \ \& \ \ldots \& \ Pre(S_n')} \quad (\text{NEW})$$

$$\frac{\Gamma \vdash e : C' \dashv P \models P' \qquad C' \ instanceof \ C}{\Gamma \vdash e : C \dashv P \models P'} \quad (\text{SUB})$$

$$\frac{\begin{array}{c} \Gamma = \texttt{this} : Name, \ x_1 : C_1, \ \ldots, \ x_n : C_n \qquad \Gamma \vdash e : C \dashv P \models P' \\ \texttt{verify} \ Ds \vdash (\Gamma \ \& \ Pre(S) \ \& \ P) \models (P' \ \& \ Post(S)) \end{array}}{Ds; \ Name \vdash S \ \texttt{method} \ C \ m(C_1 \ x_1 \ldots C_n \ x_n) \ e; \ : OK} \quad (\text{MOK})$$

$$\frac{}{Ds; \ Name \vdash S \ \texttt{method} \ C \ m(C_1 \ x_1 \ldots C_n \ x_n); \ : OK} \quad (\text{ABsMOK})$$

$$\frac{\begin{array}{c} Body = \{\texttt{interface?} \ [Cs] \ M_1 \ldots M_n\} \\ Ds; Name \vdash M_1 : OK \ldots Ds; Name \vdash M_n : OK \end{array}}{Ds; Name \vdash Body \ : OK} \quad (\text{BODYTYPED})$$

Fig. 2. Expression typing rules

Definition 3 (Methods Composition). $Ms_1 + Ms_2 = Ms$
- $(M \ Ms_1) + Ms_2 = M \ (Ms_1 + Ms_2)$
  if $methName(M) \notin dom(Ms_2)$
- $(M_1 \ Ms_1) + (M_2 \ Ms_2) = M_1 + M_2 \ (Ms_1 + Ms_2)$
  if $methName(M_1) = methName(M_2)$
- $\emptyset + Ms = Ms$

Definition 4 (Method Composition). $M_1 + M_2 = M$
- $S \ \texttt{method} \ C \ m(C_1 \ x_1 \ldots C_n \ x_n) \ e; \ + \ S' \ \texttt{method} \ C \ m(C_1 \ \_ \ldots C_n \ \_);$
  $= \ S \ \texttt{method} \ C \ m(C_1 \ x_1 \ldots C_n \ x_n) \ e;$
  if $Pre(S')$ implies $Pre(S)$ and $Post(S)$ implies $Post(S')$
- $MH_1; \ + \ MH_2 \ e; \ = \ MH_2 \ e; \ + \ MH_1;$
- $S \ \texttt{method} \ C \ m(C_1 \ x_1 \ldots C_n \ x_n); \ + \ S' \ \texttt{method} \ C \ m(C_1 \ \_ \ldots C_n \ \_);$
  $= \ S \ \texttt{method} \ C \ m(C_1 \ x_1 \ldots C_n \ x_n);$
  if $Pre(S')$ implies $Pre(S)$ and $Post(S)$ implies $Post(S')$
- $S \ \texttt{method} \ C \ m(C_1 \ x_1 \ldots C_n \ x_n); \ + \ S' \ \texttt{method} \ C \ m(C_1 \ \_ \ldots C_n \ \_);$
  $= \ S' \ \texttt{method} \ C \ m(C_1 \ x_1 \ldots C_n \ x_n);$
  if $(Pre(S)$ implies $Pre(S')$ and $Post(S')$ implies $Post(S))$
  and not $(Pre(S')$ implies $Pre(S)$ and $Post(S)$ implies $Post(S'))$

Definition 5 (Body Abstraction). $Body[\texttt{makeAbstract} \ m]$
  $\{[Cs] \ Ms_1 \ S \ \texttt{method} \ C \ m(Cxs)_{\text{-}}; \ Ms_2\}[\texttt{makeAbstract} \ m]$
  $= \{[Cs] \ Ms_1 \ S \ \texttt{method} \ C \ m(Cxs); \ Ms_2\}$

$$\frac{D'_1 \dots D'_n \vdash D_1 \Downarrow D'_1 \quad \dots \quad D'_1 \dots D'_n \vdash D_n \Downarrow D'_n}{D_1 \dots D_n \Downarrow D'_1 \dots D'_n} \quad \text{(FlatTop)}$$

$$\frac{Ds;\ Name \vdash E \Downarrow Body \qquad \text{if } Name \text{ of form } C \text{ then } abs(Body) = S\ T\ x_1();\dots S\ T\ x_n();}{Ds \vdash Name = E \Downarrow Name = Body} \quad \text{(DFlat)}$$

$$\frac{\begin{array}{c} Body = \{\texttt{interface?}\ [Cs]\ M_1 \dots M_n\} \\ Body' = \{\texttt{interface?}\ [Cs]\ M_1 \dots M_n\ Ms\} \\ Ms = \{\Sigma allMeth(Ds,\ Cs,\ m) \mid m \in dom(Cs) \text{ and } m \notin dom(Body)\} \\ Ds;\ Name \vdash Body' : OK \end{array}}{Ds;\ Name \vdash Body \Downarrow Body'} \quad \text{(BFlat)}$$

$$\frac{}{Ds;\ Name \vdash t \Downarrow Ds(t)} \quad \text{(tFlat)}$$

$$\frac{Ds;\ Name \vdash E_1 \Downarrow Body_1 \qquad Ds;\ Name \vdash E_2 \Downarrow Body_2}{Ds;\ Name \vdash E_1 + E_2 \Downarrow Body_1 + Body_2} \quad \text{(+Flat)}$$

$$\frac{\begin{array}{c} Ds;\ Name \vdash E \Downarrow Body \qquad Body = \{[Cs]\ \overline{M}_1\ S\ \texttt{method}\ C\ m(C_1\ x_1 \dots C_n\ x_n)\text{-};\ \overline{M}_2\} \\ Body' = \{[Cs]\ \overline{M}_1\ S\ \texttt{method}\ C\ m(C_1\ x_1 \dots C_n\ x_n);\ \overline{M}_2\} \end{array}}{Ds;\ Name \vdash E[\texttt{makeAbstract}\ m] \Downarrow Body'} \quad \text{(AbsFlat)}$$

Fig. 3. Flattening rules

FlatTop. The first rule flattens a set of declarations $D_1 \dots D_n$ to a set $D'_1 \dots D'_n$. We express this rule in a non-computational way: we assume to know the resulting $D'_1 \dots D'_n$, and we use them as a guide to compute them. Note that if there is a resulting $D'_1 \dots D'_n$ then it is unique; flattening is a deterministic process and $D'_1 \dots D'_n$ are used only to type check the results. They are not used to compute the shape of the flattened code.

Non computational rules like this are common with nominal type systems [27] where the type signatures of all classes and methods can be extracted before the method bodies are verified.

DFlat. This rule flattens an individual definition by flattening the trait expression. When the flattening produces a class definition, we also check that the body denotes an instantiable class; a class whose only abstract methods are valid getters. The function $abs(Body)$ returns the abstract methods.

BFlat. It may look surprising that the $Body$ does not flatten to itself. This represents what happens in most programming languages, where implementing an interface implicitly imports the abstract signature for all the methods of that interface. In the context of verification also the specification of such interface methods is imported. In concrete, $Body'$ is like $Body$, but we add Ms by collecting all the methods of the interfaces that are not already present in the $Body$.

Moreover, we check that all the methods defined in the class respect the typing and the specification defined in the interfaces: if a class has S `method Foo foo();` or S `method Foo foo() e;` and there is a S' `method Foo foo();` in the interface, then S must respect the specification S'. The system then checks that the $Body$ is well-typed and verified by calling $Ds;\ Name \vdash M_i : OK$

TFlat. A trait t is flattened to its declaration $Ds(t)$.

+FLAT. The composition of two expression E_1 and E_2, where both expressions are first reduced to $Body_1$ and $Body_2$, results in the composition of these bodies as defined in Definition 2.

ABSFLAT. An expression E where one method m is made abstract flattens to a $Body'$. We know that E flattens to $Body$. The only difference between $Body$ and $Body'$ is that the one method m is abstract in $Body'$. In $Body$, the method can be abstract or concrete.

3.4   Soundness of the Trait-based CbC Process

In this section, we formulate our main result of the TraitCbC process. We prove soundness of the flattening process with a parametric logic. The proofs of the lemmas and theorems are in the technical report [41]. We claim that if you have a language without code reuse and with sound and modular PhV verification then the language supports CbC simply by adding traits to the language. That is, traits intrinsically enable a CbC program construction process.

To prove soundness of the refinement process of TraitCbC (Theorem 2: Sound CbC Process) as exemplified in Sect. 2, we have to show that the flattening process is correct (Theorem 1: General Soundness). In turn, to prove General Soundness, we need two lemmas which state that the composition of traits is correct (Lemma 1) and that a trait after the `makeAbstract` operation is still correct (Lemma 2).

In Lemma 1, we have well-typed definitions Ds, and two well-typed and verified traits in Ds, and the resulting trait/class is also well-typed and verified.

Lemma 1 (Composition correct).
If $Ds(t1) = Body_1$, $Ds(t2) = Body_2$, $Ds(Name) = Body$, $Ds; t_1 \vdash Body_1 : OK$,
$Ds; t_2 \vdash Body_2 : OK$, and $Body_1 + Body_2 = Body$,
then $Ds; Name \vdash Body : OK$

Lemma 2 shows that if we have a well-typed and verified trait, the operation `makeAbstract` results in a trait/class that is also well-typed and verified.

Lemma 2 (MakeAbstract correct).
If $Ds(t) = Body$, $Ds(Name) = Body'$, $Ds; t \vdash Body : OK$,
*   and $Body[\text{makeAbstract } m] = Body'$,*
then $Ds; Name \vdash Body' : OK$

With these Lemmas, we can prove Theorem 1. Given a sound and modular verification language, then all programs that flatten are well-typed and verified. In a modular verification language, a method can be fully verified using only the information contained in the method declaration and the specification of any used method. Moreover, our parametric logic must support at least a commutative and associative *and* (but of course other ways to merge knowledge could work too) and a transitive *implication* (but of course other forms of logical consequence could work too).

Theorem 1 (General Soundness).
For all programs Ds where Ds flattens to Ds', and Ds' is well-typed;
that is, forall $Name = Body \in Ds'$, we have $Ds'; Name \vdash Body : OK$.

We now show that the TraitCbC process is sound. Theorem 2 states that starting with one abstract method and a set of verified traits, the composed program is also verified.

Theorem 2 (Sound CbC Process).
Starting from a fully abstract specification t_0, and some refinement steps $t_1 \ldots t_n$, we can write $C = t_0 + \cdots + t_n$ as our whole CbC refinement process; where $t_0 + t_1$ is the application of the first refinement step. If we use CbC to construct programs, we can start from verified atomic units and get a verified result. Formally, if $t_0 = \{MH\}$ $t_1 = \{Ms_1\}$ $\ldots$ $t_n = \{Ms_n\}$ are well-typed, and

$$
\begin{array}{lll}
t_0 = \{MH\} & & t_0 = \{MH\} \\
t_1 = \{Ms_1\} \ \ldots \ t_n = \{Ms_n\} & \Downarrow & t_1 = \{Ms_1\} \ \ldots \ t_n = \{Ms_n\} \\
C = t_0 + \cdots + t_n & & C = Body
\end{array}
$$

then $C = Body$ is well-typed.

Proof. This is a special case of Theorem 1.

Theorem 2 shows clearly that trait composition intrinsically enables a CbC refinement process: A object-oriented programming language with traits and a corresponding specification language supports an incremental CbC approach.

Table 1. Comparison of TraitCbC with classical CbC

	Classic CbC	TraitCbC
Language	Additional rules for a programming language.	Programming language with traits. Needs specification language.
Tool support	Pen and paper. Some specialized tools available.	Relies on prevalent PhV verification tools.
Construction Rules	Specific refinement rules.	Refinement by composition of traits.
Debugging	Guarantees the correctness of each refinement step. Only refinements without abstract statement are directly verified.	Guarantees the correctness of each refinement step. Each method is specified such that each refinement can directly be verified.
Proof complexity	Many, but small proofs .	Any granularity of proofs.
Reuse	Refinement steps cannot be reused; only fully implemented methods can.	Each verified method in a trait can be reused.
Applications	Focuses on small but correctness-critical algorithms.	As TraitCbC is based on PhV, it can be used in areas of PhV. Additionally, traits are beneficial for incremental development approaches and development of software product lines.

4   Trait-Based Correctness-by-Construction in Comparison to Classical CbC

In this section, we discuss the benefits of TraitCbC in comparison to classical CbC. To do this, we describe classical CbC first.

Classical correctness-by-construction (CbC) [19,30,37] is an incremental approach to construct programs. CbC uses a *Hoare triple* specification {P} S {Q} stating that if the precondition P holds, and the statement S is executed, then the statement terminates and postcondition Q holds. The CbC refinement process starts with a Hoare triple where the statement S is abstract. This abstract statement can be seen as a hole in the program that needs to be filled. With a set of refinement rules, an abstract statement is replaced by more concrete statements (i.e., statements in the guarded command language [19] that can contain further abstract statements). The process stops, when all abstract statements are refined to concrete statements so that no holes remain in the program. As each refinement rule is sound and each correct application of a refinement rule guarantees to satisfy the starting Hoare triple, the resulting program is correct-by-construction [30]. The CbC process is strictly tied to a set of predefined refinement rules. A programmer cannot deviate from this concept. To apply a refinement rule, it has to be checked that conditions of the rule application are satisfied. This is done by pen-and-paper or with specialized tools [42].

In Table 1, we compare TraitCbC and classical CbC:

Language. The classical CbC approach is external to a programming language. It needs the definition of refinement rules. TraitCbC is usable with languages that have traits, a specification language, and a corresponding verification framework. In this work, we focus on object-orientation, but the general TraitCbC programming guideline presented in this paper is also suitable for functional programming environments using abstract and concrete functions with specifications instead of traits and methods.

Tool Support. To use one of the approaches, tool support is desired. For classical CbC, mostly pen and paper is used. There are a few specialized tools such as CorC [42], tool support for ArcAngel [38], and SOCOS [4,5]. These tools force a certain programming procedure on the user. This procedure can be in conflict with their preferred programming style. For TraitCbC, tools for post-hoc verification can be reused. There are tools for many languages such as Java [3], C [16], C# [7,8]. Other languages are integrated with their verifier from the start, e.g., Spec# [8] and Dafny [32]. TraitCbC as presented in this paper is a core calculus, designed to show the feasibility of the concept. We believe that scaling up TraitCbC to a complete programming language reusing existing verification techniques would be feasible and would result in a similarly expressive verification process, but supporting more flexible program composition. In Sect. 5, we show how a prototype can be constructed by using the KeY verifier [3].

Construction Rules. To construct a program, classical CbC has a strict concept of refinement rules. A programmer cannot deviate from the granularity of the rules. In contrast, PhV does not give a mandatory guideline how to construct programs. TraitCbC is a bridge between both extremes. Programs can be constructed stepwise as with classical CbC, but if desired, any number of refinement steps can be condensed up to PhV based programming.

Debugging. If errors occur in the development process, TraitCbC gives early and detailed information. By specifying the method under development and any abstract method that is called by this method, we can directly verify the correctness of the method under development. We assume that the introduced abstract methods will be correctly implemented in further refinement steps. With each step, the programmer gets closer to the solution until finally all abstract methods are implemented. Classical CbC relies on the same process, but here the abstract statements (similar to our abstract methods) are not explicitly specified by the programmer. Additional specifications in classical CbC are introduced only with some rules such as an intermediate condition in the composition rule. Then, these specifications are propagated through the program to be constructed. When arriving at a leaf in the refinement process, the correctness of the statement can be guaranteed. The problem in classical CbC is that all refinement steps where abstract statements occur cannot be verified directly. In the worst case, a wrong specification is found only after a few refinement steps.

Proof Complexity. TraitCbC can have the same granularity and also the same proof effort as classical CbC, since each method implementation can correspond to just one refinement step. The advantage of TraitCbC is that programmers can freely implement a method body. They must not stick to the same granularity as in the classical CbC refinement rules. As in PhV, they can implement a complete method in one step. The programmer can balance proof complexity against verifier calls.

Reuse. If we want to reuse developed methods or refinement steps, the approaches differ. In classical CbC, no refinement steps can be reused. A fully refined method can be reused in both approaches. For TraitCbC, we can easily reuse even very small units of code, since they are represented as methods in the traits.

Applications. The classical CbC approach does not scale well to development procedures for complete software system. Rather, individual algorithms can be developed with CbC [50]. As soon as we scale TraitCbC to real languages, we have the same application scenarios as PhV. As argued by Damiani et al. [18] traits enable an incremental process of specifying and verifying software. Bettini et al. [10] proposed to use traits for software product line development and highlighted the benefits of fine-grained reuse mechanisms. Here, TraitCbC's guideline is suitable for constructing new product lines step by step from the beginning.

Summary. In summary, TraitCbC bridges the gap between PhV and CbC. It enables a CbC process for trait-based languages without introducing refinement rules. The concrete realization of specifying and verifying methods is similar to PhV, but additionally to PhV, TraitCbC provides an incremental development process. This development process combined with the flexibility of traits allows correct methods to be developed in small and reusable steps. Moreover, we have introduced a core calculus and proved that the construction and composition of trait-based programs is correct.

5   Proof-of-Concept Implementation

In this section, we describe the implementation, which instantiates TraitCbC in Java with JML [31] as specification language and KeY [3] as verifier for Java code. Our trait implementation is based on interfaces with default implementation. Our open source tool is implemented in Java and integrated as plug-in in the Eclipse IDE.[4]

---

[4] Tool and evaluation at https://github.com/TUBS-ISF/CorC/tree/TraitCbC.

Besides this prototype, other languages with a suitable verifier, such as Dafny [32] and OpenJML [17], can also be used to implement TraitCbC.

In Listing 1, we show the concrete syntax. Each method in a trait is specified with JML with the keywords **requires** and **ensures** for the pre- and postcondition. To verify the correctness of programs, we need two steps. First, we verify the correctness of a method implemented in a trait w.r.t. its specification. Second, for trait composition, our implementation checks the correct composition for all methods (cf. Definition 2). It is verified that the specification of a concrete method satisfies the specification of the abstract one with the same signature (cf. Definition 4). These verification goals are sent to KeY, which starts an automatic verification attempt. The syntax of trait composition is shown in line 24. In a separate tc-file, the name of the resulting trait is given and the composed traits are connected with a plus operator.

```
1    public interface MaxElement1 {
2    /*@ requires list.size() > 0;
3     @ ensures (\forall int n; list.contains(n);
4     @ \result >= n) & list.contains(\result);
5     @*/
6     public default int maxElement(List list) {
7        if (list.size() == 1) return accessHead(list);
8        if (list.element() >= maxElement(list.tail()))
9           { return accessHead(list) }
10       else { return maxTail(list) } }
11
12   /*@ requires list.size() > 0;
13    @ ensures \result == list.element();
14    @*/
15    public int accessHead(List list);
16
17   /*@ requires list.size() > 1;
18    @ ensures (\forall int n; list.tail().contains(n);
19    @ \result >= n) & list.tail().contains(\result);
20    @*/
21    public int maxTail(List list);
22   }
23
24   ComposedMax = MaxElement1 + MaxElement2
```

Listing 1. Example in our implementation

Evaluation. We evaluate our implementation by a feasibility study. First, we reimplemented an already verified case study in our trait-based language. We used the IntList [43] case study, which is a small software product line (SPL) with a common code base and several features extending this code base. Here, we can show that our trait-based language also facilitates reuse. The IntList case study implements functionality to insert integers to a list in the base version. Extensions are the sorting of the list and different insert options (e.g., front /back). We implement five methods that exists in different variants with our trait-based CbC approach. We implement the case study in different granularities. The coarse-grained version is similar to the SPL implementation we started with [43], confirming that traits are also amenable to implement SPLs as shown by Bettini et al. [10]. The fine-grained version implements the five methods incrementally with 12 refinement steps. We can reuse 6 of these steps during the construction of method variants.

We also implement three more case studies BankAccount [48], Email [25], and Elevator [39] with TraitCbC and CbC to show that it is feasible to implement object-oriented programs with both approaches. We used CorC [42] as an instance of a CbC tool. We were able to implement nine classes and verify 34 methods with a size of 1–20 lines of code. For future work, a user study is necessary to evaluate the usability of TraitCbC in comparison to CbC to confirm our stated advantages.

6   Related Work

Traits are introduced in many languages to support clean design and reuse, for example Smalltalk [20], Java [12] by utilizing default methods in interfaces, and other Java-like languages [11,33,45]. The trait language TraitRecordJ was extended to support post-hoc verification of traits [18]. The authors added specifications of methods in traits for the verification of correct trait composition and proposed a modular and incremental verification process. None of these trait languages were used to formulate a refinement process to create correct programs. They only focus on code reuse or post-hoc verification.

Automatic verification is widely used for different programming languages. The object-oriented language Eiffel focuses on design-by-contract [35,36]. All methods in classes are specified with pre-/postconditions and invariants for verification purposes. The tool AutoProof [29,49] is used to verify the correctness of implemented methods. It translates methods to logic formulas, and an SMT solver proves the correctness. For C#, programs written in the similar language Spec# [8] are verified with Boogie. That is, code and specification are translated to an intermediate language and verified [7]. For C, the tool VCC [16] reuses the Spec# tool chain to verify programs. The tool VeriFast [28] is able to verify C and Java programs specified in separation logic. For Java, KeY [3] and OpenJML [17] verify programs specified with JML. TraitCbC is parametric in the specification language, meaning that a trait-based language with a specification language and a corresponding program verifier can be used to instantiate TraitCbC. In our implementation, we use KeY [3] to prove the correctness of methods and trait composition.

Event-B [1] is a related correctness-by-construction approach. In Event-B, automata-based systems are specified and refined to a concrete implementation. Event-B is implemented in the Rodin platform [2]. In comparison to CbC by Kourie and Watson [30] as used in this paper, Event-B works on a different abstraction level with automata-based systems instead of program code. The CbC approaches of Back et al. [6] and Morgan [37] are also related. Back et al. [6] start with explicit invariants and pre-/postconditions to refine an abstract program to a concrete implementation, while Kourie and Watson only start with a pre-/postcondition specification. These refinement approaches use specific refinement rules to construct programs which are external to the programming language. With TraitCbC, we propose a refinement procedure that is part of the language by using trait composition.

Abstract execution [47] verifies the correctness of methods with abstract, but formally specified expressions. Abstract Execution is similar to our refinement procedure where abstract methods are called in methods under construction. The difference is that abstract execution extends a programming language to use any expression in the abstract part, not only method calls. Therefore, abstract execution can better reason about irregular termination (e.g., break/continue) of methods. In comparison to

TraitCbC, abstract execution is a verification-centric approach without a guideline on how to construct programs.

Synthesis of function summaries is also related [14,26,44]. Here, verification tools automatically synthesize pre-/postconditions from functions to achieve modular verification and speed up the verification time. In comparison, TraitCbC is a complete software development approach where specification and code are developed simultaneously by a developer to achieve a correct solution. Function summaries are just a verification technique.

7   Conclusion

In this work, we present TraitCbC that guides programmers to correct implementations. In comparison to classical CbC, TraitCbC uses method calls and trait composition instead of refinement rules to guarantee functional correctness. We formalize the concept of a trait-based object-oriented language where the specification language is parametric to allow a broader range of languages to adopt this concept. The main advantage of TraitCbC is the simplicity of the refinement process that supports code and proof reuse.

As future work, we want to investigate how TraitCbC can be used to construct software product lines. As proposed by Bettini et al. [10], trait languages are able to implement SPLs. We want to extend the guideline of TraitCbC to construct SPLs with a refinement-based procedure that guarantees the correctness of the whole SPL. To reduce specification effort in TraitCbC, inheritance of traits is useful. Another option is to integrate the concept of Rebêlo et al. [40] which supports the design-by-contract approach with AspectJML and integrates crosscutting contract modularization to reduce redundant specifications.

Since TraitCbC is parametric in the specification logic, TraitCbC's soundness only holds if such logic is consistent when composed in the presented manner. In particular, the logic needs to take into account ill-founded specifications and non-terminating recursion. In verification, ill-founded specifications and termination issues are often considered as a second step[5], separately from the verification of individual methods, and our prototype still does not yet take care of this second step. That means that methods are verified under the assumption that all other methods respect their contracts. If ill-founded specifications and non-terminating recursion are handled naively, verification might be unsound because of ill-founded reasoning. The technical report [41] shows that this problem is even more pervasive in the case of trait composition or any other form of multiple inheritance: naive composition of correct traits may produce incorrect results.

References

1. Abrial, J.: Modeling in Event-B - System and Software Engineering. Cambridge University Press (2010)
2. Abrial, J.R., Butler, M., Hallerstede, S., Hoang, T.S., Mehta, F., Voisin, L.: Rodin: an open toolset for modelling and reasoning in event-B. STTT **12**(6), 447–466 (2010)

---

[5] For example, Dafny approximately checks that the functions used in a specification form an acyclic graph.

3. Ahrendt, W., Beckert, B., Bubel, R., Hähnle, R., Schmitt, P.H., Ulbrich, M.: Deductive Software Verification-The KeY Book: From Theory to Practice, vol. 10001. Springer, Cham (2016). https://doi.org/10.1007/978-3-319-49812-6

4. Back, R.J.: Invariant based programming: basic approach and teaching experiences. FAOC **21**(3), 227–244 (2009)

5. Back, R.-J., Eriksson, J., Myreen, M.: Testing and verifying invariant based programs in the SOCOS environment. In: Gurevich, Y., Meyer, B. (eds.) TAP 2007. LNCS, vol. 4454, pp. 61–78. Springer, Heidelberg (2007). https://doi.org/10.1007/978-3-540-73770-4_4

6. Back, R.J., Wright, J.: Refinement Calculus: A Systematic Introduction. Springer, New York (2012). https://doi.org/10.1007/978-1-4612-1674-2

7. Barnett, M., Fähndrich, M., Leino, K.R.M., Müller, P., Schulte, W., Venter, H.: Specification and verification: the spec# experience. Commun. ACM **54**(6), 81–91 (2011)

8. Barnett, M., Leino, K.R.M., Schulte, W.: The Spec# programming system: an overview. In: Barthe, G., Burdy, L., Huisman, M., Lanet, J.-L., Muntean, T. (eds.) CASSIS 2004. LNCS, vol. 3362, pp. 49–69. Springer, Heidelberg (2005). https://doi.org/10.1007/978-3-540-30569-9_3

9. ter Beek, M.H., Cleophas, L., Schaefer, I., Watson, B.W.: X-by-construction. In: Margaria, T., Steffen, B. (eds.) ISoLA 2018. LNCS, vol. 11244, pp. 359–364. Springer, Cham (2018). https://doi.org/10.1007/978-3-030-03418-4_21

10. Bettini, L., Damiani, F., Schaefer, I.: Implementing software product lines using traits. In: SAC, pp. 2096–2102 (2010)

11. Bettini, L., Damiani, F., Schaefer, I., Strocco, F.: TRAITRECORDJ: a programming language with traits and records. Sci. Comput. Program. **78**(5), 521–541 (2013)

12. Bono, V., Mensa, E., Naddeo, M.: Trait-oriented programming in Java 8. In: PPPJ, pp. 181–186 (2014)

13. Chapman, R.: Correctness by construction: a manifesto for high integrity software. In: SCS, pp. 43–46 (2006)

14. Chen, H.Y., David, C., Kroening, D., Schrammel, P., Wachter, B.: Synthesising interprocedural bit-precise termination proofs (t). In: ASE, pp. 53–64 (2015)

15. Clements, P., Northrop, L.: Software Product Lines: Practices and Patterns. Addison-Wesley (2002)

16. Cohen, E., et al.: VCC: a practical system for verifying concurrent C. In: Berghofer, S., Nipkow, T., Urban, C., Wenzel, M. (eds.) TPHOLs 2009. LNCS, vol. 5674, pp. 23–42. Springer, Heidelberg (2009). https://doi.org/10.1007/978-3-642-03359-9_2

17. Cok, D.R.: OpenJML: JML for Java 7 by extending OpenJDK. In: Bobaru, M., Havelund, K., Holzmann, G.J., Joshi, R. (eds.) NFM 2011. LNCS, vol. 6617, pp. 472–479. Springer, Heidelberg (2011). https://doi.org/10.1007/978-3-642-20398-5_35

18. Damiani, F., Dovland, J., Johnsen, E.B., Schaefer, I.: Verifying traits: an incremental proof system for fine-grained reuse. FAOC **26**(4), 761–793 (2014)·

19. Dijkstra, E.W.: A Discipline of Programming. Prentice Hall (1976)

20. Ducasse, S., Nierstrasz, O., Schärli, N., Wuyts, R., Black, A.P.: Traits: a mechanism for fine-grained reuse. TOPLAS **28**(2), 331–388 (2006)

21. Flatt, M., Krishnamurthi, S., Felleisen, M.: Classes and Mixins. In: POPL, pp. 171–183 (1998)

22. Gries, D.: The Science of Programming. Springer, New York (1987). https://doi.org/10.1007/978-1-4612-5983-1

23. Haftmann, F., Krauss, A., Kunčar, O., Nipkow, T.: Data refinement in Isabelle/HOL. In: Blazy, S., Paulin-Mohring, C., Pichardie, D. (eds.) ITP 2013. LNCS, vol. 7998, pp. 100–115. Springer, Heidelberg (2013). https://doi.org/10.1007/978-3-642-39634-2_10

24. Hall, A., Chapman, R.: Correctness by construction: developing a commercial secure system. Softw. IEEE **19**(1), 18–25 (2002)

25. Hall, R.J.: Fundamental nonmodularity in electronic mail. ASE **12**(1), 41–79 (2005)

26. Hoare, C.A.R.: Procedures and parameters: an axiomatic approach. In: Engeler, E. (ed.) Symposium on Semantics of Algorithmic Languages. LNM, vol. 188, pp. 102–116. Springer, Heidelberg (1971). https://doi.org/10.1007/BFb0059696

27. Igarashi, A., Pierce, B.C., Wadler, P.: Featherweight Java: a minimal core calculus for Java and GJ. TOPLAS **23**(3), 396–450 (2001)

28. Jacobs, B., Smans, J., Piessens, F.: A quick tour of the VeriFast program verifier. In: Ueda, K. (ed.) APLAS 2010. LNCS, vol. 6461, pp. 304–311. Springer, Heidelberg (2010). https://doi.org/10.1007/978-3-642-17164-2_21

29. Khazeev, M., Rivera, V., Mazzara, M., Johard, L.: Initial steps towards assessing the usability of a verification tool. In: Ciancarini, P., Litvinov, S., Messina, A., Sillitti, A., Succi, G. (eds.) SEDA 2016. AISC, vol. 717, pp. 31–40. Springer, Cham (2018). https://doi.org/10.1007/978-3-319-70578-1_4

30. Kourie, D.G., Watson, B.W.: The Correctness-by-Construction Approach to Programming. Springer, Heidelberg (2012). https://doi.org/10.1007/978-3-642-27919-5

31. Leavens, G.T., Baker, A.L., Ruby, C.: JML: a Java modeling language. In: Formal Underpinnings of Java Workshop (at OOPSLA 1998), pp. 404–420. Citeseer (1998)

32. Leino, K.R.M.: Dafny: an automatic program verifier for functional correctness. In: Clarke, E.M., Voronkov, A. (eds.) LPAR 2010. LNCS (LNAI), vol. 6355, pp. 348–370. Springer, Heidelberg (2010). https://doi.org/10.1007/978-3-642-17511-4_20

33. Liquori, L., Spiwack, A.: FeatherTrait: a modest extension of featherweight Java. TOPLAS **30**(2), 1–32 (2008)

34. Liskov, B.H., Wing, J.M.: A behavioral notion of subtyping. TOPLAS **16**(6), 1811–1841 (1994)

35. Meyer, B.: Eiffel: a language and environment for software engineering. JSS **8**(3), 199–246 (1988)

36. Meyer, B.: Applying "Design by Contract". Computer **25**(10), 40–51 (1992)

37. Morgan, C.: Programming from Specifications, 2nd edn. Prentice Hall (1994)

38. Oliveira, M.V.M., Cavalcanti, A., Woodcock, J.: ArcAngel: a tactic language for refinement. FAOC **15**(1), 28–47 (2003)

39. Plath, M., Ryan, M.: Feature integration using a feature construct. Sci. Comput. Program. **41**(1), 53–84 (2001)

40. Rebêlo, H., et al.: AspectJML: modular specification and runtime checking for crosscutting contracts. In: MODULARITY, pp. 157–168. ACM, New York (2014)

41. Runge, T., Potanin, A., Thüm, T., Schaefer, I.: Traits for correct-by-construction programming (2022). https://arxiv.org/abs/2204.05644

42. Runge, T., Schaefer, I., Cleophas, L., Thüm, T., Kourie, D., Watson, B.W.: Tool support for correctness-by-construction. In: Hähnle, R., van der Aalst, W. (eds.) FASE 2019. LNCS, vol. 11424, pp. 25–42. Springer, Cham (2019). https://doi.org/10.1007/978-3-030-16722-6_2

43. Scholz, W., Thüm, T., Apel, S., Lengauer, C.: Automatic detection of feature interactions using the Java modeling language: an experience report. In: SPLC. ACM, New York (2011)

44. Sery, O., Fedyukovich, G., Sharygina, N.: Interpolation-based function summaries in bounded model checking. In: Eder, K., Lourenço, J., Shehory, O. (eds.) HVC 2011. LNCS, vol. 7261, pp. 160–175. Springer, Heidelberg (2012). https://doi.org/10.1007/978-3-642-34188-5_15

45. Smith, C., Drossopoulou, S.: *Chai*: traits for Java-like languages. In: Black, A.P. (ed.) ECOOP 2005. LNCS, vol. 3586, pp. 453–478. Springer, Heidelberg (2005). https://doi.org/10.1007/11531142_20

46. Sozeau, M., Oury, N.: First-class type classes. In: Mohamed, O.A., Muñoz, C., Tahar, S. (eds.) TPHOLs 2008. LNCS, vol. 5170, pp. 278–293. Springer, Heidelberg (2008). https://doi.org/10.1007/978-3-540-71067-7_23

47. Steinhöfel, D., Hähnle, R.: Abstract execution. In: ter Beek, M.H., McIver, A., Oliveira, J.N. (eds.) FM 2019. LNCS, vol. 11800, pp. 319–336. Springer, Cham (2019). https://doi.org/10.1007/978-3-030-30942-8_20

48. Thüm, T., Schaefer, I., Apel, S., Hentschel, M.: Family-based deductive verification of software product lines. In: GPCE, pp. 11–20. ACM (2012)

49. Tschannen, J., Furia, C.A., Nordio, M., Polikarpova, N.: AutoProof: auto-active functional verification of object-oriented programs. In: Baier, C., Tinelli, C. (eds.) TACAS 2015. LNCS, vol. 9035, pp. 566–580. Springer, Heidelberg (2015). https://doi.org/10.1007/978-3-662-46681-0_53

50. Watson, B.W., Kourie, D.G., Schaefer, I., Cleophas, L.: Correctness-by-construction and post-hoc verification: a marriage of convenience? In: Margaria, T., Steffen, B. (eds.) ISoLA 2016. LNCS, vol. 9952, pp. 730–748. Springer, Cham (2016). https://doi.org/10.1007/978-3-319-47166-2_52

Encodability Criteria for Quantum Based Systems

Anna Schmitt[1]([⊠]) [iD], Kirstin Peters[1]([⊠]) [iD], and Yuxin Deng[2]([⊠]) [iD]

[1] TU Darmstadt, Darmstadt, Germany
anna.schmitt@tu-darmstadt.de, kirstin.peters@uni-a.de
[2] East China Normal University, Shanghai, China
yxdeng@sei.ecnu.edu.cn

Abstract. Quantum based systems are a relatively new research area for that different modelling languages including process calculi are currently under development. Encodings are often used to compare process calculi. Quality criteria are used then to rule out trivial or meaningless encodings. In this new context of quantum based systems, it is necessary to analyse the applicability of these quality criteria and to potentially extend or adapt them. As a first step, we test the suitability of classical criteria for encodings between quantum based languages and discuss new criteria.

Concretely, we present an encoding, from a sublanguage of CQP into qCCS. We show that this encoding satisfies compositionality, name invariance (for channel and qubit names), operational correspondence, divergence reflection, success sensitiveness, and that it preserves the size of quantum registers. Then we show that there is no encoding from qCCS into CQP (or its sublanguage) that is compositional, operationally corresponding, and success sensitive.

Keywords: Process calculi · Quantum based systems · Encodings

1 Introduction

The technological progress turns quantum based systems from theoretical models to hopefully soon practicable realisations. This progress inspired research on quantum algorithms and protocols. These algorithms and protocols in turn call for verification methods that can deal with the new quantum based setting.

Among the various tools for such verifications, also several process calculi for quantum based systems are developed [4,5,8,18]. To compare the expressive power and suitability for different application areas, encodings have been widely used for classical, i.e., not quantum based, systems. To rule out trivial or meaningless encodings, they are required to satisfy quality criteria. In this new context of quantum based systems, we have to analyse the applicability of these quality criteria and potentially extend or adapt them.

Therefore, we start by considering a well-known framework of quality criteria introduced by Gorla in [6] for the classical setting. As a case study we want

© IFIP International Federation for Information Processing 2022
Published by Springer Nature Switzerland AG 2022
M. R. Mousavi and A. Philippou (Eds.): FORTE 2022, LNCS 13273, pp. 151–169, 2022.
https://doi.org/10.1007/978-3-031-08679-3_10

to compare *Communicating Quantum Processes* (CQP) introduced in [5] and the *Algebra of Quantum Processes* (qCCS) introduced in [18]. These two process calculi are particularly interesting, because they model quantum registers and the behaviour of quantum based systems in fundamentally different ways. CQP considers closed systems, where qubits are manipulated by unitary transformations and the behaviour is expressed by a probabilistic transition system. In contrast, qCCS focuses on open systems and super-operators. Moreover, the transition system of qCCS is non-probabilistic. (Unitary transformations and super-operators are discussed in the next section).

Unfortunately, the languages also differ in classical aspects: CQP has pi-calculus-like name passing but the CCS based qCCS does not allow to transfer names; qCCS has operators for choice and recursion but CQP in [5] has not. Therefore, comparing the languages directly would yield negative results in both directions, that do not depend on their treatment of qubits. To avoid these obvious negative results and to concentrate on the treatment of qubits, we consider CQP$^-$, a sublanguage of CQP that removes name passing and simplifies the syntax/semantics, but as we claim does treat qubits in the same way as CQP.

We then show that there exists an encoding from CQP$^-$ into qCCS that satisfies the quality criteria of Gorla and thereby that the treatment of qubits in qCCS is strong enough to emulate the treatment of qubits in CQP$^-$. We also show that the opposite direction is more difficult, even if we restrict the classical operators in qCCS. In fact, the counterexample that we use to prove the non-existence of an encoding considers the treatment of qubits only, i.e., relies on the application of a specific super-operator that has no unitary equivalent.

These two results show that the quality criteria can still be applied in the context of quantum based systems and are still meaningful in this setting. They may, however, not be exhaustive. Therefore, we discuss directions of additional quality criteria that might be relevant for quantum based systems.

Our encoding satisfies compositionality, name invariance w.r.t. channel names and qubit names, strong operational correspondence, divergence reflection, success sensitiveness, and that the encoding preserves the size of quantum registers. We also show that there is no encoding from qCCS into CQP that satisfies compositionality, operational correspondence, and success sensitiveness.

Summary. We need a number of preliminaries: Quantum based systems are briefly discussed in Sect. 2, the considered process calculi are introduced in Sect. 3, and Sect. 4 presents the quality criteria of Gorla. Section 5 introduces the encoding from CQP$^-$ into qCCS and comments on its correctness. The negative result from qCCS into CQP is presented in Sect. 6. In Sect. 7 we discuss directions for criteria specific to quantum based systems. We conclude in Sect. 8. The missing proofs are provided by a technical report in [17].

2   Quantum Based Systems

We briefly introduce the aspects of quantum based systems, which are needed for the rest of the paper. For more details, we refer to the books by Nielsen and Chuang [10], Gruska [7], and Rieffel and Polak [16].

A *quantum bit* or *qubit* is a physical system which has the two base states $|0\rangle$, $|1\rangle$. These states correspond to one-bit classical values. The general state of a quantum system is a *superposition* or linear combination of base states, concretely $|\psi\rangle = \alpha|0\rangle + \beta|1\rangle$. Thereby, α and β are complex numbers such that $|\alpha|^2 + |\beta|^2 = 1$, e.g. $|0\rangle = 1|0\rangle + 0|1\rangle$. Further, a state can be represented by column vectors $|\psi\rangle = \begin{pmatrix} \alpha \\ \beta \end{pmatrix} = \alpha|0\rangle + \beta|1\rangle$, which sometimes for readability will be written in the format $(\alpha, \beta)^T$. The vector space of these vectors is a *Hilbert space* and is denoted by $\mathcal{H}$. We consider finite-dimensional and countably infinite-dimensional Hilbert spaces, where the latter are treated as tensor products of countably infinitely many finite-dimensional Hilbert spaces.

The basis $\{|0\rangle, |1\rangle\}$ is called *standard basis* or *computational basis*, but sometimes there are other orthonormal bases of interest, especially the *diagonal* or *Hadamard* basis consisting of the vectors $|+\rangle = \frac{1}{\sqrt{2}}(|0\rangle + |1\rangle)$ and $|-\rangle = \frac{1}{\sqrt{2}}(|0\rangle - |1\rangle)$. We assume the standard basis in the following.

The evolution of a closed quantum system can be described by *unitary transformations* [10]. A unitary transformation U is represented by a complex-valued matrix such that the effect of U onto a state of a qubit is calculated by matrix multiplication. It holds that $U^\dagger U = \mathcal{I}$, where $U^\dagger$ is the adjoint of U and $\mathcal{I}$ is the *identity matrix*. Thereby, $\mathcal{I}$ is one of the *Pauli matrices* together with $\mathcal{X}$, $\mathcal{Y}$, and $\mathcal{Z}$. Another important unitary transformation is the *Hadamard* transformation H, as it creates the superpositions $\mathsf{H}|0\rangle = |+\rangle$ and $\mathsf{H}|1\rangle = |-\rangle$.

$$\mathcal{I} = \begin{pmatrix} 1 & 0 \\ 0 & 1 \end{pmatrix} \quad \mathcal{X} = \begin{pmatrix} 0 & 1 \\ 1 & 0 \end{pmatrix} \quad \mathcal{Y} = \begin{pmatrix} 0 & -i \\ i & 0 \end{pmatrix} \quad \mathcal{Z} = \begin{pmatrix} 1 & 0 \\ 0 & -1 \end{pmatrix} \quad \mathsf{H} = \frac{1}{\sqrt{2}} \begin{pmatrix} 1 & 1 \\ 1 & -1 \end{pmatrix}$$

Another key feature of quantum computing is the *measurement*. Measuring a qubit q in state $|\psi\rangle = \alpha|0\rangle + \beta|1\rangle$ results in 0 (leaving it in $|0\rangle$) with probability $|\alpha|^2$ and in 1 (leaving it in $|1\rangle$) with probability $|\beta|^2$.

By combining qubits, we create *multi-qubit systems*. Therefore the spaces U and V with bases $\{u_0, \ldots, u_i, \ldots\}$ and $\{v_0, \ldots, v_j, \ldots\}$ are joined using the *tensor product* into one space $U \otimes V$ with basis $\{u_0 \otimes v_0, \ldots, u_i \otimes v_j, \ldots\}$. So a system consisting of n qubits has a 2^n-dimensional space with standard bases $|00\ldots0\rangle \ldots |11\ldots1\rangle$. Within these systems we can measure a single or multiple qubits. Unitary transformations can be performed on single or several qubits.

The multi-qubit systems can exhibit *entanglement*, meaning that states of qubits are correlated, e.g. $\frac{1}{\sqrt{2}}(|00\rangle + |11\rangle)$. A measurement of the first qubit in the computational basis results in 0 (leaving the state $|00\rangle$) with probability $\frac{1}{2}$ and in 1 (leaving the state $|11\rangle$) with probability $\frac{1}{2}$. In both cases a subsequent measurement of the second qubit in the same basis gives the same result as the first measurement with probability 1. The effect also occurs if the entangled qubits are physically separated. Because of this, states with entangled qubits cannot be written as a tensor product of single-qubit states.

States of quantum systems can also be described by *density matrices*. In contrast to the vector description of states, density matrices allow to describe the states of open systems. We further discuss density matrices in Sect. 3.2.

3   Process Calculi

Assume two countably-infinite sets $\mathcal{N}$ of *names* and $\mathcal{V}$ of *qubit variables*. Let $\tau \notin \mathcal{V} \cup \mathcal{N}$. The *semantics* of a process calculus is given as a *structural operational semantics* consisting of inference rules defined on the operators of the language [14]. Thereby, a *(reduction) step*, written as $C \longmapsto C'$, is a single application of the reduction semantics where C' is called *derivative*. Let $C \longmapsto$ denote the existence of a step from C. We write $C \longmapsto^\omega$ if C has an *infinite sequence* of steps and $\Longmapsto$ to denote the *reflexive and transitive closure* of $\longmapsto$.

To reason about environments of terms, we use functions on process terms called contexts. More precisely, a *context* $\mathcal{C}([\cdot]_1, \ldots, [\cdot]_n) : \mathcal{P}^n \to \mathcal{P}$ with n holes is a function from n terms into one term, i.e., given $P_1, \ldots, P_n \in \mathcal{P}$, the term $\mathcal{C}(P_1, \ldots, P_n)$ is the result of inserting $P_1, \ldots, P_n$ in the corresponding order into the n holes of $\mathcal{C}$.

We use $\{y/x\}$ to denote the capture avoiding substitution of x by y on either names or qubits. The definition of substitution on names in the respective calculi is standard. Substitutions on qubits additionally have to be bijective, i.e., cannot translate different qubits to the same qubit, since this might violate the no-cloning principle. More on substitutions of qubits can be found, e.g., in [18]. We equate terms and configurations modulo alpha conversion on (qubit) names.

For the last criterion of [6] in Sect. 4, we need a special constant $\checkmark$, called *success(ful termination)*, in both considered languages. Therefore, we add $\checkmark$ to the grammars of both languages without explicitly mentioning them. Success is used as a barb, where $P\downarrow_\checkmark$ if P has an unguarded occurrence of $\checkmark$ and $P\Downarrow_\checkmark = \exists P'. P \Longmapsto P' \wedge P'\downarrow_\checkmark$, to implement some form of (fair) testing.

3.1   Communicating Quantum Processes

Communicating Quantum Processes (CQP) is introduced in [5]. We need a sub-language CQP$^-$ of CQP without name passing. We simplify the definition of CQP by removing contexts, the additional layer on expressions in the syntax and semantics, do not allow to construct channel names from expressions (though we allow to use the values obtained by measurement as channel names), and by using a monadic version of communication in that only qubits can be transmitted. CQP$^-$ is a strictly less expressive sublanguage of CQP. We claim, however that the treatment of qubits, in particular the manipulations of the quantum register as well as the communication of qubits, is the same as in CQP.

Definition 1 (CQP^-). *The CQP^- terms, denoted by $\mathcal{P}_C$, are given by:*

$$P ::= \mathbf{0} \quad | \quad P \mid P \quad | \quad c?[x].P \quad | \quad c![q].P \quad | \quad \{\tilde{q} \mathrel{*}= U\}.P$$
$$| \quad (x := \mathsf{measure}\ \tilde{q}).P \quad | \quad (\mathsf{new}\ x)P \quad | \quad (\mathsf{qbit}\ x)P$$

CQP^- configurations $\mathfrak{C}_C$ are given by $(\sigma; \phi; P)$ or $\boxplus_{0 \le i < 2^r} p_i \bullet (\sigma_i; \phi; P\{i/x\})$, where σ, σ_i have the form $q_0, \ldots, q_{n-1} = |\psi\rangle$ with $|\psi\rangle = \sum_{i=0}^{2^n-1} \alpha_i |\psi_i\rangle$, $r \le n$, ϕ is the list of channels in the system, and $P \in \mathcal{P}_C$.

(R-Measure_{CQP}) $(\sigma; \phi; (x := \text{measure } q_0, \ldots q_{r-1}).P)$
$$\longmapsto \boxplus_{0 \leq m < 2^r} p_m \bullet (\sigma'_m; \phi; P\{m/x\})$$

(R-Trans_{CQP}) $(q_0, \ldots, q_{n-1} = |\psi\rangle; \phi; \{q_0, \ldots, q_{r-1} \mathrel{*}= U\}.P)$
$$\longmapsto (q_0, \ldots, q_{n-1} = (U \otimes \mathcal{I}_{\{q_r, \ldots, q_{n-1}\}})|\psi\rangle; \phi; P)$$

(R-Perm_{CQP}) $(q_0, \ldots, q_{n-1} = |\psi\rangle; \phi; P) \longmapsto (q_{\pi(0)}, \ldots, q_{\pi(n-1)} = \prod |\psi\rangle; \phi; P\pi)$

(R-Prob_{CQP}) $\boxplus_{0 \leq i < 2^r} p_i \bullet (\sigma_i; \phi; P\{i/x\})$
$$\longmapsto (\sigma_j; \phi; P\{j/x\}) \quad \text{where } p_j \neq 0 \text{ and } r > 0$$

(R-New_{CQP}) $(\sigma; \phi; (\text{new } x)P) \longmapsto (\sigma; \phi, c; P\{c/x\}) \quad \text{where } c \text{ is fresh}$

(R-Qbit_{CQP}) $(q_0, \ldots, q_{n-1} = |\psi\rangle; \phi; (\text{qbit } x)P)$
$$\longmapsto (q_0, \ldots, q_{n-1}, q_n = |\psi\rangle \otimes |0\rangle; \phi; P\{q_n/x\})$$

(R-Comm_{CQP}) $(\sigma; \phi; c![q].P \mid c?[x].Q) \longmapsto (\sigma; \phi; P \mid Q\{q/x\})$

(R-Par_{CQP}) $\dfrac{(\sigma; \phi; P) \longmapsto \boxplus_{0 \leq i < 2^r} p_i \bullet (\sigma'_i; \phi'; P'\{i/x\})}{(\sigma; \phi; P \mid Q) \longmapsto \boxplus_{0 \leq i < 2^r} p_i \bullet (\sigma'_i; \phi'; P'\{i/x\} \mid Q)}$

(R-Cong_{CQP}) $\dfrac{Q \equiv P \quad (\sigma; \phi; P) \longmapsto \boxplus_{0 \leq i < 2^r} p_i \bullet (\sigma'_i; \phi'; P'\{i/x\}) \quad P' \equiv Q'}{(\sigma; \phi; Q) \longmapsto \boxplus_{0 \leq i < 2^r} p_i \bullet (\sigma'_i; \phi'; Q'\{i/x\})}$

Fig. 1. Semantics of CQP⁻

The syntax of CQP⁻ is pi-calculus like. It adds the term $\{\tilde{q} \mathrel{*}= U\}.P$ to apply the unitary transformation U to the qubits in sequence $\tilde{q}$ and the term $(\text{qbit } x)P$ to create a fresh qubit q_n (for $\sigma = q_0, \ldots, q_{n-1}$) which then proceeds as $P\{q_n/x\}$. The process $(x := \text{measure } \tilde{q}).P$ measures the qubits in $\tilde{q}$ with $|\tilde{q}| > 0$ and saves the result in x. The configuration $\boxplus_{0 \leq i < 2^r} p_i \bullet C_i$ denotes a probability distribution over configurations $C_i = (\sigma_i; \phi; P\{i/x\})$, where $\sum_i p_i = 1$ and where the terms within the configurations C_i may differ only by instantiating channel name x by i. It results from measuring the first r qubits, where p_i is the probability of obtaining result i from measuring the qubits $q_0, \ldots, q_{r-1}$ and C_i is the configuration of case i after the measurement. We may also write a distribution as $p_1 \bullet C_1 \boxplus \ldots \boxplus p_j \bullet C_j$ with $j = 2^r - 1$. We equate $(\sigma_0; \phi; P)$ and $\boxplus_{0 \leq i < 2^0} 1 \bullet (\sigma_i; \phi; P\{i/x\})$, i.e., if $|\tilde{q}| = 0$ then we assume that x is not free in P. We naturally extend the definition of contexts to configurations, i.e., consider also contexts $\mathcal{C}([\cdot]_1, \ldots, [\cdot]_n) : \mathcal{P}^n \to \mathfrak{C}$.

The variable x is bound in P by $c?[x].P$, $(x := \text{measure } \tilde{q}).P$, $(\text{new } x)P$, and $(\text{qbit } x)P$. A variable is free if it is not bound. Let $\text{fq}(P)$ and $\text{fc}(P)$ denote the sets of free qubits and free channels in P.

The state σ is represented by a list of qubits $q_0, \ldots, q_{n-1}$ as well as a linear combination $|\psi\rangle = \sum_{i=0}^{2^n - 1} \alpha_i |\psi_i\rangle$ which can also be rewritten by a vector $(\alpha_0, \alpha_1, \ldots, \alpha_{2^n-1})^T$. As done in [5], we sometimes write as an abbreviated form $\sigma = q_0, \ldots, q_{n-1}$ or $\sigma = |\psi\rangle$.

The semantics of CQP⁻ is defined by the reduction rules in Fig. 1. Rule (R-Measure$_{CQP}$) measures the first r qubits of σ, where $\sigma = \alpha_0 |\psi_0\rangle + \cdots + \alpha_{2^n-1} |\psi_{2^n-1}\rangle$, $\sigma'_m = \dfrac{\alpha_{l_m}}{\sqrt{p_m}} |\psi_{l_m}\rangle + \cdots + \dfrac{\alpha_{u_m}}{\sqrt{p_m}} |\psi_{u_m}\rangle$, $l_m = 2^{n-r} m$, $u_m = 2^{n-r}(m+1) - 1$, and $p_m = |\alpha_{l_m}|^2 + \cdots + |\alpha_{u_m}|^2$. As a result a probability distribution over the possible base vectors is generated, where σ'_m is the accordingly updated qubit vector. Rule (R-TRANS_{CQP}) applies the unitary operator U on the first r qubits. In contrast to [5], we explicitly list in the subscript of $\mathcal{I}$ the qubits it is applied to. As the rules (R-MEASURE_{CQP}) and (R-TRANS_{CQP}) operate on the first r qubits within σ, Rule (R-PERM_{CQP}) allows to permute the qubits in σ. Thereby, π is a permutation and $\prod$ is the corresponding unitary operator.

The Rule (R-PROB_{CQP}) reduces a probability distribution with $r > 0$ to a single of its configurations $(\sigma_j; \phi; P\{j/x\})$ with non-zero probability p_j. The rules (R-NEW_{CQP}) and (R-QBIT_{CQP}) create new channels and qubits and update the list of channel names or the qubit vector. Thereby, a new qubit is initialised to $|0\rangle$ and $|\psi\rangle \otimes |0\rangle$ is reshaped into a (2^{n+1})-vector. The remaining rules are standard pi-calculus rules and also structural congruence $\equiv$ is standard.

We inherit the type system from [5]. It ensures that two parallel components cannot share qubits, which is the realisation of the no-cloning property of qubits. To illustrate this type system, we present the rules for parallel composition, input, and output from [5]:

$$(\text{T-Par}) \ \frac{\Gamma_1 \vdash P \quad \Gamma_2 \vdash Q}{\Gamma_1 + \Gamma_2 \vdash P \mid Q} \qquad (\text{T-In}) \ \frac{\Gamma \vdash x : \hat{}[\widetilde{T}] \quad \Gamma, \tilde{y} : \widetilde{T} \vdash P}{\Gamma \vdash x?[\tilde{y} : \widetilde{T}].P}$$

$$(\text{T-Out}) \ \frac{\Gamma \vdash x : \hat{}[\widetilde{T}, \widetilde{\text{Qbit}}] \quad \forall i.\, T_i \neq \text{Qbit} \quad \forall i.\, \Gamma \vdash y_i : T_i \quad z_i \text{ distinct} \quad \Gamma \vdash P}{\Gamma, \tilde{z} : \widetilde{\text{Qbit}} \vdash x![\tilde{y}, \tilde{z}].P}$$

Rule (T-Par) ensures that parallel components cannot share qubits, where $\Gamma_1 + \Gamma_2$ implies that Γ_1 and Γ_2 do not share assignments for the same qubit. Rule (T-In) adds the types of the received values and qubits to the type environment for the continuation P such that P can use the received qubits. Therefore, Rule (T-Out) removes the transmitted qubits from the type environment of the continuation such that these qubits can no longer be used by the continuation. For the remaining rules of the type system we refer to [5]. These rules straightforwardly implement the idea that parallel components cannot share qubits. To adapt this type system to CQP^- it suffices to adapt the multiplicity in communication to the monadic case, where the message is always of type Qbit for qubits.

As an example for a CQP^- configuration and the application of the rules in Fig. 1 consider Example 1. This example contains an implementation of the quantum teleportation protocol as given in [1]. The quantum teleportation protocol is a procedure for transmitting a quantum state via a non-quantum medium. This protocol is particularly important: not only is it a fundamental component of several more complex protocols, but it is likely to be a key enabling technology for the development of the quantum repeaters [15] which will be necessary in large-scale quantum communication networks.

Example 1. Consider the CQP$^-$-configuration S

$$S = \left(q_0, q_1, q_2 = \frac{1}{\sqrt{2}}|100\rangle + \frac{1}{\sqrt{2}}|111\rangle; \emptyset; System\,(0, 1, 2, 3, q_0, q_1, q_2) \right) \text{ where}$$

$System\,(0, 1, 2, 3, q_0, q_1, q_2) =$
$\quad$(new 0)(new 1)(new 2)(new 3)$(Alice\,(q_0, q_1, 0, 1, 2, 3) \mid Bob\,(q_2, 0, 1, 2, 3))$
$Alice\,(q_0, q_1, 0, 1, 2, 3) =$
$\quad \{q_0, q_1 \mathrel{*}= \mathsf{CNOT}\}.\{q_0 \mathrel{*}= \mathsf{H}\}.(x := \mathsf{measure}\ q_0, q_1).x![a].\mathbf{0}$
$Bob\,(q_2, 0, 1, 2, 3) = (0?[y].\{q_2 \mathrel{*}= \mathcal{I}\}.\checkmark) \mid (1?[y].\{q_2 \mathrel{*}= \mathcal{X}\}.\checkmark) \mid$
$\quad (2?[y].\{q_2 \mathrel{*}= \mathcal{Z}\}.\checkmark) \mid (3?[y].\{q_2 \mathrel{*}= \mathcal{Y}\}.\checkmark)$

Alice and Bob each possess one qubit (q_1 for Alice and q_2 for Bob) of an entangled pair in state $\frac{1}{\sqrt{2}}|00\rangle + \frac{1}{\sqrt{2}}|11\rangle$. q_0 is the second qubit owned by Alice. Within this example it is in state $|0\rangle$, but in general it can be in an arbitrary state. It is the qubit whose state will be teleported to q_2 and therefore to Bob.

By Fig. 1, S can do the following steps

$$S \longmapsto^4 (|\psi_0\rangle; 0, 1, 2, 3; (Alice\,(q_0, 0, 1, 2, 3, q_2) \mid Bob\,(q_1, 0, 1, 2, 3)))$$
$$\longmapsto (|\psi_1\rangle; 0, 1, 2, 3; (\{q_0 \mathrel{*}= \mathsf{H}\}.(x := \mathsf{measure}\ q_0, q_1).x![a].\mathbf{0} \mid$$
$$Bob\,(q_2, 0, 1, 2, 3)))$$
$$\longmapsto (|\psi_2\rangle; 0, 1, 2, 3; ((x := \mathsf{measure}\ q_0, q_1).x![a].\mathbf{0} \mid Bob\,(q_2, 0, 1, 2, 3)))$$
$$\longmapsto \frac{1}{4} \bullet (q_0, q_1, q_2 = |001\rangle; 0, 1, 2, 3; (0![a].\mathbf{0} \mid Bob\,(q_2, 0, 1, 2, 3)))\boxplus$$
$$\frac{1}{4} \bullet (q_0, q_1, q_2 = |010\rangle; 0, 1, 2, 3; (1![a].\mathbf{0} \mid Bob\,(q_2, 0, 1, 2, 3)))\boxplus$$
$$\frac{1}{4} \bullet (q_0, q_1, q_2 = |101\rangle; 0, 1, 2, 3; (2![a].\mathbf{0} \mid Bob\,(q_2, 0, 1, 2, 3)))\boxplus$$
$$\frac{1}{4} \bullet (q_0, q_1, q_2 = |110\rangle; 0, 1, 2, 3; (3![a].\mathbf{0} \mid Bob\,(q_2, 0, 1, 2, 3))) = S^*,$$

with $|\psi_0\rangle = q_0, q_1, q_2 = \frac{1}{\sqrt{2}}|100\rangle + \frac{1}{\sqrt{2}}|111\rangle$, $|\psi_1\rangle = q_0, q_1, q_2 = \frac{1}{\sqrt{2}}|110\rangle + \frac{1}{\sqrt{2}}|101\rangle$, and $|\psi_2\rangle = q_0, q_1, q_2 = \frac{1}{2}|001\rangle + \frac{1}{2}|010\rangle - \frac{1}{2}|101\rangle - \frac{1}{2}|110\rangle$.

All configurations within the probability distribution in S^* have the same probability. We can e.g. choose the first one by using Rule (R-PROB_{CQP}).

$$S^* \longmapsto (q_0, q_1, q_2 = |001\rangle; 0, 1, 2, 3; (0![a].\mathbf{0} \mid (0?[y].\{q_2 \mathrel{*}= \mathcal{I}\}.\checkmark) \mid$$
$$(1?[y].\{q_2 \mathrel{*}= \mathcal{X}\}.\checkmark) \mid (2?[y].\{q_2 \mathrel{*}= \mathcal{Z}\}.\checkmark) \mid (3?[y].\{q_2 \mathrel{*}= \mathcal{Y}\}.\checkmark)))$$
$$\longmapsto (q_0, q_1, q_2 = |001\rangle; 0, 1, 2, 3; (\mathbf{0} \mid (\{q_2 \mathrel{*}= \mathcal{I}\}.\checkmark) \mid$$
$$(1?[y].\{q_2 \mathrel{*}= \mathcal{X}\}.\checkmark) \mid (2?[y].\{q_2 \mathrel{*}= \mathcal{Z}\}.\checkmark) \mid (3?[y].\{q_2 \mathrel{*}= \mathcal{Y}\}.\checkmark)))$$
$$\longmapsto (q_0, q_1, q_2 = |001\rangle; 0, 1, 2, 3; (\mathbf{0} \mid \checkmark \mid$$
$$(1?[y].\{q_2 \mathrel{*}= \mathcal{X}\}.\checkmark) \mid (2?[y].\{q_2 \mathrel{*}= \mathcal{Z}\}.\checkmark) \mid (3?[y].\{q_2 \mathrel{*}= \mathcal{Y}\}.\checkmark))) \quad \square$$

3.2   An Algebra of Quantum Processes

The algebra of quantum processes (qCCS) is introduced in [3,18] as a process calculus for quantum based systems. As qCCS is designed to model open systems, its states are described by density matrices or operators. A density operator in a Hilbert space $\mathcal{H}$ is a linear operator ρ on it, such that $|\psi\rangle^\dagger \rho |\psi\rangle \geq 0$ for all $|\psi\rangle$ and $\mathrm{tr}(\rho) = 1$, where $\mathrm{tr}(\rho)$ is the sum of elements on the main diagonal of the matrix ρ. A positive operator ρ is called a partial density operator if $\mathrm{tr}(\rho) \leq 1$. By slightly abusing notation, we use $\mathcal{V}$ to denote the current set of qubit names of a given density matrix ρ. We write $\mathcal{D}(\mathcal{H})$ for the set of partial density operators on $\mathcal{H}$. Every density matrix can be represented as $\sum_i p_i |\psi_i\rangle\langle\psi_i|$, i.e., by an ensemble of pure states $|\psi_i\rangle$ with their probabilities $p_i \geq 0$. Accordingly, the density matrix of a pure state $|\psi\rangle$ is $|\psi\rangle\langle\psi|$.

The dynamics of open quantum systems cannot be described solely by unitary transformations. Instead *super-operators* are used. Unitary transformations as well as measurement can be transformed to super-operators on density matrices. We illustrate this with the Hadamard transformation and measurement.

Example 2. Let $X \subseteq \mathcal{V}$. The super-operator that represents the Hadamard transformation on X is denoted as $\mathsf{H}[X]$, where its application to ρ is defined as $\mathsf{H}_X(\rho) = (\mathsf{H} \otimes \mathcal{I}_{\mathcal{V}-X}) \cdot \rho \cdot (\mathsf{H} \otimes \mathcal{I}_{\mathcal{V}-X})^\dagger$.

The super-operator to measure the qubits in X with the result of measurement unknown is denoted as $\mathcal{M}[X]$. Its application to ρ is defined as $\mathcal{M}_X(\rho) = \sum_m (\mathsf{P}_m \otimes \mathcal{I}_{\mathcal{V}-X})\rho(\mathsf{P}_m \otimes \mathcal{I}_{\mathcal{V}-X})^\dagger$, where P_m is the outer product of m as a base vector.

The super-operator to measure the qubits in X with the expected result i is denoted as $\mathcal{E}_i[X]$. Its application to ρ is defined as $\mathcal{E}_{i,X}(\rho) = (\mathsf{P}_i \otimes \mathcal{I}_{\mathcal{V}-X})\rho(\mathsf{P}_i \otimes \mathcal{I}_{\mathcal{V}-X})^\dagger$. If X is empty, then $\mathcal{E}_i[X]$ is the identity operator $\mathcal{I}_{\mathcal{V}}$.   □

Super-operators that go beyond the expressive power of unitary transformations are e.g. the super-operators that are used to model the noise in quantum communication. Intuitively, noise is a form of partial entanglement with an unkown environment. Note that, as in CQP, the channels that are used to transfer qubit-systems in qCCS, are modelled as noise-free channels, i.e., noise has to be added explicitly by respective super-operators as discussed in [18].

Definition 2 (Super-Operator). *Let $X \subseteq \mathcal{V}$. A super-operator $\mathcal{E}[X]$ on a Hilbert space $\mathcal{H}$ is a linear operator $\mathcal{E}$ (from the space of linear operators on $\mathcal{H}$ into itself) which is defined as $\mathcal{E}_X = \mathcal{E} \otimes \mathcal{I}_{\mathcal{V}-X}$ and therefore $\mathcal{E}_X(\rho) = (\mathcal{E} \otimes \mathcal{I}_{\mathcal{V}-X}) \cdot \rho \cdot (\mathcal{E} \otimes \mathcal{I}_{\mathcal{V}-X})^\dagger$. Further, $\mathcal{E}$ is required to be completely positive and satisfies $\mathrm{tr}(\mathcal{E}_X(\rho)) \leq \mathrm{tr}(\rho)$. For any extra Hilbert space $\mathcal{H}_R$, $(\mathcal{I}_R \otimes \mathcal{E})(A)$ is positive provided A is a positive operator on $\mathcal{H}_R \otimes \mathcal{H}$, where $\mathcal{I}_R$ is the identity operation on $\mathcal{H}_R$.*

The syntax of qCCS adds an operator to standard CCS to apply super-operators and a standard conditional, where P is executed if b is true. Further, it alters the communication prefixes such that only qubits can be transmitted via standard channels [3,18].

$$(\text{INPUT}_{\text{QCCS}})\ \langle c?x.P, \rho\rangle \xrightarrow{c?q} \langle P\{q/x\}, \rho\rangle \quad q \notin \text{fq}(c?x.P)$$

$$(\text{OUTPUT}_{\text{QCCS}})\ \langle c!q.P, \rho\rangle \xrightarrow{c!q} \langle P, \rho\rangle \qquad (\text{OPER}_{\text{QCCS}})\ \langle \mathcal{E}[X].P, \rho\rangle \xrightarrow{\tau} \langle P, \mathcal{E}_X(\rho)\rangle$$

$$(\text{COMM}_{\text{QCCS}})\ \frac{\langle P, \rho\rangle \xrightarrow{c?q} \langle P', \rho\rangle \quad \langle Q, \rho\rangle \xrightarrow{c!q} \langle Q', \rho\rangle}{\langle P \parallel Q, \rho\rangle \xrightarrow{\tau} \langle P' \parallel Q', \rho\rangle} \qquad (\text{TAU}_{\text{QCCS}})\ \langle \tau.P, \rho\rangle \xrightarrow{\tau} \langle P, \rho\rangle$$

$$(\text{CHOICE}_{\text{QCCS}})\ \frac{\langle P, \rho\rangle \xrightarrow{\alpha} \langle P', \rho'\rangle}{\langle P + Q, \rho\rangle \xrightarrow{\alpha} \langle P', \rho'\rangle} \qquad (\text{IFTHEN}_{\text{QCCS}})\ \frac{\langle P, \rho\rangle \xrightarrow{\alpha} \langle P', \rho'\rangle \quad b = \text{true}}{\langle \text{if } b \text{ then } P, \rho\rangle \xrightarrow{\alpha} \langle P', \rho'\rangle}$$

$$(\text{DEF}_{\text{QCCS}})\ \frac{\langle P\{\tilde{q}/\tilde{x}\}, \rho\rangle \xrightarrow{\alpha} \langle P', \rho'\rangle}{\langle A(\tilde{q}), \rho\rangle \xrightarrow{\alpha} \langle P', \rho'\rangle} \quad A(\tilde{x}) \overset{def}{=} P \qquad (\text{CLOSE}_{\text{QCCS}})\ \frac{\langle P, \rho\rangle \xrightarrow{\tau} \langle P', \rho'\rangle}{\langle P, \rho\rangle \longmapsto \langle P', \rho'\rangle}$$

$$(\text{INTL}_{\text{QCCS}})\ \frac{\langle P, \rho\rangle \xrightarrow{\alpha} \langle P', \rho'\rangle}{\langle P \parallel Q, \rho\rangle \xrightarrow{\alpha} \langle P' \parallel Q, \rho'\rangle} \quad \text{if } \alpha = c?q \text{ then } q \notin \text{fq}(Q)$$

$$(\text{RES}_{\text{QCCS}})\ \frac{\langle P, \rho\rangle \xrightarrow{\alpha} \langle P', \rho'\rangle}{\langle P \setminus L, \rho\rangle \xrightarrow{\alpha} \langle P' \setminus L, \rho'\rangle} \quad \text{cn}(\alpha) \cap L = \emptyset$$

Fig. 2. Semantics of qCCS

Definition 3 (qCCS). *The qCCS terms, denoted by $\mathcal{P}_q$, are given by:*

$$P ::= A(\tilde{q}) \mid \text{nil} \mid \tau.P \mid \mathcal{E}[X].P \mid c?x.P \mid c!q.P$$
$$\mid P + P \mid P \parallel P \mid P \setminus L \mid \text{if } b \text{ then } P$$

The qCCS configurations $\mathfrak{C}_q$ are given by $\langle P, \rho\rangle$, where $P \in \mathcal{P}_q$ and $\rho \in \mathcal{D}(\mathcal{H})$.

The variable x is bound in P by $c?x.P$ and the channels in L are bound in P by $P \setminus L$. A variable/channel is free if it is not bound. Let $\text{fc}(P)$ and $\text{fq}(P)$ denote the sets of free channels and free qubits in P, respectively. For each process constant scheme A, a defining equation $A(\tilde{x}) \overset{def}{=} P$ with $P \in \mathcal{P}_q$ and $\text{fq}(P) \subseteq \tilde{x}$ is assumed. As done in [18], we require the following two conditions:

$$c!q.P \in \mathcal{P}_{qCCS} \text{ implies } q \notin \text{fq}(P) \tag{Cond1}$$

$$P \parallel Q \in \mathcal{P}_{qCCS} \text{ implies } \text{fq}(P) \cap \text{fq}(Q) = \emptyset \tag{Cond2}$$

These conditions ensure the no-cloning principle of qubits within qCCS.

The semantics of qCCS is defined by the inference rules given in Fig. 2. We start with a labelled variant of the semantics from [18] and then add the Rule ($\text{CLOSE}_{\text{qCCS}}$) to obtain a reduction semantics. We omit the symmetric forms of the rules ($\text{CHOICE}_{\text{qCCS}}$), ($\text{INTL}_{\text{qCCS}}$), and ($\text{COMM}_{\text{qCCS}}$). Let $\text{cn}(\alpha)$ return the possibly empty set of channels in the label α.

Rule ($\text{OPER}_{\text{qCCS}}$) implements the application of a super-operator. It updates the state of the configuration as defined in Definition 2. To simplify the definition of a reduction semantics, we use (in contrast to [18]) the label τ.

Rule ($\text{INPUT}_{\text{qCCS}}$) ensures that the received qubits are fresh in the continuation of the input. The rules ($\text{INTL}_{\text{qCCS}}$) and ($\text{INTR}_{\text{qCCS}}$) forbid to receive qubits within parallel contexts that do posses this qubit. Rule (RES_{qCCS}) allows to do a step under a restriction. The other rules are self-explanatory.

4   Encodings and Quality Criteria

Let $\mathcal{L}_S = \langle \mathfrak{C}_S, \longmapsto_S \rangle$ and $\mathcal{L}_T = \langle \mathfrak{C}_T, \longmapsto_T \rangle$ be two process calculi, denoted as *source* and *target* language. An *encoding* from $\mathcal{L}_S$ into $\mathcal{L}_T$ is a function $[\![\cdot]\!] : \mathfrak{C}_S \to \mathfrak{C}_T$. We often use $S, S', \ldots$ and $T, T', \ldots$ to range over $\mathfrak{C}_S$ and $\mathfrak{C}_T$, respectively.

To analyse the quality of encodings and to rule out trivial or meaningless encodings, they are augmented with a set of quality criteria. In order to provide a general framework, Gorla in [6] suggests five criteria well suited for language comparison. We start with these criteria for classical systems, which are described in more detail in [17].

Definition 4 (Quality Criteria, [6]). *The encoding $[\![\cdot]\!]$ is good, if it is*

compositional: *For every operator* **op** *with arity n of $\mathcal{L}_S$ and for every subset of names N, there exists a context $\mathcal{C}_{op}^N([\cdot]_1, \ldots, [\cdot]_n)$ such that, for all $S_1, \ldots, S_n$ with $\mathrm{fv}(S_1) \cup \ldots \cup \mathrm{fv}(S_n) = N$, it holds that $[\![op\,(S_1, \ldots, S_n)]\!] = \mathcal{C}_{op}^N([\![S_1]\!], \ldots, [\![S_n]\!])$.*
name invariant: *For every $S \in \mathfrak{C}_S$ and every substitution γ on names, it holds that $[\![S\gamma]\!] = [\![S]\!]\gamma$.*
operational corresponding *w.r.t. $\preceq$:*

Complete: For all $S \Longmapsto S'$, there is T such that $[\![S]\!] \Longmapsto T$ and $[\![S']\!] \preceq T$.
Sound: For all $[\![S]\!] \Longmapsto T$, there is S', T' such that $S \Longmapsto S', T \Longmapsto T'$, and $[\![S']\!] \preceq T'$.
divergence reflecting: *For every S, $[\![S]\!] \longmapsto^\omega$ implies $S \longmapsto^\omega$.*
success sensitive: *For every S, $S \Downarrow_\checkmark$ iff $[\![S]\!] \Downarrow_\checkmark$.*

We use here a stricter variant of name invariance compared to [6], since we translate names by themselves in our encoding. Operational correspondence consists of a soundness and a completeness condition. *Completeness* requires that every computation of a source term can be emulated by its translation. *Soundness* requires that every computation of a target term corresponds to some computation of the corresponding source term.

Note that a behavioural relation $\preceq$ on the target is assumed for operational correspondence. Moreover, $\preceq$ needs to be success sensitive, i.e., $T_1 \preceq T_2$ implies $T_1 \Downarrow_\checkmark$ iff $T_2 \Downarrow_\checkmark$. As discussed in [12], we pair operational correspondence as of [6] with correspondence simulation.

Definition 5 (Correspondence Simulation, [12]). *A relation $\mathcal{R}$ is a* (weak) *labelled correspondence simulation if for each $(T_1, T_2) \in \mathcal{R}$:*

- *For all $T_1 \xrightarrow{\alpha} T_1'$, there exists T_2' such that $T_2 \xrightarrow{\alpha} T_2'$ and $(T_1', T_2') \in \mathcal{R}$.*
- *For all $T_2 \xrightarrow{\alpha} T_2'$, there exists T_1'', T_2'' such that $T_1 \Longmapsto \xrightarrow{\alpha} T_1'', T_2' \Longmapsto T_2''$, and $(T_1'', T_2'') \in \mathcal{R}$.*
- *$T_1 \Downarrow_\checkmark$ iff $T_2 \Downarrow_\checkmark$.*

T_1 and T_2 are correspondence similar, *denoted as $T_1 \preceq T_2$, if a correspondence simulation relates them.*

There are several other criteria for classical systems that we could have considered (cf. [11]). Since CQP^- is a typed language, we may consider a criterion for types as discussed e.g. in [9]. As only one language is typed, it suffices to require that the encoding is defined for all terms of the source language. We could also consider a criterion for the preservation of distributability as discussed e.g. in [13], since distribution and communication between distributed locations is of interest. Indeed our encoding satisfies this criterion, because it translates the parallel operator homomorphically. However, already the basic framework of Gorla, on that we rely here, suffices to observe principal design principles of quantum based systems as we discuss with the no-cloning property in Sect. 7.

5 Encoding Quantum Based Systems

Our encoding, from well-typed CQP^- configurations into qCCS-configurations that satisfy the conditions Cond1 and Cond2, is given by Definition 6.

Definition 6 (Encoding $\llbracket \cdot \rrbracket$ from CQP^- into qCCS).

$$\llbracket (\sigma; \phi; P) \rrbracket = \langle \llbracket P \rrbracket \setminus \phi, \rho_\sigma \rangle$$
$$\llbracket \boxplus_{0 \leq i < 2^r} p_i \bullet (\sigma_i; \phi; P\{i/x\}) \rrbracket = \langle D(q_0, \ldots, q_{r-1}; x; \llbracket P \rrbracket) \setminus \phi, \rho_\boxplus \rangle$$
$$\llbracket 0 \rrbracket = \text{nil}$$
$$\llbracket P \mid Q \rrbracket = \llbracket P \rrbracket \parallel \llbracket Q \rrbracket$$
$$\llbracket c?[x].P \rrbracket = c?x.\llbracket P \rrbracket$$
$$\llbracket c![q].P \rrbracket = c!q.\llbracket P \rrbracket$$
$$\llbracket \{\tilde{q} \mathrel{*}= U\}.P \rrbracket = U[\tilde{q}].\llbracket P \rrbracket$$
$$\llbracket (x := \text{measure } \tilde{q}).P \rrbracket = \mathcal{M}[\tilde{q}].D(\tilde{q}; x; \llbracket P \rrbracket)$$
$$\llbracket (\text{new } x)P \rrbracket = \tau.(\llbracket P \rrbracket \setminus \{x\})$$
$$\llbracket (\text{qbit } x)P \rrbracket = \mathcal{E}_{|0\rangle}[\mathcal{V}].(\llbracket P \rrbracket \{q_{|\mathcal{V}|}/x\})$$
$$\llbracket \checkmark \rrbracket = \checkmark$$

where $\rho_\sigma = |\psi\rangle\langle\psi|$ for $\sigma = |\psi\rangle$, $\rho_\boxplus = \sum_i p_i |\psi_i\rangle\langle\psi_i|$ for $\sigma_i = |\psi_i\rangle$,

$$D(\tilde{q}; x; Q) = \text{if } \text{tr}(\mathcal{E}_0[\tilde{q}]) \neq 0 \text{ then } \mathcal{E}_0[\tilde{q}].Q\{0/x\} + \ldots +$$
$$\text{if } \text{tr}(\mathcal{E}_{2^{|\tilde{q}|}-1}[\tilde{q}]) \neq 0 \text{ then } \mathcal{E}_{2^{|\tilde{q}|}-1}[\tilde{q}].Q\{2^{|\tilde{q}|} - 1/x\},$$

$\mathcal{E}_{|0\rangle}[\mathcal{V}]$ adds a new qubit $q_{|\mathcal{V}|}$ initialised with 0 to the current state ρ, $\mathcal{M}$ is measurement with the result unkown, and the super-operator $\mathcal{E}_i[Y]$ is measurement of Y with the expected result i.

The translation of configurations maps the vector σ to the density matrix ρ_σ (obtained by the outer product) and restricts all names in ϕ to the translation of the sub-term. In the translation of probability distributions, the state $\rho_\boxplus$ is the sum of the density matrices obtained from the σ_i multiplied with their respective probability. Again, the names in ϕ are restricted in the translation. The nondeterminism in choosing one of the possible branches of the probability distribution in CQP^- by (R-PROB_{CQP}) is translated into the qCCS-choice $D(\tilde{q}; x; \llbracket P \rrbracket)$ with $\tilde{q} = q_0, \ldots, q_{r-1}$, where each case is guarded by a conditional which checks whether the result of measurement is not zero, i.e., whether the respective case occurs with a non-zero probability, followed by a super-operator that adjusts the state to the respective result of measurement. Note that, the translation of a configuration $(\sigma; \phi; P)$ is a special case of the second line with an additional step to resolve the conditional, since $|\psi\rangle\langle\psi| = \sum 1 |\psi\rangle\langle\psi|$, $r = 0$ implies that $\tilde{q} = q_0, \ldots, q_{r-1}$ is empty, and thus $\mathsf{D}(\tilde{q}; x; \llbracket P \rrbracket) = \mathsf{if}\ \mathrm{tr}(\mathcal{I}[\mathcal{V}]) \neq 0\ \mathsf{then}\ \mathcal{I}[\mathcal{V}].\llbracket P \rrbracket$. An encoding example using such a qCCS-choice is given in Example 5.

The application of unitary transformations and the creation of new qubits are translated to the corresponding super-operators. Measurement is translated into the super-operator for measurement with unkown result followed by the choice $\mathsf{D}(\tilde{q}; x; \llbracket P \rrbracket)$ over the branches of the possible outcomes of measurement, i.e., after the first measurement the translation is similar to the translation of a probability distribution in the second case. Note that we combine two kinds of measurement in this translation. The outer measurement w.r.t. an unknown result dissolves entanglement on the measured qubits and ensures that the density matrix after this first measurement is the sum of the density matrices of the respective cases in the distribution (compare with $\rho_{\boxplus}$ and Example 3). The measurements w.r.t. $0 \leq i < 2^r$ within $\mathsf{D}(\tilde{q}; x; \llbracket P \rrbracket)$ then check whether the respective case i occurs with non-zero probability and adjust the density matrix to this result of measurement if case i is picked. The creation of new channel names is translated to restriction, where a τ-guard simulates the step that is necessary in CQP^- to create a new channel. The restriction ensures that this new name cannot be confused with any other translated source term name. Since in the derivative of a source term step creating a new channel the new channel is added to ϕ in the configuration, we restrict all channels in ϕ. The remaining translations are homomorphic.

Example 3. Consider $S = (\sigma; \phi; (x := \mathsf{measure}\ q_0).P)$, where $\sigma = q_0, q_1 = \frac{1}{\sqrt{2}}|00\rangle + \frac{1}{\sqrt{2}}|11\rangle = |\psi\rangle$ consists of two entangled qubits. By Fig. 1, $S \longmapsto S' = \frac{1}{2} \bullet (\sigma = q_0, q_1 = |00\rangle; \phi; P\{0/x\}) \boxplus \frac{1}{2} \bullet (\sigma = q_0, q_1 = |11\rangle; \phi; P\{1/x\})$. By Definition 6, $\llbracket S \rrbracket = \langle (\mathcal{M}[q_0].\mathsf{D}(q_0; x; \llbracket P \rrbracket)) \setminus \phi, \rho \rangle$ with $\rho = |\psi\rangle\langle\psi|$. By Fig. 2, then $\llbracket S \rrbracket \longmapsto T = \langle \mathsf{D}(q_0; x; \llbracket P \rrbracket) \setminus \phi, \mathcal{M}_{q_0}(\rho) \rangle$. Accordingly, the probability distribution in S' is mapped on a choice in T. The outer measurement $\mathcal{M}[q_0]$ resolves the entanglement and yields a density matrix that is the sum of the density matrices of the choice branches, i.e., $\mathcal{M}_{q_0}(\rho) = (|0\rangle\langle 0| \otimes \mathcal{I}_{q_1})\rho(|0\rangle\langle 0| \otimes \mathcal{I}_{q_1})^\dagger + (|1\rangle\langle 1| \otimes \mathcal{I}_{q_1})\rho(|1\rangle\langle 1| \otimes \mathcal{I}_{q_1})^\dagger$. □

By analysing the encoding function, we observe that for all source terms the type system of CQP^- ensures that their literal translation satisfies the conditions Cond1 and Cond2. Hence, the encoding is defined on all source terms.

Corollary 1. *For all $S \in \mathfrak{C}_C$ the term $\llbracket S \rrbracket$ is defined.*

Considering Fig. 1, we observe that in CQP^- we have to permute the matrix σ, in order to apply unitary transformations or measure qubits in the middle of σ. Such permutations are not necessary in qCCS. More precisely, since these steps only reorder qubits in σ, they do not change the state of the translated system modulo correspondence simulation.

Lemma 1. *If $S \longmapsto S'$ is by* (R-PERM$_{CQP}$), *then* $[\![S]\!] \preceq [\![S']\!]$ *and* $[\![S']\!] \preceq [\![S]\!]$.

In the literature, operational correspondence is often considered w.r.t. a bisimulation on the target; simply because bisimilarity is a standard behavioural equivalence in process calculi, whereas correspondence simulation is not. For our encoding, we cannot use bisimilarity.

Example 4. Consider $S = (\sigma; \emptyset; (x := \text{measure } q).P \mid Q)$, where S is a 1-qubit system with $\sigma = q = |+\rangle$ and $P, Q \in \mathcal{P}_C$ with $\text{fc}(P) \subseteq \{x\}$ and $\text{fc}(Q) = \emptyset$. By the rules (R-MEASURE$_{CQP}$) and (R-PAR$_{CQP}$) of Fig. 1,

$$S \longmapsto S' = \frac{1}{2} \bullet (\sigma = q = |0\rangle; \emptyset; P\{0/x\} \mid Q) \boxplus \frac{1}{2} \bullet (\sigma = q = |1\rangle; \emptyset; P\{1/x\} \mid Q),$$

i.e., (R-PAR$_{CQP}$) pulls the parallel component Q into the probability distribution that results from measuring q. Since our encoding is compositional—and indeed we require compositionality, the translation $[\![S]\!]$ behaves slightly differently. By Definition 6, $[\![S]\!] = \langle \mathcal{M}[q].\text{D}(q; x; [\![P]\!]) \mid\mid [\![Q]\!], \rho \rangle$, where $\text{D}(q; x; [\![P]\!]) = $ if $\text{tr}(\mathcal{E}_0[q]) \neq 0$ then $\mathcal{E}_0[q].[\![P]\!]\{0/x\} + $ if $\text{tr}(\mathcal{E}_1[q]) \neq 0$ then $\mathcal{E}_1[q].[\![P]\!]\{1/x\}$ and $\rho = |+\rangle\langle+|$, and $[\![S']\!] = \langle \text{D}(q; x; [\![P]\!] \mid\mid [\![Q]\!]), \rho' \rangle$ with $\rho' = \frac{1}{2}|0\rangle\langle0| + \frac{1}{2}|1\rangle\langle1|$. By Fig. 2, $[\![S]\!] \longmapsto T = \langle \text{D}(q; x; [\![P]\!]) \mid\mid [\![Q]\!], \rho' \rangle$, because $\mathcal{M}_q(\rho) = \rho'$. Unfortunately, $[\![S']\!]$ and T are not bisimilar. As a counterexample consider $P = x![q].0$ and $Q = (\text{new } y)0?[z].\checkmark$. The problem is, that a step on $[\![Q]\!]$ in $[\![S']\!]$ forces us to immediately pick a case and resolve the choice, whereas after performing the same step on $[\![Q]\!]$ in T all cases of the choice remain available. After emulating the first step of $[\![Q]\!]$ in $[\![S']\!]$, either we reach a configuration that has to reach success eventually or we reach a configuration that cannot reach success; whereas there is just one way to do the respective step in T and in the resulting configuration success may or may not be reached depending on the next step. Fortunately, $[\![S']\!]$ and T are correspondence similar.   □

We also present the translation of the quantum teleportation protocol in Example 1.

Example 5. By Definition 6

$[\![S]\!] = \langle (\tau.(\tau.(\tau.(P) \setminus 3) \setminus 2) \setminus 1) \setminus 0, \rho_0 \rangle$, where

$P = [\![Alice\,(q_0, q_1, 0, 1, 2, 3)]\!] \mid\mid [\![Bob\,(q_2, 0, 1, 2, 3)]\!]$,

$[\![Alice\,(q_0, q_1, 0, 1, 2, 3)]\!] = \text{CNOT}[q_0, q_1].\text{H}[q_0].\mathcal{M}[q_0, q_1].\text{D}(q_0, q_1; x; x!a.\text{nil})$,

$[\![Bob\,(q_2, 0, 1, 2, 3)]\!] = $

$\quad (0?y.\mathcal{I}[q_2].\checkmark) \mid\mid (1?y.\mathcal{X}[q_2].\checkmark) \mid\mid (2?y.\mathcal{Z}[q_2].\checkmark) \mid\mid (3?y.\mathcal{Y}[q_2].\checkmark)$, and

$\rho_0 = |\psi_0\rangle\langle\psi_0|$.

By Fig. 2, $[\![S]\!]$ can do the following steps

$[\![S]\!] \longmapsto^4 \langle (((((P) \setminus 3) \setminus 2) \setminus 1) \setminus 0, \rho_0 \rangle$

$\quad \longmapsto \langle (\text{H}[q_0].\mathcal{M}[q_0, q_1].\text{D}(q_0, q_1; x; x!a.\text{nil})) \mid\mid [\![Bob\,(q_2, 0, 1, 2, 3)]\!], \rho_1 \rangle$

$\quad \longmapsto \langle (\mathcal{M}[q_0, q_1].\text{D}(q_0, q_1; x; x!a.\text{nil})) \mid\mid [\![Bob\,(q_2, 0, 1, 2, 3)]\!], \rho_2 \rangle$

$\quad \longmapsto \langle \text{D}(q_0, q_1; x; x!a.\text{nil}) \mid\mid [\![Bob\,(q_2, 0, 1, 2, 3)]\!], \rho_3 \rangle = T^*$, with $\rho_1 = \mathcal{CNOT}_{q_0,q_1}(\rho_0)$, $\rho_2 = \mathcal{H}_{q_0}(\rho_1)$, $\rho_3 = \mathcal{M}_{q_0,q_1}(\rho_2)$, and where the qCCS-choice $\mathsf{D}(q_0, q_1; x; x!a.\mathsf{nil})$ is given by

$$
\begin{aligned}
\mathsf{D}(q_0, q_1; x; x!a.\mathsf{nil}) = \ &\text{if } \mathsf{tr}(\mathcal{E}_0[q_0, q_1]) \neq 0 \text{ then } \mathcal{E}_0[q_0, q_1].\left((x!a.\mathsf{nil})\{0/x\}\right) \ + \\
&\text{if } \mathsf{tr}(\mathcal{E}_1[q_0, q_1]) \neq 0 \text{ then } \mathcal{E}_1[q_0, q_1].\left((x!a.\mathsf{nil})\{1/x\}\right) \ + \\
&\text{if } \mathsf{tr}(\mathcal{E}_2[q_0, q_1]) \neq 0 \text{ then } \mathcal{E}_2[q_0, q_1].\left((x!a.\mathsf{nil})\{2/x\}\right) \ + \\
&\text{if } \mathsf{tr}(\mathcal{E}_3[q_0, q_1]) \neq 0 \text{ then } \mathcal{E}_3[q_0, q_1].\left((x!a.\mathsf{nil})\{3/x\}\right).
\end{aligned}
$$

To emulate the behaviour of S we choose again the first branch within $\mathsf{D}(q_0, q_1; x; x!a.\mathsf{nil})$.

$$
\begin{aligned}
T^* \longmapsto &\langle (0!a.\mathsf{nil}) \parallel \llbracket Bob\,(q_2, 0, 1, 2, 3) \rrbracket \rangle, \rho_4 \rangle \\
\longmapsto &\langle \mathsf{nil} \parallel (\mathcal{I}[q_2].\checkmark) \parallel (1?y.\mathcal{X}[q_2].\checkmark) \parallel (2?y.\mathcal{Z}[q_2].\checkmark) \parallel (3?y.\mathcal{Y}[q_2].\checkmark), \rho_4 \rangle \\
\longmapsto &\langle \mathsf{nil} \parallel \checkmark \parallel (1?y.\mathcal{X}[q_2].\checkmark) \parallel (2?y.\mathcal{Z}[q_2].\checkmark) \parallel (3?y.\mathcal{Y}[q_2].\checkmark), \rho_4 \rangle,
\end{aligned}
$$

with $\rho_4 = \mathcal{E}_{0,q_0,q_1}(\rho_3)$.   □

Except for permutation, a source term step is translated by the encoding $\llbracket \cdot \rrbracket$ into exactly one target term step. In the other direction, every target term step is translated by exactly one source term step possibly surrounded by two steps on (R-PERM$_{CQP}$) to permute qubits and put them back in the original order. From that, we obtain operational correspondence. Compositionality holds by definition and name invariance is trivially satisfied, because names are translated by themselves and the encoding does not use names for any other purpose. Divergence reflection results from operational soundness, since all source term steps are translated to a finite number of target term steps. Finally, operational correspondence and the homomorphic translation of success ensure that $\llbracket \cdot \rrbracket$ is success sensitive. With that, $\llbracket \cdot \rrbracket$ satisfies all the criteria that we discussed in Sect. 4. The corresponding proofs can be found in [17].

Theorem 1. *The encoding $\llbracket \cdot \rrbracket$ is good.*

By [12], Theorem 1 implies that there is a correspondence simulation that relates source terms S and their literal translations $\llbracket S \rrbracket$. To refer to a more standard equivalence, this also implies that S and $\llbracket S \rrbracket$ are coupled similar (for the relevance of coupled similarity see e.g. [2]). Proving operational correspondence w.r.t. a bisimulation would not significantly tighten the connection between the source and the target. To really tighten the connection such that S and $\llbracket S \rrbracket$ are bisimilar, we need a stricter variant of operational correspondence and for that a more direct translation of probability distributions to avoid the problem discussed in Example 4. Indeed [3] introduces probability distributions to qCCS and a corresponding alternative of measurement that allows to translate this operator homomorphically. However, in this study we are more concerned about the quality criteria. Hence using them to compare languages that treat qubits fundamentally differently is more interesting here. Moreover, to tighten the connection we would need a probabilistic version of operational correspondence and accordingly a probabilistic version of bisimulation. We leave the study of these probabilistic versions for future research.

6   Separating Quantum Based Systems

Since super-operators are more expressive than unitary transformations, an encoding from qCCS into CQP is more difficult.

Example 6. Consider the super-operator $\mathcal{Q}_q(\rho) = \begin{pmatrix} 1 & 0 \\ 0 & \sqrt{1+p} \end{pmatrix} \rho \begin{pmatrix} 1 & 0 \\ 0 & \sqrt{1+p} \end{pmatrix} - \begin{pmatrix} 0 & \sqrt{p} \\ 0 & 0 \end{pmatrix} \rho \begin{pmatrix} 0 & 0 \\ \sqrt{p} & 0 \end{pmatrix}$ where p is a probability. With $p = 1$ we obtain $\mathcal{Q}_q(\rho) = \begin{pmatrix} \rho_{00} - \rho_{11} & \sqrt{2}\rho_{01} \\ \sqrt{2}\rho_{10} & 2\rho_{11} \end{pmatrix}$ that sometimes behaves as identity, i.e., $\mathcal{Q}_q(|0\rangle\langle 0|) = |0\rangle\langle 0|$, and sometimes changes the qubit, e.g. $\mathcal{Q}_q(|1\rangle\langle 1|) = \begin{pmatrix} -1 & 0 \\ 0 & 2 \end{pmatrix}$, $\mathcal{Q}_q(|+\rangle\langle +|) = \begin{pmatrix} 0 & \frac{\sqrt{2}}{2} \\ \frac{\sqrt{2}}{2} & 1 \end{pmatrix}$, and $\mathcal{Q}_q(|-\rangle\langle -|) = \begin{pmatrix} 0 & -\frac{\sqrt{2}}{2} \\ -\frac{\sqrt{2}}{2} & 1 \end{pmatrix}$. To observe this strange behaviour of $\mathcal{Q}[q]$, we measure the resulting qubit using the qCCS-configuration

$$\mathsf{S_{ce}}(\rho) = \langle \mathcal{Q}[q].\text{if } \mathsf{tr}(\mathcal{E}_0[q]) \neq 0 \text{ then } \tau.\checkmark + \text{if } \mathsf{tr}(\mathcal{E}_1[q]) \neq 0 \text{ then } \tau.\mathsf{nil}, \rho \rangle$$

for the 1-qubit system $\rho = q$, where the choice allows to unguard success if 0 can be measured. We observe that $\mathsf{S_{ce}}(|0\rangle\langle 0|)$ must reach success, $\mathsf{S_{ce}}(|1\rangle\langle 1|)$ may but not must reach success, and $\mathsf{S_{ce}}(|+\rangle\langle +|)$ as well as $\mathsf{S_{ce}}(|-\rangle\langle -|)$ cannot reach success. □

An encoding from qCCS into CQP needs to emulate the behaviour of $\mathcal{Q}[q]$, which is inspired by an operator used for amplitude-damping (see e.g. [10]). Since there is no unitary transformation with this behaviour and also measurement or additional qubits do not help to emulate this behaviour on the state of the qubit (see the proof of Theorem 2), there is no encoding from qCCS into CQP that satisfies compositionality, operational correspondence, and success sensitiveness, i.e., we can use Example 6 as a counterexample to prove that there is no good encoding from qCCS into CQP. The proof of Theorem 2 is given in [17]. Note that we reason here about CQP instead of CQP$^-$, since even the full expressive power of CQP does not help to correctly emulate this super-operator.

Theorem 2. *There is no encoding from qCCS into CQP that satisfies compositionality, operational correspondence, and success sensitiveness.*

7   Quality Criteria for Quantum Based Systems

Sections 5 and 6 show that the quality criteria of Gorla in [6] can be applied to quantum based systems and are still meaningful in this setting. They might, however, not be exhaustive, i.e., there might be aspects of quantum based systems that are relevant but not sufficiently covered by this set of criteria. To obtain these criteria, Gorla studied a large number of encodings, i.e., this set of criteria was built upon the experience of many researchers and years of work.

Accordingly, we do not expect to answer the question 'what are good quality criteria for quantum based systems' now, but rather want to start the discussion.

A closer look at the criteria in Sect. 4 reveals a first candidate for an additional quality criterion. Name invariance ensures that encodings cannot cheat by treating names differently. It requires that good encodings preserve substitutions to some extend. CQP and qCCS model the dynamics of quantum registers in fundamentally different ways, but both languages address qubits by qubit names. It seems natural to extend name invariance to also cover qubit names.

As in [6], we let our definition of qubit invariance depend on a renaming policy φ, where this renaming policy is for qubit names. The renaming policy translates qubit names of the source to tuples of qubit names in the target, i.e., $\varphi : \mathcal{V} \to \mathcal{V}^n$, where we require that $\varphi(q) \cap \varphi(q') = \emptyset$ whenever $q \neq q'$.

The new criterion *qubit invariance*, then requires that encodings preserve and reflect substitutions on qubits modulo the renaming policy on qubits.

Definition 7 (Qubit Invariance). *The encoding $[\![\cdot]\!]$ is qubit invariant if, for every $S \in \mathfrak{C}_S$ and every substitution γ on qubit names, it holds that $[\![S\gamma]\!] = [\![S]\!]\gamma'$, where $\varphi(\gamma(q)) = \gamma'(\varphi(q))$ for every $q \in \mathcal{V}$.*

In [6], name invariance allows the slightly weaker condition $[\![S\gamma]\!] \preceq [\![S]\!]\gamma'$ for non-injective substitutions. In contrast, substitutions on qubits always have to be injective such that they cannot violate the no-cloning principle. Since $[\![\cdot]\!]$ translates qubit names to themselves and introduces no other qubit names, it satisfies qubit invariance for φ being the identity and $\gamma' = \gamma$. The corresponding proof is given in [17].

Lemma 2. *The encoding $[\![\cdot]\!]$ is qubit invariant.*

Note that the qubits discussed so far are so-called *logical qubits*, i.e., they are abstractions of the physical qubits. To implement a single *logical qubit* as of today several *physical qubits* are necessary. These additional physical qubits are used to ensure stability and fault-tolerance in the implementation of logical qubits. Since the number of necessary physical qubits can be much larger than the number of logical qubits, already a small increase in the number of logical qubits might seriously limit the practicability of a system. Accordingly, one may require that encodings preserve the number of logical qubits.

Definition 8 Size of Quantum Registers.) *An encoding $[\![\cdot]\!]$ preserves the size of quantum registers, if for all $S \in \mathfrak{C}_S$, the number of qubits in $[\![S]\!]$ is not greater than in S.*

Again, the encoding $[\![\cdot]\!]$ in Definition 6 satisfies this criterion, which can be verified easily by inspection of the encoding function. The full proof can be found [17].

Lemma 3. *The encoding $[\![\cdot]\!]$ preserves the size of quantum registers.*

Similarly to success sensitiveness, requiring the preservation of the size of quantum registers on literal encodings is not enough. To ensure that all reachable target terms preserve the size of quantum registers, we again link this criterion with the target term relation $\preceq$. More precisely, we require that $\preceq$ is sensible to the size of quantum registers, i.e., $T_1 \preceq T_2$ implies that the quantum registers in T_1 and T_2 have the same size. The correspondence simulation $\preceq$ that we used as target relation for the encoding $[\![\cdot]\!]$ is not sensible to the size of quantum registers, but we can easily turn it into such a relation. Therefore, we simply add the condition that $|\rho| = |\sigma|$ whenever $\langle P, \rho \rangle \mathcal{R} \langle Q, \sigma \rangle$ to Definition 5. Fortunately, all of the already shown results remain valid for the altered version of $\preceq$.

In contrast to CQP^-, the semantics of qCCS yields a non-probabilistic transition system, where probabilities are captured in the density matrices. The encoding $[\![\cdot]\!]$ translates probability distributions into non-deterministic choices. Thereby, branches with zero probability are correctly eliminated, but all remaining branches are treated similarly and their probabilities are forgotten. To check also the probabilities of branches, we can strengthen operational correspondence to a labelled variant, where labels capture the probability of a step. The challenge here is to create a meaningful criterion that correctly accumulates the probabilities in sequences of steps as e.g. a single source term step might be translated into a sequence of target term steps, but the product of the probabilities contained in the sequence has to be equal to the probability of the single source term step. We leave the derivation of a suitable probabilistic version of operational correspondence to future work.

Another important aspect is in how far the quality criteria capture the fundamental principles of quantum based systems such as the *no-cloning principle*: By the laws of quantum mechanics, it is not possible to exactly copy a qubit. Technically, such a copying would require some form of interaction with the qubit and this interaction would destroy its superposition, i.e., alter its state. Interestingly, the criteria of Gorla are even strong enough to observe a violation of this principle in the encoding from CQP^- into qCCS, i.e., if we allow CQP^- to violate this principle but require that qCCS respects it, then we obtain a negative result. Therefore, we remove the type system from CQP^-. Without this type system, we can use the same qubit at different locations, violating the no-cloning principle. As an example, consider $S = (\sigma; \phi; c![q].\mathbf{0} \mid c![q].\mathbf{0})$. Then the encoding $[\![\cdot]\!]$ in Definition 6 is not valid any more, because $[\![S]\!] = \langle (c!q.\mathsf{nil} \parallel c!q.\mathsf{nil}) \setminus \phi, \rho \rangle$ violates condition Cond2. Using S as counterexample, it should be possible to show that there exists no encoding that satisfies compositionality, operational correspondence, and success sensitiveness.

Of course, even if we succeed with this proof, this does not imply that the criteria are strong enough to sufficiently capture the no-cloning principle. Indeed, the other direction is more interesting, i.e., criteria that rule out encodings such that the source language respects the no-cloning principle but not all literal translations or their derivatives respect it. We believe that capturing the no-cloning principle and the other fundamental principles of quantum based systems is an interesting research challenge.

8   Conclusions

We proved that CQP$^-$ can be encoded by qCCS w.r.t. the quality criteria compositionality, name invariance, operational correspondence, divergence reflection, and success sensitiveness. Additionally, this encoding satisfies two new, quantum specific criteria: it is invariant to qubit names and preserves the size of quantum registers. We think that these new criteria are relevant for translations between quantum based systems.

The encoding proves that the way in that qCCS treats qubits—using density matrices and super-operators—can emulate the way in that CQP$^-$ treats qubits. The other direction is more difficult. We showed that there exists no encoding from qCCS into CQP that satisfies compositionality, operational correspondence, and success sensitiveness.

The results themselves may not necessarily be very surprising. The unitary transformations used in CQP$^-$/CQP are a subset of the super-operators used in qCCS and also density matrices can express more than the vectors used in CQP$^-$/CQP. What our case study proves is that the quality criteria that were originally designed for classical systems are still meaningful in this quantum based setting. They may, however, not be exhaustive. Accordingly, in Sect. 7 we start the discussion on quality criteria for this new setting of quantum based systems. The first two candidate criteria that we propose, namely qubit invariance and preservation of quantum register sizes, are relevant, but rather basic. Since the semantics of quantum based systems is often probabilistic, a variant of operational correspondence that requires the preservation and reflection of probabilities in the respective traces might be meaningful. Such a criterion would rule out the encoding $[\![\cdot]\!]$ presented above. More difficult and thus also more interesting are criteria that capture the fundamental principles of quantum based systems such as the no-cloning principle. Hereby, we pose the task of identifying such criteria as research challenge.

As, to the best of our knowledge, there are no well-accepted probabilistic versions of operational correspondence. As a first step we will study probabilistic versions of operational correspondence and the nature of the relation between source and target they imply.

References

1. Bennett, C.H., Brassard, G., Crépeau, C., Richard, J., Peres, A., Wootters, W.K.: Teleporting an unknown quantum state via dual classical and Einstein-Podolsky-Rosen channels. Phys. Rev. Lett. **70**, 1895–1899 (1993). https://doi.org/10.1103/PhysRevLett.70.1895
2. Bisping, B., Nestmann, U., Peters, K.: Coupled similarity: the first 32 years. Acta Informatica, 439–463 (2019). https://doi.org/10.1007/s00236-019-00356-4
3. Feng, Y., Duan, R., Ying, M.: Bisimulation for quantum processes. ACM Trans. Program. Lang. Syst. **34**(4) (2012). https://doi.org/10.1145/2400676.2400680
4. Gay, S.J.: Quantum programming languages: survey and bibliography. Mathe. Struct. Comput. Sci. **16**(4), 581–600 (2006). https://doi.org/10.1017/S0960129506005378

5. Gay, S.J., Nagarajan, R.: Communicating quantum processes. In: Proceedings of SIGPLAN-SIGACT (ACM), pp. 145–157 (2005). https://doi.org/10.1145/1040305.1040318

6. Gorla, D.: Towards a unified approach to encodability and separation results for process calculi. Inf. Comput. **208**(9), 1031–1053 (2010). https://doi.org/10.1016/j.ic.2010.05.002

7. Gruska, J.: Quantum computing. In: Wiley Encyclopedia of Computer Science and Engineering. Wiley (2008). https://doi.org/10.1002/9780470050118.ecse720

8. Jorrand, P., Lalire, M.: Toward a quantum process algebra. In: Proceedings of CF, pp. 111–119 (2004). https://doi.org/10.1145/977091.977108

9. Kouzapas, D., Pérez, J.A., Yoshida, N.: On the relative expressiveness of higher-order session processes. In: Thiemann, P. (ed.) ESOP 2016. LNCS, vol. 9632, pp. 446–475. Springer, Heidelberg (2016). https://doi.org/10.1007/978-3-662-49498-1_18

10. Nielsen, M.A., Chuang, I.L.: Quantum Computation and Quantum Information (10th Anniversary edition). Cambridge University Press, Cambridge (2010)

11. Peters, K.: Comparing process calculi using encodings. In: Proceedings of EXPRESS/SOS. EPCTS, vol. 300, pp. 19–38 (2019). https://doi.org/10.4204/EPTCS.300.2

12. Peters, K., van Glabbeek, R.: Analysing and comparing encodability criteria. In: Crafa, S., Gebler, D. (eds.) Proceedings of EXPRESS/SOS. EPTCS, vol. 190, pp. 46–60 (2015). https://doi.org/10.4204/EPTCS.190.4

13. Peters, K., Nestmann, U., Goltz, U.: On distributability in process calculi. In: Felleisen, M., Gardner, P. (eds.) ESOP 2013. LNCS, vol. 7792, pp. 310–329. Springer, Heidelberg (2013). https://doi.org/10.1007/978-3-642-37036-6_18

14. Plotkin, G.D.: A structural approach to operational semantics. Log. Algebraic Methods Program. **60–61**, 17–139 (2004)

15. de Riedmatten, H., Marcikic, I., Tittel, W., Zbinden, H., Collins, D., Gisin, N.: Long distance quantum teleportation in a quantum relay configuration. Phys. Rev. Lett. **92**, 047904 (2004)

16. Rieffel, E.G., Polak, W.: An introduction to quantum computing for non-physicists. ACM Comput. Surv. **32**(3), 300–335 (2000). https://doi.org/10.1145/367701.367709

17. Schmitt, A., Peters, K., Deng, Y.: Encodability criteria for quantum based systems (technical report). Technical report, TU Darmstadt, Germany (2022). https://doi.org/10.48550/ARXIV.2204.06068. https://arxiv.org/abs/2204.06068

18. Ying, M., Feng, Y., Duan, R., Ji, Z.: An algebra of quantum processes. ACM Trans. Comput. Log. **10**(3), 19:1–19:36 (2009). https://doi.org/10.1145/1507244.1507249

LTL Under Reductions with Weaker Conditions Than Stutter Invariance

Emmanuel Paviot-Adet[1,2], Denis Poitrenaud[1,2], Etienne Renault[3], and Yann Thierry-Mieg[1(✉)]

[1] Sorbonne Université, CNRS, LIP6, 75005 Paris, France
{emmanuel.paviot-adet,denis.poitrenaud,yann.thierry-mieg}@lip6.fr
[2] Université de Paris, 75006 Paris, France
[3] EPITA, LRDE, Kremlin-Bicêtre, France
renault@lrde.epita.fr

Abstract. Verification of properties expressed as ω-regular languages such as LTL can benefit hugely from stutter insensitivity, using a diverse set of reduction strategies. However properties that are not stutter invariant, for instance due to the use of the neXt operator of LTL or to some form of counting in the logic, are not covered by these techniques in general.

We propose in this paper to study a weaker property than stutter insensitivity. In a stutter insensitive language both adding and removing stutter to a word does not change its acceptance, any stuttering can be abstracted away; by decomposing this equivalence relation into two implications we obtain weaker conditions. We define a shortening insensitive language where any word that stutters less than a word in the language must also belong to the language. A lengthening insensitive language has the dual property. A semi-decision procedure is then introduced to reliably prove shortening insensitive properties or deny lengthening insensitive properties while working with a *reduction* of a system. A reduction has the property that it can only shorten runs. Lipton's transaction reductions or Petri net agglomerations are examples of eligible structural reduction strategies.

An implementation and experimental evidence is provided showing most non-random properties sensitive to stutter are actually shortening or lengthening insensitive. Performance of experiments on a large (random) benchmark from the model-checking competition indicate that despite being a semi-decision procedure, the approach can still improve state of the art verification tools.

1 Introduction

Model checking is an automatic verification technique for proving the correctness of systems that have finite state abstractions. Properties can be expressed using the popular Linear-time Temporal Logic (LTL). To verify LTL properties, the automata-theoretic approach [25] builds a product between a Büchi automaton

© IFIP International Federation for Information Processing 2022
Published by Springer Nature Switzerland AG 2022
M. R. Mousavi and A. Philippou (Eds.): FORTE 2022, LNCS 13273, pp. 170–187, 2022.
https://doi.org/10.1007/978-3-031-08679-3_11

representing the negation of the LTL formula and the reachable state graph of the system (seen as a set of infinite runs). This approach has been used successfully to verify both hardware and software components, but it suffers from the so called "state explosion problem": as the number of state variables in the system increases, the size of the system state space grows exponentially.

One way to tackle this issue is to consider *structural reductions*. Structural reductions take their roots in the work of Lipton [15] and Berthelot [1]. Nowadays, these reductions are still considered as an attractive way to alleviate the state explosion problem [2,14]. Structural reductions strive to fuse structurally "adjacent" events into a single atomic step, leading to less interleaving of independent events and less observable behaviors in the resulting system. An example of such a structural reduction is shown on Fig. 1a where actions are progressively grouped (see Sect. 3.1 for a more detailed presentation). It can be observed that the Kripke structure representing the state space of the program is significantly simplified.

Traditionally structural reductions construct a smaller system that preserves properties such as deadlock freedom, liveness, reachability [10], and *stutter insensitive* temporal logic [20] such as $LTL_{\setminus X}$. The verification of a *stutter insensitive* property on a given system does not depend on whether non observable events (i.e. that do not update atomic propositions) are abstracted or not. On Fig. 1a both instructions "$z = 40;$" and "$chan.send(z)$" of thread β are non observable.

This paper shows that structural reductions can in fact be used even for fragments of LTL that are *not* stutter insensitive. We identify two fragments that we call *shortening insensitive* (if a word is in the language, any version that stutters less also) or *lengthening insensitive* (if a word is in the language, any version that stutters more also). Based on this classification we introduce two semi-decision procedures that provide a reliable verdict only in one direction: e.g. presence of counter examples is reliable for lengthening insensitive properties, but absence is not.

The paper is structured as follows, Sect. 2 presents the definitions and notations relevant to our setting in an abstract manner, focusing on the level of description of a language. Section 3 instantiates these definitions in the more concrete setting of LTL verification. Section 4 provides experimental evidence supporting the claim that the method is both applicable to many formulae and can significantly improve state of the art model-checkers. Some related work is presented in Sect. 5 before concluding.

2   Definitions

In this section we first introduce in Sect. 2.1 a "shorter than" partial order relation on infinite words, based on the number of repetitions or stutter in the word. This partial order gives us in Sect. 2.2 the notions of shortening and lengthening insensitive language, which are shown to be weaker versions of classical stutter insensitivity in Sect. 2.3. We then define in Sect. 2.4 the *reduction of a language* which contains a shorter representative of each word in the original language. Finally we show that we can use a semi-decision procedure to verify shortening or lengthening insensitive properties using a reduction of a system.

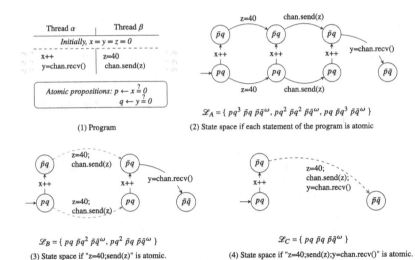

(1) Program

(2) State space if each statement of the program is atomic

$\mathscr{L}_A = \{\, pq^3\ \bar{p}q\ \bar{p}\bar{q}^{\omega},\ pq^2\ \bar{p}q^2\ \bar{p}\bar{q}^{\omega},\ pq\ \bar{p}q^3\ \bar{p}\bar{q}^{\omega}\,\}$

$\mathscr{L}_B = \{\, pq\ \bar{p}q^2\ \bar{p}\bar{q}^{\omega},\ pq^2\ \bar{p}q\ \bar{p}\bar{q}^{\omega}\,\}$

(3) State space if "z=40;send(z)" is atomic.

$\mathscr{L}_C = \{\, pq\ \bar{p}q\ \bar{p}\bar{q}^{\omega}\,\}$

(4) State space if "z=40;send(z);y=chan.recv()" is atomic.

(a) Example of reductions. (1) is a program with two threads and 3 variables. *chan* is a communication channel where *send(int)* insert a message and *int recv()* waits until a message is available and then consumes it. We consider that the logic only observes whether x or y is zero denoted p and q. (2) depicts the state-space represented as a Kripke structure. Each node is labelled by the value of atomic propositions p and q. When an instruction is executed the value of these propositions *may* evolve. (3) represents the state-space of a structurally reduced version of the program where actions of thread β "z=40;chan.send(z)" are fused into a single atomic operation. (4) represents the state-space of a program where the three actions of the original program "z=40;chan.send(z);y=chan.recv()" are now a single atomic step.

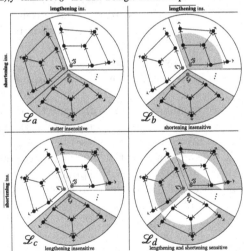

(b) Σ^{ω} is represented as a circle that is partitioned into equivalence classes of words $(\hat{r}_0, \hat{r}_1 \ldots)$. Each point in the space is a word, and some of the $\preccurlyeq$ relations are represented as arrows ; the red point is the shortest word $\underline{\hat{r}}$ in the equivalence class. Gray areas are inside the language, white are outside of it. Four languages are depicted : $\mathscr{L}_a$: equivalence classes are entirely inside or outside **a stutter insensitive language**, $\mathscr{L}_b$: the "bottom" of an equivalence class may belong to **a shortening insensitive language**, $\mathscr{L}_c$: the "top" of an equivalence class may belong to **a lengthening insensitive language**, $\mathscr{L}_d$: some languages are neither lengthening insensitive nor shortening insensitive.

2.1   A "Shorter than" Relation for Infinite Words

Definition 1 (Word). : *A word over a finite alphabet Σ is an infinite sequence of symbols in Σ. We canonically denote a word r using one of the two forms:*

- *(plain word) $r = a_0^{n_0} a_1^{n_1} a_2^{n_2} \ldots$ with for all $i \in \mathbb{N}$, $a_i \in \Sigma$, $n_i \in \mathbb{N}^+$ and $a_i \neq a_{i+1}$,*
  or
- *(ω-word) $r = a_0^{n_0} a_1^{n_1} \ldots a_k^{\omega}$ with $k \in \mathbb{N}$ and for all $0 \leq i \leq k$, $a_i \in \Sigma$, and for $i < k$, $n_i \in \mathbb{N}^+$ and $a_i \neq a_{i+1}$. a_k^{ω} represents an infinite stutter on the final symbol a_k of the word.*

The set of all words over alphabet Σ is denoted Σ^{ω}.

These notations using a power notation for repetitions of a symbol in a word are introduced to highlight stuttering. We force the symbols to alternate to ensure we have a canonical representation: with σ a suffix (not starting by symbol b), the word $aab\sigma$ must be represented as $a^2 b^1 \sigma$ and not $a^1 a^1 b^1 \sigma$. To represent a word of the form $aabbcccccc \ldots$ we use an ω-word: $a^2 b^2 c^{\omega}$.

Definition 2 (Shorter than). : *A plain word $r = a_0^{n_0} a_1^{n_1} a_2^{n_2} \ldots$ is shorter than a plain word $r' = a_0^{n_0'} a_1^{n_1'} a_2^{n_2'} \ldots$ if and only if for all $i \in \mathbb{N}$, $0 < n_i \leq n_i'$. For two ω-words $r = a_0^{n_0} \ldots a_k^{\omega}$ and $r' = a_0^{n_0'} \ldots a_k^{\omega}$, r is shorter than r' if and only if for all $i < k$, $n_i \leq n_i'$.*

We denote this relation on words as $r \preccurlyeq r'$.

For instance, for any given suffix σ, $ab\sigma \preccurlyeq a^2 b\sigma$. Note that $ab\sigma \preccurlyeq ab^2\sigma$ as well, but that $a^2 b\sigma$ and $ab^2\sigma$ are incomparable. ω-words are incomparable with plain words.

Property 1. The $\preccurlyeq$ relation is a partial order on words.

Proof. The relation is clearly reflexive ($\forall r \in \Sigma^{\omega}, r \preccurlyeq r$), anti-symmetric ($\forall r, r' \in \Sigma^{\omega}, r \preccurlyeq r' \wedge r' \preccurlyeq r \Rightarrow r = r'$) and transitive ($\forall r, r', r'' \in \Sigma^{\omega}, r \preccurlyeq r' \wedge r' \preccurlyeq r'' \Rightarrow r \preccurlyeq r''$). The order is partial since some words (such as $a^2 b\sigma$ and $ab^2\sigma$ presented above) are incomparable. □

Definition 3. *[Stutter equivalence]: a word r is stutter equivalent to r', denoted as $r \sim r'$ if and only if there exists a shorter word r'' such that $r'' \preccurlyeq r \wedge r'' \preccurlyeq r'$. This relation $\sim$ is an equivalence relation thus partitioning words of Σ^{ω} into equivalence classes.*

We denote $\hat{r}$ the equivalence class of a word r and denote $\underline{\hat{r}}$ the shortest word in that equivalence class.

For any given word $r = a_0^{n_0} a_1^{n_1} a_2^{n_2} \ldots$ there is a shortest representative in $\hat{r}$ that is the word $\underline{\hat{r}} = a_0 a_1 a_2 \ldots$ where no symbol is ever consecutively repeated more than once (until the ω for an ω-word). By definition all words that are comparable to $\underline{\hat{r}}$ are stutter equivalent to each other, since $\underline{\hat{r}}$ can play the role of r'' in the definition of stutter equivalence, giving us an equivalence relation: it is reflexive, symmetric and transitive.

For instance, with σ denoting a suffix, $\underline{\hat{r}} = ab\sigma$ would be the shortest representative of any word of $\hat{r}$ of the form $a^{n_0} b^{n_1}\sigma$. We can see by this definition that despite being incomparable, $a^2 b\sigma \sim ab^2\sigma$ since $ab\sigma \preccurlyeq a^2 b\sigma$ and $ab\sigma \preccurlyeq ab^2\sigma$.

2.2   Sensitivity of a Language to the Length of Words

Definition 4 (Language). : *a language $\mathscr{L}$ over a finite alphabet Σ is a set of words over Σ, hence $\mathscr{L} \subseteq \Sigma^{\omega}$. We denote $\bar{\mathscr{L}} = \Sigma^{\omega} \setminus \mathscr{L}$ the complement of a language $\mathscr{L}$.*

In the literature, most studies that exploit a form of stuttering are focused on *stutter insensitive* languages [9,10,18,19,24]. In a stutter insensitive language $\mathscr{L}$, duplicating any letter (also called stuttering) or removing any duplicate letter from a word of $\mathscr{L}$ must produce another word of $\mathscr{L}$. In other words, all stutter equivalent words in a class $\hat{r}$ must be either in the language or outside of it. Let us introduce weaker variants of this property, original in this paper.

Definition 5. *[Shortening insensitive]: a language $\mathscr{L}$ is* shortening insensitive *if and only if for any word r it contains, all shorter words r' such that $r' \preccurlyeq r$ are also in $\mathscr{L}$.*

For instance, a shortening insensitive language $\mathscr{L}$ that contains the word $a^3 b\sigma$ must also contain shorter words $a^2 b\sigma$, and $ab\sigma$. If it contains $a^2 b^2 \sigma$ it also contains $a^2 b\sigma$, $ab^2 \sigma$ and $ab\sigma$.

Definition 6. *[Lengthening insensitive]: a language $\mathscr{L}$ is* lengthening insensitive *if and only if for any word r it contains, all longer words r' such that $r \preccurlyeq r'$ are also in $\mathscr{L}$.*

For instance, a lengthening insensitive language $\mathscr{L}$ that contains the word $a^2 b\sigma$ must also contain all longer words $a^3 b\sigma$, $a^2 b^2 \sigma$ ..., and more generally words of the form $a^n b^{n'} \sigma$ with $n \geq 2$ and $n' \geq 1$. If it contains $\hat{r} = ab\sigma$ the shortest representative of an equivalence class, it contains all words in the stutter equivalence class.

While stutter insensitive languages have been heavily studied, there is to our knowledge no study on what reductions are possible if only one direction holds, i.e. the language is shortening or lengthening insensitive, but not both. A shortening insensitive language is essentially asking for something to happen *before* a certain deadline or stuttering "too much". A lengthening insensitive language is asking for something to happen *at the earliest* at a certain date or after having stuttered at least a certain number of times. Figure 1b represents these situations graphically.

2.3   Relationship to Stutter Insensitive Logic

A language is both shortening and lengthening insensitive if and only if it is stutter insensitive (see Fig. 1b). This fact is already used in [16] to identify such stutter insensitive languages using only their automaton. Furthermore since stutter equivalent classes of runs are entirely inside or outside a stutter insensitive language, a language $\mathscr{L}$ is stutter insensitive if and only if the complement language $\bar{\mathscr{L}}$ is stutter insensitive.

However, if we look at sensitivity to length and how it interacts with the complement operation, we find a dual relationship where the complement of a shortening insensitive language is lengthening insensitive and vice versa.

Property 2. A language $\mathscr{L}$ is shortening insensitive if and only if the complement language $\bar{\mathscr{L}}$ is lengthening insensitive.

Proof. Let $\mathscr{L}$ be shortening insensitive. Let $r \in \bar{\mathscr{L}}$ be a word in the complement of $\mathscr{L}$. Any word r' such that $r \preccurlyeq r'$ must also belong to $\bar{\mathscr{L}}$, since if it belonged to the shortening insensitive $\mathscr{L}$, r would also belong to $\mathscr{L}$. Hence $\bar{\mathscr{L}}$ is lengthening insensitive. The converse implication can be proved using the same reasoning. □

If we look at Fig. 1b, the dual effect of complement on the sensitivity of the language to length is apparent: if gray and white are switched we can see $\mathscr{L}_b$ is lengthening insensitive and $\mathscr{L}_c$ shortening insensitive.

2.4   When Is Visiting Shorter Words Enough?

Definition 7. *[Reduction] Let I be a reduction function $\Sigma^\omega \mapsto \Sigma^\omega$ such that $\forall r, I(r) \preccurlyeq r$. The reduction by I of a language $\mathscr{L}$ is $Red_I(\mathscr{L}) = \{I(r) \mid r \in \mathscr{L}\}$.*

Note that the $\preccurlyeq$ partial order is not strict so that the image of a word may be the word itself, hence identity is a reduction function. In most cases however we expect the reduction function to map many words r of the original language to a single shorter word r' of the reduced language. Note that given any two reduction functions I and I', $Red_I(Red_{I'}(\mathscr{L}))$ is still a reduction of $\mathscr{L}$. Hence chaining reduction rules still produces a reduction. As we will discuss in Sect. 3.1 structural reductions of a specification such as Lipton's transaction reduction [14, 15] or Petri net agglomerations [1,23] induce a reduction at the language level. In Fig. 1a fusing statements into a single atomic step in the program induces a reduction of the language.

Theorem 1 (Reduced Emptiness Checks). *Given two languages $\mathscr{L}$ and $\mathscr{L}'$,*

- *if $\mathscr{L}$ is shortening insensitive, then $\mathscr{L} \cap Red_I(\mathscr{L}') = \emptyset \Rightarrow \mathscr{L} \cap \mathscr{L}' = \emptyset$*
- *if $\mathscr{L}$ is lengthening insensitive, then $\mathscr{L} \cap Red_I(\mathscr{L}') \neq \emptyset \Rightarrow \mathscr{L} \cap \mathscr{L}' \neq \emptyset$.*

Proof. (Shortening insensitive $\mathscr{L}$) $\mathscr{L} \cap Red_I(\mathscr{L}') = \emptyset$ so there does not exists $r' \in \mathscr{L} \cap Red_I(\mathscr{L}')$. Because $\mathscr{L}$ is shortening insensitive, it is impossible that any run r with $r' \prec r$ belongs to $\mathscr{L} \cap \mathscr{L}'$. (Lengthening insensitive $\mathscr{L}$) At least one word r' is in $\mathscr{L}$ and $Red_I(\mathscr{L})$. Therefore the longer word r of $\mathscr{L}'$ that r' represents is also in $\mathscr{L}$ since the language is lengthening insensitive. □

With this theorem original to this paper we now can build a semi-decision procedure that is able to prove *some* lengthening or disprove *some* shortening insensitive properties using a reduction of a system.

3   Application to Verification

We now introduce the more concrete setting of LTL verification to exploit the theoretical results on languages and their shortening/lengthening sensitivity developed in Sect. 2.

3.1   Kripke Structure

From the point of view of LTL verification with a state-based logic, executions of a system (also called *runs*) are seen as infinite words over the alphabet $\Sigma = 2^{AP}$, where AP is a set of atomic propositions that may be true or false in each state. So each symbol in a run gives the truth value of all of the atomic propositions in that state of the execution, and each time an action happens we progress in the run to the next symbol. Some actions of the system update the truth value of atomic propositions, but some actions can leave them unchanged which corresponds to stuttering.

Definition 8 (Kripke Structure Syntax). *Let* AP *designate a set of atomic propositions. A Kripke structure* $KS_{AP} = \langle S, R, \lambda, s_0 \rangle$ *over* AP *is a tuple where* S *is the finite set of states,* $R \subseteq S \times S$ *is the transition relation,* $\lambda : S \mapsto 2^{AP}$ *is the state labeling function, and* $s_0 \in S$ *is the initial state.*

Definition 9 (Kripke Structure Semantics). *The language* $\mathscr{L}(KS_{AP})$ *of a Kripke structure* KS_{AP} *is defined over the alphabet* 2^{AP}. *It contains all runs of the form* $r = \lambda(s_0)\lambda(s_1)\lambda(s_2)\ldots$ *where* s_0 *is the initial state of* KS_{AP} *and* $\forall i \in \mathbb{N}$, *either* $(s_i, s_{i+1}) \in R$, *or if* s_i *is a deadlock state such that* $\forall s' \in S, (s_i, s') \notin R$ *then* $s_{i+1} = s_i$.

All system executions are considered maximal, so that they are represented by infinite runs. If the system can deadlock or terminate in some way, we can extend these finite words by an ω stutter on the last symbol of the run to obtain a run.

Subfigure (1) of Fig. 1a depicts a program where each thread (α and β) has three reachable positions (we consider that each instruction is atomic). In this example we consider that the logic only observes two atomic propositions p (true when $x = 0$) and q (true when $y = 0$). The variable z is not observed.

Subfigure (2) of Fig. 1a depicts the reachable states of this system as a Kripke structure. Actions of thread β (which do not modify the value of p or q) are horizontal while actions of thread α are vertical. While each thread has 3 reachable positions, the emission of the message by β must precede the reception by α so that some situations are unreachable. Based on Definition 9 that extends by an infinite stutter runs that end in a deadlock, we can compute the language $\mathscr{L}_A$ of this system. It consists in three parts: when thread β goes first $pq^3\ \bar{p}q\ \bar{p}\bar{q}^\omega$, with an interleaving $pq^2\ \bar{p}q^2\ \bar{p}\bar{q}^\omega$, and when thread α goes first $pq\ \bar{p}q^3\ \bar{p}\bar{q}^\omega$.

In subfigure (3) of Fig. 1a, the actions "$z = 40$; *chan.send(z)*;" of thread β are fused into a single atomic operation. This is possible because action $z = 40$ of thread β is stuttering (it cannot affect either p or q) and is non-interfering with other events (it neither enables nor disables any event other than subsequent instruction "chan.send(z)"). The language of this smaller KS is a reduction of the language of the original system. It contains two runs: thread α goes first pq $\bar{p}q^2 \ \bar{p}\bar{q}^\omega$ and thread β goes first $pq^2 \ \bar{p}q \ \bar{p}\bar{q}^\omega$.

In subfigure (4) of Fig. 1a, the already fused action "$z = 40; chan.send(z);$" of thread β is further fused with the $chan.recv()$; action of thread α. This leads to a smaller KS whose language is still a reduction of the original system now containing a single run: $pq \ \bar{p}q \ \bar{p}\bar{q}^\omega$. This simple example shows the power of structural reductions when they are applicable, with a drastic reduction of the initial language.

3.2 Automata Theoretic Verification

Let us consider the problem of model-checking of an ω-regular property φ (such as LTL) on a system using the automata-theoretic approach [25]. In this approach, we wish to answer the problem of language inclusion: do all runs of the system $\mathscr{L}(KS)$ belong to the language of the property $\mathscr{L}(\varphi)$? To do this, when the property φ is an omega-regular language (e.g. an LTL or PSL formula), we first negate the property $\neg\varphi$, then build a (variant of) a Büchi automaton $A_{\neg\varphi}$ whose language[1] consists of runs that are not in the property language $\mathscr{L}(A_{\neg\varphi}) = \Sigma^\omega \setminus \mathscr{L}(\varphi)$. We then perform a synchronized product between this Büchi automaton and the Kripke structure KS corresponding to the system's state space $A_{\neg\varphi} \otimes KS$ (where $\otimes$ is defined to satisfy $\mathscr{L}(A \otimes B) = \mathscr{L}(A) \cap \mathscr{L}(B)$). Either the language of the product is empty $\mathscr{L}(A_{\neg\varphi} \otimes KS) = \emptyset$, and the property φ is thus true of this system, or the product is non empty, and from any run in the language of the product we can build a counter-example to the property.

We will consider in the rest of the paper that the shortening or lengthening insensitive language of Definitions 5 and 6 is given as an omega-regular language or Büchi automaton typically obtained from the negation of an LTL property, and that the reduction of Definition 7 is applied to a language that corresponds to all runs in a Kripke structure typically capturing the state space of a system.

LTL Verification with Reductions. With Theorem 1, a shortening insensitive property shown to be true on the reduction (empty intersection with the language of the negation of the property) is also true of the original system. A lengthening insensitive property shown to be false on the reduction (non-empty intersection with the language of the negation of the property, hence counter-examples exist) is also false in the original system. Unfortunately, our procedure cannot prove using a reduction that a shortening insensitive property is false, or that a lengthening insensitive property is true. We offer a semi-decision procedure.

---

[1] Because computing the complement $\bar{A}$ of an automaton A is exponential in the worst case, syntactically negating φ and producing an automaton $A_{\neg\varphi}$ is preferable when A is derived from e.g. an LTL formula.

3.3   Detection of Language Sensitivity

We now present a strategy to decide if a given property expressed as a Büchi automaton is shortening insensitive, lengthening insensitive, or both.

This section relies heavily on the operations introduced and discussed at length in [16]. The authors define two *syntactic* transformations sl and cl of a transition-based generalized Büchi automaton (TGBA) A_φ that can be built from any LTL formula φ to represent its language $\mathscr{L}(\varphi) = \mathscr{L}(A_\varphi)$ [3]. TGBA are a variant of Büchi automata where the acceptance conditions are placed on edges rather than states of the automaton.

The cl closure operation *decreases stutter*, it adds to the language any word $r' \in \Sigma^\omega$ that is shorter than a word r in the language. Informally, the strategy consists in detecting when a sequence $q_1 \xrightarrow{a} q_2 \xrightarrow{a} q_3$ is possible and adding an edge $q_1 \xrightarrow{a} q_3$, hence its name cl for "closure". The sl self-loopization operation *increases stutter*, it adds to the language any run $r' \in \Sigma^\omega$ that is longer than a run r in the language. Informally, the strategy consists in adding a self-loop to any state labeled with all outgoing expressions so that we can always decide to repeat a letter rather than progress in the automaton, hence its name sl for "self-loop". More formally $\mathscr{L}(cl(A_\varphi)) = \{r' \mid \exists r \in \mathscr{L}(A_\varphi), r' \preccurlyeq r\}$ and $\mathscr{L}(sl(A_\varphi)) = \{r' \mid \exists r \in \mathscr{L}(A_\varphi), r \preccurlyeq r'\}$.

Using these operations [16] shows that there are several possible ways to test if an omega-regular language (encoded as a Büchi automaton) is stutter insensitive: essentially applying either of the operations cl or sl should leave the language unchanged. This allows to recognize that a property is stutter insensitive even though it syntactically contains e.g. the neXt operator of LTL.

For instance A_φ is stutter insensitive if and only if $\mathscr{L}(sl(cl(A_\varphi)) \otimes A_{\neg\varphi}) = \emptyset$. The full test is thus simply reduced to a language emptiness check testing that both sl and cl operations leave the language of the automaton unchanged.

Indeed for stutter insensitive languages, all or none of the runs belonging to a given stutter equivalence class of runs $\hat{r}$ must belong to the language $\mathscr{L}(A_\varphi)$. In other words, if shortening or lengthening a run can make it switch from belonging to A_φ to belonging to $A_{\neg\varphi}$, the language is stutter sensitive. This is apparent on Fig. 1b

We want weaker conditions here, but we can reuse the sl and cl operations developed for testing stutter insensitivity. Indeed for an automaton A encoding a shortening insensitive language, $\mathscr{L}(cl(A)) = \mathscr{L}(A)$ should hold. Conversely if A encodes a lengthening insensitive language, $\mathscr{L}(sl(A)) = \mathscr{L}(A)$ should hold. We express these tests as emptiness checks on a product in the following way.

Theorem 2 (Testing sensitivity). *Let A designate a Büchi automaton, and $\bar{A}$ designate its complement.*

$\mathscr{L}(cl(A) \otimes \bar{A}) = \emptyset$, *if and only if A defines a shortening insensitive language.*

$\mathscr{L}(sl(A) \otimes \bar{A}) = \emptyset$ *if and only if A defines a lengthening insensitive language.*

Proof. The expression $\mathscr{L}(cl(A) \otimes \bar{A}) = \emptyset$ is equivalent to $\mathscr{L}(cl(A)) = \mathscr{L}(A)$. The lengthening insensitive case is similar.   □

Thanks to Property 2, and in the spirit of [16] we could also test the complement of a language for the dual property if that is more efficient, i.e. $\mathscr{L}(sl(\bar{A}) \otimes A) = \emptyset$ if and only if A defines a shortening insensitive language and similarly $\mathscr{L}(cl(\bar{A}) \otimes A) = \emptyset$ iff A is lengthening insensitive. We did not really investigate these alternatives as the complexity of the test was already negligible in all of our experiments.

3.4 Agglomeration of Events Produces Shorter Runs

Among the possible strategies to reduce the complexity of analyzing a system are structural reductions. Depending on the input formalism the terminology used is different, but the main results remain stable.

In [15] transaction reduction consists in fusing two adjacent actions of a thread (or even across threads in recent versions such as [14]). The first action must not modify atomic properties and must be commutative with any action of other threads. Fusing these actions leads to shorter runs, where a stutter is lost. In the program of Fig. 1a, "z = 40" is enabled from the initial state and must happen before "chan.send(z)", but it commutes with instructions of thread α and is not observable. Hence the language $\mathscr{L}_B$ built with an atomic assumption on "z = 40; chan.send(z)" is indeed a reduction of $\mathscr{L}_A$.

Let us reason at the level of a Kripke structure. The goal of such reductions is to structurally detect the following situation in language $\mathscr{L}$: let $r = a_0^{n_0} a_1^{n_1} a_2^{n_2} \ldots$ designate a run (not necessarily in the language), there must exist two indexes i and j such that for any natural number k, $i \leq k \leq j$, $r_k = a_0^{n_0} \ldots a_i^{n_i} \ldots a_k^{n_k+1} \ldots a_j^{n_j} \ldots$ is in the language. In other words, the set of runs described as : $\{r_k = a_0^{n_0} \ldots a_i^{n_i} \ldots a_k^{n_k+1} \ldots a_j^{n_j} \ldots \mid i \leq k \leq j\}$ must belong to the language. This corresponds to an event that does not impact the truth value of atomic propositions (it stutters) and can be freely commuted with any event that occurs between indexes i and j in the run. This event is simply constrained to occur at the earliest at index i in the run and at the latest at index j. In Fig. 1a the event "z = 40" can happen as early as in the initial state, and must occur before "chan.send(z)" and thus matches this definition.

Note that these runs are all stutter equivalent, but are incomparable by the shorter than relation (e.g. *aabc, abbc, abcc* are incomparable). In this situation, a *reduction* can choose to only represent the run r instead of any of these runs. This run was not originally in the language in general, but it is indeed shorter than any of the r_k runs so it matches Definition 7 for a reduction. Note that $\hat{r}$ does contain all these longer runs so that in a stutter insensitive context, examining r is enough to conclude for any of these runs. This is why usage of structural reductions is compatible with verification of a logic such as $LTL_{\backslash X}$ and has been proposed for that express purpose in the literature [10,14].

Thus transaction reductions [14,15] as well as both pre-agglomeration and post-agglomeration of Petri nets [7,10,20,23] produce a system whose language is a reduction of the language of the original system.

For lack of space, in this paper we decided not to provide proofs that these structural transformation rules induce reductions at the language level. A formal definition involves a) introducing the syntax of a formalism and b) its semantics in terms of language, then c) defining the reduction rule, and d) proving its effect is a reduction at the language level. The exercise is not particularly difficult, and the definition of reduction rules mostly fall into the category above, where a non observable event that happens at the earliest at point a and at the latest at point b is abstracted from the trace.

Our experimental Sect. 4.2 uses the rules of [23] for (potentially partial) pre and post-agglomeration. That paper presents 22 structural reductions rules from which we selected the rules valid in the context of LTL verification. Only one rule preserving stutter insensitive LTL was not compatible with our approach since it does not produce a reduction at the language level: rule 3 "Redundant transitions" proposes that if two transitions t_1 and t_2 have the same combined effect as a transition t, and firing t_1 enables t_2, t can be discarded from the net. This reduces the number of edges in the underlying KS representing the state space, but does not affect reachability of states. However, it selects as representative a run involving both t_1 and t_2 that is longer than the one using t in the original net, it is thus not legitimate to use in our strategy (although it remains valid for $LTL_{\backslash X}$). Rules 14 "Pre agglomeration" and 15 "Post agglomeration" are the most powerful rules of [23] that we are able to apply in our context. They are known to preserve $LTL_{\backslash X}$ (but not full LTL) and their effect is a reduction at the language level, hence we *can* use them when dealing with shortening/lengthening insensitive formulae.

4   Experimentation

4.1   A Study of Properties

This section provides an empirical study of the applicability of the techniques presented in this paper to LTL properties found in the literature. To achieve this we explored several LTL benchmarks [5,6,11,13,21]. Some work [6,21] summaries the typical properties that users express in LTL. The formulae of this benchmark have been extracted directly from the literature. Dwyer et al. [5] proposes property specification patterns, expressed in several logics including LTL. These patterns have been extracted by analysing 447 formulae coming from real world projects. The RERS challenge [11] presents generated formulae inspired from real world reactive systems. The MCC [13] benchmark establishes a huge database of 45152 LTL formulae in the form of 1411 Petri net models coming from 114 origins with for each one 32 random LTL formulae. These formulae use up to 5 state-based atomic propositions, limit the nesting depth of temporal operators to 5 and are filtered in order to be non trivial. Since these formulae come with a concrete system we were able to use this benchmark to also provide performance results for our approach in Sect. 4.2. We retained 43989 model/formula pairs from this benchmark, the missing 1163 were rejected due to parse limitations of our tool when the model size is excessive ($> 10^7$ transitions). This set of roughly 2200 human-like formulae and 44k random ones lets us evaluate if the fragment of LTL that we consider is common in practice. Table 1 summarizes, for each benchmark, the number and percentage of formulae that are either stuttering insensitive, lengthening insensitive, or shortening insensitive. The sum of both shortening and lengthening formulae represents more than one third (and up to 60%) of the formulae of these benchmarks.

Concerning the polarity, although lengthening insensitive formulae seem to appear more frequently, most of these benchmarks actually contain each formula in both positive and negative forms (we retained only one) so that the summed percentage might be more relevant as a metric since lengthening insensitivity of φ is equivalent to shortening insensitivity of $\neg\varphi$. Analysis of the human-like Dwyer patterns [5] reveals that shortening/lengthening insensitive formulae mostly come from the patterns *precedence chain*, *response chain* and *constrained chain*. These properties specify causal relation between events, that are observable as causal relations between *observably different* states (that might be required to strictly follow each other), but this causality chain is not impacted by non observable events.

4.2   A Study of Performances

Benchmark Setup. Among the LTL benchmarks presented in Table 1, we opted for the MCC benchmark to evaluate the techniques presented in this paper. This benchmark seems relevant since (1) it contains both academic and industrial models, (2) it has a huge set of (random) formulae and (3) includes models so that we could measure the effect of the approach in a model-checking setting. The model-checking competition (MCC) is an annual event in its 10th edition in 2021 where competing tools are evaluated on a large benchmark. We use the formulae and models from the latest 2021 edition of the contest, where Tapaal [4] was awarded the gold medal and ITS-Tools [22] was silver in the LTL category of the contest. We evaluate both of these tools in the following performance measures, showing that our strategy is agnostic to the back-end analysis engine. Our experimental setup consists in two steps.

1. Parse the model and formula pair, and analyze the sensitivity of the formula. When the formula is shortening or lengthening insensitive (but not both) output two model/formula pairs: reduced and original. The "original" version does also benefit from reduction rules, but we apply only rules that are compatible with full LTL. The "reduced" version additionally benefits from rules that are reductions at the language level, i.e. mainly pre and post agglomeration (but enacting these rules can cause further simplifications). The original and reduced model/formula pairs that result from this procedure are then exported in the same format the contest uses. This step was implemented within ITS-tools.
2. Run an MCC compatible tool on both the reduced and original versions of each model/formula pair and record the time performance and the verdict.

For the first step, using Spot [16], we detect that a formula is either shortening or lengthening insensitive for 99.81% of formulae in less than 1 s. After this

Table 1. Sensitivity to length of properties measured using several LTL benchmarks.

Benchmark	Stutter Insens.	Length. Insens.	Short. Insens.	Others	Total
Spot [5,6,21]	63 (67%)	17 (18%)	11 (1%)	3 (3%)	94
Dwyer et al. [5]	32 (58%)	13 (23%)	9 (16%)	1 (1.81%)	55
RERS [11]	714 (35%)	777 (38%)	559 (28%)	0	2050
MCC [13]	24462 (56%)	6837 (14%)	5390 (12%)	7300 (16%)	43989

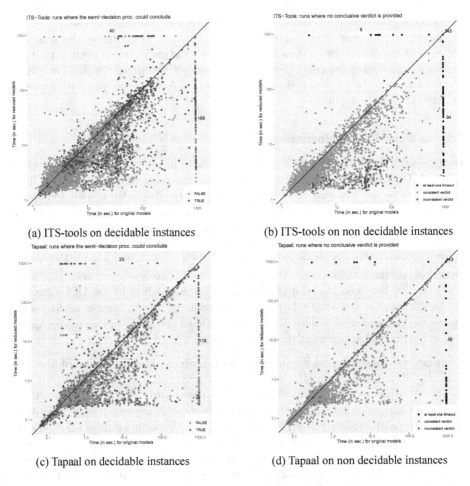

(a) ITS-tools on decidable instances

(b) ITS-tools on non decidable instances

(c) Tapaal on decidable instances

(d) Tapaal on non decidable instances

Fig. 1. Experiments on the MCC'2021 LTL benchmark using the two best tool of the MCC contest: Tapaal and ITS-tools. Figures (a) and (c) contain the cases where the verdict of the semi-decisions procedures is reliable, and distinguish cases where the output is True (empty product) and False (non empty product). (b) and (d) display the cases where the verdict is not reliable and distinguish cases where the output is inconsistent with the ground truth from cases where they agree.

analysis, we obtain 12 227 model/formula pairs where the formula is either short-ening insensitive or lengthening insensitive (but not both). Among these pairs, in 3005 cases (24.6%) the model was resistant to the structural reduction rules we use. Since our strategy does not improve such cases, we retain the remain-ing 9 222 (75.4%) model/formula pairs in the performance plots of Fig. 1. We measured that on average 34.19% of places and 32.69% of the transitions of the models were discarded by reduction rules with respect to the "original" model, though the spread is high as there are models that are almost fully reducible and some that are barely so. Application of reduction rules is in complexity related to the size of the structure of the net and takes less than 20 s to compute in 95.5% of the models. We are able to treat 9222 examples (21% of the original 43989 model/formula pairs of the MCC) using reductions. All these formulae until now could not be handled using reduction techniques.

For the second step, we measured the solution time for both reduced and original model/formula pairs using the two best tools of the MCC'2021 contest. A full tool using our strategy might optimistically first run on the reduced mod-el/formula pair hoping for a definitive answer, but we recommend the use of a portfolio approach where the first reliable answer is kept. In these experiments we neutrally measured the time for taking a semi-decision on the reduced model vs. the time for taking a (complete) decision on the original model. We then clas-sify the results into two sets, decidable instances are shown on the left of Fig. 1 and instances that are not decidable (by our procedure) are on the right. On "decidable instances" our semi-decision procedure could have concluded reliably because the formula is true and the property shortening insensitive or the for-mula is false and the property lengthening insensitive. Non decidable instances shown on the right are those where the verdict on the reduced model is not to be trusted (or both the original and reduced procedures timed out).

With this workflow we show that our approach is generic and can be easily implemented on top of any MCC compatible model-checking tool. All experi-ments were run with a 950 s timeout (close to 15 min, which is generous when the contest offers 1 h for 16 properties). We used a heterogeneous cluster of machines with four cores allocated to each experiment, and ensured that exper-iments concerning reduced and original versions of a given model/formula are comparable.

Figure 1 presents the results of these experiments. The results are all pre-sented as log-log scatter plots opposing a run on the original to a run on the reduced model/formula pair. Each dot represents an experiment on a model/-formula pair; a dot below the diagonal indicates that the reduced version was faster to solve, while a point above it indicates a case where the reduced model actually took longer to solve than the original (fortunately there are relatively few). Points that timeout for one (or both) of the approaches are plotted on the line at 950 s, we also indicate the number of points that are in this line (or corner) next to it.

The plots on the left (a) and (c) correspond to "decidable instances" while those on the right are not decidable by our procedure. The two plots on the top correspond to the performance of ITS-tools, while those on the bottom give the results with Tapaal. The general form of the results with both tools is quite similar confirming that our strategy is indeed responsible for the measured gains in performance and that they are reproducible. Reduced problems *are* generally easier to solve than the original. This gain is in the best case exponential as is visible through the existence of spread of points reaching out horizontally in this log-log space (particularly on the Tapaal plots).

The colors on the decidable instances reflect whether the verdict was true or false. For false properties a counter-example was found by both procedures interrupting the search, and while the search space of a reduced model is a priori smaller, heuristics and even luck can play a role in finding a counter-example early. True answers on the other hand generally require a full exploration of the state space so that the reductions should play a major role in reducing the complexity of model-checking. The existence of True answers where the reduction fails is surprising at first, but a smaller Kripke structure does not necessarily induce a smaller product as happens sometimes in this large benchmark (and in other reduction techniques such as stubborn sets [24]). On the other hand the points aligned to the right of the plots a) and c) (189 for ITS-tools and 119 for Tapaal) correspond to cases where our procedure improved these state of the art tools, allowing to reach a conclusion when the original method fails.

The plots on the right use orange to denote cases where the verdict on the reduced and original models were the same; on these points the procedures had comparable behaviors (either exploring a whole state space or exhibiting a counter-example). The blue color denotes points where the two procedures disagree, with several blue points above the diagonal reflecting cases where the reduced procedure explored the whole state space and thought the property was true while the original procedure found a counter-example (this is the worst case). Surprisingly, even though on these non decidable plots b) and d) our procedure should not be trusted, it mostly agrees (in 95% of the cases) with the decision reached on the original.

Out of the 9222 experiments in total, for ITS-tools 5901 runs reached a trusted decision (64 %), 2927 instances reached an untrusted verdict (32 %), and the reduced procedure timed out in 394 instances (4 %). Tapaal reached a trusted decision in 5866 instances (64 %), 2884 instances reached an untrusted verdict (31 %), and the reduced procedure timed out in 472 instances (5 %). On this benchmark of formulae we thus reached a trusted decision in almost two thirds of the cases using the reduced procedure.

5   Related Work

Partial Order vs Structural Reductions. Partial order reduction (POR) [9,18,19,24] is a very popular approach to combat state explosion for *stutter insensitive* formulae. These approaches use diverse strategies (stubborn sets, ample sets, sleep sets...) to consider only a subset of events at each step of the model-checking while still ensuring that at least one representative of each stutter equivalent class of runs is explored. Because the preservation criterion is based on equivalence classes of runs, this family of approaches is limited only to the stutter insensitive fragment of LTL (see Fig. 1b). However the structural reduction rules used in this paper are compatible and can be stacked with POR when the formula is stutter insensitive; this is the setting in which most structural reduction rules were originally defined.

Structural Reductions in the Literature. The structural reductions rules we used in the performance evaluation are defined on Petri nets where the literature on the subject is rich [1,2,7,10,20,23]. However there are other formalism where similar reduction rules have been defined such as [17] using "atomic" blocks in Promela, transaction reductions for the widely encompassing intermediate language PINS of LTSmin [14], and even in the context of multi-threaded programs [8]. All these approaches are structural or syntactic, they are run prior to model-checking per se.

Non Structural Reductions in the Literature. Other strategies have been proposed that instead of structurally reducing the system, dynamically build an abstraction of the Kripke structure where less observable stuttering occurs. These strategies build a *KS* whose language *is* a reduction of the language of the original *KS* (in the sense of Definition 7), that can then be presented to the emptiness check algorithm with the negation of the formula. They are thus also compatible with the approach proposed in this paper. Such strategies include the Covering Step Graph (CSG) construction of [26] where a "step" is performed (instead of firing a single event) that includes several independent transitions. The Symbolic Observation Graph of [12] is another example where states of the original *KS* are computed (using BDDs) and aggregated as long as the atomic proposition values do not evolve; in practice it exhibits to the emptiness check only shortest runs in each equivalence class hence it is a reduction.

6   Conclusion

To combat the state space explosion problem that LTL model-checking meets, structural reductions have been proposed that syntactically compact the model so that it exhibits less interleaving of non observable actions. Prior to this work, all of these approaches were limited to the stutter insensitive fragment of the logic. We bring a semi-decision procedure that widens the applicability of these strategies to formulae which are *shortening insensitive* or *lengthening insensitive*. The experimental evidence presented shows that the fragment of the logic covered by these new categories is quite useful in practice. An extensive measure using the models, formulae and the two best tools of the model-checking competition 2021 shows that our strategy can improve the decision power of state of the art tools, and confirm that in the best case an exponential speedup of the decision procedure can be attained. We also identified several other strategies that are compatible with our approach since they construct a reduced language. In further work we are investigating how non trusted counter-examples of the reduced model could be confirmed on the original model.

References

1. Berthelot, G., Lri-Iie: Checking properties of nets using transformations. In: Rozenberg, G. (ed.) Advances in Petri Nets 1985, pp. 19–40. Springer-Verlag, Berlin/Heidelberg (1986). https://doi.org/10.1007/BFb0016204
2. Berthomieu, B., Le Botlan, D., Dal Zilio, S.: Counting Petri net markings from reduction equations. Int. J. Softw. Tools Technol. Transfer **22**(2), 163–181 (2019). https://doi.org/10.1007/s10009-019-00519-1
3. Couvreur, J.-M.: On-the-fly verification of linear temporal logic. In: Wing, J.M., Woodcock, J., Davies, J. (eds.) FM 1999. LNCS, vol. 1708, pp. 253–271. Springer, Heidelberg (1999). https://doi.org/10.1007/3-540-48119-2_16
4. David, A., Jacobsen, L., Jacobsen, M., Jørgensen, K.Y., Møller, M.H., Srba, J.: TAPAAL 2.0: integrated development environment for timed-arc petri nets. In: Flanagan, C., König, B. (eds.) TACAS 2012. LNCS, vol. 7214, pp. 492–497. Springer, Heidelberg (2012). https://doi.org/10.1007/978-3-642-28756-5_36
5. Dwyer, M.B., Avrunin, G.S., Corbett, J.C.: Property specification patterns for finite-state verification. In: Ardis, M. (ed.) Proceedings of the 2nd Workshop on Formal Methods in Software Practice (FMSP 1998), pp. 7–15. ACM Press, March 1998. https://doi.org/10.1145/298595.298598
6. Etessami, K., Holzmann, G.J.: Optimizing Büchi automata. In: Palamidessi, C. (ed.) CONCUR 2000. LNCS, vol. 1877, pp. 153–168. Springer, Heidelberg (2000). https://doi.org/10.1007/3-540-44618-4_13
7. Evangelista, S., Haddad, S., Pradat-Peyre, J.-F.: Syntactical colored petri nets reductions. In: Peled, D.A., Tsay, Y.-K. (eds.) ATVA 2005. LNCS, vol. 3707, pp. 202–216. Springer, Heidelberg (2005). https://doi.org/10.1007/11562948_17
8. Flanagan, C., Qadeer, S.: A type and effect system for atomicity. In: PLDI, pp. 338–349. ACM (2003)
9. Godefroid, P., Wolper, P.: A partial approach to model checking. Inf. Comput. **110**(2), 305–326 (1994)
10. Haddad, S., Pradat-Peyre, J.: New efficient Petri nets reductions for parallel programs verification. Parallel Process. Lett. **16**(1), 101–116 (2006)
11. Howar, F., Jasper, M., Mues, M., Schmidt, D., Steffen, B.: The RERS challenge: towards controllable and scalable benchmark synthesis. Int. J. Softw. Tools Technol. Transfer **23**(6), 917–930 (2021). https://doi.org/10.1007/s10009-021-00617-z
12. Klai, K., Poitrenaud, D.: MC-SOG: an LTL model checker based on symbolic observation graphs. In: van Hee, K.M., Valk, R. (eds.) PETRI NETS 2008. LNCS, vol. 5062, pp. 288–306. Springer, Heidelberg (2008). https://doi.org/10.1007/978-3-540-68746-7_20
13. Kordon, F., et al.: Complete results for the 2021 edition of the model checking contest, June 2021. http://mcc.lip6.fr/2021/results.php
14. Laarman, A.: Stubborn transaction reduction. In: Dutle, A., Muñoz, C., Narkawicz, A. (eds.) NFM 2018. LNCS, vol. 10811, pp. 280–298. Springer, Cham (2018). https://doi.org/10.1007/978-3-319-77935-5_20
15. Lipton, R.J.: Reduction: a method of proving properties of parallel programs. Commun. ACM **18**(12), 717–721 (1975)
16. Michaud, T., Duret-Lutz, A.: Practical stutter-invariance checks for ω-regular languages. In: Fischer, B., Geldenhuys, J. (eds.) SPIN 2015. LNCS, vol. 9232, pp. 84–101. Springer, Cham (2015). https://doi.org/10.1007/978-3-319-23404-5_7

17. Pajault, C., Pradat-Peyre, J.-F., Rousseau, P.: Adapting Petri nets reductions to Promela specifications. In: Suzuki, K., Higashino, T., Yasumoto, K., El-Fakih, K. (eds.) FORTE 2008. LNCS, vol. 5048, pp. 84–98. Springer, Heidelberg (2008). https://doi.org/10.1007/978-3-540-68855-6_6

18. Peled, D.: Combining partial order reductions with on-the-fly model-checking. In: Dill, D.L. (ed.) CAV 1994. LNCS, vol. 818, pp. 377–390. Springer, Heidelberg (1994). https://doi.org/10.1007/3-540-58179-0_69

19. Peled, D.A., Pratt, V.R., Holzmann, G.J. (eds.): Partial Order Methods in Verification, Proceedings of a DIMACS Workshop, DIMACS Series in Discrete Mathematics and Theoretical Computer Science, vol. 29. DIMACS/AMS (1996)

20. Poitrenaud, D., Pradat-Peyre, J.-F.: Pre- and Post-agglomerations for *LTL* model checking. In: Nielsen, M., Simpson, D. (eds.) ICATPN 2000. LNCS, vol. 1825, pp. 387–408. Springer, Heidelberg (2000). https://doi.org/10.1007/3-540-44988-4_22

21. Somenzi, F., Bloem, R.: Efficient Büchi automata from LTL formulae. In: Emerson, E.A., Sistla, A.P. (eds.) CAV 2000. LNCS, vol. 1855, pp. 248–263. Springer, Heidelberg (2000). https://doi.org/10.1007/10722167_21

22. Thierry-Mieg, Y.: Symbolic model-checking using ITS-tools. In: Baier, C., Tinelli, C. (eds.) TACAS 2015. LNCS, vol. 9035, pp. 231–237. Springer, Heidelberg (2015). https://doi.org/10.1007/978-3-662-46681-0_20

23. Thierry-Mieg, Y.: Structural reductions revisited. In: Janicki, R., Sidorova, N., Chatain, T. (eds.) PETRI NETS 2020. LNCS, vol. 12152, pp. 303–323. Springer, Cham (2020). https://doi.org/10.1007/978-3-030-51831-8_15

24. Valmari, A.: A stubborn attack on state explosion. In: Clarke, E.M., Kurshan, R.P. (eds.) CAV 1990. LNCS, vol. 531, pp. 156–165. Springer, Heidelberg (1991). https://doi.org/10.1007/BFb0023729

25. Vardi, M.Y.: Automata-theoretic model checking revisited. In: Cook, B., Podelski, A. (eds.) VMCAI 2007. LNCS, vol. 4349, pp. 137–150. Springer, Heidelberg (2007). https://doi.org/10.1007/978-3-540-69738-1_10

26. Vernadat, F., Michel, F.: Covering step graph preserving failure semantics. In: Azéma, P., Balbo, G. (eds.) ICATPN 1997. LNCS, vol. 1248, pp. 253–270. Springer, Heidelberg (1997). https://doi.org/10.1007/3-540-63139-9_40

Computing Race Variants in Message-Passing Concurrent Programming with Selective Receives

Germán Vidal$^{(\boxtimes)}$ ⓘ

VRAIN, Universitat Politècnica de València, Valencia, Spain
gvidal@dsic.upv.es

Abstract. Message-passing concurrency is a popular computation model that underlies several programming languages like, e.g., Erlang, Akka, and (to some extent) Go and Rust. In particular, we consider a message-passing concurrent language with dynamic process spawning and *selective* receives, i.e., where messages can only be consumed by the target process when they match a specific constraint (e.g., the case of Erlang). In this work, we introduce a notion of *trace* that can be seen as an abstraction of a class of *causally equivalent* executions (i.e., which produce the same outcome). We then show that execution traces can be used to identify message *races*. We provide constructive definitions to compute message races as well as to produce so-called *race variants*, which can then be used to drive new executions which are not causally equivalent to the previous ones. This is an essential ingredient of state-space exploration techniques for program verification.

1 Introduction

Software verification and debugging are recognized as essential tasks in the field of software development. Not surprisingly, a recent study [27] points out that 26% of developer time is spent reproducing and fixing code bugs (which adds up to $61 billion annually). The study also identifies *reproducibility* of bugs as the biggest challenge to fix bugs faster. The situation is especially difficult for concurrent and distributed applications because of nondeterminism. In this context, traditional testing techniques often provide only a poor guarantee regarding software correctness.

As an alternative, *state-space exploration* techniques constitute a well established approach to the verification of concurrent software that basically consists in exploring the reachable states of a program, checking whether a given property holds (like some type of deadlock, a runtime error, etc.). This is the case, e.g., of *model checking* [7], where properties have been traditionally verified using a

This work has been partially supported by grant PID2019-104735RB-C41 funded by MCIN/AEI/ 10.13039/501100011033, by *Generalitat Valenciana* under grant Prometeo/2019/098 (DeepTrust), and by French ANR project DCore ANR-18-CE25-0007.

ⓒ IFIP International Federation for Information Processing 2022
Published by Springer Nature Switzerland AG 2022
M. R. Mousavi and A. Philippou (Eds.): FORTE 2022, LNCS 13273, pp. 188–207, 2022.
https://doi.org/10.1007/978-3-031-08679-3_12

model of the program. More recently, several *dynamic* approaches to state-space exploration have been introduced, which work directly with the implementation of a program. *Stateless model checking* [12] and *reachability testing* [22,26] are examples of this approach. In turn, reproducibility of bugs has been tackled by so-called *record-and-replay* debuggers. In this case, a program is first instrumented so that its execution produces a *log* as a side-effect. If a problem occurs during the execution of the program, one can use the generated log to play it back in the debugger and try to locate the source of the misbehavior.

In this work, we focus on an asynchronous *message-passing* concurrent programming language like, e.g., Erlang [9], Akka [2] and, to some extent, Go [13] and Rust [25]. A running application consists of a number of processes, each with an associated (private) *mailbox*. Here, processes can only interact through (asynchronous) message sending and receiving, i.e., we do not consider shared-memory operations. Typically, there is some degree of nondeterminism in concurrent executions that may affect the outcome of a computation. For instance, when two processes send messages to another process, these messages may sometimes arrive in any order. These so-called *message races* play a key role in the execution of message-passing concurrent programs, and exploring all feasible combinations of message sending and receiving is an essential component of state-space exploration techniques.

In particular, we consider a language with so-called *selective* receives, where a process does not necessarily consume the messages in its mailbox in the same order they were delivered, since receive statements may impose additional constraints. For instance, a receive statement in Erlang has the form

$$\texttt{receive } p_1 \texttt{ [when } g_1] \ \rightarrow t_1; \ \ldots; \ p_n \texttt{ [when } g_n] \ \rightarrow t_n \texttt{ end}$$

In order to evaluate this statement, a process should look for the *oldest* message in its mailbox that matches a pattern p_i and the corresponding (optional) guard g_i holds (if any);[1] in this case, the process continues with the evaluation of expression t_i. When no message matches any pattern, the execution of the process is *blocked* until a matching message reaches its mailbox.

Considering a message-passing concurrent language with selective receives is relevant in order to deal with a language like Erlang. Unfortunately, current approaches either do not consider selective receives—the case of reachability testing [21] which, in contrast, considers different ports for receive statements—or have not formally defined the semantics of the language and its associated *happened-before* relation—the case of Concuerror [5], which implements a stateless model checker for Erlang that follows the approach in [1,3,4].

In this paper, we introduce a notion of *trace* that is tailored to message-passing execution with dynamic process spawning and selective receives. Our traces can be seen as an extension of the *logs* of [19,20], which were introduced in the context of causal-consistent *replay* (reversible) debugging in Erlang. In particular, the key extension consists in adding some additional information to the events of a trace, namely the identifier of the target process of a message and

---

[1] If the message matches several patterns, the first one is considered.

its actual value for *send* events, and the actual constraints of a receive statement for *receive* events. In this way, we can identify not only the communications performed in a program execution but also its message races (see the discussion in the next section).

In contrast to other notions of trace that represent a particular interleaving, our traces (analogously to the *logs* of [19,20] and the *SYN-sequences* of [21]) record the sequence of actions performed by each process in an execution, ignoring the concrete scheduling of all processes' actions. These traces can easily be obtained by instrumenting the source code so that each process keeps a record of its own actions. The traces can be seen as an abstraction of a class of executions which are *causally equivalent*. Roughly speaking, two executions are causally equivalent when the executed actions and the final outcome are the same but the particular scheduling might differ. We then introduce constructive definitions for computing message races and *race variants* from a given trace. Here, race variants are denoted by a (possibly partial) trace which can then be used to drive a new program execution (as in the replay debugger CauDEr [10]). Moreover, we prove that any execution that follows (and possibly goes beyond) the computed race variant cannot give rise to an execution which is causally equivalent to the previous one, an essential property of state-space exploration techniques.

The paper is organized as follows. After some motivation in Sect. 2, we formalize the notions of *interleaving* and *trace* in Sect. 3, where we also provide a declarative definition of message race and prove a number of properties. Then, Sect. 4 provides constructive definitions for computing message races and race variants, and proves that race variants indeed give rise to executions which are not causally equivalent to the previous one. Finally, Sect. 5 presents some related work and concludes.

2   Message Races and Selective Receives

In this section, we informally introduce the considered setting and motivate our definition of *trace*. As mentioned before, we consider a message-passing (asynchronous) concurrent language with selective receives. Essentially, concurrency follows the actor model: at runtime, an application can be seen as a collection of processes that interact through message sending and receiving. Each process has an associated identifier, called *pid* (which stands for process identifier), that is unique in the execution.[2] Furthermore, we assume that processes can be spawned *dynamically* at runtime.

As in other techniques where message races are computed, e.g., *dynamic partial order reduction* (DPOR) [1,11] for *stateless model checking* [12], we distinguish *local* evaluations from *global* (or *visible*) actions. Examples of local evaluations are, e.g., a function call or the evaluation of a case expression. In turn, *global* actions include the spawning of a new process as well as any event related

---

[2] In the following, we often say "process p" to mean "process with pid p".

```
proc1() -> P2 = spawn(proc2()),
           P3 = spawn(proc3(P2)),
           send({val,1},P2).
proc2() -> receive
              {val,M} when M>0 -> {ok,M};
              error -> error
           end.
proc3(P2) -> send({val,0},P2),
             send({val,2},P2).
```

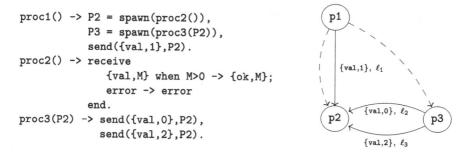

Fig. 1. A simple message-passing program

with message passing. In particular, we consider that sent messages are eventually stored in the *mailbox* of the target process. Then, the target process can *consume* these messages using a *receive* statement, which we assume is selective, i.e., it may impose some additional constraints on the receiving messages.

Example 1. Let us consider the simple code shown in Fig. 1 (we use a pseudocode that resembles the syntax of Erlang [9]). Assume that the initial process (the one that starts the execution) has pid p1 and that it begins with a call to function proc1, which first spawns two new processes with pids p2 and p3 that will evaluate the calls proc2() and proc3(P2), respectively. A call to spawn returns the pid of the new process, so variables P2 and P3 are bound to pids p2 and p3, respectively. The evaluation of proc1() ends by sending the message {val,1} to process p2. Process spawning is denoted by a dashed arrow in the diagram, while message sending is denoted by a solid arrow. Messages are *tagged* with a unique identifier (e.g., ℓ_1).

Process p3 sends two messages, {val,0} and {val,2}, to process p2. Process p2 initially blocks waiting for the arrival of a message that matches either the pattern {val,M}, i.e., a tuple whose first component is the constant val and the second component (denoted by variable M) is an integer greater than zero, or the constant error. Note that message {val,0} does not match the constraints of the receive statement since the integer value is not greater than zero. Thus, only messages ℓ_1 and ℓ_3 can be consumed by the receive statement of process p2.

In principle, one could represent a program execution by means of a concrete *interleaving* of its concurrent actions, i.e., a sequence of *events* of the form *pid:action*. E.g., we could have the following interleaving for the program of Fig. 1:

(1) p1:spawn(proc2())   (4) p2:receive({val,1})
(2) p1:spawn(proc3(p2))   (5) p3:send({val,0},p2)
(3) p1:send({val,1},p2)   (6) p3:send({val,2},p2)

This interleaving is graphically depicted in Fig. 2a, where process spawning is omitted for clarity.

In this work, though, we opt for a different representation, which is similar to the notion of *log* (in the context of replay debugging [19,20]) and that of

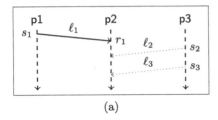 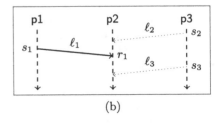

(a)   (b)

Fig. 2. Alternative interleavings for the execution of the program of Fig. 1. We have three processes, identified by pids p1, p2 and p3. Solid arrows denote the connection between messages sent and received (similarly to the synchronization pairs of [21]), while dotted arrows represent messages sent but not yet received. Time, represented by dashed lines, flows from top to bottom.

SYN-sequence (in reachability testing [21]). In contrast to interleavings (as in, e.g., stateless model checking [12] and DPOR techniques [1,11]), the advantage of using logs is that they represent a *partial order* for the concurrent actions, so that DPOR techniques are no longer needed. To be more precise, a log (as defined in [19]) maps each process to a sequence of the following actions:

- process spawning, denoted by spawn(p), where p is the *pid* of the new process;
- message sending, denoted by send(ℓ), where ℓ is a message tag;
- and message reception, denoted by rec(ℓ), where ℓ is a message tag.

In contrast to the SYN-sequences of [21], *synchronization pairs* (connecting message sending and receiving) are not explicitly considered but can easily be inferred from send/receive actions with the same message tag. Furthermore, logs include spawn actions because runtime processes are not statically fixed, which is not considered by SYN-sequences. Logs are used by the reversible debugger CauDEr [10] as part of an approach to *record-and-replay* debugging in Erlang (a popular approach to deal with the problem of reproducibility of bugs).

In practice, logs can be obtained by using an instrumented semantics (as in [19,20]) or by instrumenting the program so that its execution (in the standard environment) produces a log as a side-effect (along the lines of the technique presented in [15]). It is worthwhile to note that no centralised monitoring is required; every process only needs to register its own actions independently. For instance, a log associated with the execution shown in Fig. 1 is as follows:

$$[\text{p1} \mapsto \text{spawn(p2)}, \text{spawn(p3)}, \text{send}(\ell_1); \quad \text{p2} \mapsto \text{rec}(\ell_1); \quad \text{p3} \mapsto \text{send}(\ell_2), \text{send}(\ell_3)]$$

Unfortunately, this log does not contain enough information for computing *message races*. A first, obvious problem is that *send* events do not include the pid of the target process. Hence, even if there is a (potential) race between messages ℓ_1 and ℓ_2 to reach process p2, this cannot be determined from the log. Trivially, one could solve this problem by adding the pid of the target process to every send event, as follows (we omit spawn actions since they are not relevant for the discussion):

$$[\mathsf{p1} \mapsto \ldots, \mathsf{send}(\ell_1, \mathsf{p2}); \quad \mathsf{p2} \mapsto \mathsf{rec}(\ell_1); \quad \mathsf{p3} \mapsto \mathsf{send}(\ell_2, \mathsf{p2}), \mathsf{send}(\ell_3, \mathsf{p2})] \quad (*)$$

Now, in principle, one could say that messages ℓ_1 and ℓ_2 race for process p2 since the target is the same (p2) and there are no dependencies among $\mathsf{send}(\ell_1, \mathsf{p2})$ and $\mathsf{send}(\ell_2, \mathsf{p2})$ (s_1 and s_2 in Fig. 2a).

However, when we consider *selective* receives, the log (*) above can be ambiguous. In particular, this log represents both interleavings represented by the diagrams of Fig. 2a and Fig. 2b (where message ℓ_2 reaches first process p2 but its associated value, {val,0}, does not match the constraints of the receive statement since the guard M > 0 does not hold for M = 0). However, the diagram in Fig. 2a points out to a (potential) message race between messages ℓ_1 and ℓ_2, while the diagram in Fig. 2b suggests a (potential) message race between messages ℓ_1 and ℓ_3 instead.

In order to distinguish the executions shown in Figs. 2a and 2b one could add a new action, $\mathsf{deliver}(\ell)$, to explicitly account for the delivery of a message with tag ℓ. In this way, we would know the order in which messages are stored in the process' mailbox, which uniquely determines the order in which they can be consumed by receive statements. E.g., the actions of process p2 in the execution of Fig. 2a would be

$$[\ldots \mathsf{p2} \mapsto \mathsf{deliver}(\ell_1), \mathsf{rec}(\ell_1), \mathsf{deliver}(\ell_2), \mathsf{deliver}(\ell_3) \ldots] \quad (**)$$

while those of Fig. 2b would be as follows:

$$[\ldots \mathsf{p2} \mapsto \mathsf{deliver}(\ell_2), \mathsf{deliver}(\ell_1), \mathsf{rec}(\ell_1), \mathsf{deliver}(\ell_3) \ldots] \quad (***)$$

This approach is explored in [14], where a *lightweight* (but approximate) technique to computing message races is proposed. Unfortunately, making explicit message delivery does not suffice to allow one to compute message races in general. In particular, while it would allow us to distinguish the situation of Fig. 2a from that of Fig. 2b, we could not still determine whether there is an actual race between messages ℓ_1 and ℓ_2 or between messages ℓ_1 and ℓ_3. For instance, for the program of Fig. 1, only the message race between ℓ_1 and ℓ_3 is feasible, as explained above. For this purpose, we need to also include the actual values of messages as well as the constraints of receive statements.

In the next section, we propose an appropriate definition of *trace* (an extended log) that includes enough information for computing message races.

3 Execution Traces

In this section, we formalize an appropriate notion of trace that is adequate to compute message races in a message-passing concurrent language with dynamic process spawning and selective receives. Here, we do not consider a specific programming language but formalize our developments in the context of a generic language that includes the basic actions spawn, send, and receive.

As mentioned in the previous section, we consider that each process is uniquely identified by a pid. A message takes a *value* v (from a given domain) and is uniquely identified by a tag ℓ.[3] We further require the domains of pids, values, and tags to be disjoint. We also consider a generic domain of constraints and a decidable function match so that, for all value v and constraint cs, match(v, cs) returns *true* if the value matches the constraint cs and *false* otherwise. In Erlang, for instance, a constraint is associated with the clauses of a receive statement, i.e., it has the form $(p_1 \text{ [when } g_1] \to t_1; \ldots; p_n \text{ [when } g_n] \to t_n)$, and function match determines if a value v matches some pattern p_i and the associated guard g_i (if any) evaluates to true.

In this work, events have the form $p\!:\!a$, where p is a pid and a is one of the following actions:

- spawn(p'), which denotes the spawning of a new process with pid p';
- send(ℓ, v, p'), which denotes the sending of a message with tag ℓ and value v to process p';
- rec(ℓ, cs), which denotes the *reception* of a message with tag ℓ by a receive statement with a constraint cs.[4]

In the following, a (finite) sequence is denoted as follows: $e_1, e_2, \ldots, e_n$, $n \geq 0$, where n is the length of the sequence. We often use set notation for sequences and let $e \in S$ denote that event e occurs in sequence S. Here, ϵ denotes an empty sequence, while $S; S'$ denotes the concatenation of sequences S and S'; by abuse of notation, we use the same operator when a sequence has only a single element, i.e., $e_1; (e_2, \ldots, e_n)$ and $(e_1, \ldots, e_{n-1}); e_n$ both denote the sequence $e_1, \ldots, e_n$. Furthermore, given a sequence of events

$$S = (p_1\!:\!a_1, p_2\!:\!a_2, \ldots, p_n\!:\!a_n)$$

we let actions(p, S) denote the sequence of actions $(a'_1, a'_2, \ldots, a'_m)$ such that $p\!:\!a'_1, p\!:\!a'_2, \ldots, p\!:\!a'_m$ are all and only the events of process p in S and in the same order. Given a sequence $S = (e_1, \ldots, e_n)$, we also say that e_i *precedes* e_j, in symbols $e_i \prec_S e_j$, if $i < j$.

Now, we formalize the notions of *interleaving* and *trace*. Intuitively speaking, an interleaving is a sequence of events that represents a *linearization* of the actions of a concurrent execution, while a trace is a mapping from processes to sequences of actions (so a trace only denotes a *partial relation* on events).

Definition 1 (interleaving). *A sequence of events* $S = (p_1\!:\!a_1, \ldots, p_n\!:\!a_n)$ *is an* interleaving *with initial pid p_1 if the following conditions hold:*

1. *Each event* $(p_j : a_j) \in S$ *is either preceded by an event* $(p_i : \text{spawn}(p_j)) \in S$ *with* $p_i \neq p_j$, $1 \leq i < j \leq n$, *or* $p_j = p_1$.

---

[3] Message tags were introduced in [18] to uniquely identify messages, since we might have several messages with the same value and would be indistinguishable otherwise.

[4] Note that *receive* actions represent the *consumption* of messages by receive statements rather than their delivery to the process' mailbox. Observe that the order of message delivery and message reception might be different (see, e.g., messages ℓ_1 and ℓ_2 in Fig. 2b).

2. *Each event* $(p_j : \mathsf{rec}(\ell, cs)) \in S$ *is preceded by an event* $(p_i : \mathsf{send}(\ell, v, p_j)) \in S$, $1 \le i < j \le n$, *such that* $\mathsf{match}(v, cs) = true$.

3. *For each pair of events* $p_i : \mathsf{send}(\ell, v, p_j)$, $p_j : \mathsf{rec}(\ell, cs) \in S$, *we have that, for all* $p_i : \mathsf{send}(\ell', v', p_j) \in S$ *that precedes* $p_i : \mathsf{send}(\ell, v, p_j)$, *in symbols*

$$p_i : \mathsf{send}(\ell', v', p_j) \prec_S p_i : \mathsf{send}(\ell, v, p_j)$$

either $\mathsf{match}(v', cs) = false$ *or there is an event* $p_j : \mathsf{rec}(\ell', cs') \in S$ *such that* $p_j : \mathsf{rec}(\ell', cs') \prec_S p_j : \mathsf{rec}(\ell, cs)$.

4. *Finally, for all event* $p_i : \mathsf{spawn}(p_j)$, p_j *only occurs as the argument of* spawn *in this event, and for all event* $p_i : \mathsf{send}(\ell, v, p_j)$, ℓ *only occurs as the argument of* send *in this event (uniqueness of pids and tags).*

The first two conditions in the definition of interleaving are very intuitive: all the actions of a process (except for those of the initial process, p_1) must happen after its spawning, and each reception of a message ℓ must be preceded by a sending of message ℓ and, moreover, the message value should match the receive constraint. The third condition is a bit more involved but can be explained as follows: the messages sent between two given processes should be delivered in the same order they were sent. Thus, if a process p_j receives a message ℓ from process p_i, all previous messages sent from p_i to p_j (if any) should have been already received or their value should not match the constraint of the receive statement. The last condition simply ensures that pids and tags are unique in an interleaving, as mentioned before.

Example 2. Consider the program of Example 1. A possible interleaving is

$$\mathsf{p1:spawn(p2)}, \ \mathsf{p1:spawn(p3)}, \ \mathsf{p1:send}(\ell_1, v_1, \mathsf{p2}), \ \mathsf{p2:rec}(\ell_1, cs_1),$$
$$\mathsf{p3:send}(\ell_2, v_2, \mathsf{p2}), \ \mathsf{p3:send}(\ell_3, v_3, \mathsf{p2})$$

which can be graphically represented by the diagram of Fig. 2a.

An interleaving induces a *happened-before* relation [17] on events as follows:

Definition 2 (happened-before, independence). *Let* $S = (e_1, \ldots, e_n)$ *be an interleaving. We say that* $e_i = (p_i : a_i)$ *happened before* $e_j = (p_j : a_j)$, $i < j$, *in symbols* $e_i \leadsto_S e_j$, *if one of the following conditions hold:*

1. $p_i = p_j$ *(i.e., the actions of a given process cannot be swapped);*
2. $a_i = \mathsf{spawn}(p_j)$ *(i.e., a process cannot perform an action before it is spawned);*
3. $a_i = \mathsf{send}(\ell, v, p_j)$ *and* $a_j = \mathsf{rec}(\ell, cs)$ *(i.e., a message cannot be received before it is sent).*

If $e_i \leadsto_S e_j$ *and* $e_j \leadsto_S e_k$, *then* $e_i \leadsto_S e_k$ *(transitivity). If neither* $e_i \leadsto_S e_j$ *nor* $e_j \leadsto_S e_i$, *we say that the two events are independent.*

Given an interleaving S, the associated happened-before relation $\leadsto_S$ is clearly a (strict) partial order since the following properties hold:

- No event may happen before itself (irreflexivity) since $e_i \leadsto_S e_j$ requires $i < j$ by definition.[5]
- If $e_i \leadsto_S e_j$ we have $i < j$ and, thus, $e_j \leadsto_S e_i$ is not possible (asymmetry).
- Finally, the relation $\leadsto_S$ is transitive by definition.

In the following, we say that two interleavings are *causally equivalent* if they have the same events and only differ in the swapping of a number of independent events. Formally,

Definition 3 (causal equivalence). *Let S_1 and S_2 be interleavings with the same initial pid. We say that S_1 and S_2 are* causally equivalent, *in symbols $S_1 \approx S_2$, if S_2 can be obtained from S_1 by a finite number of swaps of consecutive independent events.*

We note that our notion of causal equivalence is similar to that of *trace equivalence* in [23] and that of causally equivalent *derivations* in [19,20].

The causal equivalence relation on interleavings is an *equivalence relation* since it is trivially reflexive ($S \approx S$ holds for all interleavings), symmetric ($S_1 \approx S_2$ implies $S_2 \approx S_1$ by considering the same swaps in the reverse order), and transitive ($S_1 \approx S_2$ and $S_2 \approx S_3$ implies $S_1 \approx S_3$ by considering first the swaps that produce S_2 from S_1 and, then, those that transform S_2 into S_3).

It is worthwhile to note that not all independent events can be swapped if we want to produce a valid interleaving. Let us illustrate this point with an example:

Example 3. Consider the interleaving shown in Example 2 that is graphically represented in the diagram of Fig. 2a. Here, we might perform a number of swaps of independent consecutive events so that we end up with the following causally equivalent interleaving:

$$p1\!:\!spawn(p2), \quad p1\!:\!spawn(p3), \quad p3\!:\!send(\ell_2, v_2, p2), \quad p1\!:\!send(\ell_1, v_1, p2),$$
$$p2\!:\!rec(\ell_1, cs_1), \quad p3\!:\!send(\ell_3, v_3, p2)$$

which corresponds to the diagram of Fig. 2b. In this case, we were able to swap the events $p1\!:\!send(\ell_1, v_1, p2)$ and $p3\!:\!send(\ell_2, v_2, p2)$ because they are independent and, moreover, the resulting interleaving does not violate condition (3) in Definition 1 since $match(v_2, cs_1) = false$.

In contrast, we could not swap $p1 : send(\ell_1, v_1, p2)$ and $p3 : send(\ell_3, v_2, p2)$ since the resulting sequence of events

$$p1\!:\!spawn(p2), \quad p1\!:\!spawn(p3), \quad p3\!:\!send(\ell_2, v_2, p2), \quad p3\!:\!send(\ell_3, v_3, p2),$$
$$p1\!:\!send(\ell_1, v_1, p2), \quad p2\!:\!rec(\ell_1, cs_1)$$

would not be an interleaving because it would violate condition (3) in Definition 1; namely, we have $match(v_3, cs_1) = true$ and, thus, event $p2\!:\!rec(\ell_1, cs_1)$ would not be correct in this position (message ℓ_3 should be received instead).

---

[5] Note that repeated events in an interleaving are not allowed by Definition 1.

In general, we can easily prove that the swap of two independent events in an interleaving always produces a valid interleaving (according to Definition 1) except when the considered events are both send with the same source and target pids. In this last case, it depends on the particular interleaving, as illustrated in the previous example.

A straightforward property is the following: causally equivalent interleavings induce the same happened-before relation, and vice versa.

Lemma 1. *Let S, S' be interleavings with the same initial pid. Then, we have $S \approx S'$ iff $\leadsto_S = \leadsto_{S'}$.*

While interleavings might be closer to an actual execution, it is often more convenient to have a higher-level representation, one where all causally equivalent interleavings have the same representation. For this purpose, we introduce the notion of *trace* as a mapping from pids to sequences of actions. Here, the key idea is to keep the actions of each process separated.

First, we introduce some notation. Let τ be a mapping from pids to sequences of actions, which we denote by a finite mapping of the form

$$[p_1 \mapsto A_1; \ldots; p_n \mapsto A_n]$$

Given an interleaving S, we let

$$tr(S) = [p_1 \mapsto \mathsf{actions}(p_1, S); \ldots; p_n \mapsto \mathsf{actions}(p_n, S)]$$

where $p_1, \ldots, p_n$ are the pids in S. We also let $\tau(p)$ denote the sequence of actions associated with process p in τ. Also, $\tau[p \mapsto A]$ denotes that τ is an arbitrary mapping such that $\tau(p) = A$; we use this notation either as a condition on τ or as a modification of τ. We also say that $(p : a) \in \tau$ if $a \in \tau(p)$. Moreover, we say that $p_1 : a_1$ *precedes* $p_2 : a_2$ in τ, in symbols $(p_1 : a_1) \prec_\tau (p_2 : a_2)$, if $p_1 = p_2$, $\tau(p_1) = A$, and a_1 precedes a_2 in A; otherwise, the (partial) relation is not defined.

Definition 4 (trace). *A trace τ with initial pid p_0 is a mapping from pids to sequences of actions if $tr(S) = \tau$ for some interleaving S with initial pid p_0.*

One could give a more direct definition of trace by mimicking the conditions of an interleaving, but the above, indirect definition is simpler.

A trace represents a so-called *Mazurkiewicz trace* [23], i.e., it represents a *partial order relation* (using the terminology of model checking [12]), where all linearizations of this partial order represent causally equivalent interleavings. In particular, given a trace τ, we let $\mathsf{sched}(\tau)$ denote the set of all *causally equivalent* linearizations of the events in τ, which is formalized as follows:

Definition 5. *Let τ be a trace with initial pid p_0. We say that an interleaving S with initial pid p_0 is a linearization of τ, in symbols $S \in \mathsf{sched}(\tau)$, if $tr(S) = \tau$.*

The following property is a trivial consequence of our definition of function sched:

Lemma 2. *Let* S, S' *be interleavings with the same initial pid and such that* $\mathsf{actions}(p, S) = \mathsf{actions}(p, S')$ *for all pid* p *in* S, S'. *Then,* $tr(S) = tr(S')$.

Proof. The proof is a direct consequence of the definition of function tr, since only the relative actions of each process are recorded in a trace.

The next result states that all the interleavings in $\mathsf{sched}(\tau)$ are indeed causally equivalent:

Theorem 1. *Let* τ *be a trace. Then,* $S, S' \in \mathsf{sched}(\tau)$ *implies* $S \approx S'$.

Proof. Let us consider two different interleavings $S, S' \in \mathsf{sched}(\tau)$. By the definition of function tr and Definition 5, S and S' have the same events and the same initial pid. Also, both interleavings have the same relative order for the actions of each process. Moreover, by definition of interleaving (Definition 1), we know that all events $p\!:\!a$ of a process (but the initial one) must be preceded by an event $p'\!:\!\mathsf{spawn}(p)$, and that all receive events $p\!:\!\mathsf{rec}(\ell, cs)$ must be preceded by a corresponding send event $p'\!:\!\mathsf{send}(\ell, v, p)$. Therefore, the happened-before relation induced from S and S' must be the same and, thus, $S \approx S'$ by Lemma 1. $\square$

Trivially, all interleavings in $\mathsf{sched}(\tau)$ induce the same happened-before relation (since they are causally equivalent). We also say that τ induces the same happened-before relation (i.e., $\leadsto_S$ for any $S \in \mathsf{sched}(\tau)$) and denote it with $\leadsto_\tau$.

The following result is also relevant to conclude that a trace represents *all and only* the causally equivalent interleavings.

Theorem 2. *Let* τ *be a trace and* $S \in \mathsf{sched}(\tau)$ *an interleaving. Let* S' *be an interleaving with* $S' \notin \mathsf{sched}(\tau)$. *Then,* $S \not\approx S'$.

Proof. Assume that S and S' have the same events and that $\mathsf{actions}(p, S) = \mathsf{actions}(p, S')$ for all pid p in S, S' (otherwise, the claim follows trivially). Let us proceed by contradiction. Assume that $S' \notin \mathsf{sched}(\tau)$ and $S \approx S'$. Since $\mathsf{actions}(p, S) = \mathsf{actions}(p, S')$ for all pid p in S, S', we have $tr(S) = tr(S')$ by Lemma 2. Thus, $S' \in \mathsf{sched}(\tau)$, which contradicts our assumption. $\square$

Example 4. Consider the following trace τ, where we abbreviate $\mathsf{send}(\ell_i, v_i, p_i)$ as s_i and $\mathsf{rec}(\ell_i, cs_i)$ as r_i:

$$[\; \mathsf{p1} \mapsto \mathsf{spawn}(\mathsf{p3}), \mathsf{spawn}(\mathsf{p2}), \mathsf{spawn}(\mathsf{p4}), \mathsf{spawn}(\mathsf{p5}), r_5, s_7; \quad \mathsf{p2} \mapsto s_2;$$
$$\mathsf{p3} \mapsto r_1, s_3, r_2, r_4, s_5, r_6; \quad \mathsf{p4} \mapsto r_3; \quad \mathsf{p5} \mapsto s_1, s_4, s_8 \qquad]$$

A possible execution following this trace is graphically depicted in Fig. 3, where spawn actions have been omitted for clarity. Moreover, we assume that arrowheads represent the point in time where messages are delivered to the target process. Despite the simplicity of traces, we can extract some interesting conclusions. For example, if we assume that τ is the trace of a terminating execution, we might conclude that messages ℓ_7 and ℓ_8 are *orphan* messages (i.e., messages that are sent but never received) since there are no corresponding events r_7 and

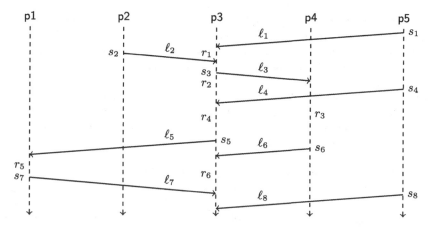

Fig. 3. Message-passing diagram. Processes (pi, $i = 1, \ldots, 5$) are represented as vertical dashed arrows, where time flows from top to bottom. Message sending is represented by solid arrows labeled with a tag (ℓ_i), $i = 1, \ldots, 8$. Note that all events associated with a message ℓ_i have the same subscript i.

r_8 in τ. A possible interleaving in $\mathsf{sched}(\tau)$ that follows the diagram in Fig. 3 is as follows:

$$\mathsf{p}_1 : \mathsf{spawn}(p_3), \;\; \mathsf{p}_1 : \mathsf{spawn}(p_2), \;\; \mathsf{p}_1 : \mathsf{spawn}(p_4), \;\; \mathsf{p}_1 : \mathsf{spawn}(p_5),$$
$$\mathsf{p}_5 : s_1, \;\; \mathsf{p}_3 : r_1, \;\; \mathsf{p}_2 : s_2, \;\; \mathsf{p}_3 : s_3, \;\; \mathsf{p}_3 : r_2, \;\; \mathsf{p}_5 : s_4, \;\; \mathsf{p}_3 : r_4,$$
$$\mathsf{p}_4 : r_3, \;\; \mathsf{p}_3 : s_5, \;\; \mathsf{p}_4 : s_6, \;\; \mathsf{p}_1 : r_5, \;\; \mathsf{p}_3 : r_6, \;\; \mathsf{p}_1 : s_7, \;\; \mathsf{p}_5 : s_8$$

By swapping, e.g., events $\mathsf{p}_2 : s_2$ and $\mathsf{p}_3 : s_3$ we get another interleaving in $\mathsf{sched}(\tau)$, and so forth. Note that $\mathsf{p}_2 : s_2$ and $\mathsf{p}_3 : s_3$ are independent since $\mathsf{p}_3 : s_3 \prec_\tau \mathsf{p}_3 : r_2$.

In the following, we assume that the actions of a process are uniquely determined by the order of its receive events (equivalently, by the order in which messages are delivered to this process). To be more precise, given a sequence of messages delivered to a given process, the actions of this process are deterministic except for the choice of fresh identifiers for the pids of spawned processes and the tags of sent messages, which has no impact on the outcome of the execution. Therefore, if we have two executions of a program where each process receives the same messages and in the same order, and perform the same number of steps, then the computations will be the same (identical, if we assume that the same process identifiers and message tags are chosen).

The following notion of *subtrace* is essential to characterize message races:

Definition 6 (subtrace). *Given traces τ, τ' with the same initial pid, we say that τ' is a subtrace of τ, in symbols $\tau' \ll \tau$, iff for all pid p in τ, τ' we have that the sequence $\tau'(p)$ is a prefix of the sequence $\tau(p)$.*

Intuitively speaking, we can obtain a subtrace by deleting the final actions of some processes. However, note that actions cannot be arbitrarily removed since the resulting mapping must still be a trace (i.e., all linearizations must still be interleavings according to Definition 1). For instance, this prevents us from deleting the sending of a message whose corresponding receive is not deleted.

Let us conclude this section with a *declarative* notion of message race:

Definition 7 (message race). *Let τ be a trace with $\tau(p) = a_1, \ldots, a_n$ and $a_i = \mathsf{rec}(\ell, cs)$, $1 \le i \le n$. There exists a message race between ℓ and ℓ' in τ iff there is a subtrace $\tau' \ll \tau$ such that $\tau'(p) = a_1, \ldots, a_{i-1}$ and $\tau'[p \mapsto a_1, \ldots, a_{i-1}, \mathsf{rec}(\ell', cs)]$ is a trace.*

Informally speaking, we have a message race whenever we have an execution which is a prefix of the original one up to the point where a different message is received.

Consider, e.g., the trace in Example 4. If we assume that the value of message ℓ_4 matches the constraints cs_2 of receive $r_2 = \mathsf{rec}(\ell_2, cs_2)$, i.e., $\mathsf{match}(v_4, cs_2) = true$, we have a race between ℓ_2 and ℓ_4 since we have the following subtrace τ'

$$[\; \mathsf{p1} \mapsto \mathsf{spawn}(\mathsf{p3}), \mathsf{spawn}(\mathsf{p2}), \mathsf{spawn}(\mathsf{p4}), \mathsf{spawn}(\mathsf{p5}), \cancel{s_6}, \cancel{s_7}; \quad \mathsf{p2} \mapsto s_2;$$
$$\mathsf{p3} \mapsto r_1, s_3, \cancel{r_2}, \cancel{r_4}, \cancel{s_5}, \cancel{r_6}; \quad \mathsf{p4} \mapsto r_3; \quad \mathsf{p5} \mapsto s_1, s_4, s_8 \;]$$

and $\tau'[\mathsf{p3} \mapsto r_1, s_3, \mathsf{rec}(\ell_4, cs_2)]$ is a trace according to Definition 4.

4   Computing Message Races and Race Variants

In this section, we introduce constructive definitions for computing message races and *race variants* from a given execution trace. Intuitively speaking, once we identify a message race, a race variant is a *partial* trace that can be used to drive the execution of a program so that a new interleaving which is not causally equivalent to the previous one is obtained. Computing message races and race variants are essential ingredients of a systematic state-space exploration tool.

First, we introduce the notion of *race set* that, given a trace τ and a message ℓ that has been received in τ, computes all the messages that race with ℓ in τ for the same receive (if any). It is worthwhile to note that race sets are defined on traces, i.e., message races do not depend on a particular interleaving but on the class of causally equivalent interleavings represented by a trace.

Definition 8 (race set). *Let τ be a trace with $e_r = (p\!:\!\mathsf{rec}(\ell, cs)) \in \tau$. Consider a message $\ell' \ne \ell$ with $e'_s = (p'\!:\!\mathsf{send}(\ell', v', p)) \in \tau$ such that $\mathsf{match}(v', cs) = true$. We say that messages ℓ and ℓ' race for e_r in τ if*

- *e_r does not happen before e'_s, i.e., $e_r \not\prec_\tau e'_s$;*
- *for all event $e''_s = (p'\,:\,\mathsf{send}(\ell'', v'', p)) \in \tau$ such that $e''_s \prec_\tau e'_s$ either $\mathsf{match}(v'', cs) = false$ or there exists an event $(p\,:\,\mathsf{rec}(\ell'', cs'')) \in \tau$ with $(p\!:\!\mathsf{rec}(\ell'', cs'')) \prec_\tau (p\!:\!\mathsf{rec}(\ell, cs))$.*

We let $\mathsf{race\_set}_\tau(\ell)$ denote the set all messages that race with ℓ in τ.

Intuitively speaking, the definition above requires the following conditions for messages ℓ and ℓ' to race for a receive statement e_r:

1. The target of both messages must be the same (p) and their values should match the constraint cs in e_r (note that we already know that the value of message ℓ matches the constraint of e_r since τ is a trace).
2. The original receive event, e_r, cannot happen before the sending event e'_s of message ℓ'. Otherwise, we had a dependency and removing e_r would prevent e'_s to happen (in a well-formed trace).
3. Finally, we should check that there are no other messages sent by the same process (and to the same target) that match the constraint cs and have not been received before e_r (since, in this case, the first of such messages would race with ℓ instead).

Given a trace τ and a receive event $p : \text{rec}(\ell, cs) \in \tau$, a naive algorithm for computing the associated race set, $\text{race\_set}_\tau(\ell)$, can proceed as follows:

- First, we identify the set of events of the form $p' : \text{send}(\ell', v', p)$ in τ with $\ell' \neq \ell$, i.e., all *send* events where the target process is p and the message tag is different from ℓ.
- Now, we remove from this set each *send* event $p' : \text{send}(\ell', v', p)$ where $p : \text{rec}(\ell, cs) \leadsto_\tau p' : \text{send}(\ell', v', p)$.
- We also remove the events $p' : \text{send}(\ell', v', p)$ where $\text{match}(v', cs) = false$.
- Finally, for each subset of *send* events from the same process, we select (at most) one of them as follows. We check for each *send* event (starting from the oldest one) whether there is a corresponding *receive* event in p which precedes $p : \text{rec}(\ell, cs)$. The message tag of the first *send* event without a corresponding *receive* (if any) belongs to the race set, and the remaining ones (from the same process) can be discarded.

Example 5. Consider again the trace τ from Example 4. Let us focus on the second receive event of process p3, denoted by r_2. Here, we have five (other) messages with the same target (p3): $\ell_1, \ell_4, \ell_6, \ell_7$ and ℓ_8. Let us further assume that the values of all messages match the constraint of r_2 except for message ℓ_4. Let us analyze each message separately:

- Message ℓ_1 is excluded from the message race since there exists a corresponding receive event, r_1, and $r_1 \prec_\tau r_2$. Hence, $\ell_1 \notin \text{race\_set}_\tau(\ell_2)$.
- As for message ℓ_4, we trivially have $r_2 \not\leadsto_\tau s_4$. Moreover, there is a previous event, s_1, from p5 to p3 but it has already been received (r_1). However, we assumed that the value of message ℓ_4 does not match the constraints of r_2 and, thus, $\ell_4 \notin \text{race\_set}_\tau(\ell_2)$.
- Consider now message ℓ_6. At first sight, it may seem that there is a dependency between r_2 and the sending event s_6 (since message ℓ_2 was delivered before s_3). However, this is not the case since event s_3 happened before r_2 and, thus, $r_3 \leadsto_\tau s_6$ but $r_2 \not\leadsto_\tau r_3$. Moreover, there are no previous send events in p4 and, thus, $\ell_6 \in \text{race\_set}_\tau(\ell_2)$.

– Regarding message ℓ_7, we have $r_2 \leadsto_\tau s_7$ since $r_2 \leadsto_\tau s_5$, $s_5 \leadsto_\tau r_5$ and $r_5 \leadsto_\tau$ s_7. Therefore, messages ℓ_2 and ℓ_7 cannot race for r_2 and $\ell_7 \notin \mathsf{race\_set}_\tau(\ell_2)$.

– Finally, consider message ℓ_8. Trivially, we have $r_2 \not\leadsto_\tau s_8$. Now, we should check that all previous sent messages (ℓ_1 and ℓ_4) have been previously received or do not match the constraints of e_r, which is the case. Therefore, $\ell_8 \in \mathsf{race\_set}_\tau(\ell_2)$.

Hence, we have $\mathsf{race\_set}_\tau(\ell_2) = \{\ell_6, \ell_8\}$.

As mentioned before, computing message races can be useful to identify alternative executions which are not causally equivalent to the current one. Ideally, we want to explore only one execution (interleaving) per equivalence class (trace). For this purpose, we introduce the notion of *race variant* which returns a (typically partial) trace, as follows:

Definition 9 (race variant). *Let* $\tau[p \mapsto A; \mathsf{rec}(\ell, cs); A']$ *be a trace with* $\ell' \in$ $\mathsf{race\_set}_\tau(\ell)$. *The* race variant *of* τ *w.r.t.* ℓ *and* ℓ', *in symbols* $\mathsf{variant}_\tau(\ell, \ell')$, *is given by the (possibly partial) trace*

$$\mathsf{rdep}(A', \tau[p \mapsto A; \mathsf{rec}(\ell', cs)])$$

where the auxiliary function rdep *is inductively defined as follows:*

$$\mathsf{rdep}(A, \tau) = \begin{cases} \tau & \text{if } A = \epsilon \\ \mathsf{rdep}(A', \tau) & \text{if } A = \mathsf{rec}(\ell, cs); A' \\ \mathsf{rdep}(A'; A'', \tau[p \mapsto \epsilon]) & \text{if } A = \mathsf{spawn}(p); A', \ \tau(p) = A'' \\ \mathsf{rdep}(A'; A^*, \tau[p \mapsto A'']) & \text{if } A = \mathsf{send}(\ell, v, p); A', \ \tau(p) = A''; \mathsf{rec}(\ell, cs); A^* \\ \mathsf{rdep}(A', \tau) & \text{if } A = \mathsf{send}(\ell, v, p); A', \ \mathsf{rec}(\ell, cs) \notin \tau(p) \end{cases}$$

Intuitively speaking, $\mathsf{variant}_\tau(\ell, \ell')$ removes the original receive action $\mathsf{rec}(\ell, cs)$ from τ as well as all the actions that depend on this one (according to the happened-before relation). Then, it adds $\mathsf{rec}(\ell', cs)$ in the position of the original receive.

Example 6. Consider again the execution trace τ from Example 4, together with the associated race set computed in Example 5: $\mathsf{race\_set}_\tau(\ell) = \{\ell_6, \ell_8\}$. Let us consider ℓ_6. Here, the race variant $\mathsf{variant}_\tau(\ell_2, \ell_6)$ is computed from $\mathsf{rdep}((r_4, s_5, r_6), \ \tau[\mathsf{p3} \mapsto r_1, s_3, \mathsf{rec}(\ell_6, cs)])$ as follows:

$$\begin{aligned}
&\mathsf{rdep}((r_4, s_5, r_6), \ \tau[\mathsf{p3} \mapsto r_1, s_3, \mathsf{rec}(\ell_6, cs)]) \\
&= \mathsf{rdep}((s_5, r_6), \ \tau[\mathsf{p3} \mapsto r_1, s_3, \mathsf{rec}(\ell_6, cs)]) \\
&= \mathsf{rdep}((r_6, s_7), \ \tau[\mathsf{p1} \mapsto \mathsf{spawn}(\mathsf{p3}), \mathsf{spawn}(\mathsf{p2}), \mathsf{spawn}(\mathsf{p4}), \mathsf{spawn}(\mathsf{p5}); \\
&\qquad\qquad\qquad \mathsf{p3} \mapsto r_1, s_3, \mathsf{rec}(\ell_6, cs)]) \\
&= \mathsf{rdep}((s_7), \quad \tau[\mathsf{p1} \mapsto \mathsf{spawn}(\mathsf{p3}), \mathsf{spawn}(\mathsf{p2}), \mathsf{spawn}(\mathsf{p4}), \mathsf{spawn}(\mathsf{p5}); \\
&\qquad\qquad\qquad \mathsf{p3} \mapsto r_1, s_3, \mathsf{rec}(\ell_6, cs)]) \\
&= \mathsf{rdep}(\epsilon, \quad\ \tau[\mathsf{p1} \mapsto \mathsf{spawn}(\mathsf{p3}), \mathsf{spawn}(\mathsf{p2}), \mathsf{spawn}(\mathsf{p4}), \mathsf{spawn}(\mathsf{p5}); \\
&\qquad\qquad\qquad \mathsf{p3} \mapsto r_1, s_3, \mathsf{rec}(\ell_6, cs)])
\end{aligned}$$

Therefore, the computed race variant τ' is as follows:

$$[\; \mathsf{p1} \mapsto \mathsf{spawn}(\mathsf{p3}), \mathsf{spawn}(\mathsf{p2}), \mathsf{spawn}(\mathsf{p4}), \mathsf{spawn}(\mathsf{p5}); \quad \mathsf{p2} \mapsto s_2;$$
$$\mathsf{p3} \mapsto r_1, s_3, \mathsf{rec}(\ell_6, cs); \quad \mathsf{p4} \mapsto r_3; \quad \mathsf{p5} \mapsto s_1, s_4, s_8 \qquad\quad]$$

In the following, given traces τ, τ', if τ is a subtrace of τ', i.e., $\tau \ll \tau'$, we also say that τ' *extends* τ. Let us consider a trace τ and one of its race variants τ'. The next result states that there is no interleaving in $\mathsf{sched}(\tau'')$ that is causally equivalent to any interleaving of $\mathsf{sched}(\tau)$ for all traces τ'' that extend the race variant τ'. This is an easy but essential property to guarantee the optimality in the number of variants considered by a state-space exploration algorithm.

Theorem 3. *Let τ be a trace with $e_r = (p \colon \mathsf{rec}(\ell, cs)) \in \tau$ and $\ell' \in \mathsf{race\_set}_\tau(\ell)$. Let $\tau' = \mathsf{variant}_\tau(\ell, \ell')$ be a race variant. Then, for all trace τ'' that extends τ' and for all interleavings $S \in \mathsf{sched}(\tau)$ and $S'' \in \mathsf{sched}(\tau'')$, we have $S \not\approx S''$.*

Proof. Consider first a (possibly partial) trace τ_1 obtained from $\mathsf{rdep}(A', \tau[p \mapsto A; \mathsf{rec}(\ell, cs)])$, i.e., τ_1 is equal to the race variant except for the fact that we have not changed yet the considered receive event. Then, it is easy to see that τ_1 is a subtrace of τ, $\tau_1 \ll \tau$, since rdep just follows the happened-before relation in order to consistently remove all dependences of e_r. Note that τ_1 and τ' only differ in the receive event ($\mathsf{rec}(\ell, cs)$ in τ_1 and $\mathsf{rec}(\ell', cs)$ in τ'). Trivially, for all interleavings $S_1 \in \mathsf{sched}(\tau_1)$ and $S' \in \mathsf{sched}(\tau')$, we have $S \not\approx S'$ since the receive events $\mathsf{rec}(\ell, cs)$ and $\mathsf{rec}(\ell', cs)$ can only happen in one of the interleavings but not in both of them. Moreover, for all trace τ'' that extends τ', and for all interleavings $S'' \in \mathsf{sched}(\tau'')$ and $S \in \mathsf{sched}(\tau)$, we have $S'' \not\approx S$ since they will always differ in the receive events above. $\qquad\square$

The definitions of message race and race variant can be used as the kernel of a state-space exploration technique that proceeds as follows:

1. First, a random execution of the program is considered, together with its associated trace.
2. This trace is used to compute message races (if any) as well as the corresponding race variants.
3. Then, each computed race variant is used to drive the execution of the program up to a given point, then continuing the execution nondeterministically according to the standard semantics. We gather the traces of these executions and the process starts again until all possible executions have been explored.

A formalization of such an algorithm can be found in the context of reachability testing [21] using SYN-sequences instead of traces.

On the other hand, the *prefix-based tracing* technique for Erlang introduced in [15] could be useful to instrument programs with a (possibly partial) trace so that their execution follows this trace and, then, continues nondeterministically, eventually producing a trace of the complete execution (point 3 above). The notion of trace in [15] is different to our notion of trace, though: message delivery is explicit and traces do not include message values nor receive constraints. Nevertheless, adapting their developments to our traces would not be difficult.

The definitions of message race and race variant could also be useful in the context of causal-consistent replay debugging [19,20]. First, we note that our traces could be straightforwardly used for replay debugging since they contain strictly more information than the logs of [19,20]. However, in contrast to the original logs, our traces would allow the replay debugger CauDEr [10] to also show the message races in a particular execution, and then let the user to replay any selected race variant, thus improving the functionality of the debugger. Some ongoing work along these lines can be found in [14]. However, the traces considered in [14] are similar to those in [15] (i.e., they have explicit events for message delivery and skip message values and receive constraints). As a consequence, the races considered in [14] are only *potential* races since there are no guarantees that message values in these races actually match the corresponding receive constraints. Nevertheless, an extension of CauDEr using our traces and the associated definitions of message race and race variant could be defined following a similar scheme.

5   Discussion and Future Work

The closest approach to our notion of trace are the *logs* of [19,20], which where introduced in the context of causal-consistent *replay* debugging for a message-passing concurrent language. In this work, we have extended the notion of log with enough information so that message races can be computed. Indeed, this work stemmed from the idea of improving causal-consistent replay debugging [19,20] with the computation of message races, since this information might be useful for the user in order to explore alternative execution paths. A first implementation in this direction is described in [14], although the traces are slightly different, as discussed above.

Another close approach is that of *reachability testing*, originally introduced in [16] in the context of multithreaded programs that perform read/write operations. This approach was then extended to message-passing programs in [22,26] and later improved and generalized in [21].[6] The notion of *SYN-sequence* in reachability testing (and, to some extend, the *program executions* of [8]) share some similarities with our traces since both represent a partial order with the actions performed by a number of processes running concurrently (i.e., they basically denote a *Mazurkiewicz trace* [23]). Nevertheless, our traces are tailored to a language with selective receives by adding message values and receive constraints ([21], in contrast, considers different ports for receive statements). Moreover, to the best of our knowledge, these works have not considered a language where processes can be dynamically spawned, as we do.

Both reachability testing and our approach share some similarities with so-called *stateless model checking* [12]. The main difference, though, is that state-

---

[6] [24] also deals with message-passing concurrent programs, but only *blocking* send and receive statements are considered.

less model checking works with interleavings. Then, since many interleavings may boil down to the same Mazurkiewicz trace, *dynamic partial order reduction* (DPOR) techniques are introduced (see, e.g., [1,11]). Intuitively speaking, DPOR techniques aim at producing only one interleaving per Mazurkiewicz trace. Computing message races is more natural in our context thanks to the use of traces, since DPOR techniques are not needed. Concuerror [5] implements stateless model checking for Erlang [1,4], and has been recently extended to also consider *observational equivalence* [3], thus achieving a similar result as our technique regarding the computation of message races, despite the fact that the techniques are rather different (using traces vs using interleavings + DPOR).

Another, related approach is the detection of race conditions for Erlang programs presented in [6]. However, the author focuses on data races (that may occur when using some shared-memory built-in operators of the language) rather than message races. Moreover, the detection is based on a *static* analysis, while we consider a *dynamic* approach to computing message races.

To conclude, we have introduced appropriate notions of interleaving and trace that are useful to represent concurrent executions in a message-passing concurrent language with dynamic process spawning and selective receives. In particular, our notion of trace is essentially equivalent to a Mazurkiewicz trace, thus allowing us to represent all causally equivalent interleavings in a compact way. Despite the simplicity of traces, they contain enough information to analyze some common error symptoms (e.g., orphan messages) and to compute message races, which can then give rise to alternative executions (specified by so-called race variants, i.e., partial traces).

As for future work, we will consider the computation of message races from *incomplete* traces, since it is not uncommon that concurrent programs are executed in an endless loop and, thus, the associated traces are in principle infinite. We also plan to extend the traces with more events (like message *deliver* and process *exit*) so that they can be used to detect more types of error symptoms (like process deadlocks and lost or delayed messages).

Finally, another interesting line of research involves formalizing and implementing an extension of the causal-consistent replay debugger CauDEr [10] for Erlang in order to also show message races (our original motivation for this work). A preliminary approach along these lines can be found in [14], though the considered traces are slightly different, as mentioned above. In this context, we also plan to analyze efficiency issues and investigate the definition of efficient algorithms for computing race sets.

Acknowledgements. The author would like to thank Juan José González-Abril for his useful remarks on a preliminary version of this paper. I would also like to thank the anonymous reviewers for their suggestions to improve this work.

References

1. Abdulla, P.A., Aronis, S., Jonsson, B., Sagonas, K.: Source sets: a foundation for optimal dynamic partial order reduction. J. ACM **64**(4), 25:1–25:49 (2017). https://doi.org/10.1145/3073408
2. Akka website (2021). https://akka.io/
3. Aronis, S., Jonsson, B., Lång, M., Sagonas, K.: Optimal dynamic partial order reduction with observers. In: Beyer, D., Huisman, M. (eds.) TACAS 2018. LNCS, vol. 10806, pp. 229–248. Springer, Cham (2018). https://doi.org/10.1007/978-3-319-89963-3_14
4. Aronis, S., Sagonas, K.: The shared-memory interferences of Erlang/OTP built-ins. In: Chechina, N., Fritchie, S.L. (eds.) Proceedings of the 16th ACM SIGPLAN International Workshop on Erlang, pp. 43–54. ACM (2017). https://doi.org/10.1145/3123569.3123573
5. Christakis, M., Gotovos, A., Sagonas, K.: Systematic testing for detecting concurrency errors in Erlang programs. In: Proceedings of the 6th IEEE International Conference on Software Testing, Verification and Validation (ICST 2013), pp. 154–163. IEEE Computer Society (2013). https://doi.org/10.1109/ICST.2013.50
6. Christakis, M., Sagonas, K.: Static detection of race conditions in Erlang. In: Carro, M., Peña, R. (eds.) PADL 2010. LNCS, vol. 5937, pp. 119–133. Springer, Heidelberg (2010). https://doi.org/10.1007/978-3-642-11503-5_11
7. Clarke, E.M., Emerson, E.A., Sistla, A.P.: Automatic verification of finite-state concurrent systems using temporal logic specifications. ACM Trans. Program. Lang. Syst. **8**(2), 244–263 (1986). https://doi.org/10.1145/5397.5399
8. Cypher, R., Leu, E.: Efficient race detection for message-passing programs with nonblocking sends and receives. In: Proceedings of the Seventh IEEE Symposium on Parallel and Distributed Processing (SPDP 1995), pp. 534–541. IEEE (1995). https://doi.org/10.1109/SPDP.1995.530730
9. Erlang website (2021). https://www.erlang.org/
10. Fabbretti, G., González-Abril, J.J., Lanese, I., Nishida, N., Palacios, A., Vidal, G.: CauDEr website (2021). https://github.com/mistupv/cauder
11. Flanagan, C., Godefroid, P.: Dynamic partial-order reduction for model checking software. In: Palsberg, J., Abadi, M. (eds.) Proceedings of the 32nd ACM SIGPLAN-SIGACT Symposium on Principles of Programming Languages (POPL 2005), pp. 110–121. ACM (2005). https://doi.org/10.1145/1040305.1040315
12. Godefroid, P.: Model checking for programming languages using verisoft. In: POPL, pp. 174–186 (1997). https://doi.org/10.1145/263699.263717
13. Go website (2021). https://go.dev/
14. González-Abril, J.J., Vidal, G.: A lightweight approach to computing message races with an application to causal-consistent reversible debugging. CoRR abs/2112.12869 (2021). https://arxiv.org/abs/2112.12869
15. González-Abril, J.J., Vidal, G.: Prefix-based tracing in message-passing concurrency. In: Angelis, E.D., Vanhoof, W. (eds.) Proceedings of the 31st International Symposium on Logic-Based Program Synthesis and Transformation (LOPSTR 2021). Lecture Notes in Computer Science, vol. 13290, pp. 157–175. Springer, Cham (2021), https://doi.org/10.1007/978-3-030-98869-2_9
16. Hwang, G., Tai, K., Huang, T.: Reachability testing: an approach to testing concurrent software. In: Proceedings of the First Asia-Pacific Software Engineering Conference (APSEC 1994), pp. 246–255. IEEE (1994). https://doi.org/10.1109/APSEC.1994.465255

17. Lamport, L.: Time, clocks, and the ordering of events in a distributed system. Commun. ACM **21**(7), 558–565 (1978). https://doi.org/10.1145/359545.359563
18. Lanese, I., Nishida, N., Palacios, A., Vidal, G.: A theory of reversibility for Erlang. J. Log. Algebraic Methods Program. **100**, 71–97 (2018). https://doi.org/10.1016/j.jlamp.2018.06.004
19. Lanese, I., Palacios, A., Vidal, G.: Causal-consistent replay debugging for message passing programs. In: Pérez, J.A., Yoshida, N. (eds.) FORTE 2019. LNCS, vol. 11535, pp. 167–184. Springer, Cham (2019). https://doi.org/10.1007/978-3-030-21759-4_10
20. Lanese, I., Palacios, A., Vidal, G.: Causal-consistent replay reversible semantics for message passing concurrent programs. Fundam. Informaticae **178**(3), 229–266 (2021). https://doi.org/10.3233/FI-2021-2005
21. Lei, Y., Carver, R.H.: Reachability testing of concurrent programs. IEEE Trans. Software Eng. **32**(6), 382–403 (2006). https://doi.org/10.1109/TSE.2006.56
22. Lei, Y., Tai, K.: Efficient reachability testing of asynchronous message-passing programs. In: Proceedings of the 8th International Conference on Engineering of Complex Computer Systems (ICECCS 2002), p. 35. IEEE Computer Society (2002). https://doi.org/10.1109/ICECCS.2002.1181496
23. Mazurkiewicz, A.: Trace theory. In: Brauer, W., Reisig, W., Rozenberg, G. (eds.) ACPN 1986. LNCS, vol. 255, pp. 278–324. Springer, Heidelberg (1987). https://doi.org/10.1007/3-540-17906-2_30
24. Netzer, R.H., Miller, B.P.: Optimal tracing and replay for debugging message-passing parallel programs. J. Supercomput. **8**(4), 371–388 (1995). https://doi.org/10.1007/BF01901615
25. Rust website (2021). https://www.rust-lang.org/
26. Tai, K.: Reachability testing of asynchronous message-passing programs. In: Proceedings of the International Symposium on Software Engineering for Parallel and Distributed Systems (PDSE 1997), pp. 50–61. IEEE Computer Society (1997). https://doi.org/10.1109/PDSE.1997.596826
27. Undo Software: The Business Value of Optimizing CI Pipelines (2020). https://info.undo.io/ci-research-report

Author Index

Printed in the United States
by Baker & Taylor Publisher Services